The Summer of Theory

The Summer of Theory

History of a Rebellion, 1960–1990

PHILIPP FELSCH

Translated by Tony Crawford

polity

Originally published in German as *Der lange Sommer der Theorie* by Philipp Felsch © Verlag C. H. Beck oHG, Munich 2015

This English edition © 2022 by Polity Press

The translation of this work was funded by Geisteswissenschaften International – Translation Funding for Work in the Humanities and Social Sciences from Germany, a joint initiative of the Fritz Thyssen Foundation, the German Federal Foreign Office, the collecting society VG WORT and the Börsenverein des Deutschen Buchhandels (German Publishers & Booksellers Association).

Front endpaper: Sector boundary at Wilhemstrasse, Berlin, 1960. Copyright © Shawn McBride / Will McBride Archive
Back endpaper: The Gropius Building next to the Berlin Wall, Berlin, early 1980s © DACS, 2021

Polity Press
65 Bridge Street
Cambridge CB2 1UR, UK

Polity Press
101 Station Landing
Suite 300
Medford, MA 02155, USA

ISBN-13: 978-1-5095-3985-7

A catalogue record for this book is available from the British Library.

Library of Congress Cataloging-in-Publication Data
Names: Felsch, Philipp, author. | Crawford, Tony (Translator) translator.
Title: The summer of theory : history of a rebellion, 1960-1990 / Philipp Felsch ; translated by Tony Crawford.
Other titles: Lange Sommer der Theorie. English | History of a rebellion, 1960-1990
Description: English edition. | Cambridge, UK ; Medford, MA : Polity, [2021] | "Originally published in German as 'Der lange Sommer der Theorie' by Philipp Felsch, Verlag C. H. Beck oHG, München, 2015." | Includes bibliographical references and index. | Summary: "The story of how the German Left fell in love with theory"-- Provided by publisher.
Identifiers: LCCN 2021009973 (print) | LCCN 2021009974 (ebook) | ISBN 9781509539857 (hardback) | ISBN 9781509539871 (epub)
Subjects: LCSH: Germany (West)--Intellectual life--20th century. | Germany (West)--Politics and government--1945-1990. | Intellectuals--Germany (West)--History--20th century. | Books and reading--Germany (West) | Germany (West)--Intellectual life--French influences.
Classification: LCC DD260.3 .F4513 2021 (print) | LCC DD260.3 (ebook) | DDC 305.5/52094309045--dc23
LC record available at https://lccn.loc.gov/2021009973
LC ebook record available at https://lccn.loc.gov/2021009974

Typeset in 11 on 14 Warnock Pro
by Fakenham Prepress Solutions, Fakenham, Norfolk NR21 8NL
Printed and bound in Great Britain by CPI Group (UK) Ltd, Croydon

For further information on Polity, visit our website:
politybooks.com

'We are obsessive readers.'
Heidi Paris
(1950–2002)
and
Peter Gente
(1936–2014)

Contents

Illustrations

Acknowledgements

Although this book is mainly based on a composite of written records, it would not have been possible without numerous conversations. I thank the following people for their willingness to answer my questions: Hannes Böhringer, Peter Geble, Peter Gente†, Wolfgang Hagen, Marianne Karbe, Helmut Lethen, Michaela Ott, Wolfert von Rahden, Ulrich Raulff, Hans-Jörg Rheinberger, Cord Riechelmann, Henning Schmidgen, Edith Seifert, Walter Seitter, Georg Stanitzek, Jochen Stankowski, Ronald Voullié, Nikolaus Wegmann and all the others who have talked to me in the past few years about their experiences with theory. I especially thank Tom Lamberty and Elisa Barth of Merve Verlag for their generous help and support. My heartfelt thanks go to Stephan Schlak for the initial impulse that led to this book. I thank the staff of the Centre for Art and Media Technology in Karlsruhe, the Walter Benjamin Archives (where there are photocopies of Adorno's correspondence), the German Literature Archives in Marbach and the University Archives of Freie Universität, Berlin. I would not have been able to finish the book without a sabbatical semester funded by the Excellence Initiative of Humboldt-Universität, Berlin. For their critical reading and crucial suggestions, I thank Philipp Albers, Jan von Brevern, Martin Engelmeier, Martin Mittelmeier, Jan Mollenhauer, Moritz Neuffer, Kathrin Passig, Cornelius Reiber, Johanna Seifert and, most of all, Hanna Engelmeier. I thank Christian Werner for his dedicated photography. I thank Stefanie Hölscher for her great interest in this project. And I thank Yael Reuveny and Anne Henk for everything else.

Introduction: What Was Theory?

Sentenced to three years' imprisonment for arson in 1968, Andreas Baader discovered letter-writing. He described the torment of solitude, ranted about the guards, and asked his friends to supply him with essentials. Besides cured meats and tobacco, that meant, most of all, books. He had people send him the student movement's favourite authors, Marx, Marcuse and Wilhelm Reich, which he had only known from hearsay up to then. 'Mountains of theory, the last thing I wanted', he wrote to the mother of his daughter. 'I work and I suffer, without complaining of course.' Later, in the maximum-security prison at Stammheim, it was up to his lawyers to feed his hunger for reading material. At the time of his death, there were some 400 books in his cell: a respectable library for a terrorist who was notorious among his comrades for his recklessness. Without a doubt, Baader played the part of a jailhouse intellectual, just as he had previously played the revolutionary. Yet, at the same time, there was a great deal of seriousness in his studies. His letters indicate that he felt a need to catch up[1] – after all, the struggle to which he had dedicated himself was founded on theoretical principles.[2] In a different time, Baader would have taken up painting perhaps, or begun writing an autobiographical novel. Instead, he plunged – almost in spite of himself – into theory.

Now that the intellectual energies of '68 have long since decayed to a feeble smouldering, it is hard to imagine the fascination of a genre that captivated generations of readers. Theory was more than just a succession of intellectual ideas: it was a claim of truth, an article of faith and a lifestyle accessory. It spread among its adherents in cheap paperbacks; it launched new language games in seminars and reading groups. The Frankfurt School, post-structuralism and systems theory were best-selling brands. West German students discovered in Adorno's books the poetry of concepts. As the sixties dawned, the New Left rallied under the banner of its 'theory work' against the pragmatism of the Social Democrats: those who would change the world, they proclaimed, must start by thinking it through. But the thinking they had in mind had nothing to do with the philosophy of professors who stuck to interpreting the classic texts or the meaning of Being. It was concerned less with eternal truth and more with critiques of the dominant conditions, and under its scrutiny even the most mundane acts took on social relevance. Jacob Taubes, professor of the philosophy of religion in Berlin, saw his students reading the works of Herbert Marcuse with an intensity reminiscent of the zeal 'with which young Talmud scholars once interpreted the text of the Torah.'[3] On campus, theory conferred upon its readers not only academic capital, but also sex appeal. Marcuse led to Marx, and Marx to Hegel: those who wanted to have a say in the discussion got themselves the twenty-volume Suhrkamp edition of Hegel's complete works.[4] Only after the shock of the terrorists' debacle in Stammheim and Mogadishu did any doubts about the canon of the '68 generation mature into open resistance. New thinking came to Germany from Paris and did away with the tonality of dialectics. The books of Deleuze and Baudrillard called for a different kind of reading from those of Marx and Hegel. They seemed to have a more important purpose than the search for truth, and in the course of the 1980s theory metamorphosed into an aesthetic experience. And when ecology laid constraints of quantities and limits on the speculative imagination of the seventies, thorny philosophy set out to infiltrate the art world.

The first impetus to write this book dates from several years ago. In the spring of 2008, the editor of a journal of intellectual history called me to ask for an article on the German publishing house Merve. The editor was planning an issue about West Berlin, the walled-in city on the front lines of the Cold War, which Merve had supplied with theory for twenty long years. Peter Gente, the founder of Merve, had retired from publishing and sold his papers to an archive to finance his sunset years in Thailand, and so the time seemed ripe for historical retrospection.[5] Although I wasn't a Berliner, Merve was a byword to me too. There was no way I could refuse.

Merve has been called the 'Reclam of postmodernism' – Reclam, of course, are the publishers of the 'Universal Library', the yellow, pocket-sized standard texts that no German student can do without. Merve was the German home of postmodernism, and practically owned the copyright to the German word for 'discourse'.[6] Merve had made a name for itself in the 1980s, primarily with translations of the French post-structuralists. Its cheaply glued paperbacks were a guarantee of advanced ideas, and the pop-art look of their un-academic styling was ahead of its time. The coloured rhombus on the cover of the *Internationaler Merve Diskurs* series was a well-established logo whose renown rivalled that of the rainbow rows of Suhrkamp paperbacks.

I remember well the first Merve titles I read. It wasn't easy, in Bologna in the mid-1990s, to get them by mail order. My intention had been to spend a semester there studying with Umberto Eco, but Eco's lectures turned out to be a tourist attraction. Whatever the famous semiotician was saying into his microphone at the far end of the lecture hall was easier to assimilate by reading one of his introductory books. In retrospect, that was a stroke of luck, because it forced me to look for an alternative. And the search for a more intense educational experience led me – twelve years after his death – to Michel Foucault. My Foucault wasn't bald and didn't wear turtlenecks, and although he occasionally spoke French, his Italian accent was unmistakable. But his grand rhetorical flourishes and his tendency to overarticulate his words are engraved in my memory. In his best moments, he came very close to the original. Valerio Marchetti had heard the original Foucault at the Collège de France in the early 1980s, if I remember correctly, and absorbed – as I was later able to verify on YouTube – his way of talking as well as his way of thinking. He was a professor of early modern history at the University of Bologna. His lecture course, which was attended by very few students, was devoted to a topic only a Foucauldian could have come up with: 'Hermaphroditism in France in the Baroque Period'. I was spellbound on learning of the seventeenth-century debates in which theologians and physicians had argued about the significance of anomalous sex characteristics.[7] I had never heard of such a thing at my German university, where philosophy students read Plato and Kant. I hung on Marchetti's every word, attending even the Yiddish course that he taught for some reason, and started reading the literature he cited: Michel Foucault, Paul Veyne, Claude Lévi-Strauss, Georges Devereux ... I waited weeks for the German translations to arrive in the post. I read more than I have ever read since, and collected excerpts on coloured file cards. In the heat of the Italian summer, the 'microphysics of power' and the 'iceberg of history' stuck to my forearms.[8]

In 2008, I hadn't touched these books in years. Their spines crumbled with a dry crackle when I opened them. Inside I discovered vigorous pencil marks, reminding me what a revelation theory had been to me in those days. But at a decade's remove, that experience seemed strangely foreign: it seemed to belong to an intellectual era that was now irretrievably past. I went to Karlsruhe to have a look at the materials that Peter Gente had turned over to the Centre for Art and Media Technology. In the forty heavy boxes that had not yet been opened – much less catalogued – perhaps I would find a chapter of my own Bildungsroman. They contained the publisher's correspondence with the famous – and the less famous – Merve authors, along with the paper detritus that lined the road to over 300 published titles: newspaper clippings, notes, budgets, dossiers ... While Gente rested, I supposed, in the shade of coconut palms, I immersed myself in his papers. Only gradually did I realize that what I was looking at were not the typical assets of a liquidated business: it was the record of an epic adventure of reading.

The oldest documents dated back to the late 1950s, when Gente discovered the books of Adorno. That discovery changed everything. For five years, the young man ran around West Berlin with *Minima Moralia* in his hand, before he finally got in touch with the author. By then, Gente was in the middle of the New Left's theoretical discussions, combing libraries and archives in search of the buried truth of the labour movement. He was everywhere, cheering Herbert Marcuse in the great hall of Freie Universität, demonstrating with Andreas Baader in Kurfürstendamm, running into Daniel Cohn-Bendit in Paris a few weeks before May of '68. Later, he had discussions with

Toni Negri, sat in jail with Foucault, put up Paul Virilio in his shared flat in Berlin. There was never any question that he belonged to the movement's avant-garde – yet he kept himself in the background. It was a long time before he found his role; he didn't care to play the part of an activist, nor that of an author. 'Tried to intervene, but wasn't able to do so' was his summary of the year 1968.[9]

From the beginning, Gente had been, above all, a reader. The scholar Helmut Lethen, who had known him since the mid-1960s, called him the 'encyclopaedist of rebellion'.[10] He knew every ramification of the debates of the interwar period; he knew how to lay hands on even the most obscure periodicals; his comrades' key readings were selected on his recommendation. Compared with Baader – whom he supplied with books in Stammheim Prison – Gente embodied the opposite end of the movement: the man I met in 2010, and questioned about his past, interacted with the world through text.[11] In preparation for our conversations, he would arrange books, letters and newspaper articles, and he picked them up in turn as he talked, to underscore one point or another. In the echo chamber of the theories that he mastered as no other, he had found his vital element. Professor Jacob Taubes, a gifted reader in his own right who counted Gente among his disciples, attested in 1974 to Gente's talent for 'dealing intensively with unwieldy texts'.[12] One of the peculiarities of the theory-obsessed '68 generation is that hardly any theoreticians originated in their ranks. 'As they silenced their fathers, they allowed their grandfathers to be heard again – preferably those who had been exiled',[13] the cultural journalist Henning Ritter wrote. Was he thinking of Peter Gente, who had served alongside him as a student assistant to Taubes in the 1960s? From that perspective, Gente was the ideal New Leftist: a partisan of the class struggle mining the archives.[14]

Gente travelled to Paris and brought back texts by Roland Barthes and Lucien Goldmann, authors no one knew in Berlin. Towards the end of the sixties, when the leftist book market began booming, he picked up odd editorial jobs. But he didn't find his life's theme until, in his mid-thirties, he decided to start his own business: in 1970, he and some friends and comrades founded the publishing company Merve Verlag. Initially, they called themselves a socialist collective. As their political beliefs evolved, however, the organization of their work

2 Heidi Paris and Peter Gente, West Berlin, around 1980.

changed as well. For two decades, Merve shaped the theory scene of West Berlin and West Germany. From the student movement's latecomers to the avant-garde of the art world, everyone got their share of dangerous thinking: Italian Marxism, French post-structuralism, a dash of Carl Schmitt, topped off with Luhmann's sober systems theory.

But Merve probably never would have been anything more than just a minuscule leftist publisher whose products occasionally turn up in Red second-hand bookshops if Gente hadn't met Heidi Paris. In the masculine world of theory, where women were all too often reduced to the roles of mothers or muses, she was a pioneer.[15] She led the group's publishing policy in new directions, contributing to the dissolution of the collective. From 1975 on, she was Gente's partner both in work and in a personal relationship. The couple composed Merve's legendary long-sellers, established authors such as Deleuze and Baudrillard in Germany, and steered their publishing house into the art world, where it has its habitat today. They produced books that didn't want to be read at university; they transformed readers into fans, and authors into philosophical fashion icons. They worked on film projects with Blixa Bargeld and Heiner Müller; they did the rounds of the Schöneberg clubs with Martin Kippenberger.[16] As well-entrenched members of the theory crowd, they coexisted with a like-minded milieu whose centre of gravity was the university, but whose orbit passed through Berlin's smart night spots. Or vice versa. In the 1980s, the Merve paperbacks were required reading in this milieu.

'We are almost never in Paris and are happy living in Berlin,' Heidi Paris and Peter Gente wrote in 1981 to the New York professor Sylvère Lotringer.[17] West Berlin was an ideal location for the publishers. Speculative thinking flourished in the city's exceptional political conditions. The Merve culture grew lavishly between the bars and discos of Schöneberg and the lecture halls of Dahlem. Berlin in the sixties had been a bastion of the New Left; in the seventies, it became a biotope of the counter-culture. And in the eighties, as the Cold War ideologues faded to spectres, postmodernism dawned. Hegel himself had held the Prussian capital to be the home of the World Spirit; his critical heirs thought it nothing less – although the existence of the 'enclave on the front lines,' as Heidi Paris once called her city, actually seemed to contradict Hegel's theory.[18]

The history of the publishing couple of Gente and Paris is inseparably connected with West Berlin, yet it is more than an intellectual milieu study of the city. People in Germany tend to equate the heyday of theory with what was known as 'Suhrkamp culture': the phrase was coined in 1973 by the English critic George Steiner, referring to the catalogue of the Frankfurt publishing house Suhrkamp as the canon of West Germany.[19] And, in fact, Suhrkamp played a crucial part in shaping and propagating the genre, as we shall see. Their policy of producing theory in paperback was one thing that made a project such as Merve possible in the first place. But because the Berlin publishers never blossomed out into a company with employees, proper bookkeeping and the imperative of profitability, the files I discovered in Karlsruhe afford a different perspective: they recount the long summer of theory from a user's point of view. All their lives, the Merve publishers and their friends identified themselves as avid readers. Accordingly, Merve was not just a publisher, but a reading group, a fan club – a reception context.

That fact is an invaluable advantage for my project of writing the history of a genre: to understand the success of theory since the sixties, examining how it was read and used is at least as important as its content[20] – which has long since been studied in any case – as the recently published memoirs of some former theory readers have pointed out.[21] Perhaps certain texts had a power of suggestion that was even greater than their systematic argument. This preliminary intuition, and the methodological choice which follows from it, are not aimed at adding yet another interpretation to the history of twentieth-century philosophy.[22] This book recounts the formative experiences of Peter Gente, the odyssey of the Merve collective, and the discoveries of Gente and Paris. It follows the course of their readings, their discussions and their favourite books – but it does not seek to penetrate the grey contents of those texts. The history of science has long had its eye on 'theoretical practice', to use the Merve author Louis Althusser's term for the business of thinking. Following him and others, that history has learned to pay attention to the media, institutions and practices of knowledge.[23] Why should this approach not prove fruitful for the theory landscape of the sixties and seventies, the environment in which it was originally formulated?[24] In 1978, Michel Foucault developed the concept of philosophical reporting – 'le reportage d'idées', a form devoted to the real history of thought. 'The world of today is crawling with ideas', he wrote, 'that are born, move around, disappear or reappear, shaking up people and things.' Hence, there is always a need 'to connect the analysis of what we think with the analysis of what happens.'[25] This book's purpose is precisely that.

1965

THE HOUR OF THEORY

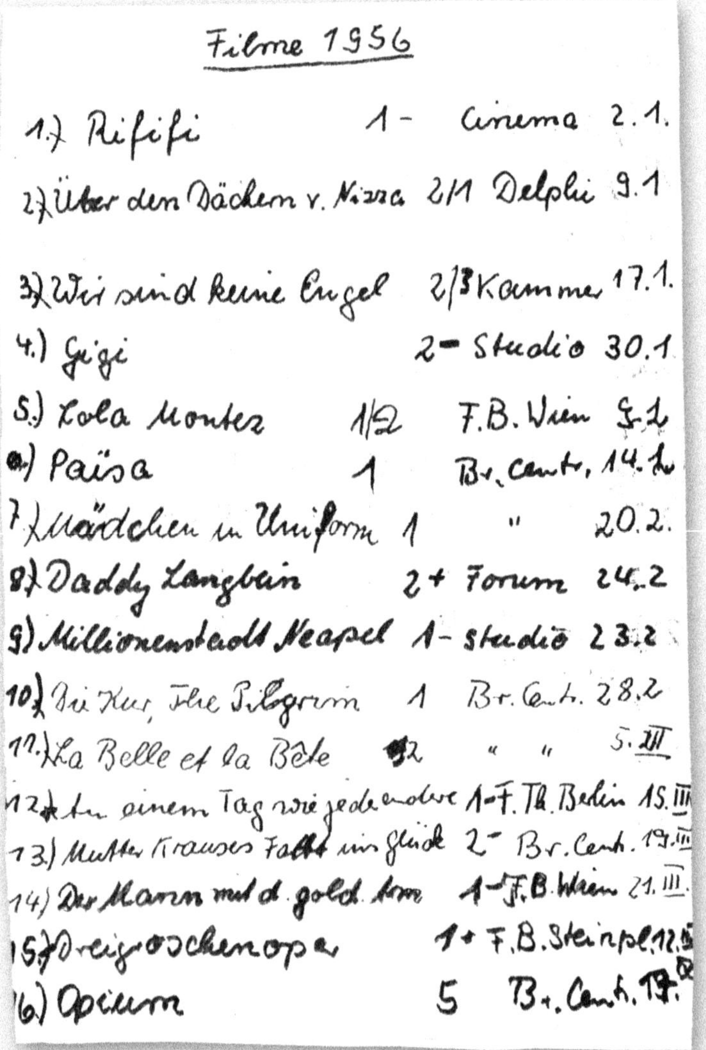

Filme 1956

1.)	Rififi	1-	Cinema	2.1.
2.)	Über den Dächern v. Nizza	2/1	Delphi	9.1
3.)	Wir sind keine Engel	2/3	Kammer	17.1.
4.)	Gigi	2-	Studio	30.1
5.)	Lola Montez	1/2	F.B. Wien	9.1
6.)	Paisà	1	Br. Centr.	14.1
7.)	Mädchen in Uniform	1	"	20.2.
8.)	Daddy Langbein	2+	Forum	24.2
9.)	Millionenstadt Neapel	1-	Studio	23.2
10.)	Bei Kur, The Pilgrim	1	Br. Centr.	28.2
11.)	La Belle et la Bête	2	" "	5.III
12.)	An einem Tag wie jeder andere	1-	F.Th. Berlin	15.III
13.)	Mutter Krausens Fahrt ins Glück	2-	Br. Cent.	19.III
14.)	Der Mann mit d. gold. Arm	1-	F.B. Wien	21.III
15.)	Dreigroschenoper	1+	F.B. Steinpl.	12.[illegible]
16.)	Opium	5	Br. Cent.	17.[illegible]

3 Peter Gente goes to the cinema, 1956.[1]

1

FEDERAL REPUBLIC OF ADORNO

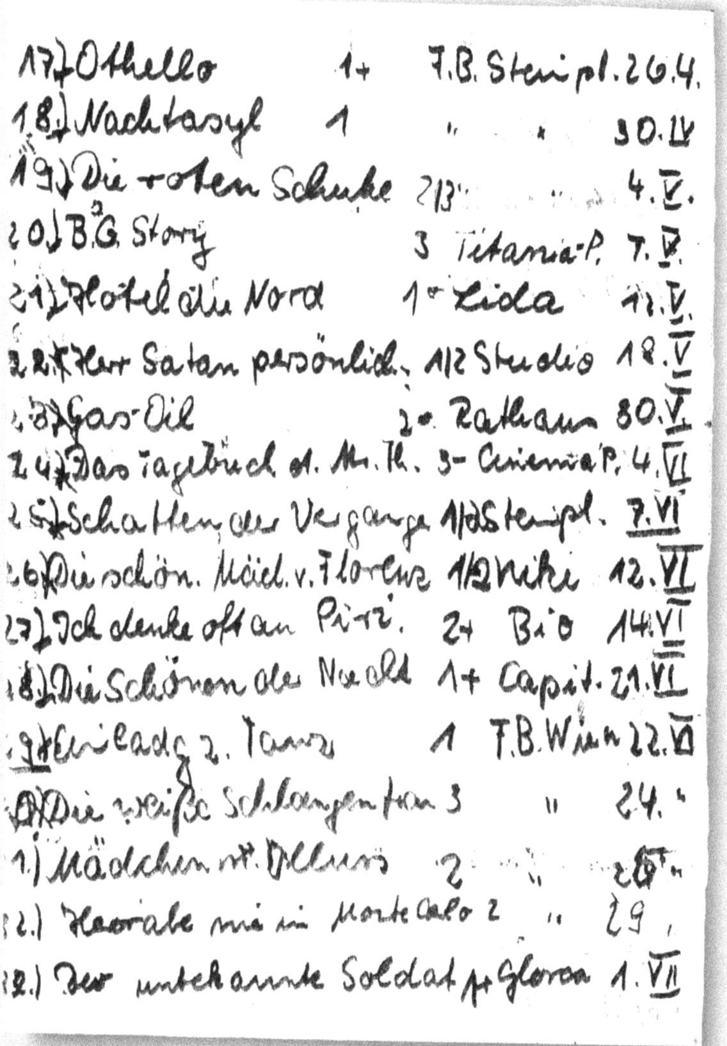
17.) Othello 1+ F.B. Steinpl. 26.4.
18.) Nachtasyl 1 " " 30.IV
19.) Die roten Schuhe 2/3 " " 4.V.
20.) B.G. Story 3 Titania-P. 7.V.
21.) Hotel du Nord 1+ Lida 11.V.
22.) Herr Satan persönlich 1/2 Studio 18.V
23.) Gas-Oil 2+ Rathaus 30.V
24.) Das Tagebuch d. Mr. Th. 3- Cinema P. 4.VI
25.) Schatten der Vergangenheit 1/2 Steinpl. 7.VI
26.) Die schön. Mädch. v. Florenz 1/2 Niki 12.VI
27.) Ich denke oft an Piroschka 2+ Bio 14.VI
28.) Die Schönen der Nacht 1+ Capit. 21.VI
29.) Einladung z. Tanz 1 F.B. Wien 22.VI
30.) Die weiße Schlangenfrau 3 " 24. "
31.) Mädchen mit Dollars 2 " 26. "
32.) Heirate mich in Monte Carlo 2 " 29.
33.) Der unbekannte Soldat 1+ Gloria 1.VII

While Radio Free Berlin was broadcasting Nikita Khrushchev's secret speech, Peter Gente went to the cinema. As the radio waves rose into the evening sky, informing listeners on both sides of the divided city about the crimes of Stalinism, the curtain opened on *Beauties of the Night*, a comedy by René Clair about a young composer escaping into dreams of success and beautiful women, losing his connection to reality – until the end of the film, when he comes to his senses just in time to face real life.[2] Gente was ecstatic, and gave the film a grade of '1+' in his culture diary. He went to the cinema often in those days, and also visited Berlin's theatres, concert halls and cultural centres. He had discovered his passion for culture after moving with his parents to the metropolis from the Soviet-occupied provinces. He began reading novels with the zeal of a late bloomer, and invested what money he earned at his summer jobs in admission tickets.[3] Herbert von Karajan was the director of the Berlin Philharmonic. The Berliner Ensemble was an unbeatably affordable theatre at the unofficial exchange rate between Western and Eastern marks, and Brecht himself still watched from his box. And the cinemas showed films from France and Italy that broke with the aesthetics of the pre-war generation.[4] On the eve of the Nouvelle Vague, Gente surrendered to the spells of Fellini, Hitchcock, Orson Welles and Jean Cocteau. 'Read bourgeois novels; consumed culture generally' was his summary of this period in a later self-criticism before his socialist comrades.[5]

Karl Marx once commented that the Germans are philosophically contemporary with the present day, but not historically.[6] In Gente's life too, major political events were only background noise. Although he lived at the epicentre of the Cold War, he hardly seems to have noticed Khrushchev's speech, which heralded a thaw in the East and a disenchantment among the intellectual left in the West.[7] But perhaps Berlin was precisely the wrong place to develop a stable sense of reality. There were too many realities coexisting here: the ruins of the World War, and the monuments of the post-war economic miracle; the Kurfürstendamm in the West with its cafés full of buttercream cakes, and the Stalin-Allee in the East with its socialist gingerbread housing blocks. To Maurice Blanchot, whom Gente later counted among his favourite authors, Berlin 'was not ... just one city, or two cities,' but 'the place in which the question of a unity which is both necessary and impossible confronts every individual who resides there, and who, in residing there, experiences not only a place of residence but also the absence of a place of residence'.[8]

This is what it sounds like when a geopolitical situation invites metaphysical speculation. But, in 1956, Gente did not yet see the world in the light of theory. In a round script that betrays his youth, he kept a record of his evenings at the cinema and the theatre, and the minimalistic prose of his lists seems to quiver with pent-up desire. Gente was burning to find a place for himself in the world of the arts,[9] and his readings soon influenced him to limit his search to the canon of high culture. In the year of the thaw, however, his taste had not yet matured. His diary mixes musicals with auteur cinema, Puccini with Hollywood and Brecht. It was up to him to discover a common denominator. In the meantime, he awarded the performances grades from 1 to 5 – the scale used by German secondary schools, including the one he had recently left. The numbers were a relatively modest instrument of cultural criticism, taking no notice of highbrow or lowbrow categories. At the same time, Susan Sontag, negligibly older, was already jotting savvy mini-reviews in her diary as she made her own cultural rounds in Chicago.[10] Gente's marks went no higher than the superlative '1++' for Giorgio Strehler's adaptation of *Harlequin, Servant of Two Masters,* performed by the visiting Piccolo Teatro of Milan, and no lower than the moderate '3' for Puccini's *La Bohème*. He was an easy grader who repeatedly had to expand his scale upwards because, worshipper of culture, he had started out awarding too many 1s.

Reflections from Damaged Life

The following year, in 1957, Gente had an awakening. It occurred, however, not in the cultural sphere where he was seeking his future, but at the base, in wage labour. The scene is symptomatic of the young West Germany, which was already approaching full employment in the second half of the 1950s. On the assembly line of the Siemens factory in Spandau, where Gente worked to support himself while studying law – in accordance with his father's wishes – he listened to two of his fellow students talking about a certain Adorno, whom they seemed for some reason to consider absolutely essential. Exactly what it was that captured his attention, he couldn't remember later on. But the impression it made was certainly deep. 'Adorno challenged earlier life', Gente's later self-criticism states tersely.[11] He got a copy of Adorno's best-known book, *Minima Moralia*, and couldn't put it down, although he understood hardly any of its impenetrable aphorisms.[12] Yet the author, claiming that only thoughts 'which do not understand themselves' can be true, apparently saw the hermetic tone as part of his message.[13] The difficult language, yielding its meaning only to patient reflection, contributed to the influence of a book which made those Gente had read before it seem irrelevant.[14]

In 1957, Adorno's 'reflections from damaged life', as *Minima Moralia*'s subtitle calls them, were still an insider tip. Six years after its publication, there was little to indicate that the book would be a philosophical hit, selling over 120,000 copies to date. In the middle of the post-war boom, between Opel Rekords and ice cream parlours, Gente was unsettled by it – by the way of thinking of a little-known Frankfurt philosophy lecturer who saw only disaster wherever he looked. 'Life does not live', reads the epigram, like a warning, on the first page; the pages that follow contain variations on that paradox. Condensing his experience of American exile into miniatures, Adorno exposes modern life as a state of deception. What seems to be alive and authentic is in reality long dead; the apparent aspiration to progress is caused by a ghostly compulsion to keep moving.[15] It is a post-cataclysmic world we are living in. 'The disaster does not take the form of a radical elimination of what existed previously', a key passage reads – 'rather the things that history has condemned are dragged along dead, neutralized and impotent as ignominious ballast'. Hence the macabre atmosphere of *Minima Moralia*: its pages are populated by the undead. Among the figures whose eerie 'post-existence' Adorno exposes are the achievements of the preceding bourgeois era – such as liberalism, socialism and the hospitality industry, which reached a state of rigor mortis with the advent of room service. Adorno discovers the ghastliest signs of decay in the tiniest details of day-to-day life – hence his now famous observations that the inhabitants of the Enlightened hemisphere no longer know how to give gifts, to be at home in their homes, or to close a door. 'The world is systematized horror' is his judgement of the present. That condemnation had the sinister weight, two decades before *Apocalypse Now*, of Coppola's Colonel Kurtz watching a snail crawl along a razor's edge. Meanwhile, German radios played the sentimental songs of the Austrian rover Freddy Quinn.[16]

In the depressing post-war atmosphere of 1950s Germany, Adorno made it plain that there was 'no longer anything harmless and neutral': his diagnosis of a society paralysed to death stood against the backdrop of the German genocide.[17] Elsewhere, he wrote about the primal scene of the ghostly life: 'In the concentration camps, the boundary between life and death was eradicated. A middle ground was created, inhabited by living skeletons and putrefying bodies.'[18] Images like these must have conjured up childhood memories in Peter Gente. Towards the end of the war, prisoners from a nearby labour camp had turned up in his home town of Halberstadt. Children passed around the rumours of underground factories where these figures assembled aircraft – their parents said not a word about them. In return, Gente said nothing about his parents for the rest of his life. The rupture – precipitated not least by his reading of Adorno – was too deep for him to accord them any importance beyond rejection. As a result, only a few isolated facts are known about them. Gente's father was a lawyer who had served as a lieutenant on the Eastern front and had been taken prisoner by the Red Army. His mother, from a 'very anti-Semitic family,' contributed that heritage to the marriage. Gente remembered helping his mother carry his paralysed grandmother to the basement shelter during an air raid that destroyed large parts of Halberstadt in April of 1945. The family's big house on the outskirts of the city was not hit. But when Gente's father returned from Russia six years later, his career was ruined: a former member of the Nazi Party had no hope of advancement in the legal bureaucracy of East Germany. A short time later, the family had to flee to the West – allegedly because the father's contacts with the American intelligence service had been exposed.[19]

Along with an initially small but later fast-growing number of his generation, Peter Gente made *Minima Moralia* his breviary: a book that was digestible only in small portions, but one that could be consulted in every circumstance. The dons of German universities did not know what to make of Adorno's 'painfully convoluted intellectual poetry', as Thomas Mann once called the book.[20] As a result, the influential reading experiences were extramural.[21] Later, Gente the publisher would insist on making ambulatory books – readable on the train, 'while travelling' or around town – no doubt influenced by his experience as an Adorno reader.[22] 'I carried *Minima Moralia* around with me for a good five years. Every day, always with me, a regular vade mecum.'[23] With his melancholy diagnosis of the present, Adorno instituted a new use for philosophy: his books replaced the volume of poetry in the young reader's coat pocket.

Like Thomas Mann, the first critics to review *Minima Moralia* in the fifties pointed out its poetic character. They either revealed the book to be 'secretly a lyric poem', or attested that 'only a musician' could have composed it.[24] Adorno himself later claimed, in an interview in *Der Spiegel*, to be a 'theoretical person who feels that theoretical thinking comes extraordinarily close to his artistic intentions'.[25] This was no doubt the reason for the book's great success: it catered for the poetic demand of the post-war period. In the same year in which *Minima Moralia* was published, Gottfried Benn noted that the poets had triumphed over the philosophers. Even the philosophers, he declared in his 1951 Marburg lecture on 'Problems of Lyric Poetry', now longed to write poems. 'They feel that systematic, discursive thinking has reached an impasse at the moment; consciousness can bear at the moment only something which thinks in fragments; five hundred pages of observations on truth, apt though some sentences may be, are outweighed by a three-verse poem.'[26] If this diagnosis is correct – and the number of new poetry magazines emerging in the 1950s suggests that it is – then Adorno and his philosophical aphorisms were aligned with the trend of the time.

Adorno himself would by no means have wanted his work to be misunderstood as a prose poem, however. He is known to have rejected philosophers 'borrowing from literature' and expecting 'that Being itself will speak in a *poésie* concocted of Parmenides and Jungnickel', and decried the resulting language as a 'jargon of authenticity'.[27] But Adorno went further: in a world which had passed through an apocalypse, he saw no future for poetry itself. After Auschwitz, in his notorious dictum – also dated 1951 – writing poems was a barbaric act.[28] Was he carrying this idea to its logical conclusion in *Minima*

Moralia? Was the book a subversion of the poetic form by discursive philosophy?[29] Adorno was smuggling a work of social analysis full of difficult philosophical references into his readers' reach by disguising it as literature. As the sixties progressed, they took the bait. Although Gente continued to read novels, he no longer read them as edifying tracts. Michael Rutschky, who discovered *Minima Moralia* a few years after him, wrote that Adorno's texts made 'literary writing seem completely anaemic compared with philosophy.'[30] Ten years after Gottfried Benn's premature declaration of victory, different circumstances prevailed: 'theory' – now in the singular as a mass noun – had so thoroughly co-opted poetry that it was in the process of superseding it.

Culture after Working Hours

With *Minima Moralia* as a pocket compass, Gente set off into the sixties. The young German intellectuals of that time wore Caesar bangs and simple clothes, and demonstrated their nonconformism by listening to jazz. Their attitude towards life had existentialist foundations, and Adorno's 'teaching of the good life' gave it a flavour of social critique.[31] 'Even the blossoming tree lies,' they read, 'the moment its bloom is seen without the shadow of terror.' And: 'For the intellectual, inviolable isolation is now the only way of showing some measure of solidarity.'[32] The dismay that sentences like these elicited in their readers is difficult to understand today; they sound oddly melodramatic to ears accustomed to the varieties of postmodern irony. Hence, it is with nostalgia that Michael Rutschky recalls the years when the world was still 'in perfect disorder.' With a little practice, Adorno's readers learned to apply his conceptual toolbox to situations of day-to-day life – at the risk of acting smugly superior.[33] No wonder Adorno, returning from exile, seemed to many older Germans like an avenging angel. His 'fiercely brilliant' thinking was all the more influential among the younger generation.[34]

Written in exile in California in the mid-1940s, *Minima Moralia* anticipated the post-war era's misgivings about the young West German state. The exiled Polish writer Witold Gombrowicz, who

4 Layers of time in Berlin: 'Trümmerfrauen' clearing away the rubble for the reconstruction of the Hansaviertel, 1957.

spent 1963 in West Berlin as a guest of the Ford Foundation, seems not even to have known the book's title, and yet the impressions he recorded in the divided city came surprisingly close to Adorno's assessment. Gombrowicz looked out over the trees of the Tiergarten from his fifteenth-floor apartment in the Hansaviertel tower block, took a drive down the broad boulevards to Freie Universität, and marvelled at the concrete hair-dos of the ladies in the cafés on Kurfürstendamm. 'City-spa, the most comfortable of all the known cities, where cars move smoothly without traffic jams and the people move smoothly, unhurriedly, where crowds and stuffiness are almost unknown.' Yet the cool modernism and the ahistorical atmosphere that surrounded the author instilled in him a certain anxiety. 'Death sat on my shoulder, like a bird, throughout my entire stay in Berlin'; terrible forebodings emanated from overgrown ruins. 'Only the everyday and the trifle', Gombrowicz wrote of the city where he contracted a heart ailment, 'are diabolical.'[35]

Peter Gente must have had similar feelings as he walked around town with his vade mecum in his pocket. Putting the past behind one was especially difficult in Berlin, where past and future overlapped. When Gente mentioned his new favourite author at home, his mother smelled 'Jewish subversion': she had retained her sensitivity to racial distinctions after the end of the war.[36] Her son's reaction was to drop law and enrol in philosophy, sociology and German literature. His sitting 'ten hours a day at his desk' to get through the gigantic reading load of three courses cannot be explained by political misgivings alone.[37] Adorno was more than just a moral authority breaking the silence that hung over the past: he attracted his first supporters by feeding their hunger for culture. He had noticed with surprise, after his return from exile in the United States in 1949, his Frankfurt students' zeal for 'the mind'. In a letter to Leo Lowenthal, he compared his seminar with a Talmud school: 'as if the spirits of the murdered Jewish intellectuals had descended into the German students'. Although these students had his respect – and although they helped him to feel at home in West Germany – Adorno found their political apathy worrying. People who would rather discuss poems than the state of the world, he felt, were continuing a German pattern of behaviour that prevented them from recognizing the gravity of the disaster. And yet, by the same token – such was the dialectic of Adorno's success – they were bound to be fascinated by Adorno.[38]

The work of the intellectual, Peter Gente read in *Minima Moralia*, encompassed 'what the bourgeois relegate to non-working hours as "culture"'.[39] On this point, at least, the book must have made sense to him straight away. Adorno made going to see Herbert von Karajan conducting, or to the Komische Oper, a serious matter. In order to be 'susceptible of aesthetic contemplation', he explained in one of his radio lectures, art must 'be thought through' as well.[40] Only by reflecting on its social entanglements can one activate its secret potential for emancipation. Thus, for readers like Gente who felt a vague desire to create culture themselves, Adorno had a tempting job to offer: they were expected to act as cultural critics. Even the cinema was an opportunity to practise the strenuous toil of conceptual reflection. After the awakening he had experienced in the Siemens factory, Gente never had to award school grades again. His new reading endowed him with different ways of responding altogether.[41]

Adorno is said to have been the 'trustee' of a German tradition, that of Beethoven and Hölderlin, which had been compromised and had to wait for his work to make it listenable and readable again. Perhaps it amounts to much the same thing if we say that West German post-war intellectuals not only had a weakness for culture, but also felt a need to raise the degree of thinking involved in approaching works of art. They understood Adorno's belief that, after the breakdown of civilization, culture 'in the traditional sense' must be seen as 'dead'. Only by adopting a critical distance could they accept their cultural heritage – and by the same token that heritage took on a social relevance. Joachim Kaiser wrote that nothing could be 'complicated enough' for German students. Witold Gombrowicz, spending his year in West Berlin literary and academic circles, found the intellectual climate of 1963 too 'cerebral'. Alongside the aestheticization of theory to which Adorno contributed with his books, the theorization of the aesthetic experience was the imperative of the moment.[42]

As the beneficiary of both developments, the new genre was suspected of cant. One of the first to fall under that suspicion was Adorno's antithesis, the Stuttgart philosopher of technology Max Bense. Bense's project 'Programming Beauty' was aimed at subjecting the field of aesthetics to the mathematical calculations of information theory. Like a cultural engineer, he wielded formulas to dismantle irrational faith in art. Aesthetic philosophy in Frankfurt and Stuttgart could not have been more different in tone: in Frankfurt, the critique of instrumental reason was *de rigueur*; in Stuttgart, the hard language of science ruled. But, in spite of the stylistic difference, there were striking parallels: Bense too applied his complicated formulas to works of art; he too had set aside artistic ambitions for the sake of theoretical work; his theory too was marked by an unmistakable idiom.[43] As early as the 1950s, Bense's incomprehensibility was so legendary that he became the target of a happening almost before the term was invented. In 1959, the group SPUR, the German wing of the Situationist International, announced a lecture by Bense in Munich – which the Stuttgart professor had to cancel at the last minute. Fortunately, he was able to send an audio tape, which the 300 attendees heard as a substitute – while watching a solitary glass of water on the lectern. The audience listened, could hardly believe its ears – and applauded. Only later, when Bense took legal action against the organizers, did it transpire that he had neither cancelled nor been invited in the first place. Hans-Peter Zimmer, one of the Situationists, had looted his publications and recorded a pastiche, disguising his voice. The lecture was exactly what the audience had not dared to pronounce it: pure nonsense. The discourse of theory, the sound of the sixties, had entered the period of its parody as soon as the decade began.[44]

In the Literary Supermarket

Peter Gente was fascinated with Adorno to such a point that he wanted to read everything the man wrote. Starting with his gateway drug, *Minima Moralia*, he systematically worked his way backwards to the early writings on musical aesthetics, some of which were difficult to find at that time, before the Suhrkamp edition of Adorno's collected works. Library research was necessary to reconstruct the theoretical context. Gente collated bibliographical lists as meticulously as he had kept his cultural diary (now abandoned), copying out tables of contents on the typewriter and making thick, gum-bound Xerox copies which are now almost completely faded.

And, while catching up on Adorno's past publications, Gente also had to keep up with his current production. What with the author's growing popularity and presence in the West German media, that was a time-consuming task. Together with a handful of like-minded readers – who were thought nuts by their fellow students – Gente formed an 'information syndicate' to lay hands on everything Adorno published, no matter how obscure the outlet. 'He'd just written something in *Neues Forum*, so I ran to Schöller's and bought it.'[45] (Marga Schöller's historic shop in Knesebeckstrasse was where West

Berlin's revolutionary students bought their literature before the little Red bookshops usurped the market.) The thick dossier Gente compiled as an Adorno fan would later become his seed capital as a publisher. His theory archives grew more diverse with each passing year, and eventually spawned the first Merve titles.

Among the earliest articles Gente clipped and filed is a commentary by Adorno on the 1959 Frankfurt Book Fair. In it, Adorno expressed a vague 'anxiety' that had oppressed him for some time at the sight of each season's new publications: it seemed to him that the books no longer looked like books. The covers had become 'advertising', degrading the reader to a consumer as they made their advances. They heralded the 'liquidation of the book' in 'all too intense and conspicuous colours'. A proficient stylist, Adorno needed no more than two columns to run the gamut of his cultural criticism: the diagnosis of death where life only appeared to persist; the successive moments of horror, realization and despair. For Adorno would not be Adorno if he did not finish with a dialectical sidestep and declare the industrialization of the book market inevitable. The melancholy over the deterioration of a cultural artefact 'in which truth presents itself' was all the deeper for that.[46]

Every new medium has kindled in its turn the apocalyptic discourse of the death of the book – television, in particular, and later the screen culture of the digital age.[47] In the post-war period, that discourse was first heard as a critique of the paperback book. In the same year in which Adorno reported on the Frankfurt Book Fair, the Hessian radio network broadcast Hans Magnus Enzensberger's 'analysis of paperback production', an examination of the leading German publishers' catalogues. Rowohlt's *rororo* series, named for the mass-producing rotary printing press, had entered the German market as early as 1946. From then on, paperback production had only grown, in all segments of the industry. In his critique, an attempt to grasp the significance of the paperback phenomenon, Enzensberger essentially came to the same conclusions as Adorno. He, too, saw intellectual culture deteriorating to a commodity, the reader demoted to a consumer. Of course, the fear that cheap paperbacks would be not so much read as briefly leafed through and then stuffed back onto the shelf, or even thrown away, was not limited to Germany. It was a common motif of cultural criticism wherever publishers pressed forward into the new book market – in Paris and Rome no less than in Frankfurt. The paperback seemed to be a harbinger of the global 'mass culture'.[48] What worried Enzensberger most was the reader's disenfranchisement: he thought the flood of new titles robbed readers of their ability to judge. In the 'literary supermarket', where anticipated sales took the place of the cultural canon, helpless readers were prey to the manipulations of the culture industry.[49]

Neither Enzensberger nor Adorno could have imagined in 1959 that they would owe their own success as authors to the generation of paperback readers.[50] Once *Minima Moralia* appeared in a soft cover in the early 1960s, no one carried it around in hardcover any more. Adorno later attained high sales figures in the various paperback series published by Suhrkamp. The new medium, which, from its critics' perspective, ensured the conformance of the consumer, was supplying difficult ideas – initially as contraband – to a growing readership.[51] The history of theory is not conceivable without these upheavals in the book market, and that is what makes Peter Gente, the book collector and book producer, such an exemplary figure in that history. It was the Penguin designer Hans Schmoller, a German-Jewish emigrant, who remarked in 1974 on the paradox of the 'paperback revolution': 'though in the West paperbacks have become big business, this has not prevented their publishers from giving free rein to expressing ideas strongly opposed to established political and economic systems and indeed advocating their overthrow'.[52]

Adorno Answers

After having been forgotten for an interim, Adorno was omnipresent in the 1960s.[53] He filled the lecture halls and appeared in the young mass media – most of all, radio, the German 'counter-university' of the post-war period.[54] The barely modulated voice, separating its words with tiny pauses, was unmistakable. It was a hit with the audiences of the cultural programmes and the night-time airwaves. Learning by radio how to read Hegel: such breathtakingly highbrow content sends today's cultural editors into raptures of nostalgia. It is hardly imaginable any more, Joachim Kaiser wrote for Adorno's hundredth birthday, what influence the philosopher had in those days.[55] At that time, when Kaiser himself fell under that influence, he described it in these terms: 'Anyone writing, speculating, politicizing, aestheticizing today must engage with Adorno.'[56] No one has held a comparable monopoly since. In the seventies, as Marxism grew sclerotic, Critical Theory submerged in the think-tank on Lake Starnberg – the Max Planck Institute for the Study of the Scientific-Technical World, whose second director was Jürgen Habermas – and the French came to dominate the theoretical airspace, another German generation grew accustomed to living in the philosophical provinces, dependent on onerously decrypted imports from a Mecca of theory across the Rhine. The *Weltgeist* didn't live here any more.

Before '68, when German society had maintained an eloquent silence about its recent past, it had been otherwise – this was one of history's ironies. Dangerous ideas hadn't had to be smuggled across the border then; they were right there in Frankfurt. And if you weren't one of the chosen few who personally inhabited Adorno's orbit, as Joachim Kaiser did, you could pick up the Frankfurt phone book, look up his address and write to him.[57] Adorno's philosophical presence seems in retrospect almost to have demanded direct communication. The Situationists in Munich apparently thought so too, although their missive also contains a first grain of resistance against Adorno. In 1964, five years after they had taken on Max Bense, they posted on German university buildings their famous 'lonely hearts advert', composed of excerpts from the as yet largely unknown *Dialectic of Enlightenment*, in block letters: 'THE CULTURE INDUSTRY HAS SUCCEEDED SO UNIFORMLY IN TRANSFORMING SUBJECTS INTO SOCIAL FUNCTIONS THAT, TOTALLY AFFECTED, NO LONGER AWARE OF ANY CONFLICT, THEY ENJOY THEIR OWN DEHUMANIZATION AS HUMAN HAPPINESS, AS THE HAPPINESS OF WARMTH', and more in that vein. Readers who felt the poster made them stop and think were invited to contact 'Th. W. Adorno, Kettenhofweg 123, 6 Frankfurt/Main.' Among those who wrote to the address given was the University of Stuttgart, which sent an invoice for the cost of removing the posters, although Adorno, like Bense before him, had known nothing of the Situationists' action.[58]

The 'nexus of deception' that Adorno depicts in sombre colours penetrated to the capillaries of day-to-day life. In the absence of functional differentiation, which had no place in his theory, nothing was safe from the falseness of society as a whole – and from that fact Adorno derived an almost boundless authority. The numerous unsolicited letters among his archived papers show how willing his German readers and listeners were to appeal to his expertise. His remark in *Minima Moralia* that, in a society in which 'every mouse-hole has been plugged, mere advice exactly equals condemnation' did not stop them from asking the book's author for advice in almost every imaginable circumstance.[59] He gave it, sometimes hesitantly, sometimes reluctantly, but he always made an honest effort to help. 'Intellectual people', Adorno wrote in one of his return letters, must have had a great need for spiritual guidance at that time.[60]

The questions, arriving from every state of the Federal Republic and from all social classes, make up an intellectual portrait of post-war West Germany. Doctoral candidates in philosophy sent Adorno their dissertation projects; disillusioned students turned to him in search of meaning. The expectations people had in writing to Adorno are astounding. In those days, the figure of an intellectual was still filled with promise. A law student in Tübingen who had doubts about his career assured Adorno he was 'the only man in Germany' who could 'help him to moral freedom', and hoped he might maintain 'relations of correspondence, however minimal', with him.[61] The Baroness von Gersdorff, who wrote to Adorno in 1956, made no bones about having finished her letter only after four false starts – and in the middle of the night: 'The cause of this schoolgirl uncertainty can be found in the considerable respect your books instil in me.'[62]

The letters on *Minima Moralia* alone could provide material for a brief reception history. 'I am completely mesmerized by the *Minima Moralia*', wrote a Swiss woman who had met Adorno in the high Alpine valley of Engadine. 'I read, I read again, I say yes and of course – & I am frightened and then rescued when a clear truth is simply there and I recognize it.'[63] In the 1950s, some readers used the book as their gospel. 'I have been wandering around for several months now in the glowing space of your ideas', says a letter from Wiesbaden; 'most recently I have drawn daily instruction and light from your sketched thoughts, as others read the watchwords of the Moravian Church every morning for the strength they inspire.'[64] Is it possible that Adorno's most loyal followers were those in the provinces? 'I am a teacher in a remote East Frisian village of 500 inhabitants, and I have few opportunities to receive stimulation of this kind', wrote a solitary listener who had heard him on the radio. 'Be assured that your words found attentive and eager ears even in the remotest corner!'[65]

The group of senders was not limited to young intellectuals. There were also many older Germans among the music enthusiasts who asked Adorno for musical assistance. 'I would like to know whether you consider Weber's aria "Through the Forests, through the Meadows" to be light or serious music.'[66] That question came from a woman who had known Adorno's aunt before the war. And what about the businessman from Wuppertal who assured Adorno that he was 'also a nonconformist, which you may perhaps see by the fact that I have just returned from a rather unusual sojourn, called a monastic retreat, during which I joined the community of a Benedictine abbey for a fortnight'?[67] There is no answer to this letter in the archives. As his celebrity grew in the course of the sixties, Adorno found himself more and more often in the situation of having to ward off false friends. A former classmate who felt it incumbent upon himself to point out a gap in the author's knowledge of physics was dismissed with the words:

> You are not the only one of my childhood friends to seek contact with me again after a hiatus of decades, and to be so obviously plagued by resentment that that contact is disrupted in the very moment at which it is supposed to be renewed, and in view of the fact that my name has made the rounds, I can't even defend myself properly against the resentment without being mistaken for a snob.[68]

Adorno was prompt, however, to respond helpfully to a letter that arrived in 1968 from Amorbach, the paradise of his childhood in the Odenwald forest. The girl from the stationery shop over the road from the hotel where his family had spent the summer holidays before the war asked him to intervene with the government of Lower Franconia in opposition to a planned ring road. By return post, Adorno petitioned the politicians in Würzburg to 'refrain from everything that could make this unique place ugly'.[69]

Adorno felt an obligation to answer letters, and was hence afflicted by the number he received. Again and again, he pointed out in his replies that it was not his task to interfere 'in the casuistry of anyone's specific problems'.[70] He even complained occasionally of a 'torrent of filth' pouring down on him.[71] His radio lectures were regularly followed by hate mail, and the project-initiators and amateur philosophers who wanted to involve him in their planning exercises were probably not his cup of tea, either. He had nothing to say about the 'spectral analysis of reason' which a legal counsellor from Darmstadt had thought up in a Russian prisoner-of-war camp, nor about the 'international intellectuals' unions' that a writer in Duisburg thought necessary.[72] He kept the astrologers at arm's length too, who carried on a kind of personal feud with him after the publication of his analysis, written in exile in California, of the *Los Angeles Times* horoscope rubric.[73]

Adorno's best moments as the post-war Germans' friend in need had to do with their situations of intellectual and existential distress. His correspondence with readers illustrates the strictures of a society in urgent need of the '68 generation's cultural revolution. 'Dear Professor Adorno', the moving letter of an 18-year-old Viennese art student begins:

> My homophile disposition itself would not pose me any problems if I were not confronted with an ignorant, hateful, tyrannical world which tolerates no 'difference'. It would help me a great deal if I could read something now and then that counterbalances the lies of my surroundings with a true and human attitude. Dear Professor Adorno, please send me the title and address of a good homosexual periodical so that I can subscribe to it. I am young and desperate, but I don't want to lose faith in myself.[74]

In his answer, Adorno recommended reading André Gide and encouraged the writer not to surrender 'to conformism'. However, he was unable to recommend a homosexual magazine, 'much as he would like to', as he himself felt 'not even the slightest inclination in that direction'.[75] If there seems to be a hint of antipathy here – of which

Adorno can be suspected elsewhere, too – it did not diminish the art student's gratitude. 'I was honestly surprised and startled at the length of your reply', he wrote back. 'I appreciate your service to all humanity (of which we homosexuals are only a negligible part).'[76]

A philosophy student from Berlin felt the same as she struggled to cope with the feeling of hopelessness that had possessed her after reading Adorno's works. 'Thinking about what I was reading and trying to think through other matters myself', she wrote in the summer of 1966:

> the more clearly I recognized the total negativity, the less I was able to understand how there could be any hope. I can no longer feel the exhilarating 'air of other planets' as anything but a promise of the impossible; I cannot grasp the last sentence of the *Minima Moralia*. And I can't find anyone who could help me somehow. Because I cannot bear to go on living and talking as if it were possible to lead a light-hearted personal life, I have broken off personal contacts that were of no help in my search for some possibility of hope, but only made me more desperate with their spiritual emptiness.[77]

Confronted with the potential side effects of his ideas, Adorno responded immediately. He warned his reader against doing anything rash, and suggested a personal meeting. 'The way from thinking to so-called practice', he pointed out, 'is much more convoluted than is generally imagined today.'[78] Apparently, his tactics of reassurance had the desired effect, for his correspondent was feeling much better in her next letter. She thanked him for a meeting that had changed her life – and that in the tones of a true disciple: 'You thought it somewhat odd that I should look to you of all people for consolation when I felt that "everything is so bleak"; I realized only afterward that I was not looking for hope, but for solidarity in my hopelessness.'[79]

Are Your Endeavours Aimed at Changing the World?

Peter Gente did not seek Adorno's help. In October of 1965, he wrote to him on a matter that was apparently purely philological:

> Some weeks ago I read the special issue of the journal *Sinn und Form* on Hanns Eisler. The issue contained reprinted excerpts of *Composing for the Films.* I immediately borrowed that book and was quite perplexed. Did Eisler really write it? It reads like a digression from the *Dialectic of Enlightenment*, and yet the manuscript was allegedly completed as early as 1942! I suspect that you are the real author and would be grateful for confirmation. Please allow me to send you my best wishes and very warm regards.[80]

This tone of respectful distance is how a disciple addresses his master. Adorno's answer betrays that he felt quite flattered: 'As to your suspicions concerning the book *Composing for the Films*, you have guessed the truth. I believe I can say without doing Eisler any injustice that nine tenths of the book are mine and one tenth at most was written by him.' The reason for leaving Adorno's name off the title page, he hinted, was Joseph McCarthy's campaign against supposed communists: in 1947, just before the book went to press, the House Un-American Activities Committee had begun its first hearing – against the brothers Hanns and Gerhart Eisler. 'Under these circumstances', Adorno explained, 'I felt it was right not to declare my authorship, trusting that people who took an interest in my work would notice it in any case. After so many years, you are one of the first.' In concluding, he asked Gente to treat his message as confidential, since 'in the climate currently prevailing in our country, some people would naturally try to exploit the matter.'[81]

The heads of the Frankfurt School were anxious to keep their Marxist past under wraps, not least in order to avoid risking the disfavour of their American sponsors. For that reason, they long resisted the idea of a new edition of the *Dialectic of Enlightenment*, and purged their old texts of passages that contained echoes of class struggle.[82] And that was the reason why Adorno was reluctant, in 1965, to be associated with Hanns Eisler, the recently deceased composer of East Germany's national anthem, whose brother Gerhart, just on the other side of the Berlin Wall, was a high official in the Socialist Unity Party. Although he showed fewer reservations in this regard than Max Horkheimer, Adorno too tried to avoid the stigma of communist sympathies under the West German state. Not until May of 1969, shortly before his death, did *Composing for the Films* appear under his name, published by the direct-distribution press Zweitausendeins. Adorno exposed the book's true authorship in an appendix. The letter to Gente in which he had done so four years earlier found its way into an editor's afterword in the later Suhrkamp edition of Adorno's complete works.[83] Gente, by then the publisher of Merve and still an Adorno reader, was, of course, proud of that.

And yet, for all his overt veneration of the author, Gente's intentions in formulating his letter had been quite critical. For in 1965, at the apex of his fame, Adorno's moral authority was beginning to show signs of strain. The question whether the book on film music was really the product of Adorno's pen concealed the unspoken suspicion that Adorno had foisted off his elitist, ultimately bourgeois aesthetics on the Marxist Eisler. Both Adorno and Eisler had lent their support to twelve-tone music since the 1920s; whoever had written the book in question went so far as to hold Schönberg's progressive dissonances to be the only music appropriate to the medium of film. But there was an essential political difference, as the well-read Gente knew by that time, between Adorno's and Eisler's positions. Was the function of twelve-tone composition to liberate music – without regard for audiences' tastes – from the myth of natural tonality? Or was its purpose grounded in the education of the revolutionary class? Adorno's 'Leninist listening,' as the novelist Rainald Goetz once called it, was reserved to the avant-garde.[84] To Hanns Eisler, on the other hand, whose studies with Schönberg had not prevented him from composing a harmonious anthem for the Germany of his choice, musical progress must be subservient to the socialist society. Aesthetic elitism or music for the revolutionary masses: those were the choices. The book on film scoring took Adorno's side – under Eisler's name. Since the mid-sixties, however, that side had become politically suspect.[85] Sooner or later, Gente's subtle criticism would inevitably draw after it the crucial question that Adorno heard more and more often during the last years of his life. Just a few weeks after Gente's letter, one of Adorno's students in Frankfurt asked it straight out: 'Dear Professor Adorno,' says the letter of November 1965:

> Our generation, or at least a part of it, is confronted with the harrowing experience of our parents having lived under National Socialism and

failing to explain why they put up with it, except by saying there was nothing they could have done. Hence our reflections on what meaning philosophy has, what meaning it can have, for our practice. Is theory practicable or not? Are your endeavours aimed at changing the world?[86]

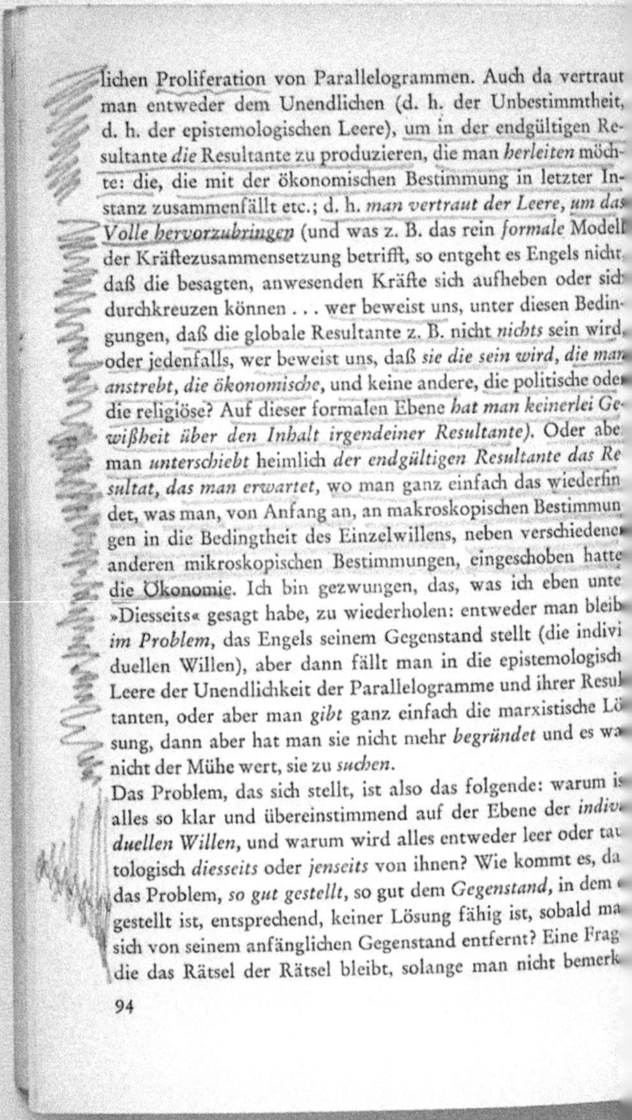
lichen Proliferation von Parallelogrammen. Auch da vertraut man entweder dem Unendlichen (d. h. der Unbestimmtheit, d. h. der epistemologischen Leere), um in der endgültigen Resultante *die* Resultante zu produzieren, die man *herleiten* möchte: die, die mit der ökonomischen Bestimmung in letzter Instanz zusammenfällt etc.; d. h. *man vertraut der Leere, um das Volle hervorzubringen* (und was z. B. das rein *formale* Modell der Kräftezusammensetzung betrifft, so entgeht es Engels nicht, daß die besagten, anwesenden Kräfte sich aufheben oder sich durchkreuzen können . . . wer beweist uns, unter diesen Bedingungen, daß die globale Resultante z. B. nicht *nichts* sein wird, oder jedenfalls, wer beweist uns, daß *sie die sein wird, die man anstrebt, die ökonomische*, und keine andere, die politische oder die religiöse? Auf dieser formalen Ebene *hat man keinerlei Gewißheit über den Inhalt irgendeiner Resultante).* Oder aber man *unterschiebt* heimlich *der endgültigen Resultante das Resultat, das man erwartet,* wo man ganz einfach das wiederfindet, was man, von Anfang an, an makroskopischen Bestimmungen in die Bedingtheit des Einzelwillens, neben verschiedene anderen mikroskopischen Bestimmungen, eingeschoben hatte: die Ökonomie. Ich bin gezwungen, das, was ich eben unter »Diesseits« gesagt habe, zu wiederholen: entweder man bleibt *im Problem*, das Engels seinem Gegenstand stellt (die individuellen Willen), aber dann fällt man in die epistemologisch Leere der Unendlichkeit der Parallelogramme und ihrer Resultanten, oder aber man *gibt* ganz einfach die marxistische Lösung, dann aber hat man sie nicht mehr *begründet* und es wa nicht der Mühe wert, sie zu *suchen*.

Das Problem, das sich stellt, ist also das folgende: warum is alles so klar und übereinstimmend auf der Ebene der *individuellen Willen*, und warum wird alles entweder leer oder tautologisch *diesseits* oder *jenseits* von ihnen? Wie kommt es, da das Problem, *so gut gestellt*, so gut dem *Gegenstand*, in dem gestellt ist, entsprechend, keiner Lösung fähig ist, sobald ma sich von seinem anfänglichen Gegenstand entfernt? Eine Frag die das Rätsel der Rätsel bleibt, solange man nicht bemerk

94

5 Louis Althusser, *Für Marx*, Frankfurt: Suhrkamp, 1968.

2

IN THE SUHRKAMP CULTURE

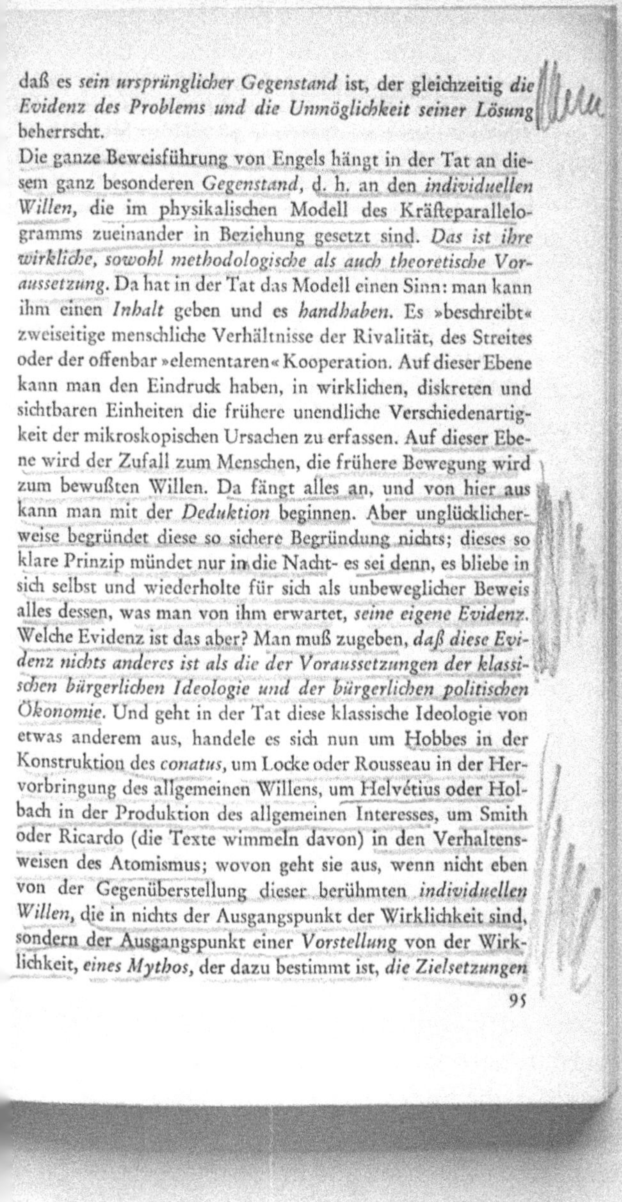

daß es *sein ursprünglicher Gegenstand* ist, der gleichzeitig *die Evidenz des Problems und die Unmöglichkeit seiner Lösung* beherrscht.

Die ganze Beweisführung von Engels hängt in der Tat an diesem ganz besonderen *Gegenstand*, d. h. an den *individuellen Willen*, die im physikalischen Modell des Kräfteparallelogramms zueinander in Beziehung gesetzt sind. *Das ist ihre wirkliche, sowohl methodologische als auch theoretische Voraussetzung*. Da hat in der Tat das Modell einen Sinn: man kann ihm einen *Inhalt* geben und es *handhaben*. Es »beschreibt« zweiseitige menschliche Verhältnisse der Rivalität, des Streites oder der offenbar »elementaren« Kooperation. Auf dieser Ebene kann man den Eindruck haben, in wirklichen, diskreten und sichtbaren Einheiten die frühere unendliche Verschiedenartigkeit der mikroskopischen Ursachen zu erfassen. Auf dieser Ebene wird der Zufall zum Menschen, die frühere Bewegung wird zum bewußten Willen. Da fängt alles an, und von hier aus kann man mit der *Deduktion* beginnen. Aber unglücklicherweise begründet diese so sichere Begründung nichts; dieses so klare Prinzip mündet nur in die Nacht- es sei denn, es bliebe in sich selbst und wiederholte für sich als unbeweglicher Beweis alles dessen, was man von ihm erwartet, *seine eigene Evidenz*. Welche Evidenz ist das aber? Man muß zugeben, *daß diese Evidenz nichts anderes ist als die der Voraussetzungen der klassischen bürgerlichen Ideologie und der bürgerlichen politischen Ökonomie*. Und geht in der Tat diese klassische Ideologie von etwas anderem aus, handele es sich nun um Hobbes in der Konstruktion des *conatus*, um Locke oder Rousseau in der Hervorbringung des allgemeinen Willens, um Helvétius oder Holbach in der Produktion des allgemeinen Interesses, um Smith oder Ricardo (die Texte wimmeln davon) in den Verhaltensweisen des Atomismus; wovon geht sie aus, wenn nicht eben von der Gegenüberstellung dieser berühmten *individuellen Willen*, die in nichts der Ausgangspunkt der Wirklichkeit sind, sondern der Ausgangspunkt einer *Vorstellung* von der Wirklichkeit, *eines Mythos*, der dazu bestimmt ist, *die Zielsetzungen*

95

It would be some time, however, before philosophy would be swept up in the maelstrom of practice, and before Adorno would be driven from the lecture hall as an obstacle to revolution by bare-breasted student activists. In 1965, theory was ascendant. In the autumn semester, Adorno lectured on negative dialectics: the event had the aura of an important event for German society. He stepped up to the lectern, aided by a female assistant. For the first time, a tape recorder was running to record his message for posterity. Adorno went all out in saying that Marx's famous Feuerbach thesis – that philosophy's duty is to change the world – was obsolete. Because theory has not metamorphosed, as predicted, into practice, because it has thus failed to be eliminated, he explained, we must assume once more that theoretical thinking is still current. In a bold figure of speech, he summarily turned Marx upside down: 'One reason why [the world] was not changed was probably the fact that it was not interpreted enough.' Only theory that is not immediately aimed at changing the world, his dialectically intricate argument implied, is able to change it at all. And where, if not here, in 'relatively peaceful' West Germany, could such a philosophical project find the necessary 'historical breathing space'?[1] It is surprising how benevolently Adorno reviewed German history. Ordinarily, he had been the harshest critic of the status quo, but now he seemed to sense a historic opportunity. The present, he assured the students who packed his lecture hall to overflowing, is 'the time for theory.'[2]

New Leftists

The lines of conflict of debates to come were already laid out in that statement. But in the autumn semester of 1965, Adorno's affirmation of pure philosophy must have been met with approval in the ranks of the New Left. If the seed Adorno had sown yielded such an abundant harvest in the sixties, it was thanks to the enthusiasm for culture among Germans born in wartime, as well as to the rise of the first theory generation.[3] In 1959, the Social Democratic Party (SPD) had adopted the Godesberg Programme, abandoning the goal of overcoming rather than reforming capitalism, and in 1961, it declared the new political course irreconcilable with the aims of its former youth organization, the Socialist German Student League (SDS), and cut off its financial support. This push-off into precarity – which would soon be cushioned by new funding for the SDS from East Germany – marked the beginning of the history of the New Left in Germany. Left in the lurch by their mother organization, the students turned their backs on the dogmas of Social Democratic folklore, sized up the conformism of the West German proletariat and, making a virtue out of necessity, rolled up their sleeves as revolutionary subjects. Thus, the early sixties saw the formation of the 'student movement', so named in analogy to the 'labour movement'. The distinguishing characteristic that set it apart from the classical left – especially in West Germany – was theory.[4]

'What is to be done?' cried the literature student Elisabeth Lenk at the 17th regular delegates' conference of the SDS in October 1962. Her answer to Lenin's famous question: work on theory. In the face of union officials who proudly claimed not to read books, in the face of a Social Democratic Party that was throwing itself at the petite bourgeoisie, the path of the New Left must lead into the vineyard of texts. Lenk urgently warned her comrades against the casual cultural critique of the nonconformists, who 'think they are performing a revolutionary act by sitting in a basement jazz bar with their Enzensberger haircuts'. The SDS needed hard, 'socialist theory'. Lenk's speech gives voice to the need for fundamental research of a kind that the Left had last undertaken in the 1920s. 'But what is socialist theory?' she asked her comrades. 'Is it the same as unadulterated Marxism? Or is it a revised Marxism, and if so, which one? Bernstein's, Kautsky's, Lenin's, or that of some Marxist-Existentialist? Or is it just the eclectic interconnection of handy bits of theory?'[5]

From this vantage, we can already see looming on the horizon the craggy ridge of text that the students of the coming years would have to climb. Under the eyes of these readers, the revolution metamorphosed into textual analysis.[6] Until its creeping exhaustion, the Left's theoretical discourse was dominated by a powerful fantasy of reprieve which looks startlingly similar to Adorno's 'breathing space': there could be no revolution, according to the credo of these years, without a theory of revolution, which neither Marx nor his successors had supplied. And building such a theory would take longer than a five-year plan. The SDS 'study groups' proposed by Elisabeth Lenk were given relatively short deadlines. Hans-Jürgen Krahl, on the other hand, the intellectual head of Frankfurt's anti-authoritarians, estimated in 1969 that it would take several decades to develop a theory of revolution.[7] That was the same year, by the way, in which Niklas Luhmann at the University of Bielefeld estimated a development time of thirty years for his 'theory of society'. After '68, once the messianic expectations had been dispelled, theory developed staying power – and not just on the left. As the catalogue of available classics grew longer, the network of references denser and the political hopes more cloudy, the practice of difficult thinking transformed into a process whose end was hardly foreseeable.

He Didn't Write

Peter Gente's path through the Red decade opens the Bildungsroman of the '68 generation. At Freie Universität, he came into contact with the West Berlin wing of the SDS; joined the cleverest leftists at Argument Club, led by the editors of *Das Argument*, Margherita von Brentano and Wolfgang Fritz Haug; read every line of Adorno ever printed; and then began a critique of the 'superstructure catechists'.[8] Back issues of the *Zeitschrift für Sozialforschung* turned up which showed that Critical Theory had been outspokenly Marxist before the war. In the Institute for Social Research in Frankfurt, Horkheimer had put these issues under lock and key, but a connoisseur in West Berlin could find them in the estate of the German Jewish political scientist Franz Neumann, the author of *Behemoth*, one of the first structural analyses of the Third Reich, published in 1942.[9] The Left's slow separation from Critical Theory in the second half of the sixties took place in the form of such archaeological digs, as students eagerly sifted the contents of the libraries and second-hand bookshops to unearth the buried truth of the labour movement.[10] Such a tranquil, studious radicalization must have suited Gente's disposition. His investigative reconstruction of Adorno's œuvre had long since made him an eminent authority in the parallel universe of obscure sources. He would later refer to himself, in a letter to his author Pierre Klossowski, as a 'monomaniacal collector'.[11] His fanatical collecting is somewhat reminiscent of the Milanese publisher Giangiacomo Feltrinelli, who drove his Citroën DS all over Europe in the 1950s to accumulate a library of the labour movement – from a first edition of More's *Utopia* to the correspondence of Palmiro Togliatti. (Later, Feltrinelli went underground, and he blew himself up under mysterious circumstances at the foot of a high-voltage pylon near Milan.)[12] In contrast to Feltrinelli, however, Gente had no penchant for luxurious or antique editions. Nor did he ever take the leap into activism. Rather, he supplied Berlin's leftist students with dangerous reading material as an 'encyclopaedist of rebellion'.[13]

In 1960, Peter Gente married the pedicurist Merve Lowien. The intellectual and the proletarian: to his comrades in the SDS, the alliance amounted to a political statement.[14] Gente's commitment went so far as to include starting a family. While others of his generation, taking advantage of the Pill, plunged into serial one-night stands, Gente became a father in 1962. In any case, his intellectual development during these years did not permit a hedonistic lifestyle. Acquiring a moustache and metal-rimmed glasses, he was gradually morphing into Walter Benjamin.[15] Such mimicry was a common phenomenon among Berlin students in those days – not only because Benjamin, a Berlin native, was a suitable candidate for the role of the local hero,[16] but because, in his later, materialist writings, Benjamin had created a revolutionary type of author, a language engineer who placed his typewriter at the service of the struggling working class: 'Does he succeed in promoting the socialization of the intellectual means of production? Does he see how he himself can organize the intellectual workers in the production process? Does he have proposals for transforming the function of the novel, the drama, the poem?'[17] Compared with the radicalism which such questions expressed, Adorno, with his penchant for Stifter and Beethoven, suddenly looked like one of the reactionary bourgeoisie.[18] Didn't the 'meditation of powerlessness' that his texts demonstrated stifle every impulse to act?[19] Wasn't the revolutionary Brecht better than Adorno's preference, Beckett? The letter that Gente wrote to Adorno in 1965 already betrays the politicization of his aesthetic repertoire. Shortly thereafter, Gente worked openly against his former favourite author in supplying the editors of the literary journal *Alternative* with original publications by Benjamin from the 1930s to demonstrate that the Frankfurt editors of Benjamin's collected works – Adorno and his student Rolf Tiedemann – were carrying out a questionable policy. The allegation that the Suhrkamp edition, principally edited by Adorno, downplayed Benjamin's conversion to Marxism by retouching key sentences caused a stir in philological politics. To his growing numbers of followers in the student movement, Benjamin was being martyred once more by the injustice of his executors.[20]

While the leftist press drew on his expertise, Gente's studies made only modest progress. The seminar papers he wrote on materialist aesthetics did not arouse his professors' enthusiasm. Peter Szondi found a 1965 paper on Lukács to contain 'approaches and suggestions that sometimes overstep the boundary between research and journalism', and marked it 'satisfactory'.[21] In spite of modest marks, Gente thought about going on to do a doctorate. The dissertation he had in mind, inspired by his reading of Benjamin, would be devoted to the failure of the bourgeois arts. But Szondi was not receptive to the topic. 'He didn't really understand what I actually wanted, and I couldn't really explain it to him, you see', Gente recalled. The idea of the end of art must have sounded as strange to Szondi as it did to Adorno.[22] Yet it was what everyone had been talking about since May '68, under the label of 'cultural revolution'. 'L'art est mort', the Parisian students had written on the walls of the Sorbonne, and Hans Magnus Enzensberger had continued their eulogy in his monthly cultural journal *Kursbuch*: 'In our day, it is not possible to identify a significant social function of literary works of art', he pronounced, causing an uproar among publishers and authors. As examples for a revolutionary literature to come, Enzensberger named the politically engaged writers Günter Wallraff and Ulrike Meinhof.[23] In view of their public reception, however, his theses were no longer suitable as a topic for a dissertation. It looks as though Peter Gente had come too late to his academic career. Or perhaps he had merely realized since his arrival at the university that he had no talent as a writer.

'He didn't write', the New York theory publisher Sylvère Lotringer would recall about his friend many years later.[24] The statement hits the central issue of Gente's life on the head – perhaps even the issue of his generation. As a budding intellectual, he had not only penetrated into the nexus of leftist tradition during the sixties, but had also been looking for his own voice. For lack of a better label, Gente identified himself at the time of Merve's founding as a 'freelance writer',[25] but, except for an article on the 'Bitterfeld Way', a current in East German workers' literature, he had written practically nothing.[26] Publishing other people's writing suited him better. At a time when the air was filled with editorial projects, there were many opportunities to do so. Gente scored his first modest coup as an editor in 1965 with a theme issue of *Alternative* on Parisian essayists. By that time, he had extended his mania for collecting to include French journals, and had unearthed texts by Roland Barthes, Claude Lévi-Strauss, Lucien Goldmann and others. Hardly anyone in Berlin knew these theoreticians, and the issue was a great success. Two years later, Gente would again demonstrate his advanced knowledge by providing the key evidence in the dispute over the Suhrkamp edition of Benjamin. Helmut Lethen, who also contributed to *Alternative* at that time, found Gente and his encyclopaedic knowledge a 'tremendous source of inspiration'. Nevertheless, Gente did not become a regular member of the editorial team: the editor-in-chief, Hildegard Brenner, would not accept the fact that he could not be persuaded to write.[27]

School of Hard Books

In 1965, shortly after the *Alternative* special issue appeared, the newly appointed Professor of Hermeneutics and Jewish Studies Jacob Taubes invited Gente into his office. Up to then, he had taken no notice of the quiet student in his seminars, but he found Gente's knowledge of the French thinkers remarkable. As a token of his appreciation, Taubes offered Gente one of his envied student assistant positions. Gente's first assignment was to unpack Taubes's library, which, he recalled, had 'arrived from New York in heavy shipping crates'.[28] At that time, it was taken for granted that a well-to-do scholar and professor would control his means of production by personal ownership.[29] To the hungry eyes of his student assistant, the encounter with Taubes's books must have been a formative experience. Taubes's library encompassed more than the canon of German philosophy and modern classics that had come to be *de rigueur* for the followers of Critical Theory. It documented the reading career of a cosmopolitan intellectual who had a penchant for giving consideration to obscure and scandalous thinkers. Taubes exuded an atmosphere of scholarly intensity in which the fate of humanity seemed to depend on the interpretation of crucial texts.[30] Rumour had it that he was able 'to grasp the content of a book infallibly by merely laying his hands on it'.[31] Among the mysteries of this colourful personality is the fact that, in spite of – or perhaps because of – this gift as a reader, he was not prominent as an author. Adorno, whose relationship with Taubes was strained, thought he was 'simultaneously highly gifted and deeply disturbed in his productivity'.[32] To the students who felt attracted to his intellectual excitement, Taubes conveyed the existential importance of theory. The Department of Hermeneutics that he established at Freie Universität 'was the centre of often wildly interdisciplinary studies, highly controversial, and a sanctuary for many who did not want to tread any predefined path', recalled Henning Ritter, who was a tutor under Taubes in the sixties.[33] One of the nonconformists broadening their intellectual horizons in this circle was the student assistant Peter Gente. Those who came under Taubes's influence were exposed to sufficient apocrypha to immunize them against the dogmatism of the student movement. They were also estranged from Adorno, whom Taubes in turn considered a 'protesting left-wing Heideggerian' with an affected style.[34] 'Who here can write as beautifully as Adorno?' he is said to have shouted repeatedly during a lecture, 'laughing eerily'.[35]

Taubes had neither Adorno's talent as a writer nor his reluctance to intervene in politics. At Freie Universität, which he saw as something like the Berkeley of Germany, Taubes took the side of the rebelling students. And yet he responded with scepticism to their utopian expectations. The activity of the SDS interested him more for its subversive energy than for its socialist background. When the Kommune I members Fritz Teufel and Rainer Langhans were made to stand trial for distributing a handbill inciting people to burn down department stores, Taubes wrote, as an amicus curiae, an evaluation of the 'surrealist provocation', situating it in the tradition of literary avant-gardes. His submission helped the communards escape a jail sentence.[36] In July of 1967, Taubes moderated a public discussion at FU with his friend Herbert Marcuse, who drew boisterous enthusiasm from the students. Taubes invited the Parisian Hegel interpreter Alexandre Kojève to Berlin the same year, who perplexed his revolutionary listeners by recommending that the best thing to do in the present situation was to learn Ancient Greek. Kojève's snobbism was incomprehensible to the '68 generation. Only initiates among Taubes's students could decipher, perhaps, that Kojève was serving up a taste of his theory of 'post-histoire'.[37] Taubes himself also knew how to subvert leftists' expectations, which sometimes made his political engagement difficult to gauge. The right-wing intellectual Armin Mohler, Taubes's friend from undergraduate days, was of the opinion that he wanted to inoculate the protest movement 'with surrealism'.[38]

Paperback Theory

Jacob Taubes also plays an important part in the history of theory in West Germany as one of the architects of the Suhrkamp culture. In 1965, when Gente arrived in his department, Taubes was in the middle of planning a new paperback series for the head of Suhrkamp, Siegfried Unseld. Three years before, Unseld had inaugurated the *edition suhrkamp*, a rainbow-coloured shelf of paperbacks that became the emblem of an intellectual era. The concept of supplying literary and philosophical titles in a pocket format had become feasible only after the death of Unseld's predecessor Peter Suhrkamp, who had staunchly refused to deal in paperbacks.[39] In 1962, Unseld's innovation was still the object of controversy at the publishing house. Among the questions debated by his advisors, who included the paperback critic Enzensberger, was whether an 'intellectual series' could afford to have bright-coloured covers. The compromise initially adopted – printing Willy Fleckhaus's cover design on a dust jacket which could be removed to reveal grey cardboard as a guarantee of intellectual solidity – says a great deal about the weight of the ideological confrontation. The *edition suhrkamp* sold well from the beginning; the philosophical titles in particular seemed to appeal to the 'younger and student readers', Unseld's target audience for the new series.[40] Authors such as Wittgenstein, Bloch and Adorno topping the sales statistics even in train-station bookshops was remarkable news.[41] Husserl's *Logical Investigations*, a fundamental text of modern philosophy, had sold just 7,500 copies by 1966. The long-term best-seller of the twentieth century, Heidegger's *Being and Time*, had sold 40,000 copies.[42] Figures like these were low compared with Suhrkamp's philosophical paperbacks: Herbert Marcuse's *Culture and Society*, which appeared in *edition suhrkamp* in 1965 as *Kultur und Gesellschaft*, sold 80,000 copies within a few years.[43]

At first, the critics of the paperback format saw its success as confirmation of their suspicions that people might buy paperbacks, but not read them.[44] But the phenomenon also admitted the opposite interpretation: perhaps the affordable books were actually revolutionizing people's reading habits; perhaps they were a medium for disseminating difficult ideas. Unseld, one of the optimists, commissioned the young luminaries of the West German social sciences to conceive another series that would serve this purpose. Jürgen Habermas, Hans Blumenberg, Dieter Henrich and Jacob Taubes were engaged as advisors and series editors to attune Suhrkamp's academic catalogue to the zeitgeist. A few years later, Unseld added Niklas Luhmann to this circle. 'The individual books should be formally appealing as well as inexpensive', the editor Karl Markus Michel wrote to the professors in January of 1965, 'and should be distinct both from the ubiquitous pocket books and paperbacks and from those traditional books that tend to crawl away and hide on bookshop shelves.'[45] The result, presented the following year at the Frankfurt Book Fair, was the *Theorie* series, whose minimalistic cover was the sober counterpoint to the candy-coloured, pop-art design of its older sister: the Suhrkamp culture's *White Album*, so to speak, to follow its *Sergeant Pepper*.[46] Of course, the *Theorie* series never became as successful as the *edition suhrkamp*. Not until the 1970s did its successor series reach a wider readership, the midnight-blue *suhrkamp taschenbuch wissenschaft* (that is, 'Suhrkamp academic paperback', or *stw* for short).[47] The *Theorie* series can be credited with a different achievement, however: its title helped to establish a new genre.

Birth of a Genre

That is not merely a retrospective observation: it was the editors' intention. Their correspondence, preserved in the German Literature Archives in Marbach, reveals an ambition to give form to a new style of thinking which was not only in tune with the times, but practically inevitable from their view of history. In the sixties, scholars had still favoured the big stories. Jacob Taubes, for one, certainly did: his arguments as one of the Suhrkamp consultants followed eschatological patterns. 'There is no doubt', he informed Karl Markus Michel in 1965, 'that philosophy today is lagging behind, condemned to "thinking back". Ethnology, linguistics, psychoanalysis, literary theory, film theory, even archaeology and history are modes in which the new consciousness is trying to express itself.'[48] The verdict that philosophy was at an end, which Taubes had phrased more drastically elsewhere, was not based on the observation of business cycles in academic scholarship: Taubes saw it, rather, as an inevitable consequence of the legacy of Hegelian dialectics, which had staked out the horizons within which the human mind, 'from Ionia to Jena', might find itself.[49] What came after it, in a society with division of labour, must necessarily take place between several disciplines. The committee of series editors cast about for a fitting name for 'that field'.[50] The 'consciousness of the present' that they wanted to capture called for a style of modern objectivity.[51] Dieter Henrich tossed 'Critique', 'Argument', 'Concept' and 'Diagnosis' into the hat.[52] Taubes proposed 'Humanitas', after the example of a series of books that he had conceived in the 1950s for Beacon Press of New York.[53] The label that finally prevailed, however, as reflecting most of the participants' ideas, was *Theorie*. One factor in the decision was no doubt the fact that the Parisian philosopher Louis Althusser had started a series called *Théorie* at Éditions Maspero in 1965.[54] Legions of French readers, and still more German ones, have him to thank for crucial reading experiences.

To readers of theory, the distinction between theory and philosophy has always been important – although not always for the historical reasons that Taubes mentioned. Taubes himself noted another critical difference – the new series, he wrote in a memo to Unseld during a flight back from Paris, should dispense with the 'professorial philosophy of philosophy professors': 'The field lies between philosophy ("indirectly"), ethnology and literature.'[55] On this point at least, Taubes knew he was in agreement with Adorno, who had also proclaimed the 'time of theory' in his 1965 lecture: both saw the academic orientation of philosophy as an obstacle to knowledge. For that reason, theory's self-conception has been, since the days of the Frankfurt School, that of a counter-discourse – against the question of Being, against the curriculum, and against the systematic philosophizing that Adorno had encountered as early as 1958 in the form of the essay: 'radical in its non-radicalism, in refraining from any reduction to a principle, in its accentuation of the partial against the total, in its fragmentary character.'[56] Siegfried Unseld also insisted on publishing only short texts in the *Theorie* series.[57] In the 1970s, Peter Gente would make even shorter forms a hallmark of Merve. Theory was evidently not just a type of content, but a whole new culture of books. The genre's form corresponded with the potential of the paperback.[58]

Referring to himself in a letter to Unseld as a 'hunting dog' for Suhrkamp, Taubes threw himself with zeal into the task of defining the intellectual profile of the new series.[59] 'He's always thinking of new things, among which there are no doubt many important, even necessary works,' Karl Markus Michel noted in 1965 after a meeting in Berlin. But he added that Taubes's proposals not only needed supervision – 'they are almost eager for supervision.'[60] 'Theory' in 1965 mainly meant critical social theory along the lines of the New Left, and the idea of Taubes's that met with the greatest approval from Michel was Karel Kosík's *Dialectics of the Concrete*, the manifesto of a humanistic materialism from the thaw of Czechoslovakia. But Unseld had intentionally put together a group of series editors with internal checks and balances. Dieter Henrich was worried that Suhrkamp might use the series that he co-edited as an 'ideological forum.'[61] 'All of that is indispensable,' he wrote to Unseld, who had set out for him what he understood by Enlightenment, 'but is it everything? Enlightenment didn't always come from "the left". And when it did, often enough it was the adversary who had provoked the best arguments, or even supplied them.'[62]

How deeply the Suhrkamp culture had intervened in the intellectual economy of West Germany can be seen from the misgivings of Hans Blumenberg. To Karl Markus Michel, he remained 'the great unknown' of the four-man editorial board: 'How will he react when we show him our planning? Will he reject titles like Kosík?'[63] In the event, Blumenberg was opposed at first, but his hostility to the project was general. The very prospect of being one of a group of series editors rubbed him up the wrong way: he had had too many bad experiences 'with collective enterprises', he intimated to Michel. A more serious impediment was his scepticism towards the development 'of our publishing industry, which is more and more turning into a brand segment'. As late as 1965, the project of an academic paperback series was still met with resistance among German scholars. It was the indefatigable Jacob Taubes who hit upon the idea of recruiting Blumenberg not only as an editor but as an author. 'Hans Blumenberg has almost finished a book with the title "The Legitimacy of the Modern Age"', Taubes wrote to Unseld in April of 1965. 'I would ask you to ring him as soon as possible. He has offers from traditional philosophy publishers. But I think we can commandeer the work for Suhrkamp.'[64] The swashbuckling metaphor was well chosen: as it happened, Blumenberg had to be coerced to publish with Suhrkamp. Although Taubes's plan called for *The Legitimacy of the Modern Age* to appear not as a paperback, but in the regular academic catalogue, Blumenberg baulked. He had no intention of entrusting his work to a publisher with a 'yet unspecified reception', which he saw as the home of 'the more rhetorical Enlightenment authors and the philosophical essayists'.[65] To Karl Markus Michel, he expressed his trepidation 'that the publisher might interfere in the preparation of the text and back matter for extraneous reasons'.[66] Blumenberg's self-image as a philosopher was incompatible with the project of harnessing intellectual goals to the needs of the audience.

Only Jacob Taubes had no such qualms. He took up his activities as a Suhrkamp advisor with the objective of 'overrunning and transforming the academic market'.[67] His tone in the reports he sent to Frankfurt from Paris and New York is thus not professorial; they read more like the situation analyses of a professional industry journalist. '*Competition* is keen', he wrote to Michel from the US, where he was taking soundings, and recommended securing as many options as possible 'because the market is rapidly being picked over from

Germany.' The publisher Rowohlt also had agents on the ground, whose monstrous salaries alone were evidence that they were expected to deliver results.[68] It is no coincidence that Taubes often slips English vocabulary, such as the word 'competition' above, into his market reports: only a knowledgeable scout would have been capable of his incisive analysis of the American culture industry.[69] His intellectual promiscuity, practically free of ideological reservations, also went well with his American habitus. As he later admitted in a book published by Merve, he even supported recruiting the ill-famed constitutional lawyer Carl Schmitt for Unseld's academic catalogue – a project which failed to overcome Habermas's resistance and Schmitt's refusal to 'enter the Suhrkamp culture' with his books.[70]

Taubes was a global player, however, concentrating his activities mainly on the international market. This was no doubt the role for which he had been chosen. And his dossiers taking stock of the theory books on the market in English and French say a great deal about the West German reception context. Who was Claude Lévi-Strauss again, the guy who landed a big hit in 1955 with *Tristes tropiques*? 'The master who connects everything and has held the interest of intellectual circles in post-Existentialist France for years. L.-S. an ambivalent phenomenon. He thinks he's the successor of Rousseau, Marx; has integrated elements of Marx, but his "structuralism" is ahistorical.' And what should one make of Serge Maillet, the young author of *The New Working Class*, a book everyone was talking about among the Parisian Left? 'Highly gifted, long in communist unions, but sees that the unions don't see that a whole new physiognomy of the working class has evolved. Apart from him, such insights are pronounced only "from the right" (since E. Jünger's *The Worker*). A talent for journalism; no professorship; not likely to get one.'[71] Perhaps it is true that Taubes was able to grasp the content of a book just by touching it. What is certain, however, is that he knew how to sketch an intellectual landscape in a few quick strokes of the pen.

Getting the four professors to sit down together proved to be a difficult task. Dieter Henrich was eager to work with Habermas, but preferably not with Blumenberg. Blumenberg in turn recoiled from collaborating with Taubes, who he thought was an 'unreliable fellow.'[72] Taubes, for his part, had the feeling that he was doing more work than the others and refused to do so 'for the same money'.[73] Nor did he make a secret of his disappointment on seeing the proofs of Blumenberg's *Legitimacy of the Modern Age*, which he had so warmly recommended to Unseld.[74] Only Habermas struck Michel as being a dependable partner 'without compulsion and without ambitions', one who 'quite spontaneously makes the most useful suggestions'. But Habermas was the one who, after a particularly tedious session with Henrich and Blumenberg, asked to be discharged from the 'bubbling cauldron' of the *Theorie* series. 'I told him very plainly', Michel reported to Unseld, 'that the series had been conceived with a view to his collaboration, and that we would not be interested in publishing it if he withdrew.'[75] The editor's desperate sigh is understandable: 'It is a shame', Michel noted, 'that we do not yet have the technical means to hold conferences without the simultaneous presence of all the participants.'[76]

In spite of the difficulties with the series editors, Unseld and Michel hammered out a first autumn list between 1965 and 1966. The market for theory seemed too promising to permit unnecessary delays. To put weight behind Suhrkamp's presence, the new series was initially supposed to be flanked by a journal in which 'in each issue, various philosophers or scholars would critically look at a major philosophical or scientific book (or a life's work)'.[77] Taubes was easily won for this project too: 'The time for a journal is well chosen, since *Merkur* and *Neue deutsche Hefte* seem to be nearing their end.' As titles for a periodical that would carry on the anticipated legacy of those cultural reviews, he suggested 'Janus' and 'Angelus novus'. The rest of his offer to Michel in August of 1965 sounded less like a collaboration than a friendly takeover. The responsible editor would be Taubes's partner, the Freie Universität philosopher Margherita von Brentano; Berlin seemed to be the best address for the editorial offices. As the chair of a well-endowed department, Taubes held out the prospect of throwing 'four to five student assistants into the journal's pot' as editorial staff – including a certain Peter Gente, whom Michel might know 'as the editor of an issue of *Alternative* on French literary theory'.[78] Thus Gente came within a hair's breadth in 1965 of landing in the Suhrkamp culture. But the journal, whether *Janus* or *Angelus novus*, never saw the light of day. Enzensberger's *Kursbuch*, which appeared in a pilot issue the same year, probably made another Suhrkamp periodical seem superfluous.

Nonetheless, the episode left a mark. Taubes's activity as an editorial advisor brought his assistant Gente into contact with the publishing world. His hope of working in publishing gradually took shape during the second half of the sixties. Gente experienced the events of the period as one of the inner circle of the student movement, from the shooting of the student Benno Ohnesorg by a policeman during protests against the Shah of Iran's visit to Berlin, to the battle between police and students in front of the Berlin courthouse in Tegeler Weg on the day of a hearing to disbar Horst Mahler.[79] But even in those tumultuous years of 1967 and 1968, Gente continued to read voraciously. In 1968, he edited a publication of Joseph Stalin's 1950 pamphlet on 'Marxism and Problems of Linguistics' for the Munich publishers Rogner & Bernhard.[80] The following year, he developed a concept for a book series of his own. In contrast to his uneven seminar papers, the business idea he pitched to publishers is surprisingly mature, reflecting the acumen of a hunter-gatherer who had been roaming the woods of the intellectual journals for the past ten years. Gente's concept was to publish theory finds 'whose prior distribution allows us to assume that the reader interest has not been exhausted' in a booklet format. He was thinking mainly of articles from foreign journals on discussions 'in which the last word has not yet been spoken'. The little book on the situation at hand: that was a logical next step from Suhrkamp's *Theorie* paperbacks, which were just asking to be outbid. Gente imagined catering for the 'demand for orientation in the social sciences among a broad diversity of readerships', audiences which 'up to now have been considered as a relatively unified public only for fiction'.[81] Gente himself had been a part of the chapter of West German intellectual history that this sentence evokes: the shift in reading habits, the declining relevance of artistic writing and the ascendancy of theoretical literature. Theory was to be devoured like novels, and hence made suitable for paperbacks: around 1970, this formula spawned a new growth market. And yet Gente did not succeed in attracting a publisher. Sooner or later, the idea arose of founding his own publishing house. West Berlin, with its low rents, was the ideal place to do so.[82]

1970

ENDLESS DISCUSSIONS

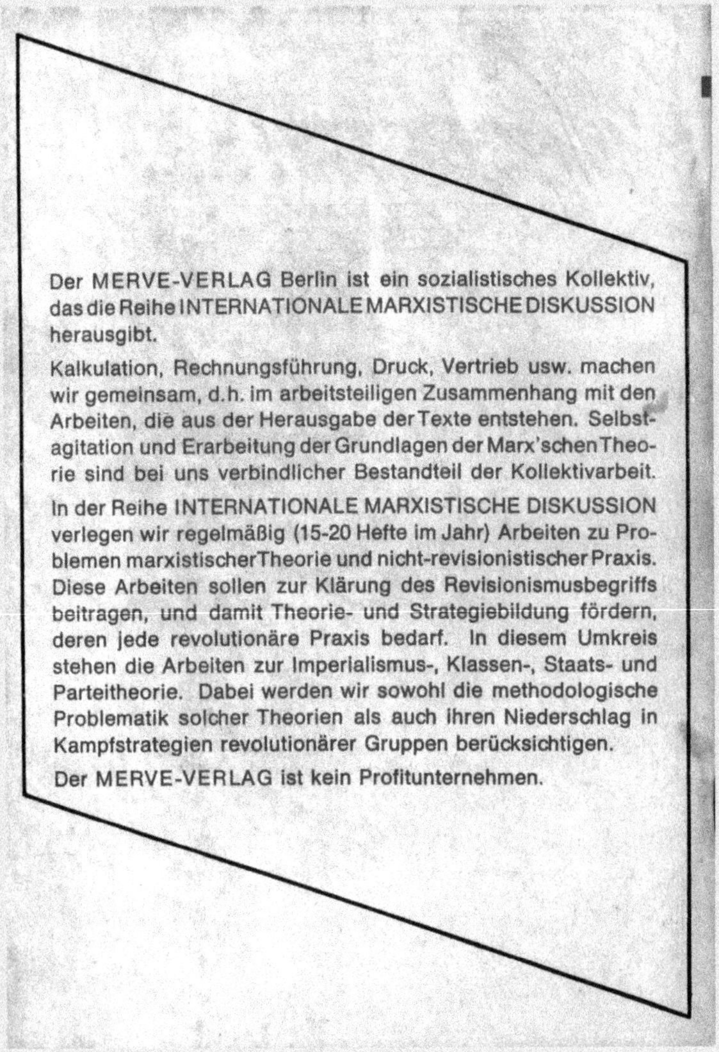

Der MERVE-VERLAG Berlin ist ein sozialistisches Kollektiv, das die Reihe INTERNATIONALE MARXISTISCHE DISKUSSION herausgibt.

Kalkulation, Rechnungsführung, Druck, Vertrieb usw. machen wir gemeinsam, d.h. im arbeitsteiligen Zusammenhang mit den Arbeiten, die aus der Herausgabe der Texte entstehen. Selbstagitation und Erarbeitung der Grundlagen der Marx'schen Theorie sind bei uns verbindlicher Bestandteil der Kollektivarbeit.

In der Reihe INTERNATIONALE MARXISTISCHE DISKUSSION verlegen wir regelmäßig (15-20 Hefte im Jahr) Arbeiten zu Problemen marxistischerTheorie und nicht-revisionistischer Praxis. Diese Arbeiten sollen zur Klärung des Revisionismusbegriffs beitragen, und damit Theorie- und Strategiebildung fördern, deren jede revolutionäre Praxis bedarf. In diesem Umkreis stehen die Arbeiten zur Imperialismus-, Klassen-, Staats- und Parteitheorie. Dabei werden wir sowohl die methodologische Problematik solcher Theorien als auch ihren Niederschlag in Kampfstrategien revolutionärer Gruppen berücksichtigen.

Der MERVE-VERLAG ist kein Profitunternehmen.

6 Charles Bettelheim, *Über das Fortbestehen von Warenverhältnissen in den 'sozialistischen Ländern'* [On the persistence of commodity relations in the 'socialist countries'], Berlin: Merve, 1970. This stapled booklet was the first publication to bear the name 'Merve Verlag'.

3

ILL-MADE BOOKS

charles bettelheim
über das fortbestehen von
warenverhältnissen in den
»sozialistischen ländern«
internationale
marxistische diskussion 1
merve verlag berlin
dm 2,—

In February of 1970, Adorno had been dead for half a year. Hans-Jürgen Krahl, the talented young theoretician of the German student movement, crashed head-on into a lorry when his car slid on an icy road north of Frankfurt. Four days later, Peter Gente, together with his wife and a friend and comrade, began printing his first book in a vacant shop in the West Berlin borough of Steglitz: *How to Read Marx's* Capital, a thin booklet by Louis Althusser in an anonymous German translation, *Wie sollen wir* Das Kapital *lesen?* The scene was set, Merve Lowien writes in her report on the Merve publishing collective, in one of the many quiet corners of the city: deserted streets, a Greek migrant worker fixing his broken-down car, and a former shop of 120 square metres filled with dust and the props and costumes of 'some departed Kreuzberg theatre group'.[1]

Berlin in the 1970s was no longer the metropolitan conflict zone where the superpowers demonstrated their symbolic superiority. The isolation of the Wall and the hardening of the Cold War fronts had driven many inhabitants away, bleeding the West half of the city dry. 'How empty Berlin was', a surprised West German visitor observed in 1968. 'The broad boulevards and avenues much too wide; the present much too thin to fill them.'[2] That emptiness was a great attraction to bohemians dreaming of a self-determined life. Nouveau Berliners, fleeing West German military service and the high cost of living in Hamburg or Stuttgart, were able to move into spacious old flats. Instead of career opportunities, West Berlin offered low rents; instead of SMEs, the project economy of the subculture. The Merve collective was a typical example of that sector, an enterprise that could afford to run in the red: '"Doing publishing" is an experiment', writes Lowien, 'which the participants should be able to abort at any time if they should find another activity more meaningful.'[3]

Krahl's death must have resounded as a dark omen in the publishers' ears as they worked with numb fingers on the unfamiliar printing press. Gente had seen Krahl earlier in Frankfurt, where he was known not only as a formidable speaker, but also as a jack-of-all-trades and a drinker who could sing along to the jukebox or drop his glass eye into his brandy glass.[4] But little had been heard of him lately. Germany's extra-parliamentary opposition disintegrated after '68 into a thousand splinter groups preaching free love or party discipline, and sounding the retreat to the urtext of Marxism. Gente, schooled in negative dialectics, found himself the editor of a book by Stalin.[5] According to Diedrich Diederichsen, seminar discussions never again attained the complexity they had had in the sixties.[6] Adorno was dead, Max Horkheimer was a mystic in Ticino, and Jürgen Habermas had accused the students of 'left-wing fascism'. Krahl's death had robbed the anti-authoritarian movement of one of its leading minds, and it seemed to be doomed to failure.[7]

Yet the dissolution of the context in which discussion had gone on did not mean that people were reading less. In the seventies, the hard core of the protest movement finally broadened into a leftist mainstream. New theory series, theory journals and theory publishers sprang up like mushrooms.[8] The appetite for Marxist classics drove the presses of a bootleg reprinting industry that turned the long-neglected source codes of the labour movement into best-selling grey-market literature. It was in this expanding Gutenberg galaxy that Merve sought its niche. The collective's name – after Gente's wife, Merve Lowien – and its legal form were chosen in the course of the first year of operations. Between then and 1976, numerous comrades joined and left the collective, among them students, tradesmen, actors, booksellers ...[9] Their mission as publishers was to supply German derivative Marxism with theory imported from abroad. Perhaps Gente, the encyclopaedic reader, secretly dreamed of becoming the intellectual conscience of the movement. The choice of Louis Althusser for the first title fits that picture, in any case. The regression back to the sources was to be retransformed once more, thanks to Althusser, into a theoretical avant-garde. No one had thought harder than he, even in the theory-mad sixties. And, unlike Adorno, Althusser did so from under the cover of Marx's urtext.

Theoretical Practice

Althusser is still remembered as the Marx exegete who subjected *Capital* to a 'symptomatic analysis' to translate its implicit philosophy, which Marx himself could only hint at, into explicit terms. The fact that this treasure raised from the depths of the nineteenth century turned out in the end to be Althusser's own philosophy – that is, structuralism of the Parisian rite – was the pay-off of Althusser's difficult work. As a member of the French Communist Party, he had been defending Marxism against its humanistic interpreters since the early sixties. The Marx with the 'human face' whom intellectuals on the European left from Sartre to Karel Kosík had found, after the end of Stalinism, in the early writings was to Althusser a particularly dangerous form of revisionism, a betrayal of the master thinker's radicalism. Using the concepts of the epistemologist Gaston Bachelard, he read Marx against the grain and detected an 'epistemological break' – it was Althusser in the sixties who made the term well known – right through the middle of Marx's complete works. Althusser willingly left Marx's 'ideological' early writings to the humanists. Only later, in *Capital*, Althusser wrote, did Marx arrive at his revolutionary 'THEORY', whose message – soundly structuralist – was a rejection of humanism, the subject and the dialectical process of history. Nowhere better than in Althusser can we read, even today, why the Parisian thinkers saw 'man' and his derivatives as dangerous ideologies: humanism always served as a universalist smokescreen under which to pursue the interests of specific groups of people.[10] If we compare Althusser's 'hyperintellectualism' with the texts of left-wing humanists, we can understand why his readers saw him as a fascinating avant-garde author.[11] There was no more radical – that is to say, more abstract – philosophy on the market.

One of the most successful coinings to come from Althusser's school of pure theory was the concept of 'theoretical practice'. 'For there is not one side of theory, a purely intellectual vision without body or materiality – and another of completely material practice which "gets its hands dirty"', he wrote in his key work *Reading Capital*, which was published in German by Rowohlt in 1972. 'This dichotomy is merely an ideological myth.'[12] Rather, he continued, theory too is a form of practice, of productive work, in which knowledge is the object produced. The fine points and fallacies of this interpretation of Marx were discussed *ad nauseam* in the 1970s. One side spun the lengthening thread of an academic reception: epistemologists following Gaston Bachelard, decrypting the dialectic of the Enlightenment in the European history of the sciences, were inspired by the concept of 'theoretical practice' to address the practical side of research, giving it the attention they had up to then reserved to ideas and theories. This new perspective, committed to the 'practical turn' and still in conflict with the history of ideas today, entered the gene pool of cultural studies via 'discursive practices', which Althusser's student Michel Foucault contributed to the discussion in his *Archaeology of Knowledge*.[13]

At the same time, Althusser's 'theoretical practice' concerned not only the sciences, but also his own existence as a Marxist intellectual. This aspect was much more important, in fact, for his contemporary reception. The concept implied, as a critical reader in West Berlin commented, that 'the thought process is in principle equivalent with the real process by virtue of having the form of practice'.[14] In a flip of the wrist, Althusser had legitimized the activity of the intellectual – whom he logically termed the 'intellectual worker'.[15] In the increasingly heated debate between theoreticians and activists which marked the late sixties, this was a valuable strategic position, repeated 'like a mantra' by Western European Marxist academics.[16] Faced with more and more enraged students, Adorno too had declared, in his 'Marginalia to Theory and Praxis': 'Thinking is a doing, theory a form of praxis; only the ideology of the purity of thinking is deceptive about it.'[17] As the editor of the *New Left Review*, Perry Anderson placed the New Left's passion for theory in a melancholy balance against its disenchantment with politics. In his view, the 'defiant theoreticism of these pronouncements' could be seen 'as a general motto of Western Marxism in the epoch after the Second World War'.[18]

The theme can easily be pursued beyond the sphere of Marxism. As long as the fascination of theory lasted, it was brought up again and again to reaffirm the relevance of philosophy. Even Niklas Luhmann, who never made a secret of his distance from the Left, paid ironic homage to his political opponents when, freshly appointed professor at the reformed University of Bielefeld, he stated in 1968 that 'work on theories is action, like any other action'.[19] The idea of theoretical practice remains influential today in the form given it by the French Left-Nietzscheans, whom Merve had begun to import into the German context in the second half of the seventies. In 1977, Merve published a conversation between Michel Foucault and Gilles Deleuze, titled *Die Intellektuellen und die Macht* – 'The intellectuals and power'

– in which the two theoreticians assured each other that they shared certain basic premises. Deleuze expressed the belief that 'representation no longer exists, there's only action – theoretical action and the practical action.' Foucault agreed, remarking that 'theory does not express, translate, or serve to apply practice: it is practice.'[20] To the Merve collective, whose contribution to changing the status quo consisted in disseminating texts, this agreement of opposites was an ideal basis for their own legitimation. 'Althusser and Foucault always claimed that their theory is practice,' Gente would later explain. 'We make books: that's our practice.'[21]

The Althusser whom Merve and other publishers had smuggled into the German discussion, with a certain delay, was on difficult footing. The conceptual Leninist, with his assertion that the real revolution takes place in the formation of theories, fell under suspicion in the seventies of playing philosophical glass bead games. 'Scholarship, withdrawn into esoteric climes, uses a verbal trick to consider itself practice,' a critic wrote in *Das Argument* in 1975.[22] The Merve collective turned on its own very first author with the publication of *Wider den akademischen Marxismus* [Against academic Marxism], a collection of polemics by the renegade Althusser student Jacques Rancière. Having got caught up in the maelstrom of 'events' in May '68 and subsequently having defected to Maoism, Rancière was mistrustful of 'Althusserism' from then on, because its originator was a professor with an academic chair. The experience of revolt and the news from China had opened Rancière's eyes:

> Without revolutionary theory there can be no revolutionary practice. We have repeated this sentence over and over again, thinking it might set our minds at ease. But now we must heed the lesson taught by the Cultural Revolution and the ideological revolt of the students: cut off from revolutionary practice, there is no revolutionary theory that is not transformed into its opposite.

And 'thus the unravelling of Marxism into opportunism is complete.'[23]

Five years later, in 1980, Althusser's life took a tragic turn. In a fit of madness, he strangled his wife, then allowed himself to be arrested and subsequently faded into the twilight of psychiatric hospitals. The violent act, committed in the apartment provided by his institution, the École normale supérieure, seemed to justify his critics retroactively: was a murder not the logical consequence of Althusser's 'theoretical antihumanism'? Was it any wonder that a declared enemy of humanity killed his wife?[24] The theoretical abstraction that Althusser had embodied fell under pathological suspicion by association. The memoirs he later wrote in his defence only made everything worse. It transpired that his writings had been the product of a long struggle against mental illness. Althusser had spent May of '68, the crucial formative moment of his students, in a psychiatric ward: this theoretician was a man driven to invent concepts that might justify an existence he felt was meaningless.[25] With brutal understatement, the Merve author Heiner Müller made his judgement in 1982: 'Althusser no longer interests me except as material.'[26]

Smash Bourgeois Copyright!

On 10 August 1973, Althusser's tragic end was still far off. He had received bad news from West Berlin and responded with an angry letter to the 'Gentlemen' – not 'Comrades' – of the tiny publisher Merve. The unauthorized translation of his essay *Freud and Lacan*, Althusser wrote, was an 'act of piracy' against which he would take legal action unless Merve retroactively offered him an 'appropriate' contract: 'Please understand the word "appropriate" in its fullest sense.'[27] The publishers must have complied, because three years later they published his essay again in a second edition. And yet purchasing rights generally went against their business model. Anyone who intended to feed the booming market for leftist movement literature with fresh text from abroad could not be overly scrupulous about niceties of copyright – anyone with zero seed capital, that is. Like other leftist publishers of that time, Merve began its existence with a hybrid business plan. There was a mission: to jump-start German Marxism out of its dogmatic standstill with boosts from Italy and France. There was a will: to man the printing press and the sales table in self-exploiting labour. And there was a historic opportunity: to earn the necessary small change with bootleg reprints. In an article on bootleg printing for the 'Mass Communications' volume of the *Enciclopedia Feltrinelli–Fischer*, the Merve collective wrote in 1974:

> The bootleg printing movement which arose at the beginning of the student movement (late 1966) in Berlin communes and political groups has expanded rapidly, not least thanks to the advanced technical means in use (offset printing). The number of groups producing Red books for the black market will have been about 25 in 1973. The number of reprinted titles was about 1000 by the end of 1971, with print runs varying between 200 and 6,000 and prices between 0.30 and 18.00 deutschemarks. Some titles have been printed in 20,000 to 30,000 copies. The prices overall are 40% to 60% below those of official printings. The reprinted texts continue to be primarily Marxist and psychological/psychoanalytical texts. The slogan 'Smash bourgeois copyright' stands for the literature producers' radical thesis that 'under the present socio-economic conditions of the culture and consciousness industry, "intellectual property", the ownership of artistic, literary and scientific work, mainly serves not the development of society as a whole, but the maximizing of capitalist profits.' A bootleg printing of 120 pages in 2,000 copies can be printed, with a working machine and with average skill, in 40 hours, gathered and bound in another 80 hours, with material costs of about 800 marks.[28]

The story of the 'literature producers' mentioned in the article may illustrate the mood in the industry. At the 1968 Frankfurt Book Fair, the leftist publishers, authors and booksellers had joined together in a syndicate. Two years later, they adopted their first set of resolutions. In addition to an appeal on economic grounds for the production of 'proletarian reprints,' the paper contained an accusation that the federal government in Bonn was producing grey literature of its own and scattering it over East Germany as anti-socialist propaganda. 'Uncopyrighted bootleg printings produced expressly for this purpose have been transported to the GDR by balloons and rockets. This total manipulation of literature has led to the denunciation of the educational function of all literature.'[29] Literature as a political scandal: the episode is an exhibit in the case brought by the '68 generation against the fine arts. The bootleggers' resolution does not indicate what titles were pirated by the government; that information must be slumbering in the intelligence service archives, if anywhere. Konsalik? Ernst Jünger? Arthur Koestler? There has not been any government statement on the issue.

Attacks on copyright began long before the digital age. In the 1970s, the pirates' political motives were no secret.[30] The Merve collective was initially one of the groups supplying the West Berlin market with bootleg books. In addition to Althusser and other contemporary authors of avant-garde theory, the Rotaprint offset machine clattering in the empty shop in Steglitz also churned out law books and classics of Marxism – Karl Korsch, Walter Benjamin, Sergei Tretyakov, Ernst Ottwalt, ... – as grey literature without a proper copyright notice. The merchandise was marketed in the left-wing bookshops and at the second-hand bookstalls in front of Freie Universität – much to the dismay of German publishers, who heaped lawsuits on the copyright pirates.[31] Some said that the feeding troughs of the illegal book trade generated millions, and financed such underground endeavours as the Red Army Faction, but such apocryphal figures were, at best, extrapolations by the political adversary. Where the reliable statistics ended, the paranoia of the seventies took over.[32] It was possible, however, to make a living by bootleg publishing. The Merve collective participated in the grey market until its own books sold well enough to finance themselves; once that point had been reached, they produced only official titles with the Merve rhombus on the cover.[33] Nonetheless, manoeuvring around copyrights remained a part of the business model. Even today, Merve is said to hold few rights, so that its assets are almost nothing but the 'Merve' brand.

The rhombus cover design, which the publishers commissioned from a graphic artist of their acquaintance, was at first a point of controversy within their own camp.[34] In the Red world of offset Gutenbergs, even a hint of corporate identity was frowned upon. The objections that the literature producers raised against bourgeois publishing were not limited to principles of copyright: the actual problem, as they saw it, was the 'exchange value' of books. That is why there is sometimes such a startling similarity between the cultural critique of the fifties and the cultural revolution of the seventies: both were opposed to the commercialization of a cultural artefact, the book. They drew opposite conclusions from that premise, however: to the '68 generation, the paperback promised not the downfall but the revolution of the book, destroying its aura and inviting the reader to subvert its obsolete functions.[35] As early as 1964, the future filmmaker Harun Farocki had written, in a review for the daily *Spandauer Volksblatt*, that the *edition suhrkamp* was where 'aesthetics triumphs over intellect' – and in the same breath proposed suitable remedies: 'So, let us remove the cover and begin by crumpling the book good and tight. Then we'll look inside it.'[36] This gesture of disrespect towards a medium which, its critics said, had always been fetishized anticipated the practice of the leftist theory publishers.[37] Ever since Wolfgang Fritz Haug's 1971 Suhrkamp best-seller *Kritik der Warenästhetik* [Critique of commodity aesthetics], which traced the expansion of the West German brand universe back to Goebbels, that practice was expressed in a derivative Marxist idiom which played off use value and exchange value against each other.[38]

The Merve collective, too, wanted to replace 'books as things' with 'functional books' – although the rhombus, strictly speaking, ran against that principle.[39] Rejecting the 'alluring design of the dominant world of consumption', as Merve Lowien put it, the Merve collective wrapped their brochures in unadorned grey.[40] Because the inside too was to be reduced to bare necessities, the page layout was an unvarying block of running text: every title published confronted the reader with a wall of type. Moreover, once the transition had been made from stapled folios to glued bindings, the books fell apart quickly. Minimalist production values and political beliefs often went hand in hand in the name of neo-Marxism. 'Our advertising', the Merve publishers wrote in the 1980s, 'consists in not being seen in certain places.'[41] In 1986, when the lead-type printing and the stitched bindings of Hans Magnus Enzensberger's book series *Die Andere Bibliothek* seemed to confirm a relapse into bibliophile ways, the Merve philosophy of 'ill-made books' required some explanation:

> Just as there is salmon in every supermarket today, the beautiful, bibliophile book has become the common, customary book, and the bad book is that of the connoisseurs, the collectors and insiders. If necessary, you can buy two copies straight away, underline in it, take it with you to the

loo or on the road, give it away, forget it somewhere, toss it out, use it for all kinds of things.[42]

Mondays, Fridays and Sundays

Following the example of the Chinese Cultural Revolution, Merve Verlag considered itself a socialist collective committed to breaking down divisions between work and life. 'We try to think through the work we do with our hands, and get our hands dirty with theory', was the publishers' motto.[43] What that meant specifically can be read in Merve Lowien's chronicle of disillusionment: she documented the publishing collective's rise and fall as a utopian social experiment. 'Female Productive Power: Is a Different Economy Possible?' [*Weibliche Produktivkraft – Gibt es eine andere Ökonomie?*] was the title of volume 65 in the series 'International Marxist Discussion' [*Internationale Marxistische Diskussion*], the only book series Merve had published since its beginning in 1970. In it, the collective's departing eponym takes stock of six years' shared subsistence labour, recounts the attempt to build a Gaulish village in the middle of late capitalism, and analyses the group dynamics that made that attempt so difficult.

To overcome the dictates of the 'social division of labour', all the comrades would have to do all the jobs, from developing the forthcoming list to accounting to shipping books to the subscribers.[44] That was not an easy objective for a young group of self-taught publishers from middle- and working-class backgrounds. 'The fungibility of all services and people', Adorno had written in *Minima Moralia*, 'and the resultant belief that everyone must be able to do everything, prove, in the existing order, fetters'[45] – as if he had foreseen the tribulations of the Merve collective. For the group's intellectuals, such as Peter Gente, operating the printing press resulted in 'aimless motor activity', his wife noted. In the 'paper arena' of the theoretical debates, meanwhile, the proletarian members fared poorly.[46] Consequently, in spite of growing sales and improved workflows, the contradictions of the society at large were reproduced within the collective: conflicts flared up over every issue imaginable.

The group's weekend retreat to reach agreement on a political position 'thoroughly failed' because someone had had the idea of bringing alcohol along. An effort to introduce the kiss of brotherhood went awry. In Paris, Gente prowled the bookshops irritably in search of new texts while his comrades displayed foolish 'leisure behaviour'. One of the comrades who had a knack for practical tasks felt he was being degraded to a 'maid' by the others.[47]

Lowien's book is full of episodes like these. Uninhibited in their communication with the world spirit, the publishers sent a copy of it to Herbert Marcuse in California. The master thinker reported in his reply of April 1977 that he had only been able to glance at *Weibliche Produktivkraft*, but there was indeed plenty to be said about the publishing collective, its concept and its working practice. 'It seems to me absolutely necessary to discuss the matter with you', Marcuse wrote, two years before his unexpected death, but a 'responsible discussion' would require a great deal of time.[48] His offer of a continuing dialogue seems the only appropriate response to the book: the psychodrama that Merve Lowien presented in her brief history took the form of an ongoing discussion itself.

Merve's series title was, after all, *Internationale Marxistische Diskussion*, which they originally set all in lower-case, after Enzensberger's style. That title was right in tune with the times. In 1970, Suhrkamp launched the *Theorie* spinoff *Theorie-Diskussion* – a red-covered series in which the famous debate between Habermas and Luhmann would soon be fought.[49] That coincidence says a great deal about how far the mood of theory in the early seventies had diverged from the academic innocence of the white-covered *Suhrkamp Theorie* books. What had happened in the meantime was '68: just as the heroic student leaders of the revolt now looked anachronistic, theory propounded in a seminar style now had a gamy aroma of 'theoreticism'. The banner of *Diskussion* signalled a focus on process rather than results, on communication rather than dogmatic doctrines. For the collectives and the base groups who had inherited the legacy of the student movement and the 'extra-parliamentary opposition', the format of the theory palaver was essential to survival. Besides its egalitarian ethic, it brought with it an invaluable strategic advantage: as long as consensus could be postponed, the dialogue could go on indefinitely.[50]

It was in discussion that the Merve collective found itself. The comrades met regularly in one or another of the members' shared flats. 'These sessions always lasted at least four, at most seven hours, without breaks, but with much consumption of coffee.' Mondays, organizational matters were on the agenda; Fridays, readings in theory; Sundays, 'self-agitation.' The ambition not just to sell books but to lead a political life made it necessary, the publishers felt, 'to keep a close eye on their own activity' in order 'to wear away', slowly but surely, 'the crutches of the old muck of the dominant ways of seeing, thinking and writing' – by constantly talking with one another. Gone were the days when Adorno had recommended inviolable solitude; forgotten was his warning against pretending it was still possible to converse meaningfully. 'Human beings arise through communication', says Lowien's book, as if stating a first article of faith. 'The end of communication means death', reads the second. The paradigm of labour on which the left had pinned its political hopes since Marx was augmented in the seventies by the paradigm of communication, and the new social theories of Luhmann and Habermas brought it to centre stage. In one of the Merve collective's Friday discussions, Peter Gente, once more displaying the greater breadth of his reading, exposed Habermas's utopia of 'dominance-free communication' as a 'liberalistic illusion' and an obfuscation of relations of power. From the radical publishers' perspective, the new head of the Frankfurt School had long since gone over to the Social Democrats' camp. But that made no difference to their own marathon discussions. There seems to have been no alternative in those days, for comrades who rejected violence, to faith in the power of communication.[51]

The Merve publishers' worst-case scenario was speechlessness – or, worse, 'silent speechlessness', to use Lowien's pleonasm, which indicates how much she feared that condition. Silence threatened when the tensions between manual and mental labourers escalated into irreconcilable differences, if not before. 'Just the thought of coming here makes me sick', one of the comrades declared at the end of an epic discussion in which he had told the others he wanted to quit. He was going to be a father soon and intended to finish his degree in education, and besides he was fed up with all the discussion. The others, obliged to accept that he was 'knackered', were losing more than just their best man at the offset machine. His departure, which had been preceded by others, placed the future of the publishing experiment in jeopardy. 'What's going to become of our political aspiration, of our collective work, if one after another just leaves?' Lowien asked desperately. A few years later, she left too.[52]

The comrades' problems can be read in the minutes they kept. The fact that their discussions are thus preserved for posterity is only a side effect of their note-taking, however: the intended purpose of their records was self-education. The minutes of their discussions were meant to be discussed in turn. The group even went to the trouble of taking minutes of their discussions of the minutes. The belief in 'mutual learning processes' underlying their political work occasioned – as in other groups – an excrescence of written material.[53] The minutes alone, wrote Lowien in a tone recalling the rigor of communist groups, 'reflect the consciousness of the group's own action, the relations of the individuals to one another, the serious attitude towards the issues, the degree of necessary discipline and the capacity to bear deprivation.'[54] In 1978, a decollectivized Peter Gente summed up: 'The dialectics drive you mad.'[55]

The love of discussion among the West German '68 generation was the late-blooming zeal of the convert. While other countries such as Britain had grown accustomed over centuries to progressively more civil manners, the Germans had never stopped rattling sabres. To make matters worse, as the frustrating process of civilization dragged on, they drank too much. *Kompromiss*, 'compromise', was a dirty word in German up until 1945, always understood to be 'sham': *fauler Kompromiss.* It took the unconditional surrender and American re-education to make discussion take root in Germany as a modern cultural technique. The students of the '68 movement took the Americans at their word and went on to invent, in a reckless overvaluation of dialogue, the utopian verb *ausdiskutieren*, 'to elucidate completely by exhaustive discussion.' No wonder a big disappointment happened sometime in the seventies. The strangely unforced force of the 'superior argument' fell into disrepute. Drinking, on the other hand, was once again highly regarded.[56]

The undaunted Merve collective, however, went on discussing until 1977. The goal of 'mediating' the 'contradictions' could no more be questioned than a mathematical axiom.[57] 'The divisions between personal and public,' Lowien writes, 'between work and leisure, between theory work and manual work, between love and philosophy, have the consequence that people are "knocked senseless", become mute and motionless, instead of becoming more and more sensitive to communication "in the course of time" and producing themselves as whole persons with imagination and self-determined power.'[58] Merve Lowien saw 'female productive power' – the title of her book – as a principle which could form the starting point of such a process of emancipation. The opposition of female and male which was manifested in the publishing collective's practice was, in her perspective, even more fundamental than the class conflict. As the title indicates, she was reconstructing her experience no longer in a Marxist framework, but in an early feminist perspective. Borrowing a metaphor from Verena Stefan's influential 1975 novel *Shedding*, she described her liberation from the patriarchal publishing collective as shedding a skin.[59] The West German women's movement found its point of leverage in the seventies by invoking the female principle as a primal force which could bring about alternative forms of socialization. The notion of a 'women's superior mode of production,' which is also a motif of Alexander Kluge's films, recalls the left-wing mythology of the proletariat, and at the same time evokes the idea of a primordial matriarchy.[60] The idea soon fell under suspicion of essentialism, thanks in considerable measure to Merve Verlag: in 1977, Merve began translating the work of the French feminist Hélène Cixous, who dissolved the polarity of the sexes in an interplay of differences.[61]

The Disorder of Discourse

Two days before the Sunday self-agitation session, the comrades regularly met to read theory. 'Learning reading' was the slogan Peter Gente proclaimed for this meeting.[62] Like the interactions between the collective's members, interaction with the texts had to be 'mediated' so that the results of the theoretical work could feed back into practice. As the only veteran of the student movement in the Merve collective, Gente compiled a reading list for the younger members that consisted of Marx, Feuerbach, Marcuse and Gente's contemporary Hans-Jürgen Krahl, who had died in a tragic accident. Perhaps the only serious theoretician to emerge from the ranks of the West German movement of '68, Krahl was especially important for the publishing collective's self-conception at the time of its founding. His 'theory of revolution', which he had only managed to foreshadow in introductory texts during his lifetime, cast a spotlight right in the middle of the group's uncontrollable dynamics, illuminating why they were so concerned with the 'how' of their theory readings.

Even the most abstract texts challenged their readers to contemplate themselves. Krahl's did so in regard to the 'organizational question', which he carried to 'dizzying theoretical heights'.[63] In the post-'68 debates, that question was a sensitive spot. Krahl had insisted on 'deploying the first seminal forms of the future society in the organization of the political struggle itself'. In this clever recursive figure – which was no more paradoxical than most attempts of that time to sneak out of the dilemma of theory and practice by dialectical paths – the 'organization' was presented as a kind of fractal image of the future classless society. In Adorno, whose seminars had given Krahl the opportunity to discover his talent for theory, only art, if anything, was accorded a comparable role. But even art's anticipation of something as yet inexpressible in words took place in an inscrutable way.[64] Krahl's organization, on the other hand, was conceived as a nexus of discussion. Only 'constant argumentative confrontation' could ensure that both the militant discipline of the avant-garde and the free spontaneity of individuals would always be realized in it: Lenin Goes Rosa Luxemburg, or Squaring the Revolutionary Circle. Krahl's conceptual efforts bound together once more what was fast falling apart in the schism between Spontis and cadres.[65] Although he states, like Marx, that the revolutionary organization cannot anticipate the 'New Jerusalem', this conciliatory formula occurs a bit too often in his work. To Krahl, the organizations of the student movement were more than a political home, especially as he had no such bourgeois attachments as a family or a fixed abode, in contrast to his colleague Rudi Dutschke.[66]

The message of Krahl's organizational utopia was clear, even to readers who did not care to join in all of its dialectical finesse. The

Merve collective's aspirations to the 'realized anticipation of emancipatory practice' meant carrying on the revolution every day between the shared flat and the printing shop.[67] Their hope for a classless society was vindicated only by the exemplary character of their own project. While the 'K-groups' – the many splinter organizations arising from the shattered student movement, generally with a K for *kommunistisch* somewhere in their abbreviations – chose the simpler path of Leninist party discipline, all others with theoretical ambitions were called upon to rethink their practice constantly. In the Merve collective, this compulsion drove the culture of discussion to an extreme:

> In the meantime, the interest in abolishing all divisions had led the group to talk about its momentary and theoretical, 'personal' and 'publishing-related' problems all at the same time. Thus a single discussion would touch on, for example, paper prices, a member's behaviour at a publishing-collective party, the political situation in Italy, the concept of class, and an urgently needed cleaning of the publishing offices.

Nothing could be cleared up by discussion under these conditions. 'The problems brought up,' Lowien continues, 'merge to form an "unbearable marmalade"'.[68]

It was in this situation that the Merve publishers discovered Michel Foucault. Towards the end of her account, Lowien quotes from his text *The Order of Discourse*, which had been published in German translation in 1974. In his inaugural lecture at the Collège de France, Foucault had examined the mechanisms which govern the production of verbal utterances in the Western societies. Dialectics, which had supplied inexhaustible material for discussion by 'mediating' the 'contradictions,' suddenly seemed spooky from this perspective. Did it not simply multiply the 'swarming abundance' of spoken and written discourses by continuously holding out the hope of a solution?[69] Was it not a particularly efficient specimen of those 'systems of multiplication of discourses' which Foucault subjected to his linguistic decluttering?[70] To another Foucault reader of those years, Friedrich Kittler, the method of reducing communication to its very existence produced a Sartrean nausea.[71] In the West Berlin publishing collective, it accelerated the loss of faith in discussion. 'They no longer made so many speeches,' Merve Lowien writes, 'but now insisted on acting events out. Hence there were tears and interruptions in the work, with no explanation.' For the publisher observing these changes from 1974 on, they amounted to a 'total withdrawal from the discourse.'[72] In relation to the goals the collective had set for itself, they were an admission of failure.

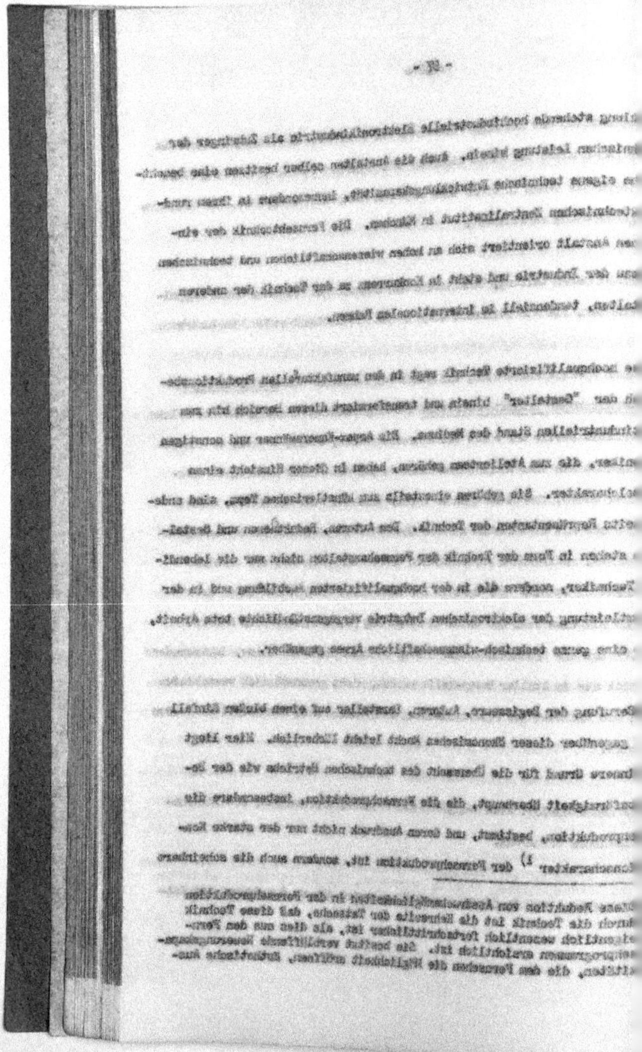

7 Oskar Negt and Alexander Kluge, *Öffentlichkeit und Erfahrung* [*Public Sphere and Experience*], Frankfurt: Suhrkamp, 1972. A preliminary draft was circulated among the Merve collective before publication.

4

WOLFSBURG EMPIRE

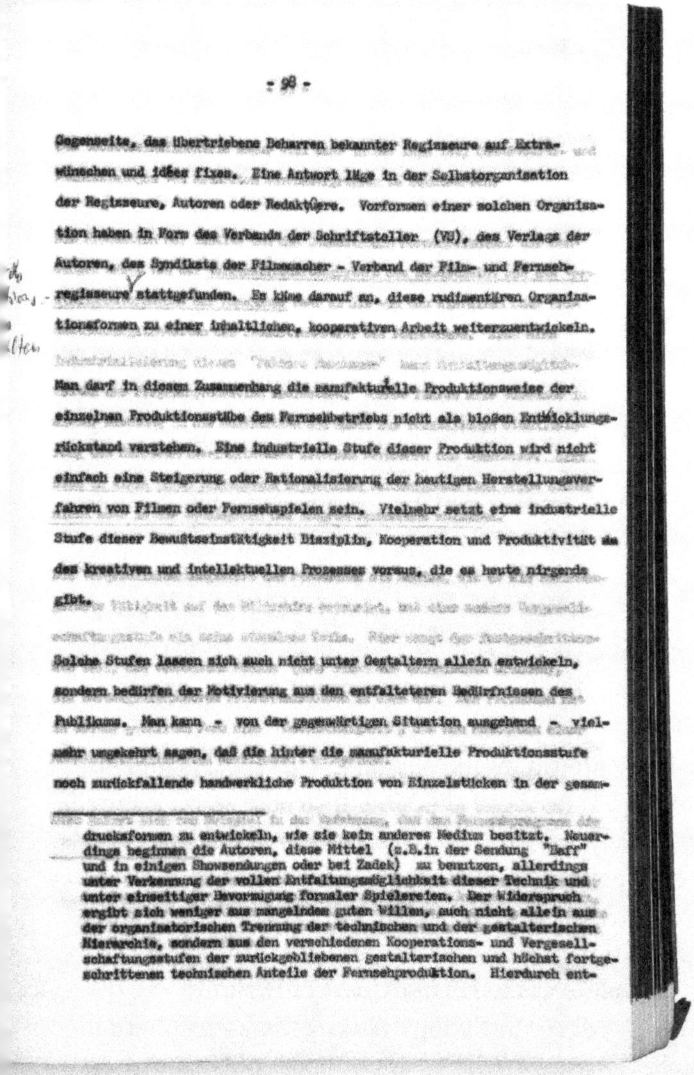

\- 98 -

Gegenseite, das übertriebene Beharren bekannter Regisseure auf Extrawünschen und idées fixes. Eine Antwort läge in der Selbstorganisation der Regisseure, Autoren oder Redakteure. Vorformen einer solchen Organisation haben in Form des Verbands der Schriftsteller (VS), des Verlags der Autoren, des Syndikats der Filmemacher - Verband der Film- und Fernsehregisseure stattgefunden. Es käme darauf an, diese rudimentären Organisationsformen zu einer inhaltlichen, kooperativen Arbeit weiterzuentwickeln.

Man darf in diesem Zusammenhang die manufakturelle Produktionsweise der einzelnen Produktionsstäbe des Fernsehbetriebs nicht als bloßen Entwicklungsrückstand verstehen. Eine industrielle Stufe dieser Produktion wird nicht einfach eine Steigerung oder Rationalisierung der heutigen Herstellungsverfahren von Filmen oder Fernsehspielen sein. Vielmehr setzt eine industrielle Stufe dieser Bewußtseinstätigkeit Disziplin, Kooperation und Produktivität des kreativen und intellektuellen Prozesses voraus, die es heute nirgends gibt.

Solche Stufen lassen sich auch nicht unter Gestaltern allein entwickeln, sondern bedürfen der Motivierung aus den entfalteteren Bedürfnissen des Publikums. Man kann - von der gegenwärtigen Situation ausgehend - vielmehr umgekehrt sagen, daß die hinter die manufakturielle Produktionsstufe noch zurückfallende handwerkliche Produktion von Einzelstücken in der gesam-

---

drucksformen zu entwickeln, wie sie kein anderes Medium besitzt. Neuerdings beginnen die Autoren, diese Mittel (z.B. in der Sendung "Baff" und in einigen Showsendungen oder bei Zadek) zu benutzen, allerdings unter Verkennung der vollen Entfaltungsmöglichkeit dieser Technik und unter einseitiger Bevorzugung formaler Spielereien. Der Widerspruch ergibt sich weniger aus mangelndem guten Willen, auch nicht allein aus der organisatorischen Trennung der technischen und der gestalterischen Hierarchie, sondern aus den verschiedenen Kooperations- und Vergesellschaftungsstufen der zurückgebliebenen gestalterischen und höchst fortgeschrittenen technischen Anteile der Fernsehproduktion. Hierdurch ent-

It would not be true, however, to say the collective had spent the first half of the seventies just talking among themselves. The aspiration to a political existence drove them not only into the loop of recursive self-agitation, but also outwards into the forest of organizations, which had been growing ever denser since '68. In 1971, Merve got in touch with the Socialist Bureau in Offenbach, a focal point of 'undogmatic leftists' who stood aloof both from the cadre parties and from the 'puttering' of the factory and neighbourhood groups.[1] The publishers also organized a seminar on the 'organizational question' at the Department of Architecture of West Berlin's Technische Universität. To advance the proliferation of the right books, they joined the Federation of Leftist Booksellers, whose members were obligated under the by-laws to invest their profits from bootleg printing in the political struggle.

Proletarian Public Sphere

There has been much speculation about the connections between the Red publishing scene and the militant underground in the 1970s. The terrorists' practice forced all other left-wing groups to take a position on the use of violence. In West Berlin, attitudes towards the urban guerrilla were often complicated by personal acquaintance. Peter Gente, for example, had known the Red Army Faction founders Andreas Baader and Ulrike Meinhof before their paths had diverged.[2] Merve's low revenues probably spared him and his comrades the dilemma of deciding whether to donate funds to the RAF. Instead, the publishing collective contributed media support. As an expression of solidarity with comrades 'who are now experiencing the full repressive violence of the capitalist state system,' Merve published in 1973 a brochure of pleadings and transcripts from the trial of the leftist lawyer Horst Mahler, the first of the RAF trials to take place at the Higher Court of Berlin.[3]

The transcripts in the Merve anthology convey the atmosphere in the courtroom, where the public seized every opportunity to express their solidarity with the prisoners. When the witness Gudrun Ensslin managed to slap the prosecutor during her testimony, the courtroom was in an uproar: a spectator jumped over the bar and ran forward;

'cops with helmets and clubs closed in'. The defendant Horst Mahler, on trial for founding a criminal association and abetting the jailbreak of Andreas Baader, discussed revolutionary strategy with the witness Ulrike Meinhof.[4] He used his closing statement to describe the horrors of the Israeli occupation in the Palestinian territories, then summed up the progress of the 'revolutionary people's war' which the RAF had brought back home to the metropolitan West. This war, the spearhead of the whole movement, was impossible 'to grasp with the customary ways of thinking of traditional theory'. Facing the public, the defendant Mahler outlined the two possible alternatives: 'The events of the armed struggle confront the Left with the choice: either resolutely to support this struggle, or to betray the proletarian revolution to the class enemy; to follow the path of the RAF, or to crawl after the Rodewalds, Negts and Röhls' – former sympathizers who had baulked at violence – 'straight up the arse of the ruling class.'[5] Like Baader, Mahler too used his time in prison to immerse himself in theory – he had his defence lawyer Otto Schily bring him the collected works of Hegel[6] – although he had roundly rejected his comrades' admonition to maintain a high level of critical reflection.

In their afterword to the trial documents, the Merve publishing collective take a position: theirs is against terrorism. Its 'avant-garde or elite principle, redeemed neither by theoretical analysis nor by emancipatory practice', runs the risk of leading to a 'reification' of violence. The publishers support their position with bibliographic references, which is typical of the debate's tone: 'A full discussion would also consider, in addition to the problem outlined here, pp. 91 ff. and 243 ff. of *Public Sphere and Experience: Analysis of the Bourgeois and Proletarian Public Sphere* by Oskar Negt and Alexander Kluge.'[7]

Placing their hope in books, not weapons, the Merve group used this work by Negt and Kluge, originally published in German as number 639 in the *edition suhrkamp* series, as one of their most important references. They had got their hands on a preliminary draft even before its publication in 1972. In it, the authors explored the historic conditions under which the experiences of class struggle could be networked to form a nexus of communication which would be subordinate neither to a revolutionary avant-garde nor to the 'media cartel', nor to any compulsory rationalization. Their goal of constituting a 'proletarian public' or 'counter-public' was influenced, at least conceptually, by the American counter-culture.[8] In a chapter on the consciousness industry, Kluge anticipated the coup he would later land in commercial media: criticizing television by means of television. In many respects, *Public Sphere and Experience* was a revision of Habermas's *Structural Transformation of the Public Sphere,* the book that had placed the issue on the left's agenda in 1962. Unlike Habermas, however, Negt and Kluge no longer believed in the superiority of the bourgeois public sphere. The rational discussion among equals which Habermas had traced back to Enlightenment London, they felt, had always been an instrument to legitimize particular, capitalist interests. But 'a public sphere that reflects the interests and experiences of the overwhelming majority of the population, insofar as these experiences and interests are real', must also admit the voices of imagination and sensuality. This is a utopia of the seventies.[9]

In the Land of Class Struggle

The theoretical territory in which the publishers manœuvred grew broader with every new author: from Althusser's theoretical practice via Krahl's organizational analysis, they had arrived at Negt and Kluge's proletarian public sphere. The recklessness with which later generations of readers would serve themselves from the 'theory drugstore' was inconceivable in the 1970s.[10] Theories had to be explored in their interrelations dialectically, which further escalated the abstraction. But, as the movement splintered and the theoretical options became more and more complex, a new beacon of hope was spied south of the Alps. As generations of German humanists had done before them, the left discovered Italy as the land of their dreams. What they sought in the south, however, was neither the rigour of classical forms nor the 'porosity' with which Naples had won Walter Benjamin's affection.[11] Italy's attraction in the seventies was rather that of an Arcadia of the class struggle. The Italian Communist Party was the strongest in Western Europe; its working class was not yet depraved by prosperity; grand-bourgeois circles in Rome and Milan cultivated revolution as radical chic. Rudi Dutschke, severely wounded by a reactionary attacker, had found refuge in Milan with Giangiacomo Feltrinelli in the spring of 1968. Fascinated by the country 'where the class struggle and the richness of life ran riot', the communard Dieter Kunzelmann visited an anarchists' camp in Sicily the following year.[12] The department store arsonists Gudrun Ensslin and Andreas Baader also fled to Italy in 1969, and were given shelter by the composer Hans Werner Henze. With no language skills or higher education, Baader felt out of place in the refined society of Rome, but he managed to steal a few of his host's silk shirts.[13]

Of course, Italy was more than just a hideout for terrorists. Over a year after May '68, the rebellion had wandered from Paris to Turin. The eyes of the left were fixed on the strikes in the Fiat factories of Mirafiori, where in 1969 the class struggle seemed to be entering a new phase. Proletarians from the Mezzogiorno and students from the University of Turin had protested – not against working conditions, but against work itself. The unions had been unable to contain the conflict. The militants' battle cry – *Vogliamo tutto!* 'We want everything!' – made the rounds of the West German left that year. Compared with what was going on in Turin, the wildcat strikes taking place in the Ruhr at the same time seemed harmless.[14] In the workers' and students' assembly, the Fiat workers themselves had spoken up: their slogan was 'Fuck the factory!' – not really a demand at all, and certainly not one that could be met by shorter hours or better pay. Instead of playing the role that had been written for the proletariat, they carried the cultural revolution into the factory halls.

When, in December of 1969, a bomb exploded in Milan, the police seized on the pretext to put a violent end to the rebellion in Turin. Only later did it transpire that the attack had been carried out by fascist extremists. The event marked the beginning of the *anni di piombo* – the leaden years, as the seventies are called in Italy. By 1980, terrorist groups of the left and the right would take hundreds of lives. The German left nonetheless clung to hopes of a revolution in the south, and an uninterrupted stream of political tourists crossed the Alps in the seventies. As late as 1982, Heiner Müller expressed the belief that Italy represented the 'future of Western Europe' because the 'conflicts' had progressed further there.[15]

The Merve collective too set out on its first Italian foray in 1971 – but without going much farther than the transit motorway through East

Germany connecting West Berlin with the West German mainland. Their destination was not Turin, Milan or Rome, but the motor city Wolfsburg, where 6,000 Italian workers assembled Volkswagens. Like their compatriots at Fiat, they came from Italy's poorer south and lived apart from their wives and families – in Wolfsburg's 'guest worker' estate, Berliner Brücke, a barracks complex enclosed in barbed-wire fences. These migrant workers were the dormant revolutionary subject that had been waiting for the spark of rebellion. Armed with Negt and Kluge, the Merve group's strategy was to establish a proletarian public sphere. They planned to start an Italian–German communication centre 'with a pub and rooms for discussion'.[16] In a case such as this, it seemed the step from theory to practice couldn't be simpler: as the strikes in Turin had shown, it all depended on getting the proletariat itself to speak up. Installing the necessary channels of communication would be enough to get things rolling in the biggest Italian settlement north of the Alps.[17]

If the plan didn't pan out, it was in part the fault of Wolfsburg's urban development. The 'atomization of the city and the parcelling of its residential space into minimal units (there aren't even pubs with rooms to hold more than fifty people)' prevented any effective organization of the proletariat.[18] But, apart from the disciplinary architecture, which they would soon be analysing with Foucault, the publishers also discovered in Wolfsburg the treacherous limits of their social and political common ground. One evening, as they lay on their mattresses on the floor, one of the group had the idea of undressing in front of the others. The attempt to engender trust and community failed miserably. In the confusion that befell the group instead, another comrade was moved to confess that he secretly dreamt of having a family and a little house and garden. That lapse led in turn to interminable discussions. Filled with new apprehension, the Merve collective went to sleep. The next day they drove back to West Berlin.[19]

The Lightness of Being Communist

In the summer of 1972, they almost went to Wolfsburg a second time – but only because Toni Negri begged for their support. He was the head of Potere Operaio, one of the Italian Operaist groups that were beginning to gain influence in West Germany as well during the Italy craze. Before Merve became established in the late seventies as the home of French philosophy, the publishing house made a name for itself by translating Operaist texts. After the example of the Mirafiori rebellion, Potere Operaio developed a theory that broke with the work ethic. Since Marx, the left had assumed that the proletarians were the avant-garde of humanity by virtue of the fact that they worked: their class consciousness and their revolutionary potential derived from their productive power. In the eyes of the Operaists, this view, held by the unions in particular, tended to perpetuate the system. By limiting the proletariat's role to rebelling against capital in the name of labour, the traditional view perpetuated the passivity of the proletariat in the class struggle. Instead, Potere Operaio and Lotta Continua advocated fighting against work itself.[20] Only a working class which refused to perform the task assigned to it could regain the initiative it had lost. Hence, the Operaists felt the best strategies were insubordination, boycott and sabotage – not just in the factories, but also in mass protests. In the *autoriduzione* campaign, the inhabitants of some working-class neighbourhoods of Turin unilaterally lowered their own rents and electricity rates.[21] Negri, in particular, who generalized the proletarian as 'society's worker', advocated extending Operaism to all areas of life. Nonetheless, labour remained his theory's critical point of reference.

In contrast to the German terrorists, who operated in isolation, the revolutionary avant-garde in Italy sought to close ranks with the base, the working masses.[22] That made them a strategic alternative in Germany, where Potere Operaio and Lotta Continua became models for the Sponti movement. 'The whole theory of the integration and embourgeoisement of the working class and the thesis that the Third World is the only revolutionary subject were swept away', recalls Daniel Cohn-Bendit, describing the shifting mood of the early seventies.[23] Through the events in Italy, the proletariat regained the favour of the German intellectuals. The cadres of the cultural revolution were now getting up at the crack of dawn to agitate at the gates of the Opel factory in Rüsselsheim or the Siemens plant in Spandau. Potere Operaio had not only an armed militant wing, but also an international office to coordinate activities abroad, and West Germany was considered an especially important territory.[24] Consequently, Toni Negri urged his West Berlin publishers in the summer of 1972 to go to Wolfsburg again as a reconnaissance troop to study the situation on the ground. 'We don't have much time', he impressed upon the Merve comrades. 'The situation in Italy is deteriorating visibly (the new government has announced that we are going to be outlawed). So our time as an "open" organization is limited, and we want to achieve something while we're still able to move. I embrace you all. Venceremos.'[25]

But a second mission to Wolfsburg did not take place – probably because the collective realized that it was not suited to serve as a revolutionary cell. Like most former Adornians, Peter Gente was immune to the idolization of the worker.[26] While Negri flirted with armed rebellion in Italy, Gente cautiously withdrew into his world of paper. Operaist titles continued to appear in Merve's publishing catalogue until 1977. That year, the Autonomia movement in Bologna triggered another wave of enthusiasm for Italy. Two years later, Negri was arrested,[27] leaving the left's decade-old hopes of Arcadia without a figurehead. The 'irrepressible lightness and joy of being communist', which Negri recalled twenty years later to the readers of his theory bestseller *Empire*, was nowhere to be found as the seventies drew to a close.[28]

A Fateful Stroke of Luck

Although sales revenues rose, and the success of the Italian titles made it possible for the first time to pay each member a stipend of 500 marks per month, the Merve collective was drifting apart. Under the smoke-screen of 'interest in the proletarian experience', the comrades sought escape in the personal and particular: listening to blues, reading Nietzsche, painting. Peter Gente, for his part, discovered nightlife. His weariness with discussion grew commensurately with his indulgence in the seductions of Berlin's bar scene. In the spring of 1974, Hans Magnus Enzensberger visited the publishing house. He listened, encouraged the group to carry on, and paid homage to Gente's and Lowien's 'successful' combination of marriage and partnership in their work.[29] It would soon become evident, though, that Enzensberger's impression no longer reflected reality. The same year, while drinking beer in a bar in Schöneberg, Gente met a student named Heidi Paris. The shy publisher would later call that meeting his 'fateful stroke of luck'.[30]

The motif of 'switching women' occurs in Lowien's 1976 account.[31] The publishers' marriage was headed for a crisis along with the tribal patriarchy of their working collective, and Heidi Paris gave them both the coup de grâce. In the mid-seventies, the collective was hitting a sandbank; that proved fertile ground for the new lover's ideas. 'In 1974, the working relationships in the publishing collective fell apart', Peter Gente recalled. 'Times of confusion. 1976: "No future"; that made sense to us straight away.'[32] The couple were soon known simply as 'Heidi and Peter' in allusion to characters from Johanna Spyri's classic children's book *Heidi* – which was popular then in a Japanese cartoon adaptation – but their symbiosis was growing on the ruins of a utopia. The socialist life project was no match for their private chemistry. As a dual mind, they composed melodious titles, developed Merve into a brand, and collaborated on a string of successful publications over almost thirty years. Their contrasting temperaments must have been an important factor, and their age difference another.

When Peter Gente had founded the publishing collective, Heidi Paris, fourteen years younger, had just left Braunschweig, where her family had a furniture shop. Her father, allegedly a former member of the Waffen-SS, is said to have replayed battles of the Second World War with tin soldiers. Like Gente, Paris had little to say about her parents – and that usually in a sarcastic tone.[33] Originally, she had come to Berlin to work in film. Instead, however, she began reading theory in seminars at Freie Universität. She exuded a headstrong intelligence that men were afraid of, Gente said. She later pursued her artistic ambitions as a curator of design exhibitions, among other things. Authors and friends who tried to describe the publishing couple's working methods emphasized his erudition and her judgement.[34] He played the encyclopaedic part, collecting every newspaper cutting that might be relevant; she responded to texts with a keen intuition. She suffered from occasional psychotic episodes – beginning with one in the late 1980s – and was repeatedly treated in hospital, which allowed her for a long time to keep the illness under control. As a member of the '68 generation, Heidi Paris came to university as Marxism was already stagnating.[35] She first encountered Michel Foucault in a tutorial offered by Henning Ritter in the winter term of 1973–4.[36] In the following year, the new author was the dowry she brought with her to the collapsing Merve collective. For Gente, who was tired of dialectics, the consequences were momentous.

The mid-seventies are a time of countless little turning points. Diedrich Diederichsen – a few years younger than Heidi Paris – tells how LSD lost its kick: in the middle of a trip, the ineffable fascination of the clouds, trees and blades of grass suddenly dissolved, and all he wanted to know was who had won the Hamburg SV match. From that moment, there was no point in turning on and tuning in any more.[37] The Merve publishers experienced comparable moments, although they are perhaps not as precisely dated, and of course they did not concern LSD or HSV. In the borough of Schöneberg, in the loft where Merve Verlag had moved sometime in the late seventies, the style of the student movement, the ideas of '68, and politics itself as the measure of all things were suddenly up for negotiation. A letter from Merve to Jean-François Lyotard dated 1976 points in both directions at once: the publishing collective is still addressing a comrade; the objective is still to 'work away' the differences between manual and mental labour. Yet traces of a different tone are detectable: instead of Italian Operaism, the letter mentions 'the recent French discussion' and political aimlessness. 'And then we laugh even while we're making books.'[38]

1977

READING FRENCH IN THE GERMAN AUTUMN

Jean-François Lyotard, 1925 geboren, während des Algerienkriegs in der linksradikalen Gruppe um die Zeitschrift "Socialisme ou Barbarie" engagiert, dann in Nanterre, jetzt an der Universität Paris-Vincennes Ordinarius für Philosophie - er ist inzwischen wohl eher ein Barbar im "Reich" des Sozialismus, und nicht nur dort, ein Fremdling, der die Grenzen des Imperiums durchlöchert und die Kategorien des Zentrums zerfleddert.

In den Texten, die hier zusammengestellt sind, schreibt er über die Minderheiten, über das vielförmige und prekäre Patchwork, das sie bilden. Er folgt ihren Listen und Finten, die die monotonen und zentralisierten Räume verdrehen, ihren Bewegungen in der verzwickten Zeit des Begehrens und schleicht sich mit ihnen in ökonomische, politische Diskurse ein, um Paradoxa zu installieren, die deren Ordnung und Logik platzen lassen.

Diese Operationen sind durch und durch bejahend, und ihre Methode ist weniger die Kritik als ein raffiniertes Spiel mit Fallen, Intensitäten und Perspektiven.

8 Jean-François Lyotard, *Das Patchwork der Minderheiten* [The patchwork of minorities], Berlin: Merve, 1977.

5

(POSSIBLE) REASONS FOR THE HAPPINESS OF THOUGHT

The publishers seem to have learned a lesson from the trouble with Althusser. Although little had changed about their nonchalance towards copyrights, their inquiry to Lyotard betrays at least an effort to get a green light from the author before publishing his book: 'We would like to bring out some texts by you in the near future. Because most of them are pieces from periodicals, we are taking advantage of the ambiguous situation and not bothering about the copyright. We do need your permission, of course. We can't pay you anything.'[1] They also seem to have found the right person this time. Unlike Althusser, Lyotard was willing to overlook the issue of rights: 'I perfectly understand your position', he wrote back immediately from Baltimore. He would inform his publisher, Christian Bourgeois, a comrade who, as luck would have it, was in financial difficulties himself at the moment, but Lyotard himself had no objection to conceding a German publication right gratis.[2]

And so the Merve team at the 1977 Frankfurt Book Fair presented to the German public a little book by an unknown author: Lyotard's 'Patchwork of minorities' – a collection of essays in form; in substance, a manifesto. It is dedicated to the 'minoritarian struggles' of women, homosexuals, the unemployed ... even 'minoritarian "researchers"' in their laboratories. In all these struggles, Lyotard writes, causes were upheld without reference to the 'CENTRE' of power; demands for meaning and truth were dropped; things happened which could no longer be accounted for in Marxist terms. The French professor, described a few years later by a surprised German journalist as an amiable older gentleman, saw a 'great patchwork of many minoritarian singularities' on the near horizon, and a confusion of little constellations in which weaknesses became strengths.[3] The weapons of the workers' movement were worn blunt, Lyotard felt. He placed his political hopes in the undocumented workers, tax dodgers and non-voters whose anarchic stance of refusal was like that of the Italian proletarians who had come up with the strategy of sabotaging work itself.[4] But the Operaists – translated and published by Merve to the last – were still acting within a Marxist worldview; Lyotard, on the other hand, abandoned the vocabulary of dialectical materialism. One of the first and most striking consequences of this paradigm shift was his rescaling of the political: what was small, and seen by the classical left as necessarily condemned to inefficacy, was suddenly promising. The semantic field of the microscopic that conquered theory around the mid-seventies – microphysics, micropolitics, microhistory too – betrays the end of faith in the power of the masses. Logically, the microtheoretician Lyotard could hardly do otherwise than come to terms with the micropublisher Merve on the matter of copyright.

The changed relations of size also dictated Merve's new appearance. The books on display at Merve's 1977 Frankfurt Book Fair stand had shrunk from the pirate printing movement's folio format to the ISO B6 postcard size still used today: 'We have switched from ISO A5 to the smaller format,' Paris and Gente explained, 'to make the break in our publishing "programme" unmistakable.'[5] Besides Lyotard, the new titles included books by Gilles Deleuze, Michel Foucault, Félix Guattari and Hélène Cixous. The bestselling German non-fiction titles in autumn of 1977 included *Der Aufmacher*, Günter Wallraff's undercover investigation at the tabloid *Bild*; Erich von Däniken's evidence of extra-terrestrial visitors; and Klaus Theweleit's *Male Fantasies* – which Rudolf Augstein called 'perhaps the most exciting German-language publication' of the season.[6] The Francophile wave at Merve Verlag did not merit a mention in Augstein's *Der Spiegel*. In the theory sector, however, it met with great interest.[7] It would be a few months yet before Paris and Gente ratified their new orientation in a new series title, but from early 1978 on, their books were labelled not *Internationale Marxistische Diskussion*, but *Internationaler Merve Diskurs*. The publishing couple took their leave of Marxism and discussion in the same breath.

All Kinds of Escapes

In the intellectual situation of 1977, many people read the new Merve books as an antidote: they supplied the best arguments against Marxism. In no other country were intellectuals processing their old beliefs as exuberantly as in France. The French were taking revenge for a frustrated love. After all, they had been the most eloquent advocates of communism in Western Europe after 1945. The tradition of the *Résistance*, Stalin's prestige as the victor over Hitler, and the deep-seated myth of revolution had long swelled the ranks of the French Communist Party.[8] After the shocks of Khrushchev's revelations and the uprising in Hungary, the socialist creed had lived on in the theory work of the New Left. Thinkers such as Lyotard had also won their intellectual reputations in those circles. Lyotard recapitulated his Marxist past in a text that Merve would have liked to have in its catalogue: until the late sixties, he had been a member first of Socialisme ou barbarie, then of Pouvoir ouvrier. In the whirlpool of the cultural revolution, he had turned away from these groups, and in the years that followed had begun formulating antitheses to the Marxist style of thought.[9]

One such antithesis was taking up the cause of a group that Marx and Engels had excluded from the revolutionary movement: the 'minorities' were, in the old terminology, nothing more and nothing less than the lumpenproletariat. Bernard-Henri Lévy was alluding to this context when, writing in the *Nouvel observateur* in 1976, he called Lyotard the leader of the 'lumpen-intelligentsia' of Vincennes – a group which included Michel Foucault, Gilles Deleuze and Félix Guattari.[10] From a Marxist perspective, the lumpenproletariat was a reactionary class. Without a homogeneous composition or shared objective interests, it consisted only of the 'refuse, offal, and wreck of all classes'.[11] To Lyotard and his supporters, that was a reason to hope that it could play the central role in the 'minoritarian struggles' to come. 'There are the communes', Deleuze explained at an anti-psychiatry conference in Milan in 1973, 'there are the marginal groups, the criminals, there are the drug addicts, there is the escape into drugs, there are all kinds of escapes, there are schizophrenic escapes, there are people who try to escape in all kinds of ways.'[12]

In the previous decade, the star of the Berlin student movement, Herbert Marcuse, had already placed a special emphasis on society's marginal groups. He thought the unintegrated outsiders were capable of sparking the uprising of the working class.[13] Deleuze's soft spot for drug addicts was less promising, however. The junkies William Burroughs wrote about in his novels were not apt to catalyse any kind of social movement. In contrast to the American civil rights movement which had served as Marcuse's point of reference, they had no agenda – except to organize their next fix.[14] They violated the social consensus, but without appealing to any higher principle. They neither represented anything nor were themselves represented by anyone. Explaining the strength of the weak in an interview with Bernard-Henri Lévy, Lyotard added, speaking for the Vincennes faculty, 'it makes one incredulous towards any representation of the little guy'.[15]

Later generations of readers have encountered the critique of representation mainly as a semiological issue which originated in the radicalization of structural linguistics: signs which refer not to reality, but reciprocally to one another – such signs, according to Ferdinand de Saussure, generated meaning in language. His successors took this idea to extremes, calling the world a text, or saying that there are free-floating signifiers. They criticized the idea that words can touch reality and explored the conditions under which reference is possible. In the 1970s, when these topics arrived in Germany, the critique of representation had also taken on an immediately political dimension: it now concerned not only questions of semiotics, but also the viability of a revolution that would be bound by the 'theoretical representation of Marxism' and the 'practical representation of the Party'. Félix Guattari, formulating these ideas in the 1977 Merve publication *Mikro-Politik des Wunsches* – the 'micropolitics of desire' – joined Lyotard in holding such a revolution to be impossible.[16]

Rejecting the idea of representation had another consequence which affected the role played by the renegades of Vincennes. In the 1960s, Adorno had claimed a universal responsibility which obliged him to take a position on the problems of West Germans. In the early eighties, Lyotard wrote a widely received article in *Le Monde* in which he laid the figure of the public intellectual to rest. After the end of the utopias, he declared, such representatives as 'thinkers who situate themselves in the position of man, humanity, the nation, the people, the proletariat, creation, or some such entity' were obsolete.[17] A short time later, Michel de Certeau – also a Merve author – went so far as to assert that those who pretend to 'represent the masses' are in reality fighting 'to educate, discipline and order them'.[18] Niklas Luhmann, too, corrected the image of the intellectual, although without striking such an accusatory tone: 'Knowing what's what', he explained in a 1987 interview on German radio, 'and combining that with the idea that one is in touch with reality, and therefore others have to follow or listen or accept authority – that is an obsolete mentality.' Merve published the interview in its first Luhmann reader. The observation that there was no longer any privileged observer in the functionally differentiated society was an excellent fit for the Merve catalogue.[19]

Intensity Is Not a Feeling

In 1978, with their second title by Lyotard, *Intensitäten* [Intensities], Paris and Gente incinerated the cardboard-grey tones of the pirate printing movement with a hot pink cover. As the seventies progressed, they had made their books not only smaller, but also more colourful. 'The colour came out beautifully,' they wrote in a letter to Lyotard. 'The printer really drifted off while he was working; maybe he absorbed too much of the text.'[20] 'Drifted' was an allusion to the author's terminology: he described his abandonment of Marxism as 'une dérive.'[21] *Intensitäten* contained several essays from the early seventies in which Lyotard had proposed the principle of intensity in opposition to representation. The mechanisms of representation, which included the institutions of the left, divided the world into pairs of opposites: capital and labour, party and class, signifier and signified. But what if, Lyotard asked, society consists of nothing but 'shifts and transformations of energy'? Lyotard was drifting out of Marxist waters back to a kind of social thermodynamics like that which had been in vogue for a time at the close of the nineteenth century. There the 'contradictions' that the New Left diagnosed became mere differences in intensity, and the posture of the critic became affirmation: instead of fighting the prevailing order, Lyotard advocated unleashing its particular energies. Capitalism, kept in check only by the equivalence principle of the exchange of commodities, was in his view a machine to destroy all the existing hierarchies.[22]

Intensitäten was a theory bestseller for Paris and Gente. Even the title contributed to the book's success: it suggested a philosophy with passion, and signalled a liberation from the conventions of dialectical reason.[23] One chapter in the pink Merve book was the print version of a lecture that Lyotard had given at the 1972 conference 'Nietzsche aujourd'hui' in Cerisy-la-Salle. At the podium of this colloquium, which would prove ground-breaking for the French reception of Nietzsche, Lyotard had paid homage to the 'men of profusion': the 'experimental painters, pop, hippies and yippies ... binned loonies. One hour of their lives', the professor declared self-critically, 'offers more intensity ... than three hundred thousand words of a professional philosopher.'[24] Carlos Castaneda might have written something similar. In some respects, Lyotard's praise of intensity seems to amount to a hippie philosophy, claiming superiority for experiences that cannot be captured in words. But in exalting the ineffable, he resorted neither to drug-induced states nor to sexual ecstasy. Nor did he recommend a primal-scream therapy: such attempts to get back to the roots were still dependent, he felt, on the principle of representation.[25]

The path that Lyotard proposed as an escape from the logic of representation led not to the hot swamps of romanticized nature, but to the cool heights of New Music, the American music that exemplified the phenomenon of intensity. Lyotard's lecture at the French Nietzsche conference praised the compositions of John Cage, who had broken more radically than Schönberg with the traditions of European music history by abandoning not just the tonal system, but also its elementary particle, the note. Cage had replaced well-tempered tones with a world of sounds that were beyond the conventions of notation – and beyond the composer's control. Lyotard saw the lack of intentionality that Cage orchestrated as the dissolution of the dichotomous order: a zone of intensity which was free of the 'Rousseauism' of the counter-culture. Thus Lyotard discerned a correspondence between Cage's music and Nietzsche's philosophy.[26]

Nietzsche, too, had countered the philosophy of his time with 'Dionysian enthusiasm', yet without worshipping emotion. In contrast to Wagner and his Romantic longing for redemption, Nietzsche had praised 'beautiful, austere form, economy' and 'Classicism'. Nietzsche thus offered a suitable blueprint for Lyotard's 'politics of intensity', which would escape from the 'theoretical terror' of dialectics, yet without succumbing to any naive belief in immediacy.[27] In 1984, Karl Heinz Bohrer defended Nietzsche against the contemporary vulgarization that pitted good emotion against evil reason – an all-too-German misreading, Bohrer found. His essay, which was aligned with the current of the Parisian Nietzscheans, was titled *Intensität ist kein Gefühl* ['Intensity is not a feeling'].[28]

Lyotard's interpretation of Nietzsche as an intense thinker builds on a French tradition going back to Georges Bataille and Pierre Klossowski, who saw Nietzsche not so much as a philosopher, but more as an author who confronted the philosophical discourse with an existential experience which was bound to destroy its order.[29] This Nietzsche reinforced and revised the difference between theory and philosophy that had been fundamental to a reader such as Peter Gente ever since the aphorisms of Adorno. 'Theoretical constructions are at the same time "dreams"', Bohrer observed. 'In their tendency towards analogy and identification with symbols, in fact, they show elements of schizophrenic obsession': this is a late-1970s insight which drew on Nietzsche.[30] Under the guidance of their French authors – in particular, Deleuze, who was especially concerned with the correct interpretation – Paris and Gente began reading Nietzsche. In 1979, they published Deleuze's 1965 introduction to Nietzsche under the title *Nietzsche: Ein Lesebuch* [Nietzsche: a reader]. 'After intensive readings in Nietzsche', they wrote to Deleuze, while translating and compiling the book, 'we think a great deal about your theory of becoming less, which opens up beautiful and unforeseen perspectives for action in view of widespread megalomania. We're doing a different kind of publishing house: small, cheap, unpretentious, off.'[31]

The Laugh of Merve

That was the new Merve sound. The image of Merve Verlag which was rapidly taking shape in the letters and editorial afterwords of this period would remain largely unchanged during the 1980s: 'We're not pros, we're bookworms.' 'We're a little shy and we have neither money nor strong elbows.' 'We happily confess to making bad and cheap books.'[32] After all the years of discussion about manual and mental labour, this couldn't-care-less attitude must have felt immensely liberating. Its watchword was a laugh. As the critique of ideology decayed, that was the mark it left on the period of transition to postmodernism: before giving way to the urbane irony of the 1980s, the tone of the theory discourse erupted in mirth. At the end of her final report on the enterprise that bore her name, Merve Lowien had quoted Derrida to say 'laughter alone exceeds dialectics' – but 'only on the basis of an absolute renunciation of meaning, an absolute risking of death.'[33] In 1977, Paris and Gente took that risk. For half a decade, they had observed a growing melancholy; in the left-wing bars, cheerfulness was considered an affront at the time the publishers discovered the Nietzschean culture of humour as an expression of their new theoretical perspective.[34] 'Those who read Nietzsche without laughing – without laughing often, richly, even hilariously,' Deleuze wrote, 'have, in a sense, not read Nietzsche at all.'[35] Lyotard too made it plain that, in the emerging 'libidinal dispositive,' it was no longer important 'to be right,' but 'to be able to laugh and dance.' Like the Situationists years before, he advocated the destruction of theory through parody.[36] Meanwhile, his West Berlin publishers cultivated their cheerfulness as a calling card for their new kind of philosophy: 'We want to be a little publisher, unpretentious and off, and we're having mad fun doing it.'[37]

That fun was most visible in the language. It developed a tendency towards wordplay and puns, as if it was having an allergic reaction to the wooden prose of neo-Marxism. In one of the first German anthologies on Deleuze and Guattari's *Anti-Oedipus*, edited by the psychoanalyst Rudolf Heinz, all of the contributors used pseudonyms with the surname 'Heinz': Norbert Heinz, Jochen Heinz, Hubert Heinz ...[38] Paris and Gente designed a bookcase made of shovel blades to accommodate their own books, like so much manure.[39] The characteristic form which that humour took in this transitional phase is perhaps that of the uncontrollable giggles. Michael Rutschky, the author of a famous essay on the melancholy of the seventies, has reminisced on his first giggling fit, caused by watching *Kentucky Fried Movie* in the cinema. A short time later, he had a similar experience seeing *The Life of Brian*.[40] Both films arrived in German cinemas in 1980, just at the close of the decade, and both were big hits, their throw-away punch lines attesting to the end of dialectics.

It was also a certain convulsive laughter that became the emblem of theory's new feeling: a laughter that came from the mouth of Michel Foucault. 'To all those who still wish to talk about man, about his reign or his liberation,' he wrote as early as 1966, in *The Order of Things*, 'to all these warped and twisted forms of reflection we can answer only with a philosophical laugh.'[41] After his death, Foucault's eulogists stylized his laugh as a trademark. 'I can just hear the echo of his *fou rire* breaking out into laughter', wrote Paris and Gente in their obituary for the daily *die tageszeitung* (better known as the *taz*).[42] Friedrich Kittler, who had met Foucault in Bayreuth but hadn't had the courage to speak to him, remembered 'a loud laugh amid a circle of young men.'[43] Michel de Certeau, who had been a friend of Foucault's, went so far as to dedicate a theory-soaked eulogy to that sound. In the most famous laugh of the period, he claimed to hear the voice of History herself laughing at those of the left who had hoped to impute to her some kind of meaning. But they knew better now; History was no more directed towards a goal than Monty Python's sketches towards a punch line. Certeau managed, in his *tour d'horizon*, to locate Foucault's other topics in his laugh: the critique of reason, the return of the body, and the liquidation of the author-subject.[44]

No wonder Foucault's *fou rire* aroused such great interest: it was right in the mainstream of ideological debates. The theory of laughter had not made significant progress in Germany since Helmuth Plessner's investigation on laughing and weeping, published during the war.[45] Why the topic was back on the agenda of the social sciences in the seventies is a question that might merit a historical study in itself. After all, the decade which fell from faith in the future is a proverbially melancholy one.

Yet laughter research was in the air, not only in philosophy, but also in education, psychology and behavioural science.[46] In September of 1974, the mandarins of the German humanities assembled in Bad Homburg. The Research Group on Poetics and Hermeneutics was devoting its seventh colloquium to 'The Comical.' As the papers indicate, the topic had been put on the agenda not only as a timeless phenomenon tangential to aesthetics, but as one of current interest to the participants. Even Hans Blumenberg, who presented his first reflections 'on the comedy of pure theory', incorporated references to the cultural revolution in his talk which were later left out of his 1987 book. Guiding his listeners through the centuries, he demonstrated how the strange business of the philosophers had amused their audiences time and time again. Ever since the Pre-Socratic Thales fell into a well while observing the stars, it had always been others who had the laughs at their expense. 'Where was there ever anything to laugh about in the milieu of philosophers, and what?' Blumenberg asked. A rhetorical question; he could hardly have anticipated a positive answer.[47]

Odo Marquard saw precisely this as the problem. In his talk, he bemoaned the 'programme of total sadness', the legacy of Critical Theory under whose weight the heads of the present day were bowed. Marquard encouraged the attending professors to participate in a limbering-up exercise which he elsewhere titled 'transcendental literature'. 'The salvation of theory is laughter', he declared, insisting that there is 'a close affinity between the comical and the theoretical'. Marquard's testimonial to mirth placed him alongside Peter Sloterdijk as a bestselling philosopher of the 1980s. Their books domesticated philosophical humour. The Nietzschean laughter which had accompanied the end of ideology was now preparing the ground for the Cynics and sceptics.[48]

'The comical', as it was being negotiated by the scholars in Bad Homburg, also had political implications. Accordingly, the podium was shared between apologists and apocalyptics. Dieter Wellershoff, invited by the organizers as a guest speaker, struck a tone of cultural criticism in his 'Theory of Nonsense'. Unlike Marquard, he felt no obligation to the legacy of the Frankfurt School: the subcultures of West Germany had long since emancipated themselves from the duty of consternation. Instead, Wellershoff saw the proliferation of an 'excessive gaiety' among 'hippies', the Dutch 'Provos', 'Zen disciples' and 'drug addicts', which to him seemed not only strange, but dangerous. With its disregard for punch lines, it undercut the standards of comedy; with its jargon of inside jokes, it excluded the uninitiated. In the rituals of 'nonsense', Wellershoff detected a regression into a 'paradise of immaturity' whose *spiritus rector* was still – as late as 1974 – Herbert Marcuse.[49]

A few years later, nonsense had left the ghetto of the drug addicts to become an acceptable mode of discourse among the advocates of French theory. Once the intellectual watershed of the late seventies had been crossed, laughter enjoyed a growing reputation, particularly in its 'low' forms. Its progress can be traced in detail in the various talks given at the symposium 'Laughing – Laughter – Smiling' ['Lachen – Gelächter – Lächeln'] organized by the sociologist and Merve author Dietmar Kamper at Berlin's Freie Universität in 1983, a scant decade after the colloquium in Bad Homburg. The 'Essay on Silliness' that Gert Mattenklott presented in Berlin may suffice as an example: he outlined a theory of forms of amusement very similar to those Dieter Wellershoff had described, but his conclusions were quite different. 'In fits of silliness,' he summed up, 'the meaningful is shaken out of the body, destroying not only all that is representative and bourgeois, but – far more radically – the order of representation itself.' He might almost have been speaking about the music of John Cage: 'Only the signifier is left, not the signified; only words or gestures, no meaning.'[50]

If the smiley face had been popular in Germany around 1980, perhaps Paris and Gente would have been handing out smiley buttons wherever they went. Instead, they left a trail of stickers with the slogan, 'Make rhizomes! – The Pink Panther.' This prompted *Der Spiegel* to print a five-page investigation on the botanical term. The trail led from Alexander Kluge and Klaus Theweleit to the West Berlin bookshop-cum-café Rhizom, to the 'tiny' publishing company Merve and its little book *Rhizom* by Gilles Deleuze and Félix Guattari. The *Spiegel* reporter concluded: 'People on the D&G kick spot one another right away; their numbers are growing.'[51]

Vague Thinkers

It looks very much as though the Merve publishers were swept up in a gold rush in the late seventies: 'We get more feedback than we used to; we've met a lot of people, and fantastic people; and we're completely exhausted.'[52] They weren't after profits; they were out to explore and exploit an El Dorado of theory that was just being discovered in Germany. Even the German women's movement was still arguing in moral universals, while in postcolonial France a new kind of thinking was flowering.[53] Although Suhrkamp had been translating the new French philosophers since the beginning of the 1970s – Foucault's *Madness and Civilization* appeared in German in 1969; Derrida's *Writing and Difference* in 1972; Deleuze and Guattari's *Anti-Oedipus* in 1974 – they were received only by an academic audience. And even at the universities, they were largely an insider tip. They had not yet reached the renegade heirs of the student movement, the 'theory-freak scene' that Merve had by this time conceived as its particular clientele.[54]

The project of importing the French to Germany was hindered by the smouldering hostility of Critical Theory. To the Frankfurt School and its minions, everything remotely associated with post-structuralism was dangerous thinking – and that was not meant as a compliment. Even a cautious approach to the French authors was impeded by their relationship to Heidegger, still *persona non grata* in West Germany, but long a leading contemporary thinker in France. Dialogue was still possible on Nietzsche at a pinch, if nothing else. But even back in the early sixties, Adorno had been up in arms over the 'heideggery' in Paris.[55] In the 1980s, Jürgen Habermas and Manfred Frank took on his indignant role. Furthermore, such a moral authority as Jean Améry, who had survived torture and imprisonment at Auschwitz, wrote in *Die Zeit* against the dark French. Foucault in particular was a dangerous obscurantist, overweening in his shimmering edifice of ideas 'like a climber in the mountains'.[56]

Thus Merve's new catalogue was bound to be edgy. A book such as *Rhizom* quickly made the rounds of the West Berlin 'scene of freaks, communes, dope-smokers and drop-outs', Peter Gente wrote to one of his authors.[57] Unlike the difficult text of *Anti-Oedipus*, *Rhizom* was an atmospheric read, intuitively understandable. 'Your loves will be like the cat and the baboon' and 'Don't bring out the General in you' were slogans that, in 1977, appealed even to readers who never would have climbed the mountains of theory looming in the distance. The maxim 'Never plant!' may have rankled the potheads, of course.[58] But the book also said it wasn't necessary to understand everything. Merve's successful diffusion strategy made sure that Deleuze and the other 'vague thinkers' found a readership: suddenly theory was selling like phonograph records.[59] That played into the hands of Suhrkamp, who marketed the authors' major works.

9 Pages 6 and 7 of Gilles Deleuze and Félix Guattari, *Anti-Oedipus*, trans. Bernd Schwibs, Winterthur: Suhrbier, 1974. Peter Gente and Heidi Paris struggled through this pirate edition for five years.

6

THE READER AS PARTISAN

I.
Die Wunschmaschinen

Es funktioniert überall, bald rastlos, dann wieder mit Unterbrechungen. Es atmet, wärmt, ißt. Es scheißt, es fickt. Das Es ... Überall sind es Maschinen im wahrsten Sinne des Wortes: Maschinen von Maschinen, mit ihren Kupplungen und Schaltungen. Angeschlossen eine Organmaschine an eine Quellemaschine: der Strom, von dieser hervorgebracht, wird von jener unterbrochen. Die Brust ist eine Maschine zur Herstellung von Milch, und mit ihr verkoppelt die Mundmaschine. Der Mund des Appetitlosen hält die Schwebe zwischen einer Eßmaschine, einer Analmaschine, einer Sprechmaschine, einer Atmungsmaschine (Asthma-Anfall). In diesem Sinne ist jeder Bastler; einem jeden seine kleinen Maschinen. Eine Organmaschine für eine Energiemaschine, fortwährend Ströme und Einschnitte. Präsident Schreber hat die Himmelsstrahlen im Arsch. *Himmelsarsch.* Und seid ohne Sorge, es funktioniert; Präsident Schreber spürt etwas, produziert etwas, und vermag darüber hinaus dessen Theorie zu entwickeln. Was eintritt sind Maschineneffekte, nicht Wirkungen von Metaphern.

Das Umherschweifen des Schizophrenen gibt gewiß ein besseres Vorbild ab als der auf der Couch hingestreckte Neurotiker. Ein wenig freie Luft, Bezug zur Außenwelt. Beispielsweise die Wanderung von Büchners Lenz. Wie anders dagegen jene Augenblicke beim guten Pastor, in denen dieser ihn nötigt, sich erneut gesellschaftlich: in Beziehung zum Gott der Religion, zum Vater, zur Mutter, anzupassen. Dort aber ist er im Gebirge, im Schnee, mit anderen Göttern oder ganz ohne Gott, ohne Vater noch Mutter, ist er mit der Natur. »Was will mein Vater? Kann er mehr geben? Unmöglich! Laßt mich in Ruhe!« Alles ist Maschine. Maschinen des Himmels, die Sterne oder der Regenbogen, Maschinen des Gebirges, die sich mit den Maschinen seines Körpers vereinigen. Ununterbrochener Maschinenlärm. »... aber er meine, es müsse ein unendliches Wonnegefühl sein, so

7

The new French authors transformed the 1970s into one big massacre: they liquidated the author; they entombed the intellectual and decreed the end of the proletariat; they rubbed out humanity like a drawing in the sand. No wonder they met with opposition. In the summer of 1978, Heidi Paris and Peter Gente sent a situation report to Paris describing the entrenched fronts and the 'anger and silence' they saw all around them: 'Rowohlt have published the first piece against the "new irrationalism". All the left periodicals are preparing something; the Marxists are rallying for the final battle.'[1] The martial vocabulary suggests antagonism, and there was just as much of it on either side. In Rowohlt's lit mag, the publication mentioned in Paris and Gente's letter, the new Merve authors were exposed once more as counter-revolutionaries.[2] The verbal escalation did little, however, to win back control over the discourse. To a generation who knew of '68 only by hearsay, and who saw the posture of Critical Theory as intellectual folklore, the charm of the Parisian renegades increased proportionately with the official warnings that they were dangerous. From the late seventies on, a growing readership awaited the latest in French discourse imported to West Germany by big Suhrkamp and little Merve.

The Death of the Author

In 1978, Merve tried to obtain perfectly legal rights to publish a text that had launched the massacre in the late sixties: Roland Barthes's 'La mort de l'auteur', still untranslated for German readers ten years after its original publication. 'Who are we and what does that have to do with texts by Roland Barthes?' Paris and Gente wrote in their letter to the Barthes translator Jürgen Hoch. They described 'the diffuse network of shared flats, bars, groups, the scene' in which their books circulated. They made a point of being not just 'amateurs', but 'marginal' to boot, and stood up as 'enthusiastic readers and incapable writers.'[3] This last confession seems to allude to the conclusion of the death certificate Barthes had issued – a point mostly forgotten today: the 'death of the author' is the price that must be paid for the 'birth of the reader.'[4] This figure of the newborn reader has remained pale beside the much more suggestive image of a polyphonous *écriture* which dissolves the author in the anonymity of a thousand codes. That may be in part the fault of Michel Foucault's prominent response of the following year, 1969 – 'What Is an Author?' – in which he set himself the task of surveying, more accurately than Barthes had done, 'the space left empty by the author's disappearance'.[5] No trace of the reader emerged in Foucault. Yet Barthes had written his obituary explicitly with a view to developing a 'theory of reading', which he began several times before his own death in 1980.[6]

Various figures have arisen out of the defunct author's ashes, notably 'writing' and its 'whole relentless theorization', as Foucault found as early as 1977.[7] From 'grammatology' to systems of 'writing down', they continue to hold an undisputed place in the middle of the postmodern theory apparatus today. In their shadow, the reader's career has been much more discreet: from Louis Althusser's *Reading Capital*, conceived as the record of a reading of Marx which Althusser had undertaken together with 'three or four comrades and friends, philosophy professors', to Roland Barthes's *Pleasure of the Text*; from Deleuze and Guattari's 'Rhizome', a school of reading, to Michel de Certeau's 1980 *Practice of Everyday Life*, which celebrated the reader as a merry poacher in the jungle of texts.[8] At the University of Constance, Hans Robert Jauss and Wolfgang Iser spelled out an aesthetics of reception; in East Berlin, the Naumann Collective, led by the Romanists Manfred Naumann and Karlheinz Barck, developed a theory of reading in actually existing socialism.[9] And Foucault himself, who had little theoretical interest in reading, is said to have answered the question of his identity as a writer, during a lecture tour of Brazil, with the words: 'Who am I? A reader.'[10]

Even Jorge Luis Borges had said reading was 'more resigned, more civil, more intellectual' than writing, because it is 'subsequent to writing'.[11] But what did the 1970s care for civility? The theoretical interest in reading can be thought of as connected with the new book market: with the theory series, the left-wing publishers, the flourishing bootleg printing industry to which pirates like Merve owed their precarious existence. In any case, the revenues earned by difficult texts multiplied rapidly in the seventies. In some respects, the period resembles the situation around 1800, when an expanding publishing industry blew apart the Bible's monopoly on readership, creating a reading audience hungry for each year's new books. And Goethe's time too had produced a theory of reading: hermeneutics, to which readers of Barthes and Foucault cultivated a cordial hostility. Working with Foucault's philosophical toolbox, Friedrich Kittler in 1979 exposed the maxims of text interpretation as a strategic gambit in the struggle for a scarce resource: attention. To ensure that his phenomenology of the mind would not drown in the new book market, Hegel had invented the hermeneutic circle: his work had to be read at least twice to be understood.[12] But wasn't Roland Barthes's intention comparable to Hegel's when he dreamed, in *The Pleasure of the Text*, of 'aristocratic readers' who would 'rediscover' the 'leisure of bygone readings': 'not to devour, to gobble, but to graze, to browse scrupulously'?[13] His own thin volume, at least, is most memorable when read in this way.

The Pleasure of the Text

Foucault's West Berlin publishers would no doubt have enjoyed his laconic self-identification as 'a reader'. Their scattered messages from this time betray how they gradually made a virtue of the adversity that they had no talent for writing. 'Only once I was free of the pressure to write myself was I able to edit other people's books', Gente recalled in an interview for the *Frankfurter Allgemeine Magazin* about his start as a publisher.[14] After he had supplied his comrades at *Alternative* with damning material, as an 'encyclopaedist of the rebellion', in the controversy over the Adorno–Tiedemann edition of Walter Benjamin, it was only his own textual sterility that had kept him from joining the journal's staff. Perhaps working with Jacob Taubes had helped him to exempt himself from the duty of authorship, for, in Taubes, Gente had met an exceptionally gifted reader who did not write. According to Henning Ritter, the reason Taubes could not write books was because they would not have satisfied his standards as a reader.[15] It seems as though Taubes passed on this dilemma to his disciples: Ritter himself, who, to Taubes's dismay, refused to write a doctoral dissertation, is as good an example as Gente.[16] But Gente seems only slowly to have taken leave of the idea that perhaps he was a closet writer after all, abandoning it definitively only in the course of the seventies. 'We as a publishing collective do not write', a Merve editorial of 1975 proclaims, exhibiting a budding self-image. Heidi Paris – like Gente a passionate reader – had just come aboard.[17] Under her influence, Gente's receptive talent became the new Merve mantra: 'We're not professionals, we're bookworms'; 'We are obsessive readers and monomaniac collectors'; 'Why do we publish this or that book? Because we can't write ourselves.'[18]

If there was a seed crystal of this new pleasure of the text, it must have been the reading group formed in 1976 in which Paris and Gente struggled for five years through a bootleg edition of *Anti-Oedipus*, Deleuze and Guattari's 'introduction to the non-fascist life'.[19] The revolutionary moment of that reading experience is apparent in the participants' memoirs: 'The experience of collective reading is tremendous.'[20] Manfred Frank, who tried a few years later in his lectures to avert the danger posed by *Anti-Oedipus*, situated its influence 'in the whisperings of fan clubs or sectlike groups on the margins of the academic scene'.[21] Who could have said it better? The renegade academics who met with the publishers week in and week out to read Deleuze were fans. 'We met once a week at the home of one of the participants and read *Anti-Oedipus* right through from beginning to end', Peter Gente recalled. 'We didn't prepare; no one took minutes; we just read continuously, sentence for sentence, in a book.'[22]

No minutes, no preparation, no self-agitation: the discipline that the socialist publishing collective had shown gave way in the mid-seventies to a remarkable nonchalance. And yet there are other unmistakable tones too in Gente's retrospection: the *Anti-Oedipus* group clung to the text, taking turns reading aloud, proceeding linearly 'from beginning to end', 'sentence by sentence'. That sounds not so much anti-Oedipal as Old-European. Communal reading aloud, the thoughtful progression through the text: these are techniques best known from Protestant Bible readings. 'We trust in the musicality of the language as speech', Gente explained elsewhere. 'In the Middle Ages, that connection went without saying. It got lost only in the course of written culture.'[23] Just like Barthes, who dreamt of the 'leisure of bygone readings', the Merve publishers strove to revive a pre-modern culture of books.[24] No doubt that had something to do with their fascination with Nietzsche, from whose books they drew the insistence on slow and ruminative reading to get to the core of the language's intensity.[25] When Paris and Gente encourage their readers, in the editorial afterword to Wolfgang Müller's *Geniale Dilletanten*, to read the book in a loud voice, they do so as Nietzscheans.[26] They had gathered their initial experience with this technique in the *Anti-Oedipus* reading group, which broke with the asceticism of hermeneutic readings. After an evening in which one sentence after another had resonated, the readers headed out into the night, where they talked still more 'and, most of all, laughed'.[27] Over the Christmas holidays of 1977, the avant-garde *Anti-Oedipus* group adjourned its readings to Italy, the promised land of a hedonistic left.

Group experiments with books were no rarity in the late seventies. And literary texts too offered an opportunity to revise the practice of theory. One bounteous source on the reading atmosphere of the times is the account published by Helmut Lethen and Hans-Thies Lehmann in 1978 of a collective reading of Brecht poems. It documents the efforts of two leftist literary scholars to emancipate themselves from their own standards. The reading was to focus not on the poems' 'political use value', but on the 'pleasure of the text'. After working as an editor at *Alternative*, Lethen had disappeared in the early seventies into the milieu of the communist splinter parties. The Brecht seminar he and Lehmann offered at Freie Universität was a step on his way to dropping out. The two instructors encouraged their students to give

10 Peter Gente (second from left) reading *Mille plateaux* by Gilles Deleuze and Félix Guattari, Poland, 1994.

up their materialist perspective and give free rein to their associations instead. With Brecht as their jumping-off point, the group discussed 'feelings of abandonment, anti-authoritarian lust for destruction, ambivalent feelings.' They let themselves drift in the warm waters of wishful rebelliousness. The more relaxed theoretical approach brought with it a feeling of flowing.[28]

Children's Books

The motto the Merve publishers followed in their readings was 'intensity.' Of course, in the Nietzschean energy theory brought into circulation by Deleuze and Lyotard, this principle did not at first appear to be applicable to the use of books. As the advocate of the lumpenproletariat, Lyotard had played the role of the anti-intellectual during the Nietzsche colloquium in Cerisy-la-Salle: the 'men of profusion' he heralded were 'more Nietzschean than Nietzsche's *readers*.' But the reversal followed right behind: what, the man of books had paused to wonder, might an '*intensive reading* of Nietzsche' look like?[29] His answer is like the one spelled out by Deleuze and Guattari a few years later in *Rhizom*, a key text of the Merve culture and in many passages a school of intense reading: 'We will never ask what a book means,' they wrote; 'we will ask what it functions with, in connection with what other things it does or does not transmit intensities.'[30] The wish for emancipation from the ethics of understanding in the name of intensity went so far that Deleuze and Guattari retroactively declared their *Anti-Oedipus* a children's book. Although it was undeniably arcane, and cost Paris and Gente five years of precious reading time, the authors insisted that their libido manifesto neither required any prior knowledge nor presupposed a hermeneutical attitude: 'Félix says that our book is addressed to people who are now between 7 and 15 years old.'[31] When have children ever been taken as seriously again as they were in the seventies?

But to Manfred Frank, the scholar of German Romanticism, the concept did not hold water. The 'pee-pee-kaa-kaa language' he found in *Anti-Oedipus* struck him as 'artificially infantilized' at best.[32] Deleuze and Guattari too had doubts about their work, although for other reasons. Perhaps it was, they had to concede, in spite of its Rabelaisian hyperbole 'still too serious a book, too intimidating.'[33] Or perhaps its readers had simply misunderstood it. *Rhizom* is thus the logical attempt to offer recommendations for a correct reading: 'Find in a book the excerpts you can make something of. We no longer read and write in the traditional way. There is not a death of the book, but a new kind of reading. There is nothing in a book to understand, but a great deal that you can make something of. Take what you want!'[34] The idea of revolutionizing the use value of books is at least as old as the paperback, yet Deleuze and Guattari take this idea a step further in their discourse of intensity. Their school of reading is aimed at destroying the order of representation by doing away with the dualism of text and world. But instead of declaring the world a book, they take the opposite path, bringing books as far into the world as possible. In this way, they allowed their readers to be radical simply by reading.[35]

For a habitual reader such as Peter Gente, the new Parisian thinking was an act of liberation: 'I was no longer subject to these compulsions, no longer burdened by this guilt, these eternal self-justifications.'[36] The dilemma of the sixties had consisted in mediating between the theory of the lecture halls and the practice of the street. In the new style of thinking, the two came together all by themselves. A generation of hungry theory readers who had indulged their addiction only at the price of a guilty conscience were suddenly confronted with vigorous theories of reading. Even Louis Althusser in his day had come, through labyrinthine reflections, to the conclusion that Marxism is at bottom nothing else but a theory of reading. In May of '68, he had been beaten round the head with this theorem and accused of 'theoreticism.' But the praise of reading gained the upper hand in the seventies. Roland Barthes, having laid the author in his grave, stylized the reader in 1973 as the *Homo novus* of the present: 'Imagine someone,' he wrote in *The Pleasure of the Text*,

> who abolishes within himself all barriers, all classes, all exclusions ... who mixes every language, even those said to be incompatible ... who remains passive in the face of Socratic irony ... and legal terrorism (how much penal evidence is based on a psychology of consistency!). Such a

> man would be the mockery of our society: court, school, asylum, polite conversation would cast him out: who endures contradiction without shame? Now this anti-hero exists: he is the reader.[37]

We can imagine the feeling with which the anti-hero Gente read these lines. After the artists of intensity, a new figure was taking the stage of theory, one which must have been all too familiar to him. The lover of difficult texts, relegated to a role at the bottom of the food chain by both the revolution and the literature industries – the role of a timid character, a coward, a recipient – suddenly the vicissitudes of the new decade were playing into his hands. 'Changer la vie!' – perhaps the May '68 slogan was only about reading after all.[38]

A Different Mode of Production

'We as a publishing collective do not write ourselves,' the Merve comrades had proclaimed in the mid-seventies. 'What we learn and experience in our day-to-day work, what we want, is visible in our texts – which we do not write ourselves. Reception, then, means not the accumulation of quantitative knowledge, but the process in which experiences which were unspoken up to now become public. Such reception constitutes a different mode of production.'[39] Written at a time when the publishers were in the process of breaking away from dialectical materialism, this insistence indicates that they were working on building a mythology. According to Marx, only productive labour was able to generate added value, and the future of humanity depended on that Promethean power.[40] But the New Left, having rediscovered the Marxian paradigm of production in the course of its philological excavations, was doubtful as to that paradigm's protagonists. Applying their conceptual inventiveness in the effort to discern a revolutionary subject in post-industrial society, they brought an army of new producers into the world, from the 'literature producer' to the 'knowledge producer' to the 'producer' of the left-wing public sphere found in Negt and Kluge. Even 'desiring-production,' which Deleuze and Guattari conceived as the 'deterritorialization of all forms of production,' belongs to a period whose key political dichotomy was the distinction between productive and unproductive. Perhaps that's one reason why it hasn't aged well.[41]

The praise of reading that Roland Barthes intoned turned the myth of the proletariat upside down. Growing louder through the 1970s, it reached its fullest articulation in another key Merve text, one which is among the most successful titles on the backlist today: Michel de Certeau's *Kunst des Handelns*, published in the original French in 1980 and in Merve's German edition, after tedious translation work by Ronald Voullié, in 1988. (The English translation, *The Practice of Everyday Life*, was published in Berkeley in 1984.) In the tradition of Henri Lefebvre and the Situationists, Certeau had dogged the heels of the 'common man' and written an almost 400-page panegyric on his underestimated creativity. In contrast to Foucault, who saw modern individuals as dominated by the techniques of punitive power, Certeau was interested in their ways and means of covertly escaping the enclosure of dispositives. Thus the seductive substance of his book is made up of the 'victories of the "weak" over the "strong" ... clever tricks, knowing how to get away with things, "hunter's cunning," manœuvres, polymorphic simulations, joyful discoveries, poetic as well as warlike,' and so on. This sounds suspiciously like Lyotard's patchwork of minorities, but the situation had changed since 1977. Unlike the Nietzscheans of the seventies, Certeau was no longer interested in hippies, junkies or crazies – in a word, in 'groups associated with the "counter-culture"'. His pathos of subversion was reserved for a marginal group that had long since taken society's centre stage: the consumer. 'Marginality today is no longer limited to minority groups, but is rather massive and pervasive ... A marginal group has now become a silent majority.'[42] It is significant that Certeau wrote his book on a commission from the French Ministry of Culture to research consumer behaviour.[43]

Heidi Paris is said to have opposed publishing *The Practice of Everyday Life* for a long time. She may well have doubted that an evening in front of the television set or a walk through the supermarket could offer opportunities for individual self-assertion. Didn't the glorification of day-to-day life amount to ennobling the philistines? In the early 1980s in West Germany, in any case, it was a trend that was difficult to resist. The history of the everyday was finding its way into the universities. Walter Kempowski was gathering material for *Das Echolot*, his chronicle of ordinary lives during the Second World War; Michael Rutschky brought out his journal *Der Alltag*, 'Day-to-day life'. Only Hans-Ulrich Wehler, the Bielefeld doyen of social history, found that what the micro-historians called the leaven of history tasted more like 'musty gruel'.[44] Peter Gente disagreed. In spite of his partner's resistance, he clung to *The Practice of Everyday Life* until, in 1988, it finally appeared, the thickest book Merve had ever published. That would have pleased Certeau, who did not live to see it. He had appreciated 'the nimble, agile, un-academic style' of the Berliners' books, 'which scans like a dance or a conversation'.[45] The correspondence between author and publishers bears witness to an easy agreement. The Jesuit Michel de Certeau was impressed by the tactics of the little publishing house. And if Gente, for his part, persisted, instinctively claiming the book for Merve, perhaps that was because of an eerie feeling of recognition: although Certeau made a point of avoiding 'actors who possess proper names' in order to do justice to the 'anonymous hero' of day-to-day life, the anti-hero of his book is none other than Gente himself.[46]

As an old Spontaneist, of course, Gente would hardly have identified with the role of the tenant, the television spectator or the housewife – protagonists of that day-to-day art of living whose underestimated potential Certeau brought to light. But, at the same time, he must have recognized himself in every detail of Certeau's figure of the reader. 'The reader ... is thus a novelist', he read in *The Practice of Everyday Life*:

> He deterritorializes himself, oscillating in a nowhere between what he invents and what changes him. Sometimes, in fact, like a hunter in the forest, he spots the written quarry, follows a trail, laughs, plays tricks, or else, like a gambler, lets himself be taken in by it. Sometimes he loses the fictive securities of reality when he reads: his escapades exile him from the assurances that give the self its location on the social checkerboard.

Among all the heroes of day-to-day life, this reader was not just Certeau's favourite: in a society completely 'made into a book', he represents the virtues of the consumer. Reading, Certeau writes, has always been a 'misunderstood activity' overshadowed by writing, the reader upstaged as a 'passive' recipient by the writer. No longer willing to acquiesce in this mythical system 'that distinguishes authors, educators, revolutionaries, in a word "producers," in contrast with those who do not produce', Certeau reversed the conventional roles: he not only dismissed the author in favour of the reader, but he also surreptitiously cast the reader in the role of the author, producing the book in the act of reading it. Admittedly, this is an author who no longer has the identity of a subject. 'The reader takes neither the position of the author nor an author's position. He invents in texts something different from what they "intended." He detaches them from their (lost or accessory) origin. He combines their fragments and creates something unknown in the space organized by their capacity for allowing an indefinite plurality of meanings.'[47]

Lying on Water

Barthes's 'new man' of the seventies, indulging in his pleasure of the text, reappeared in Certeau's ministerial commission as the prototype of the cunning consumer. Over the intervening two decades, the relation between reader and consumer had rotated through 180 degrees. They had first met in the late 1950s, when the ascendancy of the paperback seemed to threaten the future of culture and Hans Magnus Enzensberger observed with concern that even the reader in the 'literary supermarket' was in danger of being degraded to a consumer.[48] The '68 generation took him at his word, recycling his worst fears into a formula for subversion. Although the critique of commodity aesthetics and the glorification of the ascetic producer were still dominant,[49] deserting consumers were crisscrossing the theory landscape as early as the late sixties. In the same year in which Barthes proclaimed the death of the author and the birth of the reader, Jean Baudrillard published his dissertation *Le système des objets*. Written under Henri Lefebvre, the work struck chords critical of ideology which must have resonated with readers familiar with Marxism: the modern consumer society was found to be suffering from alienation, the dominance of exchange value and the erosion of use value.[50] In the closing chapter, however, the author drew a surprising conclusion: 'Consumption is surely *not* that passive process of absorption and appropriation which is contrasted to the supposedly active mode of production', but rather 'an activity consisting of the systematic manipulation of signs'.[51]

The decade that followed would boost the protagonist of that activity to an unexpected celebrity. The period was marked not only by fantasies of dropping out and returning to the sources, but also by a redistribution of agency and a theoretical abseiling from the high ridge of revolution. As the myth of the productive class dissolved in the runoff of Marxism, the bricoleurs and borderliners, dilettantes and consumers conquered its post-utopian power of action.[52] In 1978, as Certeau was putting the results of his consumer survey on paper, Foucault immersed himself in the neoliberalism of the Chicago School and found it both unsettling and fascinating. He discovered in the writings of the later Nobel laureate Gary Becker 'a very interesting theory of consumption', he reported to his audience at the Collège de France, involving an active, entrepreneurial consumer who invests his human capital to produce his own satisfaction.[53] It is fair to assume that this entrepreneur of the self was an inspiration of Foucault's late work on the subjectivity of the artist of existence. And it is undeniable that the entrepreneur producing his own satisfaction sometimes looked surprisingly like the poachers in the forest of signs whom Merve imported as role models for the new disorder. As an economist of the Reagan era, of course, Becker drew different political conclusions. But that makes the coincidence all the more startling that he too first wrote down his ideas in the spring of 1968.[54]

As a *Minima Moralia* reader, Peter Gente would have run across Adorno's scepticism towards the left's faith in production as early as the 1950s. Adorno had presented a 'social-democratic ideal of the personality' which was modelled through and through on 'the laws of production' in the guise of 'heavily-bearded Naturalists', of the 'uninhibited, vital, creative man'. Adorno's famous and enigmatic counter-utopia – 'lying on water and looking peacefully at the sky' – is faintly reminiscent of the 'minoritarian' marginal groups' chilling-out in the seventies. But Adorno's condemnation of the culture industry stood in the way of any appreciation of the consumer.[55]

In his *Cool Conduct*, Helmut Lethen – years after his break with Maoism – exhumes a figure originally described in the 1950s by the American sociologist David Riesman: the 'other-directed character', whom Lethen loosely renames the 'radar type'. This is a consumer who, drifting through the world of commodities, stumbles upon unexpected opportunities for autonomy in the niches of conformism. The radar type, Lethen writes, 'engages in tireless information-gathering, in a cult of nonchalance and "fun morality"'. The radar type's temperament is sceptical of political illusions, tending towards autonomy, but never heroism.[56] With this description in hand, it is not hard to spot the reader Gente, sitting on a folded-out shopping trolley surrounded by stacks of periodicals in a loft in the West Berlin borough of Schöneberg. The stereo system emits the scrap-metal sounds of Einstürzende Neubauten. The scene is nothing short of emblematic of consumer empowerment.

The insular city inspired its inhabitants to work with the materials at hand. While its business sector atrophied, West Berlin became a dream landscape of bricolage. In the 1980s, Heidi Paris began to explore design. She was particularly interested in the Berlin school of the ready-made, and organized exhibitions in Merve's publishing offices in Crellestrasse featuring repurposed objects from day-to-day life, such as the punkish *Consumer's Rest Lounge Chair*, which Stiletto, a graduate of West Berlin's fine arts academy, had made out of a shopping trolley with a minimum of deformation. 'It's not how it used to be in the 1960s, when mass production brought with it the big disposable movement', Paris explained in one of her opening talks. 'In the present day, as a century is gradually coming to a close, we are a bit more humble again towards objects; we're trying to assimilate them again.'[57] The humility of appropriation came at the end of a long political process of liquidation. The publishers called on their readers too to repurpose things in the 1980s: they recommended using their 'ill-made books' in the toilet, on the train, and 'for all kinds of things' – for everything but culture in the classical sense.[58]

It was the nightmare that the critics of the paperback revolution had decried, but returning this time as a publisher's programme. Even Enzensberger, who had found cheaply glued paperbacks unreadable years before, insisted in 1976 on the recipient's 'right to leaf back and forward, to skip whole passages, to read sentences against the grain ... to draw conclusions from the text of which the text knows nothing ... and to throw the book in which it is printed into the corner at any time he likes.'[59] The art of reading required irreverence. This development had long since been foreseen by an oracle on the shores of Lake Constance: a market study conducted for the German Publishers' Association by the Allensbach Institute found, as early as 1968, that the modern reader no longer pursued the passion of reading in the interiors of bourgeois leisure, but reached for a paperback whenever a fleeting 'vacuum of control' opened up – in the underground, at bedtime, or in waiting rooms: 'This immersion and the attitude of constant readiness: the successful book reader recalls the lifestyle of the partisans.'[60]

7

FOUCAULT AND THE TERRORISTS

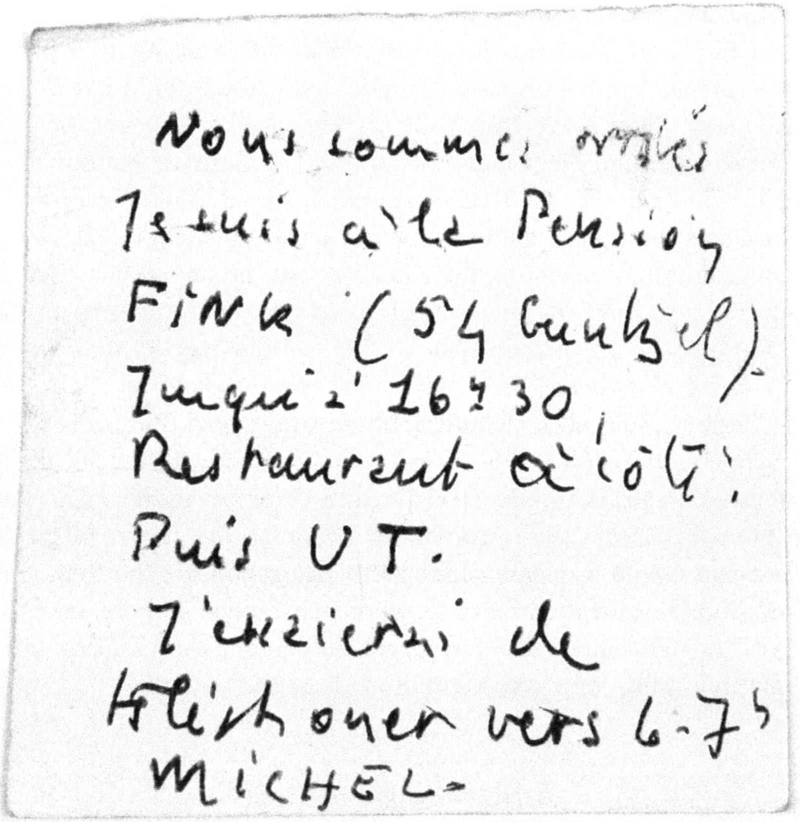

Nous sommes arrivés
Je suis à la Pension
Finck (54 Güntzel).
Jusqu'à 16h30
Restaurant à côté;
Puis U T.
J'essaierai de
téléphoner vers 6-7h
MICHEL.

11 Michel Foucault in West Berlin, Güntzelstrasse, Pension Finck, 1978.

The film anthology *Germany in Autumn* exhibits Rainer Werner Fassbinder wandering through the brown interiors of his flat, mostly nude, chain-smoking and constantly on the telephone, trying to stay up to date and form an opinion on the events that have since gone down in history as the 'German Autumn'.[1] The RAF kidnapping of Hanns Martin Schleyer in September of 1977, followed by the hijacking of Lufthansa Flight 181 and the climactic events in Mogadishu and Stammheim Prison in October, marked a turning point in the political and intellectual disposition of West Germany. The German Autumn also left its mark on the history of Merve Verlag. Like many things in Germany, 'theory' was not the same after 1977.

Heidi Paris and Peter Gente witnessed the German Autumn from the Frankfurt Book Fair. That year's parade of publishers, authors and journalists took place without any particular conviction. The writer Reinhard Lettau, reporting for *Die Zeit*, had the impression that the industry was carrying on its business as usual only to keep up the appearance of its own relevance.[2] The events that mattered were happening elsewhere. Three days after the hijacking of Flight 181, the German chancellor Helmut Schmidt summoned the authors Max Frisch, Heinrich Böll and Siegfried Lenz, together with the Suhrkamp publisher Siegfried Unseld, straight from Frankfurt to the chancellery in Bonn to discuss the terrorists' motivation.[3] The copyright pirates Paris and Gente were not among this delegation. At the Book Fair, they stood out for the first time, with their French authors, from the crowd of leftist literature producers, but under the circumstances, their publishing coup gave them little pleasure.

A Schweppes in Paris

'It was horrible', Gente told Michel Foucault a few days later. From Frankfurt, the Merve team had driven their old Mercedes directly to Paris to pay a visit to their new author. Among the high points of the business trip was an afternoon in a flat overloaded with books in Rue de Vaugirard in the 15th arrondissement. The atmosphere was heavy with cigarette smoke; the telephone rang incessantly. Foucault, who turned out to be a cordial host, offered tea and tonic water, the soft drink of French progressives, and had no objection to his German guests' turning on a tape recorder. He was used to that from his lectures at the Collège de France.[4] The publishers, who had been joined at Foucault's by the Italian political scientist Pasquale Pasquino and the translators Walter Seitter and Hans-Joachim Metzger, wanted to discuss publishing prospects: they were mainly interested in winning Foucault's support for a project to launch an international theory journal. But the conversation digressed again and again; soon they were talking about nothing but the RAF.

Unintimidated by Foucault's presence, Gente spoke impromptu in broken French about the German Autumn. He explained how West Germany had turned into a police state, which was in keeping with the terrorists' strategy. But the 'Left Social Democrats', who echoed the rejection of violence that Böll and Grass had reaffirmed at the Book Fair, were completely obsessed with the state. 'The state, the state, that's the real problem', Gente summarized the left's position, and went on to outline the alternative: the future of rebellion was elsewhere. It was discernible in the 'scene' – Gente pronounced it like an American word rather than the French *scène* or German *Szene* – of Spontis, freaks and rural communes. The practice of people in that scene was not terrorism, but an everyday 'illegalism': the scene had long since turned its back on the state. And Foucault's writings, which Merve had publicized in the scene in the past year, were being read enthusiastically. The German Language Society selected the new usage of *Szene* as its 1977 Word of the Year, ahead of the runners-up *Terrorismus*, 'terrorism', and *Sympathisant*, 'sympathizer'.

Foucault listened carefully, but he was not persuaded by Gente's praise of the West Berlin lumpenproletariat. Heiner Müller, who had visited Foucault in Paris the same year, had a similar experience, finding Foucault interested only in East Germany's dissidents and West Germany's terrorists. All other topics that had to do with Germany prompted him only to digress. 'What was fascinating', Müller recounts, 'was how Foucault dissolved the present that was congealing before our eyes in a whirlpool of differences that constantly formed different compounds. He did this while lying on a white rug.'[5] Gente, too, remembered Foucault lying on the floor with his arms crossed behind his head as he picked up the loose threads that his German reader had rather clumsily laid out, and wove them ad lib into his grand discourse of biopower, in which even the RAF was no more than an episode.[6]

'As late as the seventeenth century,' Foucault's striking voice can be heard saying on the tape, 'terror was a perfectly acceptable instrument of government.' Going back to the Sun King to explain Baader–Meinhof: that was exactly the kind of historical analysis that made Foucault so fascinating. Its very chronology shows that he situates political conflict on a deeper level. Foucault's books usually ended with the nineteenth century, where Marx had only started looking at specific cases.[7] This archaeological bent might contribute to Foucault's acceptance in academia in the 1990s, but it did not make him any less up to the minute in October of 1977. To his German visitors, Foucault's historicism only reinforced their impression of his contemporary relevance. He told them how the authoritarian state of old Europe had given way to a modern regime whose power no longer rested on physical violence, but rather on ensuring the 'security' of the population. 'This power,' said Foucault, 'is a power that protects you, assures your life, assures your health, secures you against theft, secures you against murder.' As his allusions indicate, he was working on further developing the concept of 'biopower' which he had introduced in his 1976 book *The Will to Knowledge*. The new power, he continued, was based on a modern society which had succeeded in fooling its enemies for 200 years. On the assumption that the façade of the welfare state still concealed Hobbes's Leviathan, those enemies had chosen the path of terror to expose the state's true nature.

In Foucault's view, that strategy, which the RAF was still pursuing in 1977, was devoid of any avant-garde impulse. Its logic could be traced back to the episteme of the eighteenth century, when physicians still thought they could cure a disease by inducing a critical fever. Mentioning Andreas Baader in the same breath as Xavier Bichat, the clinician of the French Revolutionary period, was one of Foucault's surprising lateral connections. The terrorists' error, he explained, lying on the rug, was that they reduced the question of power – 'naturalistically' – to the question of violence. They were committed to a struggle against an imaginary *ancien régime*. Ergo their attacks necessarily failed to harm the modern state, which had replaced the rule of terror with much more effective mechanisms of control. Like

Lyotard, although on the basis of different considerations, Foucault recommended rescaling the field of the political. Paris and Gente had perceived this as early as 1976, when they titled their first Foucault booklet *Mikrophysik der Macht*: the 'microphysics of power'.

The Parisian philosopher's later induction into academic spheres has almost effaced the attraction he first exerted on German Spontis. Foucault not only sent legions of young historians to the archives to write the annals of biopolitics; he also armed urban nomads in the late seventies with the bow and arrow. A theory that revoked the great state machine's privilege of power, that pulverized power and scattered it everywhere, lent justification even to the tiniest neighbourhood group. Power was too volatile for the German federal police to stockpile it, yet it lay in the streets where anyone might pick it up.[8]

To the other French theoreticians, the RAF was an avant-garde whose senseless violence was helping to demolish the regime of representation.[9] To Foucault, on the other hand, the RAF looked like a relic of the nineteenth century. The information that Baader had taken on the code name 'Captain Ahab' in prison might have offered him the perfect corroboration of his assessment. Foucault is said to have quarrelled with Deleuze so bitterly over German terrorism that the two were not on speaking terms for years.[10] Accusing the 'urban guerrilla' of atavism was in keeping with Foucault's structuralist temperament. His teacher Althusser had been indignant at Foucault's dismissal of Marxism as a doctrine that swims 'in nineteenth-century thought like a fish in water'. Washed up on the beach of the present, that is, it stops breathing.[11] It is not surprising that Foucault has been said to have an evil eye: his way of looking at the articles of faith in the left's catechism fossilized them.[12]

The effect of that gaze on Peter Gente was electrifying. 'He became a figure who was constantly in one's mind, to whom one sometimes even tried to justify one's own actions', he wrote about his relation to Foucault – the first thinker since Adorno whom he internalized as an authority. 'A pull arises, a fixation, symptoms of a love.' And yet his author, Gente added, was anything but a simple guy. He was worlds apart from the habitus of the Berlin Spontis. From his external appearance to his handwriting, with each letter well separated from the others, the overall impression he made was one of severity. He suffered from mood swings; he had little patience; he had a penchant for lecturing that sometimes made him seem arrogant, even when he was lying on the floor. But the philosopher whom Gente got to know in the late seventies was one who reflected even on his own faults. Foucault might interrupt himself, for example, to digress spontaneously on the phenomenon of bad temper.[13] He was a doctor's son, and anything that came within reach of his attention was subjected to the 'over-intense brightness' of his diagnostics.[14]

'Reading Foucault is a drug, a head rush. He writes like the devil', Heidi Paris commented on her intellectual adventure in 1979 in an early issue of the *taz*.[15] This was a thinker on the historic scale of Marx, but in a whole new kind of coordinate system. Ulrich Raulff, who heard Foucault in 1976 at the Collège de France, felt as if he was present at a meeting of Walter Benjamin and Carl Schmitt. The 'darkly critical and intensely mythic' sound of Foucault's discourse made Raulff a disciple on the spot.[16] After the smouldering fire of dialectics, which had boiled the theory of the seventies down to the bland gruel of leftist anti-ideological critique, Foucault must have offered an irresistible mixture of perceptive acuity and nuance. His concepts seemed tailored to fit history much more closely than the brands off the Marxist rack, such as 'reification' or 'relations of production', to say nothing of 'contradictions' and their 'mediation'. Perhaps the seventies really were similar to the Decisionists' 1920s that Raulff was reminded of: that too had been a time of demolished certainties and decaying philosophical customs, when the hunger for experience brought forth not only brooding melancholy, but also, in its best moments, a sharpened sense of reality. That, in any case, was what Foucault claimed for his analyses.[17]

Political Tourists

After a good two hours – during which they obtained their host's agreement to publish another book with Merve, along with the promise of a return visit in Berlin in the near future – the publishers left the flat in Rue de Vaugirard. It would not be long before their next meeting. Foucault wanted to find out for himself about the situation in Germany, and so he and his partner Daniel Defert went to Berlin for a

12 Michel Foucault and Heidi Paris at the Tunix Conference, Berlin, 1978.

13 Michel Foucault and Peter Gente at the Tunix Conference, Berlin, 1978.

long weekend in December of 1977.[18] It is hard to imagine the city at that time in colour, what with the grey of Berlin winters and the memory of the black-and-white wanted posters. After the drama of the German Autumn, the mood on the left was dark. Even if the terrorists' strategy had been based on an eighteenth-century paradigm, it had borne bitter fruit: West Germany now wore the trappings of a police state.[19] The open letter by the pseudonymous 'Mescalero from Göttingen', confessing a 'secret joy' after the RAF's assassination of the federal prosecutor Siegfried Buback, contributed to the blanket suspicion of terrorist sympathies cast upon all parts of the leftist scene.[20] By a great deal of luck, Hanns Martin Schleyer's kidnappers had slipped through the dragnet directed by the federal chief of police, Horst Herold, and the milieu that was suspected of covering their operations was made to feel the state's nervousness all the more. In the winter of 1977, police rolled out regularly to search shared flats and to follow up the tips of motorists who thought they had recognized one of the fugitives at a petrol station. The police pressure in turn brought the terrorists more supporters. 'Through a moralism, and in the face of an experience of repression, it quickly goes in Baader–Meinhof's direction', Gente had explained to Foucault in Paris. 'Once they've been beaten up, they're strung out, almost paranoid.'

The Merve publishers tried to treat the Left's hangover with Nietzschean merriment. They showed their guests around the divided city by day and the bars of Schöneberg by night. As a cultural highlight, there was a film evening in the Arsenal art cinema featuring *Moi, Pierre Rivière*, René Allio's film based on Foucault's research about a French farm boy who had murdered his family with a kitchen knife in 1835 and subsequently been caught in the net of criminological discourses.[21] Ulrich Raulff, whose initiation at the Collège de France eventually led to a doctoral dissertation on Foucault's *Discipline and Punish*, and who translated Foucault for both Merve and Suhrkamp, took a series of photos at the Arsenal showing the guest in discussion with the audience. More will remain of Foucault than his hairstyle; after thirty years of posthumous reception history, there is no doubt of that. But, inversely, what would he be without the bald head and turtleneck that are firmly linked to our image of his philosophy? Raulff's photos show the iconic Foucault, embodying intellectual intensity with his energetic chin and his sweeping hand gestures. In his charismatic way of speaking, Raulff saw the revival of a centuries-old scholastic tradition.[22]

Allio's Foucault adaptation, praised by critics as an ethnography of rural France under the July Monarchy, was topical in Peter Gente's view as a contribution to the debate on violence and terrorism. But the film was also able to raise many questions simply 'because it tells a story that happened'.[23] According to Michael Rutschky, the seventies were characterized by a hunger for reality that was fed by cinema: moving pictures helped to wear down derivative Marxism, he wrote, by establishing forms of discussion that remained on the visible surface of events instead of descending into their deeper meanings.[24] But, apart from film and its ability to create presence, Gente, with his emphatic realism, pointed out a phenomenon that was characteristic of Foucault specifically: in his hands, an obscure episode from the dusty archives took on political relevance. You could almost call it 'the Foucault effect'. Peter Sloterdijk once accorded Foucault a special rank as a 'discourse founder'. And, indeed, he had succeeded – as only Leopold von Ranke before him – in turning the archives, the houses of records, into the source of a new poetry.[25]

Vermin

Foucault's 1977 visit to Berlin is memorable not least because it involved the forces of order in both their East and West German varieties. The political tourists' programme included an outing to East Berlin. As they were leaving the capital of the German Democratic Republic at the Friedrichstrasse Station border crossing in the evening, Foucault and Defert were taken aside by the People's Police and searched. The officers were especially interested in a man called Rudolf Virchow, whose name appeared on a note they found in Foucault's coat pocket. Who was this Virchow? One of the eloquent Frenchman's East Berlin contacts? Or was it a reference to a meeting in West Berlin's Virchow Hospital? The policemen can't be blamed, of course: how could they have known they were questioning a famous epistemologist who was on familiar terms with the classics of the history of science?

'It concerned a book by Rudolf Virchow that was published in 1871,' Foucault reported, with bitter irony, to the Paris correspondent of *Der Spiegel* on his return. 'Perhaps somewhere in East Germany today there is someone called Rudolf Virchow who is wondering why he is under suspicion of communicating with two Frenchmen he's never heard of.'

Foucault attached more importance to an event that occurred two days later in West Berlin. On finishing breakfast at the Hotel Vier Jahreszeiten, he, Defert and the two Merve publishers suddenly found themselves surrounded by heavily armed police. A guest at the next table had discreetly raised the alarm because he thought Heidi Paris looked like the RAF terrorist Inge Viett. Such incidents must have happened mainly to women in those days, since the RAF was the only radical-left group with more female members than male.[26] The suspects, who looked like intellectuals, were arrested and interrogated, spending hours in the hands of the police even though it was soon evident that they were not the persons being sought. Describing the experience for *Der Spiegel*, Foucault saw in it a 'ritual of accusation' that seemed to him 'much more troubling' than the East German methods. In the East, the People's Police spread late-Stalinist terror, while the government agencies of West Germany, acting in the name of its citizens, and in response to their call, produced a climate of denunciation in which Foucault detected the signs of biopolitics. 'The big eyes of the state were upon us because someone in a hotel lobby was of the opinion that we looked odd. We felt like vermin.'[27]

On Tunix Beach

The days with Foucault inspired his publishers to 'cheerful activity,' as they reported to him a short time later: 'We are no longer struck speechless by your ferocity and playfulness on the theoretical field; we have found our voice, and we are having fun thinking, speaking and doing.'[28] There was no lack of opportunities to do so: after the depression which had followed the German Autumn, the West Berlin scene was now buzzing like a startled beehive. The terrorists had failed, and so had their adversary the state, since it could no longer shake off the suspicion that the political prisoners in Stammheim had been murdered. In January of 1978, the 'wake of the radical Left' in which Merve was 'drifting' poured into the great Tunix Conference, held at Berlin's Technical University.[29] Some 20,000 battle-weary revolutionaries made the pilgrimage from all corners of West Germany for the mass emigration – in the words of the organizers' invitation – from Chancellor Helmut Schmidt's 'Model Germany' to 'Tunix Beach'. Once again, the attractive alternative was a southern coastline of the mind. Over the drumming of the *Stadtindianer*, or 'Urban Indians' – whose feathers, modelled after the Italian *Indiani metropolitani*, were by this time being worn by German Spontis – Tunix buried the idea of revolution, and the ethics of activism along with it.[30] 'We just want to kind of enjoy, to me that's political as well, just want to, like, live', said an anonymous participant to a radio microphone. For three winter days, the concrete castles of TU, West Berlin's Technische Universität straddling the great avenue that stretches westward from the Brandenburg Gate, housed a motley marketplace of drop-out fantasies: from the commune in the country to magic mushroom therapy to catching your own fish on the beaches of the Algarve. The 'alternative' movement had officially taken shape as a subculture.[31]

The Berlin Senator for Higher Education, Peter Glotz, took the podium and bemoaned the young people's escapism. The editors of the radical left-wing monthly *konkret* commented that 'actually the people piping along so merrily can only make you sad'. But the melancholy cultivated by the left was precisely what the organizers were tired of. 'The stench of the bureaucracy, the reactors and the factories has been in our noses for a long time now', they wrote in their proposal of a new direction. 'We've had enough of being commanded, our thoughts controlled, our ideas, our homes, our passports, our clocks cleaned. We've done with being canned and cut down and normalized. We're all leaving!'[32] The idea of abandoning the political arena to the enemy as 'their game', theoretically traceable back to the workers' autonomy of the Italian Operaists, reached a climax in 1978 in a break from the majority culture.[33] But the post-Marxist throng also included working groups on gay rights, the conception of a nationwide ecologist party, and the founding of the collectively managed left-wing daily *die tageszeitung* – 'the daily newspaper' – soon to be universally known as the *taz*. As if by accident, little Merve found itself for a moment at the centre of attention, introducing the guest star Michel Foucault.

'It would be terrible', Paris and Gente had written to Daniel Defert, 'if the conference in Berlin became a vehicle to reintroduce an RAF romanticism, when what we need is to overcome the apathy that the RAF has produced.'[34] For that reason, they would do everything to bring their new Parisian friends to Tunix in Berlin. Lyotard pleaded persistently that he had too much work to do; he admitted he currently lacked the 'morale' to support such 'amusements'. 'I think you have produced enough text in 1977 and can afford to take a spontaneous weak-end in Berlin', the publishers boldly answered.[35] They invited the shy Deleuze – also in vain. In the end, French philosophy was represented at the event in Berlin by Félix Guattari, André Glucksmann and Michel Foucault. The photos of the Tunix Conference are classic Foucault iconography: Foucault with Spontis; Foucault on the steep terraces of lecture-hall seats, his ascetic figure oddly out of place amid all the long-haired participants. What is missing is Foucault the speaker: unlike Marcuse in 1967, he did not take the podium in Berlin, although his reputation had preceded him, even in West Germany in 1978. He talked with Klaus Hülbrock from Göttingen, the pseudonymous 'Mescalero' whose identity was no secret in the radical scene.[36] In the official Tunix programme, Foucault was named only as a participant in a workshop on antipsychiatry; the organizers apparently had not planned a talk by the author of *The Will to Knowledge*.[37] Their abstinence, and his, is a clear indicator of the historical gap that divided the '68 generation from their older siblings: the young people mistrusted the leadership role of their own intellectuals. If Foucault went on to become known as their leading philosopher, it was only because he found the corresponding theoretical concepts for that mistrust.

1984

THE END OF HISTORY

14 *Traverses: Revue trimestrielle*, 32 (1984).

8

CRITIQUE OF PURE TEXT

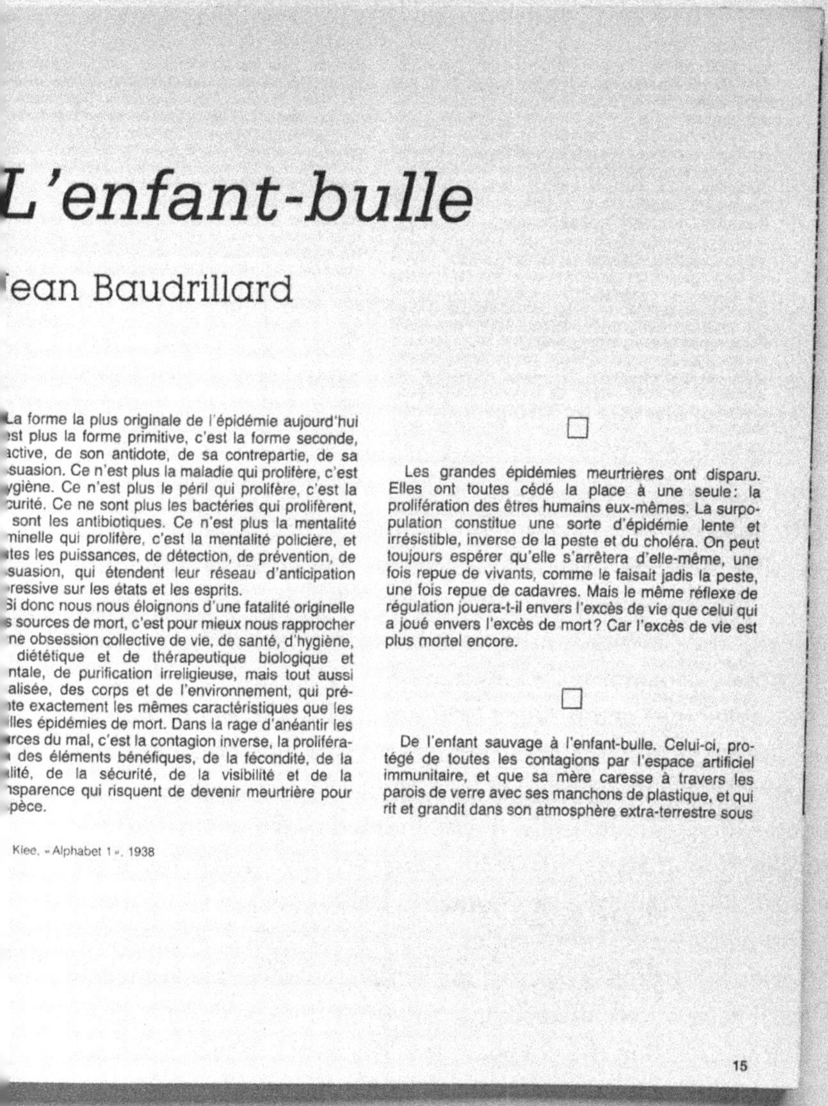

L'enfant-bulle

'ean Baudrillard

La forme la plus originale de l'épidémie aujourd'hui ɪst plus la forme primitive, c'est la forme seconde, ɪctive, de son antidote, de sa contrepartie, de sa ·suasion. Ce n'est plus la maladie qui prolifère, c'est ygiène. Ce n'est plus le péril qui prolifère, c'est la curité. Ce ne sont plus les bactéries qui prolifèrent, sont les antibiotiques. Ce n'est plus la mentalité minelle qui prolifère, c'est la mentalité policière, et ıtes les puissances, de détection, de prévention, de ·suasion, qui étendent leur réseau d'anticipation ·ressive sur les états et les esprits.

Si donc nous nous éloignons d'une fatalité originelle s sources de mort, c'est pour mieux nous rapprocher ne obsession collective de vie, de santé, d'hygiène, diététique et de thérapeutique biologique et ntale, de purification irreligieuse, mais tout aussi alisée, des corps et de l'environnement, qui pré- ıte exactement les mêmes caractéristiques que les illes épidémies de mort. Dans la rage d'anéantir les ırces du mal, c'est la contagion inverse, la proliféra- ı des éléments bénéfiques, de la fécondité, de la ılité, de la sécurité, de la visibilité et de la ısparence qui risquent de devenir meurtrière pour pèce.

Klee, « Alphabet 1 », 1938

□

Les grandes épidémies meurtrières ont disparu. Elles ont toutes cédé la place à une seule: la prolifération des êtres humains eux-mêmes. La surpopulation constitue une sorte d'épidémie lente et irrésistible, inverse de la peste et du choléra. On peut toujours espérer qu'elle s'arrêtera d'elle-même, une fois repue de vivants, comme le faisait jadis la peste, une fois repue de cadavres. Mais le même réflexe de régulation jouera-t-il envers l'excès de vie que celui qui a joué envers l'excès de mort? Car l'excès de vie est plus mortel encore.

□

De l'enfant sauvage à l'enfant-bulle. Celui-ci, protégé de toutes les contagions par l'espace artificiel immunitaire, et que sa mère caresse à travers les parois de verre avec ses manchons de plastique, et qui rit et grandit dans son atmosphère extra-terrestre sous

15

'Dear Michel,' begins Heidi Paris and Peter Gente's letter to Foucault, written two months after the end of the Tunix Conference:

> We haven't been in touch for a while. For a long time after Tunix we were left with a great void, a paralysis, and had trouble getting on with our work. We're only resurfacing now. What bothered us was that at Tunix we slipped into the theoretical centre, although we would have preferred to act outside it, on the margins. We made the mistake of succumbing to the fascination of international movement fetishism, to the point of reheating the movement myth ourselves.[1]

Stepping with their author into the spotlight of the assembled Sponti public should have been the publishers' dream come true. But, instead of seizing the opportunity and winning new readers, they were annoyed. Their insistence on a marginal role reflects the idiom of the new French theory. 'Marginal,' in the political topography of those years, is a position neither in the middle of the action, nor at the forefront, where the revolutionary avant-garde once peered ahead into the future. In refusing to launch a new movement with their texts, Paris and Gente were rejecting their role as leftist publishers. Were they manœuvring themselves into a performative contradiction? Was that the reason for the perplexity they mention in their letter to Foucault? The Parisian authors whose German translations had brought a growing esteem to their little publishing venture since 1977 upheld the pathos of intensity in opposition to the hierarchical structures of representation. But if the only way to increase the efficacy of intensity was to found yet another movement – then, paradoxically, it was doomed to remain ineffective.

As Jürgen Habermas found in his *Observations on the 'Spiritual Situation of the Age'*, published in German in 1979 as the one-thousandth title in the *edition suhrkamp* series, the period after the upheaval of the German Autumn was crawling with 'imprecise phenomena'.[2] The political camps were diversifying; the front lines were difficult to locate. That imprecision did not spare the Merve publishers. Thinkers who wanted to liberate theory from the clutches of Marxism were sometimes separated only by nuances from those who wanted to bury it with short shrift.

The Master Thinkers

At the Tunix Conference, Paris and Gente had also made the acquaintance of André Glucksmann, a Parisian renegade who had scored a philosophical best-seller the previous year with his book *The Master Thinkers*. They wrote in a letter to Jacques Rancière that they hoped to win the young author for their series, but Glucksmann never did publish with Merve.[3] *The Master Thinkers* appeared in the context of the intellectual chain reaction that was sparked in France by the publication of Alexander Solzhenitsyn's *Gulag Archipelago*, the book that opened the show trial of Marxism.[4] But not only that: Glucksmann and the other *nouveaux philosophes* proclaimed themselves enemies of theory itself. They were beyond the command of their post-structuralist teachers: the strategy of a Lyotard, a Deleuze or a Guattari of subverting the 'terror' of leftist theory by formal experiments had merely transposed the mode of difficult ideas into a different key. Glucksmann and cohorts, on the other hand, threw out the baby with the bathwater. Their escape route from Marxist orthodoxy led not to the experimental spaces of aesthetics, but to the solid ground of a philosophical realpolitik. They declared war on the 'intellectual apparatchiki' who had been 'indispensable for the propagation of the great Final Solutions of the 20th century.' With their journalistic style, which contributed significantly to their huge success, they left no doubt that they would have nothing to do with the suspension of common sense. Glucksmann had a special argument in store for German readers: theory – from Hegel to Marx to the now generally admired Nietzsche – was a sickness that came from the land of Nazism: 'The "Germany" where Fascisms are born is not a territory or a population, but a text and an attitude to texts.'[5]

It is no wonder that the author of that line never ended up at Merve – nor did he find admission into the Suhrkamp culture. A person who trained such weapons on the spirit of text was a danger to the theory publishers' business model. To an older generation representing the legacy of Critical Theory, *The Master Thinkers* provided the latest confirmation that philosophy from France was equivalent to 'hostility to theory.'[6] From Glucksmann to Foucault, all of those thinkers were tarred with the same brush. How curious today that it was once possible to dismiss Foucault's œuvre as a 'politicization of the primal scream'.[7] The motivation of critics such as Oskar Negt and Jean Améry is more understandable, however, if we imagine the atmosphere at the Tunix festival: the 'alternative' generation celebrating their rejection of the class society were at the same time turning their backs on the impositions of theoretical abstraction. 'Balance, rigorous argument, dialectics and contradiction – I couldn't care less about all that', the 'Mescalero from Göttingen' had written. The commentators agreed that his weariness reflected a collective state of mind.[8] Glucksmann's black book of the *Master Thinkers* – itself 'important ... more as theatrical action ... than as a system of ideas' – lent this state of mind the weight of a 300-page pamphlet.[9]

The 'urban Indians' who in 1978 had beat their drums in protest against police terror and legal blacklisting had now found their new theme: for many people, the Tunix Conference rang in the age of Green ideas. The establishment of environmentalism marked the beginning of the end of the era of grand philosophical schemes, and the dawn of a raw empiricism of becquerel units, thyroid tests and soil samples.[10] The proliferation of theory fatigue among the heirs of the student movement after the German Autumn is evident in the reactions of the publishing industry. After over a decade of expansion, the leftist Gutenberg galaxy now seemed for the first time to be in danger of contracting. 'The potential for political protest has concentrated elsewhere and gets its strength precisely from the non-programmatic nature of action', the editors of *Alternative* concluded in 1982, and shut down their journal for lack of reader interest.[11]

Not all theory publishers chose that path. It would be a mistake to suppose that the mode of difficult ideas dissolved in the acid rain of the 1980s, but it did change its location, its terms and its objects. And, most of all, it changed its style. Theory emerged from the crisis of the left with a new sound and a new aesthetics: those which have ensured its survival to the present day. The outlines of this intellectual fashion revolt first took shape in the publishing underground. Paris and Gente were not driven into bankruptcy, nor did they consider adopting the ecological paradigm shift. Although the Merve catalogue does contain a few Green books – a presentation of the intentional communities movement in rural West Germany, and Claus Leggewie's book, long since forgotten, on the environmental movement in France – even *Für die Vögel* [For the birds], a 1984 Merve title, is misleading. That book contains interviews with John Cage, who could hardly be proffered as an ecological author, even if he had retired to the countryside in the 1950s to gather mushrooms. After the long road of theory that the West Berlin publishers had travelled since the sixties, the way back to nature was impassable. There was no more room in their conceptual world for fantasies of escape and return to the roots.[12]

Adults Only

No one is better equipped to gauge the breach that gaped between ecology and theory than Jean Baudrillard, whose writings of the 1980s belonged to the *bon ton* of the *Internationaler Merve Diskurs* series. *Kool Killer oder Der Aufstand der Zeichen* was the first instalment of Merve's lucrative Baudrillard medley, appearing in the autumn of 1978. Besides the legendary title essay on the New York graffiti scene – 'a thousand youths armed with marker pens and cans of spray-paint are enough to scramble the signals of urbania and dismantle the order of signs'[13] – the volume contains a discussion between Baudrillard and French environmentalists, originally published in *Libération*. Baudrillard rips the Greens apart, accusing them of wanting the system to survive 'in a well-tempered form', and explaining that their crisis-alarmism does nothing to prevent the catastrophe, but in fact spreads the screen of political control wider. The activists hadn't expected him to be so discourteous. 'Everyone's got the atomic bomb. That's haywire. What can we do?' was their philosophically lame reply. We get the feeling, as with Niklas Luhmann's attempt a few years later to give the new social movements in West Germany a systems-theoretical leg up, that two language games have drifted far apart. But while Luhmann didn't want to accept the idea 'that strong political engagement must prove itself by shallow thinking', Baudrillard refused to consider engagement as an option at all.[14] This got his opponents' hackles up: 'I'd like to ask you something: How is social change possible at all, in your opinion ...?' Whereupon the former German teacher and self-taught sociologist answers that no social change is necessary since society itself is dying out.[15]

Baudrillard's flagrant fatalism was a provocation to the ecologists. 'Besides, I think it is going to end' was the *ceterum censeo* with which he parried their efforts to uphold the Green principle of hope. His texts were crawling with disasters: traffic accidents, earthquakes, terrorism and cancer. Paul Virilio, corroborating Baudrillard's eschatology in his parallel field of the history of technology, felt that the business of theory must limit itself in future to 'reporting on excesses, disasters and catastrophes, shocks of the age we have to live in.' To provide a channel for these macabre chronicles, he conceived the publication of a 'journal of disaster.'[16]

Unlike the post-history of other theoreticians such as Alexandre Kojève and Arnold Gehlen, Baudrillard's and Virilio's end of history came with drums and fanfares. Their diametrical differences notwithstanding, this plutonism was a bond between the theoreticians and their favourite Green antagonists. Besides, it opened up the final opportunities for action. It is significant that Baudrillard's German translator Gerd Bergfleth had to ask his author to put a date on the apocalypse: 'Has this state already been reached, or is it still ahead of us?'[17] Baudrillard would not be pinned down. Sometimes, the cataclysm seemed to have already taken place; sometimes, he morbidly longed for it. As zealous as he was in collecting evidence for his nightmarish vision that the times had lost all contact with reality, he was just as radical in his strategic appeal to exacerbate the situation: 'Things must be pushed to the limit, where quite naturally they collapse and are inverted,' he wrote in his major work *Symbolic Exchange and Death*, from which Merve published a first excerpt in Hans-Joachim Metzger's German translation in 1979.[18] In view of the complete 'domination of the code,' Baudrillard recommended the senseless act of violence as the only subversive act possible. Hence his fascination with the Baader–Meinhof terrorists in Stammheim and, at the same time, with the New York graffiti writers whose 'symbolic disorder' confronted the system with a message 'to which it cannot respond.'[19] Gerd Bergfleth, in his afterword to *Symbolic Exchange and Death*, saw in Baudrillard's books an 'extremism … which Foucault and Deleuze and Lyotard cannot match.'[20]

Other readers felt similarly. Peter Gente found that the paranoia of Baudrillard's method was matched by his recklessness as a theoretician.[21] In his drive to declare the status quo obsolete, Baudrillard spared not even the icons of subversion. He wrote in his polemic *Forget Foucault* that the molecular philosopher himself had 'helped establish a systematic notion of power along the same operational lines as desire, just as Deleuze established a notion of desire along the lines of future forms of power.'[22] Without a doubt, Baudrillard's daring theses would be corrected often enough. In his dismissal of Foucault, however, we must concede that his intuition was prophetic: it is a commonplace of New Left social criticism today that the rebellion of desire in the seventies provided blueprints for agile capitalism.[23]

The leftist Nietzscheans of the seventies had invoked desire as the revolutionary principle; in its place, Baudrillard set the figure of death. His thinking was darker and harder, in keeping with the darkening of the zeitgeist. In the face of all the signs flying about, theory that would resist co-optation by the code must wield symbolic terror. 'All that remains for us is theoretical violence,' Baudrillard explained, pleading for the 'radicalization of hypotheses' to escape the mode of significant discourse.[24] In his later work, he remained true to this principle by surpassing himself: he abandoned both his anthropologically grounded critique of the society of simulation and his academic self-image – which was not highly developed anyway – so that his books during the 1980s became increasingly mercurial. In reply to the Merve translator who asked him for missing bibliographical references, he asked, 'Les lecteurs ont-ils tellement besoin de se référer?'[25] To Manfred Frank, that was tantamount to 'theoretical neglect.'[26]

However, in his defeatism, granting no reprieve to the dying referent even in his own work, Baudrillard proves himself a thinker with the courage of his convictions: his texts offer at least the insight that the theoretical discourse itself is suffering from an inflation of signs. Digging in the footnotes of his magnum opus, we find the suggestion that the contemporary theories – 'Deleuze, Lyotard, etc.' – have lost their use value. Now bankrupt, their residual significance consists in the fact that they 'serve as signs for one another. It is pointless to insist on their coherence with some "reality", whatever that might be.'[27]

It was Roman Jakobson who observed, echoing Nietzsche's critique of historicism, that the late nineteenth century was the time of a dizzying proliferation of signs. When it eventually transpired that words were no longer backed by reality, they suffered a drastic devaluation. But all attempts to restore confidence in paper language, Jakobson found in the 1930s, had failed.[28] Would it be mistaken to read Baudrillard's early texts as a modernization of this verdict? Foucault, too, had devoted his inaugural lecture at the Collège de France to 'systems of discourse multiplication.'[29] A genre that had enjoyed continuous growth since the days of the student revolts, Baudrillard reported, was now detached from reality and valueless. Was the hot product of left-wing publishing drowning in its own textual deluge?

Gilles Deleuze and Félix Guattari had tried to cure Freudo-Marxism not only of its Oedipus complex, but also of its elitist airs. Hence, they aspired to produce theory for children – for illiterates, no less. Baudrillard, however, wrote for adults only. His philosophical style triggered a sudden drop in temperature. 'Le stress est total. Keep cool!' he advised his West Berlin publishers from sunny Santa Barbara, California.[30] The recommendation can be seen as a philosophical maxim. In 1983, the physiognomist of the Frankfurt School, Peter Sloterdijk, attributed the attitude of 'concernedness,' perpetuated by the environmental and peace movements, to the hypersensitive body of Adorno: 'There was scarcely anything that took place in the "practical" world that did not inflict pain on it or was spared being suspected of brutality.'[31] Baudrillard, whose diary *Cool Memories* is teeming with erotic interludes and international flights, dashed through the world like a breezy berserker. Fluttering between Tokyo, Los Angeles and São Paulo, he embodied the frenzy of contemporary life, and only in contemplative moments found the time to doubt whether it could be healthy in the long run to be 'constantly imploding.'[32] It is remarkable that a theoretical affinity connects the sturdy frequent flyer with the sensitive Adorno: in the dominance of appearance and in the disappearance of the incommensurable, Adorno too had discerned the signatures of a lull at the end of history which made any change in conditions illusory. Nonetheless, it went against his intellectual temperament to accept this state with coolness; in his lucid moments, Adorno had even allowed himself to imagine the world in a state of redemption. But Baudrillard, the fatalist, serenely observed the world after its decline and fall.[33]

Sola Scriptura

In the apocalyptic 1980s, Baudrillard's theory, which painted the end of history as losing touch with reality, thrived as though it was under a greenhouse effect.[34] 'He's up and coming', wrote Lorenz Lorenz, reviewing the latest Merve booklet in 1983 for the Munich theory fanzine *Elaste*. 'A book by him should definitely be lying around somewhere when guests come over.'[35] Ten years earlier, he might have made a similar recommendation for Adorno's books, but the advice seems still more fitting in regard to Baudrillard: if his works became the 'coffee-table books of the early 1980s', as Thomas Meinecke once wrote, it was not only because of their up-to-the-minute topics – it was also because they were so easy to browse in.[36] They were among the pioneers of a new aesthetic, a change in how theory was used, which is still with us today. And if neither Baudrillard nor Virilio has been admitted to the pantheon of the Suhrkamp culture, it is not only for reasons of substance – as in Glucksmann's case. Their books were persistently foreign to a canon based on the deification of the printed word.

In coining the term 'Suhrkamp culture', George Steiner's intention was not just to praise the influential Frankfurt publishing house. His 1973 review in the *Times Literary Supplement* also expressed the fear that Suhrkamp's edition of Adorno's complete works, just launched in the *stw* series, might elevate the author to the Elysium of unread classics: 'Twenty tomes of Adorno is a lot.'[37] And, in fact, the Suhrkamp culture did have a monumental streak: the pillars of the new series were the big complete-works editions. Just two years before Adorno's turn, Suhrkamp had published twenty volumes of Hegel. The flow of ink was oceanic, with nary an illustration amid the thousands of lines of text. Looking backward from our iconophile present, what springs to our attention in Suhrkamp's programme is the wall of type. What Siegfried Unseld established as the canon of West Germany was a sea of grey. 'The text alone!' is still the credo of his widow and successor today.[38] The imperialism of text is all the more conspicuous where Suhrkamp did condescend to print illustrations: the reproduction of Velázquez's *Las Meninas* in the Suhrkamp edition of Foucault's *The Order of Things*, for example, is so miserable that one cannot help suspecting vandalism. Most of the details discussed in the fifteen pages of the opening chapter can only be guessed. Clouds of grey have completely swallowed one of the Spanish Infanta's ladies-in-waiting. Suhrkamp's iconoclasm was the result of faith in the power of theory, and the result, from a present-day perspective, is as sober as a Protestant church. What remains is an impression of intellectual rigour bordering on austerity. This attitude reached its climax in the grey pages of neo-Marxism at the time of its full flowering: in the literature of '68, pictures served to illustrate treacherous illusions.

Somewhere along the way between then and now, a paradigm shift must have taken place. The 1980s were the decade of a quasi-Catholic Counter-Enlightenment.[39] Compared with earlier times, publications in contemporary cultural studies are as lavish as exhibition catalogues, to say nothing of the accompanying racks of cultural journals. Their elaborate layouts signal, no less than the ascendancy of iconographic studies, that we have left the era of the Suhrkamp culture behind us. And not just since the 1990s, when the talk of a 'pictorial turn' began: that term merely ratified an intellectual development that had long since flowed into the mainstream. To grasp the roots of the urge to escape social criticism's wall of type, we must reach back further to the days of theory fatigue in the late 1970s, when the future of the genre seemed to depend less on new ideas than on a new style of thinking.

Aesthetics of Counter-Enlightenment

In the thrill of treading new theoretical ground, the Merve publishers had always kept an eye out for like-minded authors. In 1977, they had written to a number of West German intellectuals and university lecturers whom they counted among the pioneers of the new style of philosophy, soliciting texts which 'build on the theories of several French authors whom we and others have published intensively in recent years'.[40] Their mailing, aimed at stimulating participation in an anthology, was addressed to such diverse recipients as the former Situationist Frank Böckelmann, the Foucault translators Walter Seitter and Ulrich Raulff, the actor Hans Zischler – who had also been a founding member of the Merve collective – and the Marburg professor of education Dietmar Kamper.

The initiative from West Berlin bore its first fruit in 1978 in *Das Schillern der Revolte* [The glitter of revolt], a scarlet-bound collection of essays which promised to explore new strategies of subversion in the face of 'more and more labyrinthine' relations of power: 'lateral thinking, reversing the rules, wearing disguises, striking up laughter, left-handed planning, bursting knots instead of tying them tighter, exploiting contradictions, breaking new ground, chasing dreams of the future, running the hedgehog to his death (instead of the hare), etc.'[41] Obviously, the authors had been infected with the wordplay of the rebellion of desire. By the time their book appeared, their ambitions had long since grown. Now they were discussing the project of a joint 'journal of desire' to take up the legacy of the *Kursbuch* and other flagships of the New Left.[42] There could be no doubt about the new journal's intellectual orientation: the objective was to cultivate Parisian philosophy in the German-speaking countries, not just in translation, but also in native assimilation. Thus, the market studies, memos and concept papers that were sent back and forth between Munich, Marburg and West Berlin are concerned less with thematic considerations than with the search for a new theory design.

The urge for innovation was aimed first of all at language, which, the secessionists felt, had been leached barren in the years of class struggle. A 'trial of new techniques of writing and presentation' was necessary, Dietmar Kamper wrote, 'which have been developed more in art and literature, in theatre and film.'[43] In the 1980s, the desire to shake off the jargon of derivative Marxism led not only to an approximation of literary forms, but also, especially in the German-speaking countries, to baroque stylistic lapses. To those who missed the voice of critique, theory was becoming indistinguishable from the parody of theory.[44] 'Let us at last write ruthlessly for once,' was the credo of the would-be editors, who boldly admitted to being 'a group of people who don't want to grow up.'[45] Dietmar Kamper's style in particular was a red rag to the academic left. Klaus Laermann's *ad personam* harangue against 'the raving ramblings of obscurantism', which appeared in *Merkur* in 1985, was a polemical high point. The philologist Laermann no doubt would have liked to strangle his colleagues – 'but how can you fight a duel with pulp?'[46] The pompous discursive recklessness that Laermann found so dangerous also seeped into the proposed titles for the projected journal. Many variants, from *Myzel* ('Mycelium') to *Fraglos* ('Unquestionably', with undertones of 'Unquestioning' or 'Ask away!') to *Abfälle der Macht* ('Detritus of power'), were discussed and discarded before the group finally agreed on *Tumult*, with the blatantly miscuing subtitle *Zeitschrift für Verkehrswissenschaft*: 'Journal of transport science' would be the contemporary reading, but surely the editors' meaning was the slightly archaic 'Studies of social intercourse'? The pilot issue of *Tumult* was finally published by Merve in 1979, after a two-year gestation period. According to Frank Böckelmann, its title had the advantage of expressing 'an unintentional, involuntary flowing together and apart, in contrast to *Aufruhr* ["uprising"], *Revolte* ["revolt"], *Rebellion*'.[47]

But merely defying the linguistic conventions of the left did not seem sufficient in the intellectual situation of that time. The ambitions of the *Tumult* editors were aimed rather at breaking out of the order of discourse altogether – as if the drop in value after the theory boom had necessitated a complete currency reform. Walter Seitter, for example, dreamt of texts 'which would not universally presuppose that the reader can/must/wants to read at all – after the kind of reading and writing which has been drummed into us and has left us speechless. Hence we are trying to develop accessory lenses out of words and lines, pictures and pages.'[48] The trip to Paris that Seitter took in October of 1977 together with the two Merve publishers was aimed, not least, at recruiting Michel Foucault's involvement in such a medium. In the early aftermath of Stammheim and Mogadishu, Seitter explained to Foucault the idea of a journal which would cross the 'language of thinking' with the 'language of the visible' to serve up a 'cocktail' of text and images.[49]

But Foucault was more interested in discussing the Red Army Faction. In view of the recent events, his visitors can hardly have been surprised. Nonetheless, the episode also reveals something about Foucault: as an inhabitant of libraries, and one whose work – for all his interest in images – kept to the written sphere, he was not particularly interested in formal experiments.[50] And, in any case, such experiments were not happening in the vicinity of Parisian universities. The publishing innovation that inspired the *Tumult* editors took place at the Centre Pompidou, which had landed in 1977 in the middle of Paris's Beaubourg quarter like a spaceship – or perhaps like an oil refinery. In doing so, it had absorbed a number of older institutions, including the Centre de création industrielle, publishers of the quarterly journal *Traverses*. *Traverses* supplied a mixture of theory, design and archival finds which grew more variegated with every issue, and had nothing in common with the purism of left-wing theory journals. This became especially noticeable once Jean Baudrillard, Paul Virilio and Michel de Certeau had joined the editorial board. From the mid-seventies, many of their own works also appeared in *Traverses*.[51] To its German readers, *Traverses* exemplified the state of the art.

Ulrich Raulff offered a thorough appraisal of the Parisian precursor in the pilot issue of *Tumult*. On leafing through *Traverses*, the young Foucault translator must have had the feeling of peering into the afterlife of the Suhrkamp culture. The staff was composed of equal parts of theoreticians, artists and designers. When the artist Bernard Lagneau joined the masthead, he became the first art director whose day job consisted of building machines out of papier-mâché. *Traverses* was so opulent and so tactile, it too seemed to want to rise from the paper page into three dimensions. The aspiration to make visible 'the medium "journal" in its physicality, as an aesthetic object in its own right', as one of the German memos puts it, seemed to have been substantially achieved in Paris.[52]

To borrow a term from Gérard Genette, who began thinking about the ancillary trappings of the book about this time, what was happening could be called a proliferation of the paratext.[53] The Catholic Virilio betrayed in an interview that he had only agreed to participate in *Traverses* 'because it worked with images'.[54] Like Baudrillard, Virilio allowed his books to grow graphically, sprinkling them with photos and *objets trouvés* which seemed not so much to illustrate the text as to fragment it. Evidently, he considered these materials equally endowed with the potential to engender knowledge. 'So if pictures are readable by the same rules and with the same discipline as texts, we should take advantage of that and work with images in a way that is not illustrative', read the corresponding resolution of the *Tumult* editors.[55] That credo, transposed from a design principle to a heuristic one, describes the agenda of visual studies down to the present. The ascendance of visual studies from the nineties on was always accompanied by the epistemologically and theologically motivated protest against the 'dirty' and 'boring ploy of illustration'.[56]

Raulff discerned the birth of a new language of theory in the 'material compounds' of 'images, concepts and objects' which he discovered in *Traverses*. The way it worked, he explained in his manifesto disguised as a salute to the Parisian forerunner, was 'to short-circuit highly sophisticated fields with others that are frivolous, banal, ordinary'. An eclecticism of this kind was able to elicit a *choc* which could 'shake things out of their customary structure'.[57] We hear Walter Benjamin and the echo of the historical avant-gardes, yet at the same time the idea of breaking down the borders between high and low recalls the aesthetics of 1960s pop culture.[58] From another perspective, it was rooted, of course, in the technical capabilities of the photocopier, of which Ulrich Giersch, another member of the *Tumult* circle, later wrote that it had dissolved the boundaries between the different signs.[59] It is understandable that the *Tumult* editors, before coming to an agreement with Merve, had tried to persuade Jörg Schröder to publish their journal: it was between the quince-yellow book covers of Schröder's publishing company, März Verlag, that the layout style of the American underground press had been transplanted to West Germany. Schröder's hedonistic publishing agenda was miles apart from the ascetic bootleg business of the New Left, however, and the separation of 'high' and 'low' styles was insurmountable until the 1980s. Only in the crisis ensuing from the critique of commodity aesthetics did the mode of bricolage infiltrate high theory.[60]

This is demonstrated by countless publications created using scissors and glue since the late seventies: Klaus Theweleit's *Male Fantasies*, Oskar Negt and Alexander Kluge's *History and Obstinacy* and Peter Sloterdijk's *Critique of Cynical Reason* are just a few of the best-known among them. In Frankfurt, too, books were now being made with pictures only loosely associated with the running text. But the new style of publications was at odds with the Suhrkamp business model. Peter Sloterdijk recalls that he had to supply the illustrations for his 1983 best-seller himself, which explains their very uneven quality. They did things better at Beaubourg. On the editorial staff of *Traverses*, theoreticians worked together with graphic designers to build an *objet d'art* on glossy paper. Little Merve discovered how much time and money that involved: the production of *Tumult* strained the publishers' resources as early as the second year.[61] The utopia of the cheap, universally accessible book, brought into the world by the paperback revolution of the sixties, could not coexist with the new coffee-table books.

A Little Materialism

And yet, in spite of its departure from the primacy of text, *Traverses* did not go far enough for the German reviewer. With its 'slightly boring juxtaposition of texts and images', Raulff wrote, *Traverses* was ultimately, 'in spite of all intentions', still a 'text journal'. But to what extent was it possible – in print – to escape the medium of text? Theory around 1980, pressed by the inflation of signs and the devaluation of the printed word, was looking for ways to escape the flatworld of its textual existence. Where there had once been text, there should now be things. The model to be emulated in this regard was once again Parisian. Although the exhibitions on day-to-day culture, design and advertising which the Centre de création industrielle had been organizing since the seventies seemed to Ulrich Raulff to be marked by a 'blithe affirmation of technology', it was the same institution, now integrated in the Centre Pompidou, which invented the theory exhibition, and with it the role of the theoretician-curator.[62] Paul Virilio had been a pioneer with his 1975 photo show on bunker archaeology on the Atlantic coast of France – and he was subsequently engaged as an editor of *Traverses*.[63] In 1985, Jean-François Lyotard followed suit with *Les Immatériaux*, at the time the most expensive exhibition ever produced by the Centre Pompidou. To Lyotard, the appeal of swapping the author's role for that of the curator consisted in 'abandoning the traditional medium of the book for a change'. In the century to come, he explained to Derrida in an interview, books would no longer be important anyway.[64] Derrida, of all people, is not likely to have been convinced that the book would soon be antiquated, but, five years later, he in turn curated the exhibition *Mémoires d'aveugle* at the Louvre. At the same museum, the historian of literature and medicine Jean Starobinski curated an opulent show on gift-giving in 1994. More recently, the tradition has been carried on most prominently by Bruno Latour. *Iconoclash*, the major retrospective he curated in 2002 in Karlsruhe, was dedicated to the modern academy's hostility to images: apparently the front lines had not moved much in the meantime. More than twenty years after the critique of neo-Marxist iconoclasm, Latour expressed the hope of arriving in a world beyond the controversy over images.[65]

The need to 'acknowledge things as things' which Ulrich Raulff had articulated was by definition a materialistic one. It is a small-form materialism which has found its way into the gene pool of cultural studies as the 'material turn'. The tangibility of signs, the preference for things, the reading of images and a proximity to art coalesced into a philosophical style which is still able to generate research programmes today. It made its debut towards the end of the seventies in the form of an elegy: small-form materialism arose from the ashes of its older namesake; it began as a dance on the extinct craters of Marxism.[66] To do justice to things, Raulff writes, we must stop treating them as reifications – a well-known synonym 'for evil' in the language of dialectical materialism, at least since Lukács.[67] It would seem as though the grand narratives of the 1980s had been betrayed by their hollow concepts – as if our talk of 'materialities' or 'practices' merely referred to sunken artefacts of leftist culture.

As late as the 1970s, the narrative of class struggle had achieved an astounding temporalization of complexity, and the grey page of running text was the corresponding typographical form. As that order of discourse eroded, it released an abundance of unbound materials which arranged themselves into the *mille tableaux* that Raulff and Seitter admired in the pages of *Traverses*. For their own journal, they favoured 'documentary montages, interviews, combined fragments of picture and text, excavations and counterfeits'.[68] That list, effortlessly extendable, catalogues the disorderly layout of postmodernism. An essay by Wolf Lepenies on Gottfried Benn's static feeling of history is dated 1982. Lepenies wrote the text in the dramatic present, which surely must have been more than a stylistic choice. And, indeed, the intellectual atmosphere that Lepenies extrapolates from Benn's writings turns out to be a portrait of the author's own present: 'Now we have to depend on what is available and regroup the intellectual resources. Bricoleurs are needed, and kaleidoscopic thinking is the mode of the hour in a time with no prospects for development.'[69]

'Crosswise' or 'lateral' is the spatial vector with which this philosophy was fondest of identifying itself. Before 'lateral thinking' arrived in business literature in the course of the 1980s, it symbolized the subversive break with Marxism. Around 1980, cutting 'across culture' – as the motto of *Traverses* proclaimed – was a clear rejection of the lengthwise sections of historical philosophy. 'The avant-garde, abstraction through reason, "ideas" in general are reincorporated into the refractory material of anthropology, psychology and ethnology', Karl Heinz Bohrer noted in his 1979 analysis of theory fatigue in Habermas's *Observations on the 'Spiritual Situation of the Age'*, which appeared in German at the same time as the pilot issue of *Tumult*. 'Things have become mightier than words. ... It would be wrong to assume that this alternative has been theoretically decided in favour of things. Yet the cultural climate smacks of it.'[70]

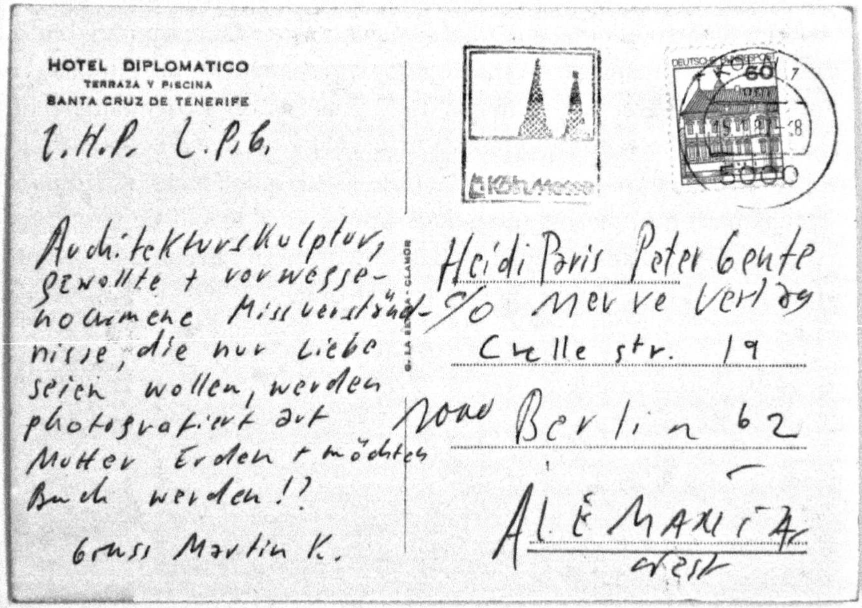

HOTEL DIPLOMATICO
TERRAZA Y PISCINA
SANTA CRUZ DE TENERIFE

L.H.P. L.P.G.

Architekturskulptur, gewollte + vorweggenommene Missverständnisse, die nur Liebe seien wollen, werden photografiert auf Mutter Erden + möchtes Buch werden!?

Grüssi Martin K.

Heidi Paris Peter Gente
c/o Merve Verlag
Crelle str. 19
1000 Berlin 62
ALEMANIA
West

15 Architectural misunderstandings would like to become a book: Martin Kippenberger sends greetings from Tenerife, 1987.

9

INTO THE WHITE CUBE

Tom Lamberty, who took over Merve Verlag from Heidi Paris and Peter Gente, expressed the opinion in a 2014 interview with the *taz* that it was high time for theory to get 'out of the art pigeonhole'.[1] One needn't share Lamberty's conclusion to concur with his perception: difficult ideas have their place today mainly in the world of art.[2] The most extensive Merve assortments have long since been found not in Red bookshops, but in museum shops and art bookshops. And while the art world cloaks itself in a cloud of theory, theory continues to become more and more like art. For its fortieth anniversary – to which Peter Gente flew in from Thailand – the *Internationaler Merve Diskurs* series was exhibited as a total work of art at the Falckenberg Collection in Hamburg. The white walls of the former Phoenix factory in Hamburg's southern borough of Harburg were adorned with a frieze of all 336 titles that Merve had published up to then.[3] *e-flux* too, the global mailing list that keeps the art world up to date on its events, claims to be nothing less than a work of art. In the dialect known as 'International Art English', analysed by the sociologists Alix Rule and David Levine, it drags around clichés of theory discourse wherever it goes.[4] Theory and art, such cases indicate, have entered a symbiotic relationship which leaves them mutually dependent.[5]

And yet, for a long time, they had been fierce rivals. In the twentieth century, art and philosophy had made a sport out of pronouncing each other dead, on the authority of Hegel and other master thinkers. In his lectures on aesthetics, Hegel had proclaimed that art had reached its end and must pass on the torch of knowledge to precisely that philosophy which he was developing before his audience. The avant-gardes of the twentieth century paid him back in his own coin, tossing philosophy onto the scrapheap of history. Joseph Kosuth, a pioneer of conceptual art, declared that art was the heir of philosophy as an instrument of reflection.[6] When Kosuth's manifesto appeared in 1969 with its agenda-setting title 'Art after Philosophy', the German '68 generation were weaving art's funeral wreath.[7] Arthur C. Danto, perhaps the most consistent adopter of the Hegelian thesis of art history as finite, took the birth of neo-Expressionism some ten years later as an opportunity to declare art defunct yet again. Having completed its mission of exploring the essence of art through art, nothing remained for art to do but to putter along contentedly to the end of its days.[8] It did so, and perhaps is doing so still – and theory is helping it. In the *Posthistoire* that Danto predicted, the two would make peace. The annals of Merve are a good source of clues as to how this alliance came about. Its beginnings lay in a series of momentous encounters in 1979.

The Mountain of Truth

'We're doing great, and we're full of enterprise,' Paris and Gente wrote to Foucault in May of 1979. A year after the Tunix Conference, their good spirits had returned. 'Actually, it started with Harald Szeemann's Monte Verità exhibition.'[9] As the left was setting sail to seek alternative islands, the Swiss curator Szeemann held up a mirror to its face. His travelling exhibition, which appeared in West Berlin in the Akademie der Künste in the spring of 1979, was devoted to the esoterics, artists and anarchists of the early twentieth century who had turned Monte Verità on the shores of Lago Maggiore in southern Switzerland into one of the world's first drop-out colonies. As Szeemann put it in the exhibition catalogue, Monte Verità was a pot-pourri of '600 visions of Paradise.'[10] In other words, it was the historical counterpart of the imaginary Tunix Beach. In the West Berlin of 1979, in any case, it was impossible not to draw contemporary parallels. 'In the total work of art, the *weltanschauung*, the *leitmotiv* of what they did there in Ascona, all so wonderfully "alternative", we couldn't help laughing out loud at ourselves,' the publishers reported to Paris. *Voilà*: they were laughing again! Because connections to Ticino were complicated, Paris and Gente booked a flight to another former drop-out spot, Capri, and used their holiday to write an enthusiastic two-page review of Szeemann's exhibition for the *taz*. Their article culminated in an appeal to all the 'Spontis, freaks, gays, women's libbers' and the 'drug scene' to go and seek self-knowledge at the Akademie der Künste. Although they found the survey on the whole too academic – 'the exhibition could have done with a few palm trees, shade, Wagner, a lawn to lie on and rest, with birds chirping'[11] – this was not an obstacle to the opportunity for worthwhile reflection, they found.

The *taz* editors added a note expressing their concern that Szeemann's 'historicization and museum packaging' might tend to neutralize the political energy of the alternative movement. That critique was a symptom of the Berlin left's anxious unfamiliarity with the art world. It took no notice of the curator's self-image: with his flowing beard, Szeemann would have fit right in at Monte Verità. Although he thought the dream of the ideal, alternative society was doomed to failure, his work brought that same dream to a kind of fruition in the experimental space of art. 'I was able to show in the exhibition,' he later explained, 'that the ideal society existed here, even if it did not exist in reality.'[12] Over ten years, he had managed to capture the revolutionary zeitgeist in the museum again and again: his exhibitions transformed '68 into art events. They were also the best presentations of the American neo-avant-gardes, which puzzled European audiences with their 'concepts' and 'actions'. In Berne, where Szeemann had the Californian earth artist Michael Heizer tear up the asphalt in front of the Kunsthalle, Swiss farmers dumped their aesthetic judgement on the site in the form of a truckload of slurry. In Cologne, where a cow was supposed to calve in his exhibition on Happenings and Fluxus, the veterinary inspectors intervened. Szeemann can take credit for having invented the figure of the artist-curator who composes exhibitions as total works of art. The importance of that figure in revitalizing the institution of the museum cannot be overestimated.[13]

Szeemann's 'Mountain of Truth' was also an attempt to capture and revive the utopian spirit by bursting the boundaries of the museum.[14] Hence, he had originally conceived the exhibition to be held on the hallowed ground of Monte Verità itself, and had the site's magnetic anomalies confirmed by the geological bureau of the Canton of Ticino in Bellinzona. But the travelling exhibition at the Akademie der Künste in West Berlin also broke with the conventions of curating. Modern classics such as Hugo Ball and Oskar Schlemmer collided with crackpots from obscure regions of esoterica. Paintings and gardening implements, books and robes, ideas and furniture were woven into a single fabric. The 'museum of obsessions' which Szeemann declared to be his lifelong project did away with the division between art and not-art: anything might be included, whether high culture, clutter or commodity form, as long as it had heretical intensity. After the increasing intellectualization that art had undergone since the end of the Second World War, objects were making their comeback – and the museum along with them – in Szeemann's exhibitions, just as in the Centre Pompidou.[15] The Futurists, in their day, had wanted to burn down the museum as a bastion of the aesthetics of autonomy. Most of the avant-gardes of the twentieth century considered it suspect, for that matter, as a locus of bourgeois auratization. Apart from such exceptions as André Malraux's 'imaginary museum', new visions of the museum did not arise until the 1970s. The need for a new cabinet of wonders grew proportionately as faith in progress waned.[16]

Peter Gente had discovered Szeemann's review of Monte Verità by accident: Janos Frecot, a former flat-mate, had contributed to the catalogue, and aroused Gente's curiosity by his remark that 'a whole mountain' was being exhibited in Italian Switzerland. The show came to Berlin a short time later. The publishers' delight is understandable: someone had arranged images and objects in a collage of materials that looked much more appropriate to the intellectual situation than the worn-out medium of text. Someone had reclaimed the museum as a playing field of the same 'intensity' that their French authors advocated.[17] Moreover, Szeemann orchestrated an alienation effect using exhibition techniques, which allowed him to shield himself with a cool irony against the warm, fuzzy, alternative current.

Pleased with Paris and Gente's review in the *taz*, Szeemann immediately sent Merve a selection of his statements of principle 'so that the contact won't break off between resourceful minorities'. At this point, if not before, it was clear that they spoke the same language. In the summer of 1980, Gente travelled on short notice to Ascona, where Szeemann had taken up residence during his research for the exhibition because he found the magnetic anomalies personally stimulating. Szeemann readily agreed to publish a book of collected occasional texts, supplied his visitor with 'towers of manuscripts', and handed him the house keys, as he was just leaving on travels of his own. The selection Gente made in the course of a week was published as the 100th book in the *Internationaler Merve Diskurs* series with the title *Museum der Obsessionen* – 'Museum of obsessions'. The jubilee book with gold rhombus on the cover marked another turning point in Merve's history. After the year of theory fatigue, new options were opening up in the art world. 'Maybe many people won't understand it,' Paris and Gente wrote in the editorial afterword intended to make their new author credible to their readership.[18] Measured against Merve's former aspirations, the voluntary move to the museum after ten years spent publishing theory might be seen as an admission of total failure.

Be Smart – Take Part

Under the influence of the recent Monte Verità experience, Gente had confessed to Foucault two years before publishing *Museum der Obsessionen* that he hadn't gone to 'any art exhibition for 15 years.'[19] His admission is typical for a member of the German '68 generation. Art had played no major part in the West Berlin student movement, apart from some actions by members of Kommune I – a planned pudding attack on Hubert Humphrey, an aerial leafleting of Mao's Little Red Book – which were traceable via Dieter Kunzelmann to the influence of the Situationists. And those communards had been a thorn in the side of the SDS since 1967 anyway. From the political activists' point of view, even the avant-garde of the Happenings, whose explicit goal was to subvert art through social critique, was on the side of the reactionary bourgeoisie. The performance artist Wolf Vostell, who would later work with Szeemann as well, barely escaped a beating in the autumn of 1967 when he unfurled a roll of wallpaper in front of Freie Universität with a photo of Benno Ohnesorg bleeding from his head wound. 'We looked at Vostell with indignation,' recalls Helmut Lethen, who a short time later enrolled in the German department at FU – almost a communist cell in itself. 'He seemed like a ghost of the *bohème* that we thought was dead and buried.'[20] Peter Gente's reservations about 'the *bohème*' were certainly not as pronounced as those of the cadre Lethen, but his distance from the art world was just as great.

Art and leftist politics could coincide only where a strong figure or an alignment of local factors concentrated the zeitgeist:[21] in Düsseldorf, for example, where Joseph Beuys worked, or in Berne, where Harald Szeemann provoked the farmers.[22] And in Vienna, where the cultural revolution of Viennese Actionism culminated in an artistic scandal. In West Berlin, on the other hand, revolutionary culture was in the firm grip of the iconoclasts. Günter Brus, one of the Vienna Actionists who sought refuge from the Austrian authorities in West Germany's eastern enclave in 1969, found he had no future there as an artist: West Berlin lacked galleries, a proper art fair and an audience. 'Somehow, I felt lonely among these provincial groups, among these Kreuzberg pub crowds, half hippie ghosts. What annoyed me the most was the quasi-abstract discussions in which the language swallowed itself, the opposite of our *Schmäh*, the manic Viennese sarcasm.'[23] The discourse Brus describes is the opposite of the excrescence that Foucault and Baudrillard would diagnose some years later. Accustomed to baroque Viennese conversation, Brus experienced the sound of theory as a desiccation of the language. The 'provincial groups' he encountered in Berlin might well have included the Merve collective, but in the early seventies their circles did not yet overlap.

An art scene something like those that existed in Cologne or Düsseldorf developed in West Berlin only towards the end of the seventies. In 1977, a group of art students opened a gallery as a kind of self-help project 'in the toughest territory in the city', at Moritzplatz in Kreuzberg.[24] Their pictures – colourful, expressive, with urban and body motifs – took leave of the conceptual avant-garde, so that they were not only a critical success, but soon a commercial one as well: unlike happenings, oil paintings could be bought. Helmut Middendorf, one of the founders, called his large canvases 'painted intensity'. The critic for *Die Zeit* observed that the gallery of the 'new Fauves' was filled with 'an ecstasy like that in discos'. The comparison is aptly chosen inasmuch as the group cultivated its nocturnal debaucheries as a distinguishing characteristic. The up-and-coming generation set itself apart from the ascetic neo-avant-garde not only in their paintings, but in their style of living and working. The fact that Beuys had never been seen drunk in a bar suddenly became an objection to his art. Like most Expressionists, the *Neue Wilde* celebrated their excesses as a catalyst of their expression. In a word: they made nightlife into an institution of the art world. As if to proclaim that agenda, one of their first exhibitions at Moritzplatz was titled 'Alkhol, Nikotin fff ...'.[25]

A title like that could have come from Martin Kippenberger, who, together with a few other Hamburg artists, moved to West Berlin in 1977. Kippenberger was not susceptible to the pathos of the Kreuzberg neo-Expressionists,[26] but he did share with them an aversion to the intellectual asceticism which had dictated that art must reflect on art. In Berlin, Kippenberger earned a reputation primarily as a publican and an impresario: he took over the management of the Kreuzberg punk club SO36 in 1979, after locals had demolished the interior in protest against the price of beer. Kippenberger also had a go at the genre of business art.[27] In the same year, he opened 'Kippenberger's Bureau', an agency for services ranging from 'brokerage' to 'consulting' to 'pictures'. The enterprise recalled the short-lived Bismarc Media GmbH, which the publisher Jörg Schröder of März Verlag had founded in 1970 for the express purpose of producing nothing tangible. Frieder Butzmann, a young musician who ended up at one of Kippenberger's agency parties, realized at the time 'that opening a shop, a gallery, a record company or a guesthouse can be art too'.[28] Perhaps just being in West Berlin was enough. In the early 1980s, Heidi Paris and Peter Gente also began using the term 'art' in the new broad sense: as they became comfortable in the expanding art scene, they discovered the 'art of making books'.[29]

In 1979, the same year they discovered Szeemann, they met Kippenberger and persuaded him to design a magazine for Merve's tenth anniversary. At that time, artists' books had a prominent place in Kippenberger's work.[30] Thomas Kapielski, a contributing author, has described the 'cultish' reverence displayed towards the Merve publishers among the Berliner *bohème*: 'Members of sublime circles quibbled obsessively over interpretations of the smart publisher's cryptic rhombi.' The wild night shifts that Kippenberger assigned his writers to compile the jubilee magazine also appear in Kapielski's recollections.[31] The magazine, titled *Schlau sein – dabei sein* ('Be smart, take part', perhaps) ultimately contained equal parts of French theory and snippets of experimental literature and artists' contributions: a collage of text and images hovering between all genres. It was in keeping with the credo that the publishers adopted at that time: 'To make things in ignorance of what they are',[32] a phrase Adorno had formulated to define 'the aim of every artistic utopia today'. By now, *Schlau sein – dabei sein* has become an *objet d'art* itself: it was exhibited in the major Kippenberger retrospective in Berlin at Hamburger Bahnhof in 2013. The thin book stood there among all the other books that are an integral part of Kippenberger's œuvre

– including *Frauen* [Women], the second Kippenberger title published by Merve. The 1980 photo book containing no text at all shows how far the theory publishers had drifted from their core business in just a few years. Sending the book to the feminist bookshops of Germany, which were among Merve's long-standing distributors from Sponti days, was nothing less than a provocation. What other reaction besides outrage could a macho's gallery of real and imagined conquests elicit? The moment when the feminist booksellers returned *Frauen* is significant: it marks a complete divorce from politics – even in the form of those little struggles that Lyotard and the French authors had focused on – and an affirmation of art, in whose institutions the publishers were to find their new sphere of circulation. 'We are talked about in the theatre, literature and art scene as a well-kept secret', the publishers wrote to an acquaintance in New York in 1981.[33]

Merve almost published a third Kippenberger, by the way. In 1987, the artist proposed a book on 'architectural sculpture': 'intentional + anticipated misunderstandings that aspire to be only love'.[34] For some reason, the proposal did not bear fruit, and Kippenberger's *Psychobuildings* was published the following year by Walther König – with a reversed Merve rhombus on the cover: proof, if any was needed, that Merve was now a classic brand.

The publishers' aesthetic transgressions were the responsibility of Heidi Paris. She did not share the iconoclasm of the '68 generation that shaped her partner's outlook. In the 1980s, she worked as a curator herself, organizing exhibitions on Berlin ready-made design. At the same time, she continued to experiment with the book form. None of the theory magazines created under her direction, with titles such as *Solo, Dry* and *Stop Art*, ever went beyond its first issue. If we postulate that these pilot issues were not publishing failures, but part of an aesthetic strategy, then she was trying out the principle of the series and its discontinuation. The series holds a place in the history of avant-gardes; it was apt to provoke doubts about both the aura of the unique object and the effects of mass production.[35] In the lectures and opening talks that Heidi Paris gave during the 1980s, she spoke again and again about her interest in serial art forms. Almost tenderly, she favoured limited editions which managed to hover between aura and reproducibility. 'Every series – a little family': the phrase betrays her aesthetic sympathies, which guided her in her 'art of making books' as well. From 1984 at the latest, when Harald Szeemann's exhibition *Der Hang zum Gesamtkunstwerk* [The inclination to the total work of art] was shown at Charlottenburg Palace, she came to an agreement with Peter Gente to view their book series *Internationaler Merve Diskurs* as a serial *Gesamtkunstwerk*.

As the Merve translator Marianne Karbe emphasizes, the Fluxus artists with their 'multiples' were an important influence.[36] Paris's mission as a publisher had come a long way from the 1970s utopia of the theory paperback – selling the greatest possible number of copies, even of difficult texts. Aware that her reception was limited to a small circle of initiates, she now saw herself as producing limited editions of objects situated between theory and art.[37] 'In the manner of their composition', Paris explained, their books were 'hard to describe as books'.[38] When the only issue of her magazine *Solo* appeared in 1981, the *taz* welcomed the 'texts by R. Barthes, W. Seitter, Laurie Anderson, S. Lotringer, P. Virilio and other branches of the mythic cult-ur-tribe of still wildly proliferating thought, reproducing the dramatization of theories in soli-performance. On glossy paper with black-and-white photo series, pleasant to the eye and delightful to read, *Solo* is a felicitous single issue'.[39]

German Issues

The 'dramatization of theories' aptly referred to here was the order of the day – not just in Berlin, but also in the neo-avant-garde capital, New York. After their encounters with Szeemann and Kippenberger, 1979 also brought the Merve publishers a copy of the theory journal *Semiotext(e)*, which the literature professor Sylvère Lotringer had been editing at Columbia University for some years. They must have realized immediately that an intellectual parallel development was going on in the US which they could not afford to ignore. Peter Gente immediately wrote to Lotringer to bring Merve Verlag to his attention: both Merve and *Semiotext(e)* were involved in transforming theory into art. In Lotringer's case, that activity seems in retrospect the almost inevitable consequence of a transatlantic university career which had begun with a dissertation under Roland Barthes at the

École pratique des hautes études and culminated in the early 1970s, after various intermediate stations, in a professorship at Columbia University. Manhattan brought Lotringer into contact with the art world. 'When I arrived in New York I was very struck talking to people like John Cage and Merce Cunningham. I discovered that they were the real thinkers in America ... coming up with something that was very close to what French post-'68 theory had come up with, especially Foucault, Deleuze and Guattari.' But, instead of pursuing this similarity in the formation of aesthetic theory – as Lyotard did, for example – Lotringer decided to make himself 'available' to the American artists, because he found their work more concrete than the texts of the Parisian Left-Nietzscheans.[40] In 1975, Lotringer brought Foucault and Lyotard to New York, together with Deleuze and Guattari, and had them discuss madness and prisons with John Cage and William Burroughs in a symposium titled 'Schizo-Culture.' The meeting, which was attended by many other New York artists and academics, including the art theoretician Arthur C. Danto, was a great success – or a huge debacle, as the French guests seemed to think at first, as the hundreds of activists, patients and former prisoners who streamed onto the Columbia campus transformed most of the talks into an uninterrupted uproar. Guattari refused to lead his panel because he saw a room filled with 'microfascisms', and disappeared with a part of the audience into the foyer. Foucault, who was accused by the audience of working for the CIA, came to the ambivalent conclusion that the colloquium marked the end of the sixties.[41]

Lotringer's *Semiotext(e)*, founded in 1974 as a journal of semiotics, became a more continuous forum for communication between New York art and Parisian theory. In the course of the seventies, the journal morphed into a large-format magazine, designed with the help of Lotringer's artist friends, and published authors such as Martine Barrat and Kathy Acker side by side with Deleuze and Baudrillard. The editors invented the artist interview as a format to get artists to talk. Lotringer has said about *Semiotext(e)*, 'Each issue was a way of "doing theory" the way artists "do art", by establishing between found material, displaced documents, original essays, interviews, photographs, quotes, and so on, what Cage called a "non-relationship" and Deleuze and Guattari a "nondisjunctive synthesis".'[42] This created a different variety of French theory which never made it to the departments of American universities. Lotringer spurned as academic the 'textual fetishism' of a Derrida or a Paul de Man, who pushed theory closer to poetry.[43] His frame of reference was not literature, but the New York art scene, in which the boundaries between artistic and theoretical production became fluid in the 1980s.

To reflect on the nature of art by artistic means: that had been the avant-gardes' purpose.[44] Arthur C. Danto, who sat alongside Lyotard on the podium of the 'Schizo-Culture' conference, wrote that 'the objects approach zero as their theory approaches infinity, so that virtually all there is at the end *is* theory, art having finally become vaporized in a dazzle of pure thought about itself.'[45] Zero objects had been achieved by the conceptual art of the sixties, which refused to produce material works of art at all. 'Being an artist now means to question the nature of art', Joseph Kosuth wrote in his 1969 manifesto quoted above.[46] After a half-century of avant-garde experiments, art had finally attained the immateriality of theory.

Theory, meanwhile, which took the place of neo-Marxism at the turn of the 1980s, longed for the materiality of art works – as if it would claim the aura, to use Benjamin's term, that it had single-handedly beaten out of art. This crossover is not to be confused, however, with the return to aesthetics that marked the philosophical discourse of the 1980s. What was happening, or was supposed to be happening, on the richly pictorial pages of *Traverses*, *Tumult* and, perhaps most explicitly, *Semiotext(e)* was the transubstantiation of theory into art.[47]

The letter Gente wrote to Lotringer drew no reaction at first, but several months later came an enthusiastic reply urging an exchange of texts and future collaboration. In the editorial offices of *Semiotext(e)*, preparations for the next issue had begun: it would be devoted to Germany after the turning point of the German Autumn. The German situation, and its Berlin form in particular, seemed to Lotringer to be a matter of general interest, and especially American interest, for the 'future of politics in late capitalism.'[48] In his letter to Gente, he describes what the issue is to include:

> Description of the alternative networks; the position of the Frankfurt School in the German political climate; the various struggles going

> on (housing, nuclear weapons) and their character compared with the sixties, both in Germany and in the US; the Baader–Meinhof legacy and the attitude of the 'alternatives' toward this kind of action; relations to Italy (Autonomia) and to the French theories (Foucault, Deleuze/Guattari); the special situation of Berlin; politics and cinema, etc.[49]

To collate material on these topics, Lotringer needed partners on-site, especially since he wasn't familiar with German affairs.[50] The Merve publishers took on that role: 'We are in the process of contacting possible authors for *Semiotext(e)* and collecting important recent texts,' they wrote in their next letter.[51] Lotringer later recalled the 'basket of articles' out of which Gente, like a magician, had pulled out the appropriate texts: 'He instinctively knew what would be good, and the selection of authors we made together is probably one of the best that could have been done at the time.'[52]

Indeed, leafing through *The German Issue* of *Semiotext(e)* is like travelling back to Schöneberg in the year 1982, and not only because a black-and-white photo strip runs like a Berlin Wall right through the book, halfway down each page. All the key topics are covered: music, the RAF, the Nazi legacy, the alternative scene, Turkish Kreuzberg, Berlin night life ... The spectrum of authors ranges from the pop star Annette Humpe to Hans Magnus Enzensberger, from Alexander Kluge to Romy Haag, and from Ulrike Meinhof to Hans-Jürgen Syberberg. The local sound bites mixed in with the chorus of intellectuals lend the issue a kind of street credibility. To round it out, there are articles by French theoreticians and a series of artist interviews – here again, interviews are essential to Lotringer's work: Christo talks about his lifelong project of wrapping the Reichstag building; William Burroughs explains the fascination of terrorism; Heiner Müller talks about time-travelling in Berlin's S-Bahn trains between Karlshorst in the East and Charlottenburg in the West.

The Island of *Posthistoire*

Among the surprises that Peter Gente pulled out of his stock and that found their way into Lotringer's *German Issue* was 'The Word Berlin,' the essay by Maurice Blanchot quoted on pages 12–13. Blanchot had written it in 1961 when the Wall was built, and it had first been published in 1964 in the Italian literary journal *Il Menabò di letteratura*. Twenty years later, Paris and Gente read the two or three pages as a certificate of Berlin's advantage as an intellectual location. In addition to the English version that was printed in *Semiotext(e)*, they also commissioned a German translation and distributed it to their readers as a special not-for-sale edition. Blanchot found that Berlin posed a problem to 'every thinking human being'. In the city on the front lines of the Cold War, he saw the scandal of an existential experience of division, which he circumscribed alternately as the absent centre, as 'the impossibility of speaking', as the suspension of meaning. Blanchot's words made Berlin into the metropolis of post-structuralism – a philosophical position in bricks and mortar.[53]

It is no wonder Paris and Gente felt the text was so important. 'We are almost never in Paris and are happy living in Berlin', they wrote coyly in their letter to Lotringer.[54] Their affirmation resonates with the certainty of being in the right place at the right time. From the very start, West Berlin with its low rents and its eager readership had assured their livelihood as leftist publishers. Not until the 1980s, however, did it become an icon of the present in the talk of other towns, including both New York and Paris. The publishers now received more frequent visits from their Parisian authors. The postmodern theoreticians – Baudrillard, Lyotard, Virilio – seem to have been particularly attracted to Berlin, having been invited there by their first German readers.[55] Another reason, however, was that the city exuded a special fascination. Lyotard was thoroughly delighted when he came to Dietmar Kamper's seminar in January of 1983 to present his recently published diagnosis of the present, *The Postmodern Condition*. He wrote to Paris and Gente afterwards that he had glimpsed in Berlin 'the true avant-garde'.[56] What Lyotard found so contemporary may be what Heiner Müller hints at in his interview with Sylvère Lotringer for *The German Issue*. Commenting at length on the intellectual atmosphere of his home town, Müller emphasizes one motif: 'One can see the end of history more clearly from here.'[57]

In his book *City of Quartz*, Mike Davis asks where Los Angeles intellectuals get their predilection for dystopian futures. From the *bohème* of the 1920s to the exiles of Critical Theory to the authors of L.A. Noir, they have dreamed ever-changing versions of the urban nightmare.[58] Apparently, there are cities that shape a style of thinking – and one of those cities is West Berlin. But if Los Angeles inspired its inhabitants to paint a bleak future, Berlin evoked still darker feelings of history. It would be hard to find a place in 'the post-war' that would have been better suited to erode faith in the future.[59] Even Gottfried Benn, returning in 1945 to the ruins of the German capital from the province of Brandenburg, could not shake the impression of having arrived in history's afterlife. With 'dust storms in summer' and 'nettles as tall as a man on the pavements', his *Posthistoire* suggested what an overgrown Mayan temple might look like east of the Elbe. 'They will be drawing ideological draperies around political, historical symbols here for a while yet,' Benn predicted, 'but actually, it's all over. Something is no longer in order.'[60]

As it turned out, Benn was right about the draperies. During the Cold War, the Western Allies redecorated their half of the city as a shop window of the West. Witold Gombrowicz landed in 1963 on an island of comfort 'whose living standard is higher than that of the United States'. But between the new buildings, the shell-riddled monuments of the World War jutted into the cityscape like witnesses of stone. Instead of the cool modernism that the planners intended, the poet experienced an infernal 'mixing of time'.[61] The tabula rasa that Wolf Jobst Siedler bemoaned in his contemporaneous essay *Die gemordete Stadt* [The murdered city] did not quite seem to be realizable in Berlin.[62] Financially dependent on West Germany, the city lacked the money to carry forward its reconstruction. Moreover, reservations about redevelopment in Berlin were fed by the shadows of the past.[63] Michael Rutschky wrote that the '68 generation flocked to the 'ruin of German history' not only to escape West German military service – a West Berlin address was an automatic exemption – but also for 'quasi-philosophical reasons', because its draughty emptiness and shrapnel-scarred façades were a memorial against the historical amnesia of their parents.[64] At the same time, they were a promise of unobstructed opportunities – which went hand in hand with low rents – as the diversity of alternative lifestyles in the city attests. The '68 generation reappraised the past and believed in the future – and the future did not have much to offer in the way of local colour.[65] Only as the utopian reserves were used up could the city once more become an allegory of the zeitgeist. One could see the end of history more clearly from West Berlin.

If Gottfried Benn was the poet of Berlin's *Posthistoire,* then David Bowie would be its postmodern prophet. In 1976, after a European tour, he moved to Schöneberg and recorded three LPs in two years. In his previous home in Los Angeles, he had spent most of his time in the future, living on milk and cocaine as the 'Thin White Duke'. In West Berlin, on the other hand, he rummaged through the props of the twentieth century. He was fascinated by Expressionism, the Nazis and the Wall, which made a division not only between two territories, but between two time capsules. On the vacant site of the former *Führerbunker,* he was said to have been seen trying out a Nazi salute – not as a political gesture, but as the expression of an altered temporal state. Having arrived in Europe tired of the future, Bowie in Berlin was trying out different costumes, playing the trendsetter of a broad present which encompassed the whole century. To him, the

16 The site of Berlin's former central railway station, Anhalter Bahnhof, 1980s.

iconography of the Third Reich was only a particularly drastic historic symbol.[66]

In the cities of West Germany, the last traces of war damage had disappeared in the course of the previous decade behind concrete façades. The contrast made Berlin's vacant building sites, bounded by brick firewalls, all the more conspicuous.[67] In the 1980s, they became the object of a sometimes nostalgic, sometimes apocalyptic analysis of the present which inferred from the urban geology a loss of the future and a return to the past. 'As always at Berlin dinners, conversation turned exclusively and passionately on Berlin', the cultural sociologist Nicolaus Sombart noted in his diary during his fellowship at the Berlin Institute for Advanced Study in Grunewald in 1982/3. 'Dead, destroyed, diseased city, or most interesting and promising city in Germany, in Western Europe even, experimental zone, laboratory, "utopia".' Sombart's diary allows us to trace his conversion to the local style of thinking: 'Only now do I get the discourse about the "postmodern"', he wrote, after seven months in Berlin.[68]

The Trouble with Duchamp

Sombart's conversion took place amid the social rounds of openings, late nights and erotic adventures. But it also had an academic component in the form of Dietmar Kamper's seminars. Kamper had been a professor of sociology at Freie Universität since 1979, the year in which the pilot issue of *Tumult* was published. In the spring term of 1982 and the following winter term, he and Jacob Taubes offered a seminar on the 'Aesthetics of Post-Histoire'. FU was then the only place in Germany where such a seminar could have been held. In Frankfurt, preparations were under way for a major conference on Adorno, even as the postmodern era was dawning in Berlin.[69] From Baudrillard to Benn, from Lyotard to Gehlen, from Spengler to Kojève – Kamper and Taubes examined everyone who had a word to say on the topic. Lyotard and Derrida even came to Berlin in person as guest lecturers. The seminar, aimed at 'fixing the position of the present', to use Jacob Taubes's phrase, was a theory event that attracted not just students.[70] Like Sombart, Paris and Gente too made the pilgrimage south to the

FU campus in Dahlem to discuss the end of history. After all, many of the authors under discussion – and the organizers – were in their catalogue.

Staking out the field in his opening lecture, Taubes limited himself to commenting on a footnote by Alexandre Kojève which had been omitted from a Suhrkamp edition. Even before the war, Kojève had deduced the advent of *Posthistoire* from Hegel's writings in his famous lectures on the *Phenomenology of Spirit*. It was not until the 1950s, however, on a mission to Japan, that he first actually encountered a posthistorical condition: not in Stalin's Soviet Union nor in the affluence of the American consumer society did he witness history at its end, as he had previously supposed, but in the aestheticism of the Japanese upper class. The existence of a class which had shed all substantive beliefs to exist in a sphere of perfect refinement indicated to Kojève the possibility of snobbism for all. The 'Japanization of the Occident' seemed to him to be inevitable. Walter Benjamin had identified an aestheticization of the political in fascism; Jacob Taubes, spelling out the implications of Kojève's laconic footnote on Japan, detected an 'aestheticization of truth' in *Posthistoire*. After the end of objective conflicts, history could continue only in the 'as if' mode. In this situation, aesthetic judgement became the model for all other kinds of judgement. Taubes traced this tendency as far back as Kant. He could have rounded out his summary of the situation with an appendix on the transformation of theory into art which was then taking shape in Berlin.[71]

It was also taking shape in the seminar. Developing a theory of *Posthistoire* necessarily implied experimenting with the form of theory. That is, it did so in the Kamper current at least, which was given to 'wild thinking'.[72] The seminar brought face to face, in the form of its two lecturers, the old and the new German social sciences. While Taubes drew his great arc of the philosophy of history, Kamper was busy liquidating the grand narratives. In that regard, he provided the best example of the aestheticization of truth.[73] During the course, the question arose 'whether the Seminar on the Aesthetics of Posthistoire itself will be considered as an artistic production in progress'.[74] There was disagreement among the participants on that matter. The tensions that arose between the different language games were released towards the end of the semester in a session devoted to Marcel Duchamp.

On Peter Gente's recommendation, Kamper had invited Bruno Hoffmann, a Duchamp specialist from Hanover who had translated little-known texts by the artist from the 1910s into German.[75] Hoffmann read these texts to the seminar participants while showing slides of the *Large Glass*, which Duchamp had been working on at the time he wrote them. Although they were absurdly cryptic artist's texts, Hoffmann had not planned to comment on them, nor to hold a discussion afterwards. He seemed to see his reading itself as an artistic performance. When it had gone on for an hour with no end in sight, the following discussion began. I present it here verbatim because it exemplifies the confusion then reigning between theory and art.

Faber:	May I ask how long this is going to be? (Hoffmann continues.)
	We get the gist by now ... (Hoffmann continues; heckling is heard; after a brief pause, Faber begins again.)
	You can see a hundred things like this every night in Berlin.
	(Hoffmann continues unperturbed.)
	...
Bolz:	First of all, many thanks to Faber. I was having an anxiety attack for an hour there, which Faber has snapped me out of. Apparently, we've reached the point where the avant-garde – and once upon a time there was an avant-garde – has become a nightmare.
Faber:	Surrealism is dead.
Lipowatz:	It's run out of love petrol.
Kamper:	No, it wasn't funny ...
Wulf:	The anxiety was evidently part of the performance. The meaning remains to be determined; we should bear with the reading until it's finished.
X:	We shouldn't bear with fascism until it's finished ...
Bolz:	By now, surrealism has an anaesthetic function. We're not in a museum. Adorno – (laughter drowns out the rest of the sentence). Surrealism – this presentation

makes it crystal clear to me – is definitively obsolete. Only flipped-out, theoryless people get off on it any more.

Hoffmann: What has my presentation got to do with surrealism?

Kamper: Well, I listened to it as an alchemistic discourse.

Hoffmann: (Puts the lights out and starts to read again; someone switches the lights back on; they go on and off a few times; Hoffmann resumes reading.)

Thiessen: Lights on or off! (Another tussle over the lights; some of the audience leave the room.)

Lewitscharoff: If a fat Saxon were to give this reading in Saxon dialect, it would be good. It depends on the artist performing.

Hoffmann: (Turns off the lights; after another scuffle he manages to get the lights left off for a while and resumes reading. In the back corner of the room, someone turns the lights back on. A big bearded student stands up and threatens the person who turned on the lights. A staring contest ensues, which the bearded student loses; he steps away, still surly. There is an animated discussion in the corner.)

Snatches of the dispute: Granddad!
Go to the East, why don't you ...
You're being childish ...

Hoffmann: (Manages to turn out the lights again for a while. He resumes; there is fidgeting and muttering in the room.)

The bearded student: We're in a bad temper – and besides, the time is almost up ...

Hoffmann: (Soldiers on.)

Bolz: (Gets up, goes to the slide projector.) I'm the organizer! (Pulls the plug.)

A man: That's terror!

Althaus: Yes, but what is terror exactly? I think we should all talk about that.

Hoffmann: (Plugs the projector in again.)

Lewitscharoff: A lecturer should be either beautiful, intelligent, or funny. This was none of it.

A. Dill: We've had far more boring lectures in this seminar

without anyone pulling the plug. Why now, all of a sudden?

Kamper: I think what's happening here has to do with the content. Why is it supposed to be surrealism? It's a new way of talking about everyday things. An unaccustomed way, certainly – but I don't understand why that scares Mr Bolz so much?

Bolz: In 1913, a lecture like this was scandalous; today it's not any more ...

A woman: My stomach has a reaction to it.

A woman: Theory is afraid of its disenfranchisement and so it can't even listen for 2½ hours ...

Lipowatz: What's happening here is the total terror of the university's search for meaning. It is intolerable for the academic discourse to be interrupted. The very fact that this lecture shows no recognizable coherence is a pleasant break for the discourse.

Hoffmann: Believe me, it is very unhealthy not to watch my presentation to the end ...

A woman: Hoffmann has withdrawn from us – in an autistic way ... (Other brief comments accuse Hoffmann of refusal, ignorance and selfishness.)

Hoffmann: I translated these texts into German; they are the only ones in the world. They are the product of a work that has been lost for 80 years. I have gone through these texts for four years.

A woman: And now it's your Bible ...

Kamper: Someone used the term 'refusal': what does the refusal consist of in this presentation?

A blonde woman: There should have been an opportunity to ask questions.

Kamper: But he's speaking. He's not speaking about speaking, that's all. That ought to be permissible. That doesn't constitute a refusal.

Lewitscharoff: ... but a question of talent.

Althaus: It was just too long ... It's absurd to accuse the participants of being afraid for their theory.

A man:	Hoffmann's language wasn't boring at all; it was poetic. It just wasn't edited. The opposition here is between individuality and collective terror.
Alioko:	I admire how aggressively and how seriously this event has been received.
Bolz:	Spontaneity must not be made into an agenda – that would really be simply ridiculous.
Kamper:	There certainly was laughter ...
A woman:	We have to have the right to interrupt boring lectures.
A man:	Of course there's no regaining the spontaneity, but a presentation like this is still better than a theoretical lecture. It was a practical reconstruction of an event. (Hoffmann offers salt to selected persons.) The text was splendid.
	...
Bolz:	Put it in a museum.[76]

17 Endpapers of Ernst Jünger, *Auf den Marmorklippen*, Hamburg: Hanseatische Verlagsanstalt, 1939.

10

PRUSSIANISM AND SPONTANEISM

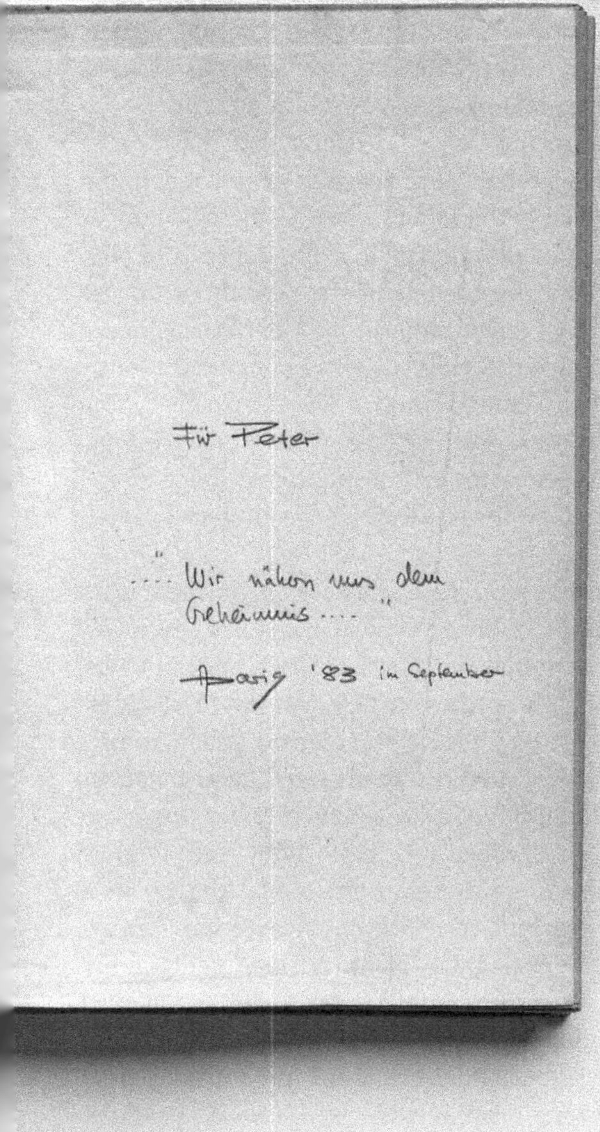
Für Peter
... "Wir nähern uns dem Geheimnis ...."
'83 im September

In the 1980s, theory migrated into the white cubes of the art galleries, where it is still most comfortable today. But the 'aestheticization of truth' which Jacob Taubes identified as the signature of *Posthistoire* also coincided with another trend – one which does not seem to be necessarily related. At the time, the relevance of art was growing just as fast as interest in right-wing thought, almost as if the two automatically went together. The receding insistence on anti-ideological principles is not sufficient to explain this coincidence. 'The Left are now starting to read the Right,' Peter Gente had said as early as October 1977 in explaining the West German situation to Foucault. 'There are some on the Left who realize that that can be useful.'[1] Interest in authors who had until recently been condemned as reactionaries was expressed in the same forums as the new hunger for pictures. In the shadow of Francophilia, a longing for German sounds was heard even in the discussions of the *Tumult* group. 'As much as we are impressed by French philosophy,' one of the concept papers reads, 'we want to trace the severed lines of our inhibitions.'[2] These lines led from the cities to the uplands of West Germany, where intellectuals who had been entranced by Nazism had taken refuge. One of them was Ernst Jünger, who lived in the forest lodge of the Stauffenbergs at Wilflingen, at the southern edge of the Swabian Mountains.

From Paul Virilio to Jünger was just a little step. Virilio's texts returned to positions of heroic nihilism typical of the late seventies. His fascination with the 'original accident' echoed the Futurists' exhilaration of speed. Virilio's studies of the 'history of disaster' recall the Promethean myth of the interwar period which Jünger forged in *The Worker* and later adapted to changed circumstances in his *Waldgang*, the 'walk in the woods' in which the *Titanic* served as a metaphor for modern civilization: 'Here light and shadow stridently collide: the hubris of progress with panic; the greatest comfort with destruction; automation with disaster, which appears in the form of a traffic accident.'[3] Likewise, in Virilio's conception, the motor of modernism was not labour – as the Marxists believed – but technology; not production, but destruction, drove the world on its course. 'Modernity surfaces not as filiation, as Foucault would say, as genealogy. It surfaces only as surprise, chance, accident.

Hence the rejection of libraries, unless one fishes out of them, as out of rubbish bins, pieces of women, pieces of lorries, Vaubans and Flying Fortresses.'[4] The passage also contains a very casual critique of the academic habitus, which could just as easily have been written by Jünger. 'Nothing is more informative', Jünger had written in 1932 in *The Worker*, 'than a quarter of an hour standing at a traffic junction.'[5]

Jünger is also audible in the background of *Tumult*. His voice seems to resonate in the titles of projected and published issues: 'Schools of the Elites', 'Forests', 'The Metastases of State-Owned Libido', 'The Planet'....[6] Surfing the post-structuralist wave, *Tumult* authors nonetheless cultivated a certain undertone. 'Close collaboration with foreign authors should not keep us from working with German traditions and experiments as well', Walter Seitter wrote.[7] For the issue on 'Forests', the editors planned to undertake a 'walk in the woods' with Jünger.[8]

In 1978, Karl Heinz Bohrer published his study on Jünger's aesthetics of terror. In 1982, Jünger received the City of Frankfurt's Goethe Prize. After years of political suspicion, the 'terrible chemist's son from Hanover', as Helmut Lethen called him, had received his literary rehabilitation.[9] Not long after, Heidi Paris gave her partner a copy of Jünger's *roman à clef*, *On the Marble Cliffs*. Even Joschka Fischer, who joined the Green Party in 1982, took Jünger's side in the controversy that broke out over his Goethe Prize. In his defence of Jünger in Daniel Cohn-Bendit's left-wing magazine *Pflasterstrand*, Fischer recalled Jünger's interpretations as insider tips of the cultural revolution:

> The more militant the rebellions became, the more the 'combatant', the 'fighter', came to the fore, the more obvious the parallels became. Later, when 'subjectivity', the politics of the first person, had long since become fashionable, one read Ernst Jünger again – this time, Jünger the LSD author. And later still, when the class struggle had at last given way to Don Juan or East Asian enlightenment, the New Left's third eye stared at the cosmic disciple Jünger – to say nothing of Jünger's affinity with the pre-industrial world and his critique of civilization.[10]

War in the Time of Total Peace

The *Tumult* team, meanwhile, were not interested in Jünger's critique of civilization, nor were they susceptible to the fascination of his books, because they were still willing to take up the political struggle. They read him as an aristocratic anarchist and a diagnostician of *Posthistoire*. War, which he had once called the axis on which everything turns, interested them more as an aesthetic phenomenon.[11] Heiner Müller had visited Jünger in Wilflingen in the 1980s and considered him a fellow 'disaster lover', which he saw as grounds for general concord. War had usurped the place of sexuality before Jünger had had the opportunity to know women; to Müller, this biographical influence was a 'problem of the century'.[12] Perhaps for Jünger's new readers the constellation was reversed: after sexual liberation – after the rhetoric of sexual liberation had decayed, in the '78 generation's ears, to folklore, if not harassment – the 'phantasm of the military' reawakened with new power. In the 'total peace' of the time, it existed as a fascinating hidden truth, which Virilio had identified as the essence of nuclear deterrence.[13] The attempts to analyse culture on the basis of war, which are so frequent in the 1980s, can thus be understood as a consequence both of the decline of Freudo-Marxism and of the growing strength of the peace movement.

The theoretical references of such analyses go back a long way in the Franco-German history of ideas. Ulrich Raulff, who contributed to *Tumult* an analysis of the times in the form of an excursus on the soldierly virtue of *Schneid* – roughly translatable as dash, verve, derring-do – had in 1976, during his DAAD scholarship to the Collège de France, seen Foucault stand the Prussian military theoretician Clausewitz on his head, claiming that politics is the continuation of war by other means: 'War is the motor behind institutions and order. … we have to interpret the war that is going on beneath peace'.[14] Virilio's books contained the same thing in different words. The kind of cultural analysis that his readers advocated in peaceful West Germany was intended to account, finally, for 'the militaristic in us' – but no longer in the abstract terms of class struggle.[15] The Marxists based their analyses not on war, but on labour; hence they gave priority to the economic sphere. In the history that Foucault and Virilio reconstructed, violence played a more fundamental role than the act of production.

Foucault traced the origins of his martial conception of history as far back as the seventeenth century. But his inspirations can be found in the more recent past. One of them is the work of Alexandre Kojève, the theoretician of *Posthistoire* who introduced Parisian intellectuals to Hegel in the 1930s.[16] Kojève's Hegel had little in common, however, with the idealist philosopher who observed the mind coming into its own over the course of the millennia. He resembled rather an anthropologist of violence *avant la lettre*, revealing the war that went on under the cover of peace. Kojève made the history Hegel had developed in the *Phenomenology of Spirit* into humanity's struggle for recognition. This struggle always necessitated subjection before the stable conditions of the economic could arise. Thus, the chapter on the dialectics of master and servant was at the centre of Kojève's interpretation of Hegel.

Kojève's lectures were always well received by his audience – who included Georges Bataille, Jacques Lacan and Pierre Klossowski. He did not invalidate Hegel on philological grounds, but set him in relation to the present situation of the world. Kojève's anthropological perspective appealed to the advocates of the Durkheim school.[17] And, not least, Kojève's Hegel was easy to connect to Nietzsche, whose reception in France was then at a first peak. Nietzsche, too, pitted slaves against masters, and Nietzsche's *Genealogy of Morals* told a story of continuous violence.[18] Its echo was heard in Foucault's 1976 lectures.[19] Since Kojève, and since Nietzsche, reflection upon war as the truth of history has accompanied the discourse of French intellectuals like a basso continuo. The 'war-machines' that Deleuze opposed to the 'State apparatus', and the '*polemological* analysis of culture' which Michel de Certeau advocated in *The Practice of Everyday Life*, are equally good examples.[20]

In the 1930s, this 'brutal conception of history' had migrated from Germany to France;[21] in the 1980s, it returned to Berlin. In an article in *Tumult*, Ulrich Raulff interpreted the disco as a battlefield.[22] Writing in the *Archiv für Begriffsgeschichte* [Archives of conceptual history], the Merve author Hannes Böhringer exposed the military origins of the metaphorical term 'avant-garde'.[23] But the greatest audience for the Heraclitic paradigm – in Germany at least – was achieved by Friedrich Kittler. Since the 1980s, a generation of disciples has learned from his books that all technology is born in war, and that the entertainment industry in particular must be seen as an 'abuse of army equipment'.[24]

Machiavelli in Westphalia

The *Tumult* editors who wanted to trace the 'severed lines' back to the German history of philosophy ended up not only in Ernst Jünger's Wilflingen, but also in Plettenberg in southeastern Westphalia with the scholar of constitutional law Carl Schmitt. After the Marxist boom had subsided, Schmitt was even more rewarding to movements of leftist seekers than Jünger, who had once described 'struggle as an inner experience' and subsequently made himself comfortable in the cosmic equanimity of his late works. Schmitt was a theoretician, not a man of letters, and he shared the 'boundless faith in the idea' which was so familiar to the heirs of the student movement.[25] Intellectuals 'who have fallen silent amid the clattering of liberal, left and Spontaneist prayer wheels and lost contact with one another' – Frank Böckelmann's characterization of the *Tumult* circle – pronounced Schmitt's name like a secret watchword.[26] In 1982, Nicolaus Sombart, who was working on a Schmitt book himself, ran into people planning to publish on Schmitt wherever he went in West Berlin. 'I have to get moving', he noted, 'and finish my Carl Schmitt, or I'll end up like Scott discovering the South Pole.'[27] Schmitt's concept of the political could be wielded to beat back the hegemony of the social sciences.[28] In the light of his Catholic history of philosophy, the future turned out to be deferred. A theory premised on an enemy and on war fell on the open ears of Foucault's and Virilio's readership. And its Decisionism, after zig-zagging dialectics, promised new intellectual energy – reason enough for it to appear in the *Tumult* contributors' analyses. In fact, Schmitt's concepts permeate the pages of *Tumult* like a watermark. The katechon that is delaying the end of the world? To Walter Seitter, the term is merely a synonym for structure.[29] The absence of soldierly virtue in the nuclear death zone? To Ulrich Raulff, it was a symptom of the triumph of irregular warfare.[30]

Peter Gente asked himself at the time 'why I so enjoy reading an author like C. S.' – and not as a newcomer.[31] In the course of Gente's broad reading, his attention had been drawn to the constitutional law expert early on. His initiation was probably the *Theory of the Partisan,* Schmitt's 1963 return to political writing from his post-war 'inner exile'. Having continued his studies of world affairs, Schmitt traced the historic lines that led back from Mao via Lenin to the partisan struggle against Napoleon, practised by the Spaniards and theoretically analysed by the Prussians. From a footing deep in the historical space, Schmitt viewed the Vietnam War in the context of its significance for universal history.[32] The fact that it was a reactionary who stylized the guerrilla as a 'figure of the world-spirit' put his readers between the fronts.[33] By rights, Schmitt's theory should have come from the left. Soon after he had published it, the youth of '68 began marching through the city centres chanting 'Ho, Ho, Ho Chi Minh', and it wasn't long before they were discussing the concept of the urban guerrilla. No doubt many of them at first overlooked the silent expert, who was writing not about Che Guevara, but about the Prussian generals Clausewitz and Gneisenau. Schmitt believed his book could not have been written 'from any other standpoint than Prussia'.[34] But after 1970, when he appeared as the knowledgeable interview partner of the Maoist Joachim Schickel in an anthology titled *Guerrilleros, Partisanen: Theorie und Praxis,* Schmitt was no longer an insider tip.[35] During the seventies, his writings turned up on the extended reading lists of the communist splinter groups.[36] To many a cadre yearning for the outbreak of the worldwide ideological war, they were an intellectual step towards militancy. Both 'incisively rational' and 'apocalyptically feverish', they conjured a 'climate of decision', overlaying West Germany's day-to-day life with images of a state of emergency that seemed about to occur at any moment.[37] Moreover, readers who premised their intellectual existence on the axiom of class struggle could learn from Schmitt that the act of declaring someone an enemy was a politically essential one – and, in fact, an anthropological universal.[38]

Although his texts had circulated earlier in some parts of the left spectrum, Schmitt was not widely rediscovered until the 1980s. All of the attempts from that time to understand the attraction of his proposed theories emphasize his overdetermined language, which generated an aura of danger. Nicolaus Sombart, who had met Schmitt before the war in his parents' home in Grunewald at the west end of Berlin, made an effort to analyse the 'oscillation between conceptual discourse and image magic' into its component parts.[39] Armin Mohler resorted to a term from art history: *Kern-Exaktheit*, or 'central precision,' with its implication of peripheral fuzziness.[40] Günter Maschke, a renegade of the student movement who had metamorphosed into a stalwart Schmittian in the course of the seventies, felt he had to shield his eyes from the 'overintense brightness in whose light the objects under examination take on an ambiguous shimmer.'[41]

Schmitt's language was crucial to Peter Gente too: 'He can write amazingly well, better than Heidegger and Jünger together.'[42] Schmitt also fascinated him as a philosophical *poète maudit*, and he was not ashamed to name him alongside Giordano Bruno, Spinoza and Sade: 'That's the kind of philosopher I love. And there are very few of them today.'[43] Gente's declaration of love follows Schmitt's own self-styling: this was a man who had dealt with the break in his biography after 1945 by identifying with the figures of famous victims. He called his house in Plettenberg 'San Casciano' in allusion to Machiavelli's home-in-exile. As the eighties and his Renaissance began, Schmitt was still living in that obscurity, present mainly by his absence. Rumours circulated among insiders about contacts established, letters answered and confidential conversations.[44] Walter Seitter sent his habilitation thesis – on the transformations of the political since the Middle Ages – to Plettenberg. He can quote from Schmitt's reply even today: Schmitt had never heard of Jacques Lacan, an important reference, alongside Foucault, in Seitter's dissertation.[45]

Nicolaus Sombart was struck by the celebrity Schmitt enjoyed in Berlin intellectual circles in 1982. During his fellowship at the Berlin Institute for Advanced Study, he wrote down his recollections of their encounters in the 1930s. A paternal friend of the family, Schmitt had given the young Sombart an initiation in his philosophy on long walks through the Grunewald forest. 'He felt himself the bearer of a secret,'

Sombart noted, 'an "initiate" in the Gnostic sense.' In his memoirs, Sombart described the charisma of an intellectual tempter who, drawing on his immense erudition, was searching for the pattern of world history. The task he gave his disciple with every book he placed in his hands was to find the concealed key statement. '*Arcanum*', Sombart writes, 'was one of his favourite words.'[46]

The Wild Academy

It was the watchword of an intellectual life that sought no publicity. To the intellectuals in the Merve publishers' circles, it was an enticing alternative. They had been trying since the mid-seventies to tear down the hierarchies of representation by propagating a theory that did not speak in others' name. The *Anti-Oedipus*, which had accompanied their efforts like a handbook for five years, was addressed to children and even illiterates. But in 1981 the reading group disintegrated almost overnight after someone had had the idea of bringing a video camera and taping one of their meetings. Seeing the video was disconcerting: the practice of intensive reading suddenly didn't seem to be in keeping with the times.[47] Still, rejecting the pretensions of the avant-garde didn't necessarily have to mean letting the discourse overflow its banks: it might also mean being intentionally obscure.[48] 'The initiative group identifies not as an avant-garde, influencing some target groups', the *Tumult* editors had written in their founding phase. 'We don't see ourselves as facing a PUBLIC SPHERE composed of the common reasoning of representative intellectuals.'[49] Thus, they edited their journal with their backs to the audience.[50] In the course of the 1980s, Peter Gente too began making his books ultimately for himself.

'We draw nearer to that secret', his partner Heidi Paris wrote to him in 1983 on the flyleaf of Ernst Jünger's *On the Marble Cliffs*.[51] Her inscription was an allusion to a passage in which Jünger's narrator refers to his initiation in the arcana of natural history.[52] The Merve publishers, in search of a new role model, hit upon the figure of the initiate. A distinctive feature of their theory discourse had always been its detachment from common sense. Since Adorno, if not before, thinking that would go beyond the status quo had to be difficult.

Yet the utopia of the '68 generation also included the hope that that difficult philosophy would someday be self-evident. What else were intellectuals supposed to be but philosophical pioneers pointing the way to a better future? Out of the crisis of faith in the revolution, however, grew the identity crisis of its trailblazers. After the German Autumn, the heirs of the student movement withdrew from the 'nexus of discussion'. From the shards of shattered concepts, they put together Epinal sheets of printed images. The art world granted them asylum so that they could go on doing theory. Did this development necessarily bring with it a sectarian attitude, an intentionally esoteric pose? In West Berlin in the 1980s, the capital of *Posthistoire*, theory was cultivated as enigma.

In 1983, Dietmar Kamper founded the *Wilde Akademie* – the 'Savage', 'Fauve' or 'Wild Academy'. Most of its members came from the *Tumult* circle. 'The "Wild Academy" has no programme', the founding declaration reads. 'Its name appears paradoxical only if "academy" is understood as an agency beyond the university, at the spearhead of advanced civilization, devoted to driving back the wilderness.' Even the choice of meeting places made it plain that the members understood the word otherwise: they gathered in various West Berlin galleries, in a loft in Charlottenburg, at the Hotel Kempinski. Matinees and midnight sessions were held to take in 'texts, photos, films, music, drinks'. But, although the symposia were supposed to have the opulence of banquets, Kamper insisted on a distinction between them and the 'Dionysian academies' of ancient Greece: 'While those were boiling hot, the "Wild Academy" steams with cold.' It was unquestionably an institution of the cool zeitgeist. The 'intensity' which it required of its rector was thus 'chilled'.[53]

Nicolaus Sombart, attending a 'topological symposium' on the 'Location and Structure of Hell' at the Kempinski, was surprised by the hip young types who 'shelled out 50 deutschmarks with never a grumble for such an event' – and that on a Sunday morning. He noted the contrast between their 'miscut' punk hairdos and the liveried waiters, and found the quality of the buffet worth a special mention. 'Keynote presentation by Bazon Brock, who gave a slide lecture. As always with him, a mixture of brilliant aperçus and *n'importe quoi*, up to and including crude nonsense, but presented with aplomb

18 The Wild Academy at the buffet, Kassel, 1984.

and apparently well received.'[54] The Kempinski was a good place to exorcise the spirit of academic Marxism. Kamper's bosom enemy Klaus Laermann observed the entry of hedonism in the theory scene with a critical eye. 'Those who find the esotericism of nonsense funny are free to do so. In view of more than two million unemployed and the secure salaries of civil servants, I find it not funny, but shameful and cynical to found a supposedly "wild" academy whose chief purpose is to propagate high hogwash.' In addition to the events in Berlin, conferences in Venice, Toulouse and Palermo came to Laermann's attention. In a time 'in which most doctoral candidates don't know how they are to pay for their heating coal,' he considered such 'fancy-shmancy conferences' scandalous. Hence he closed his tirade in the *Merkur* with an appeal to Kamper's employer, Freie Universität, to stop funding his activities with tax revenues.[55]

A look at the Academy's unofficial journal may give an indication of the models it looked to for orientation. The fourth issue of *Tumult* was devoted to the 'schools of the elites,' and contained articles on the Cistercian order, occult Judaism and the Collège de Sociologie, where Georges Bataille, Roger Caillois and others had tried in the

1930s to establish a politics of the sacred. The theme of the issue speaks for the editors' intuition of the problems of the times.[56] 'Elite or avant-garde?' is the title of a long interview with Jacob Taubes in the middle of the issue. With his usual flair for the philosophy of history, Taubes develops an antagonism between two European knowledge cultures: one heathen-elitist, in which truth is a privilege of initiates, and one Christian-avant-gardist, in which truth is a reward promised to the willing and industrious. 'A *new* concept of philosophy begins with Hegel: the path to truth is hard – "conceptual work" is work! – but ultimately *everyone* can take part in it.' Taubes traced the struggle between exoteric and esoteric knowledge that had marked the history of German philosophy and German universities. Nietzsche had revitalized pagan elitism, he said, in opposition to Hegel and Christianity. The proximity of Max Weber's and Stefan George's circles in Heidelberg had led to a confrontation in the 1920s. The democratization of the university in the sixties? A victory of the Weber faction. The founding of the Berlin Institute for Advanced Study in Grunewald? A 'revenge' of the George school which filled Taubes with concern – after he had been called on to advise that institution by Berlin's senator for higher education, Peter Glotz. Taubes interpreted the rhetoric of 'excellence' as a return to a heroic myth of science which did away with the achievements of the student movement; he was staunchly opposed to it.[57]

Taubes's analysis, in which he distinguished the elite from the avant-garde as different ideal types, was not limited to the political controversy of the Berlin Institute for Advanced Study: it can also be understood as a commentary on the intellectual climate of West Berlin. The prophets of *Posthistoire* were bidding farewell to the avant-gardist posture of the Enlightenment. Instead, they liked to stylize themselves as the keepers of arcane knowledge – although usually in an ironic, as-if mode.

In Search of the Punctum

Taubes himself, however, was also fond of wearing the nimbus of hermetic knowledge. He initiated his students in the arcana of the history of philosophy, bewildering as that might be in a professor who sympathized with the cultural revolution. His conception of traditional philosophy was characterized by a distinction between exoteric and esoteric interpretations which lay concealed under its superficial meaning.[58] 'Each work of the philosophical tradition carried in it a secret to be unlocked, and that alone constituted its *raison d'être*', Henning Ritter recalled. 'Taubes asked young students who interested him about their most important reading experience, rather than what year the second edition of the *Critique of Pure Reason* was published. He shared his personal preferences with them and urged them to search every important work for that sentence for the sake of which it was written.'[59] In this way Taubes was able to charge the classics with an existential gravity that seemed strangely antiquated, especially in the light of the contemporary reform of the universities. Kojève's remark 'that the future of the world and hence the meaning of the present and the importance of the past ultimately depend on the present-day interpretation of the Hegelian writings' could just as well have come from Taubes.[60] The search for the critical word or sentence – the punctum, to use Roland Barthes's word – transformed this urgency into a philological method.[61]

Only at first glance was such a method similar to that of the critique of ideology which set out to expose class interests behind an apparent reification. Furthermore, it had little in common with that empowerment of the recipient which ratified the death of the author. Taubes's art of interpretation was not intended as indiscriminate looting: it set narrow restrictions on the play of meanings. Those who were admitted to the circle of his disciples acceded to the enjoyment of eye-opening readings.[62] And they inevitably came into contact with a number of authors whom no one in West Berlin read in those days, except Taubes. In his seminars, he often mentioned Leo Strauss, who had taught him privately in New York in the 1940s: the theoretician of the political, later influential as the mentor of American neo-conservatives, had written a whole book on the difference between overt and covert interpretations.[63] But Taubes read Carl Schmitt still more intensively than he read Strauss – Schmitt, too, was a thinker in search of hidden key sentences.[64] Not until the 1980s did Taubes publicly declare Schmitt's work to be 'head and shoulders above all the scribblings of intellectuals.'[65] Among his students, however, he had long since left no doubt as to his appreciation of Schmitt, which was indeed the reason for Schmitt's special reception history in West Berlin intellectual circles. Taubes, who habitually called himself an 'arch-Jew', was the most valuable advocate of Schmitt, once the legal counsellor of the Third Reich. Taubes's student assistant Peter Gente, while unpacking Taubes's library from the crates in which it had been shipped from New York, had made the surprising discovery of personally inscribed copies of Schmitt's books as early as the mid-sixties.[66]

Jacob Taubes's Best Enemy

Soon afterward, Taubes's Department of Hermeneutics saw something still more perplexing than that implausible intellectual link: the professor circulated a letter Walter Benjamin had written to Carl Schmitt. In December of 1930, in the midst of the crisis of the Weimar Republic, the favourite author of the Berlin left had sent his book on German tragedy to the right-wing legal scholar for his information – with a note saying how much he was indebted to Schmitt's work. For a generation burning to take up the interrupted traditions of radical left philosophy, the letter contained intellectual dynamite: the revolutionary had extended his hand to the reactionary theorist of the political state of emergency. The edition of Benjamin's correspondence published by Suhrkamp in 1966 contained no trace of such a letter. But why was the leftist professor Taube detonating this charge amidst his students? Was he trying to rattle their political certainties? To recommend Schmitt as a remarkable thinker? And how had he come into possession of Benjamin's letter in the first place, and his inscribed copies for that matter? As Taubes's assistant, Gente would have been in a position to ask him these questions – 'and yet at the time I didn't dare ask Taubes about his personal relations with Schmitt.'[67]

The riddle was not solved until after Schmitt's death twenty years later, when Taubes published a kind of personal obituary in the *taz*. Peter Gente, who was still close to his former mentor, smelled an opportunity to publish an intellectual *roman à clef*. 'We met Taubes at the Kreuzberg restaurant "Exil"; he agreed without hesitation.' Thus encouraged, the Merve publishers followed the traces of a secret history of ideas, corresponding with Schmitt's disciple Armin Mohler, accompanying Taubes to Paris for a panel on Schmitt's legacy – they 'had many conversations and parties',[68] according to the editorial note in the resulting Merve book *Gegenstrebige Fügung* [Union of opposites], in which the Jewish eschatologist writes on his 'fragile relations' with the anti-Semite from Westphalia. For the first time, light was shed on the proximity between two political arch-enemies linked by apocalyptic theology. 'Carl Schmitt appealed to me as an apocalyptic of the counterrevolution', Taubes explained to his astonished readers. 'As an apocalyptic, I knew, and know, that we are related. We share that experience of time and history as a respite, as a reprieve.'[69]

The thin Merve volume plays a weighty part in Taubes's work: it was his first book-length publication since his 1947 doctoral thesis on Western eschatology, four decades before. The occasional pieces that had accumulated in the meantime did not meet Taubes's own standards.[70] And yet it was not given to him to hold the account of his intellectual adventure in his own hands: he died in spring of 1987, shortly before it went to press. He had isolated himself academically, Armin Mohler wrote in his obituary; 'only a close circle of "unconditional" disciples stand by him. The postmodern Merve Verlag is run by persons from this circle.'[71] Taubes's efforts to include Carl Schmitt in the Suhrkamp *Theorie* series had been thwarted by the resistance of his fellow editor Habermas.[72] But one of his students, whom he almost managed to place with Suhrkamp, later founded his own publishing house, and his publishing policy helped to transform Schmitt retroactively into a theory author after all. Seen in this light, *Internationaler Merve Diskurs* would seem to be the late revenge of Jacob Taubes.

Dr. Dirk Baecker
Schäferstraße 15
48oo Bielefeld 1
Tel. o521/87o931

den 5. August 1987

Merve Verlag GmbH
Crelle Str. 22
1ooo Berlin 62

Sehr geehrte Verlagsleiter,

vor einigen Jahren, es war wohl 1981 nach meiner Rückkehr von einem Studienjahr in Paris, habe ich Ihnen schon einmal geschrieben, wie erfreulich ich Ihren innovatorischen Wagemut auf dem deutschen Buchmarkt finde. Ich dachte damals vor allem an die Einführung von Übersetzungen einiger Arbeiten von Virilio und Baudrillard, die ja inzwischen in aller Munde sind.

Heute würde ich Ihnen gerne meinerseits zwei Buchprojekte vorstellen, die sehr gut in Ihre Tradition innovativen Traditionsverzichts passen würden.

Im ersten Projekt handelt es sich um einen kleinen Band mit den gesammelten Interviews von Niklas Luhmann. Sie haben sicherlich mitverfolgt, zum Beispiel in der FR und in der taz, daß Luhmann einen sehr kühlen und ironischen, manchmal bissigen und in der Selbstkommentierung an "Monsieur Teste" erinnernden Interviewstil entwickelt hat, der diesem Genre wieder etwas literarischen Schwung verleiht. Allesamt immer etwas launige, auf Tagesgeschehen und -eindrücke bezogene Kommentare, können sie doch auch als Einführungen in den spezifisch luhmannschen Theoriestil dienen. Es liegen einige in Italien (Unità, Rinascità) und einige bei uns erschienene Interviews vor, die zusammen einen schönen kleinen Band ergeben könnten.

Beim zweiten Projekt handelt es sich die verlegerische Großtat der Übersetzung und erstmaligen Zusammenstellung von Artikeln von einem der pfiffigsten und spielerischsten Vertreter

-2-

19 Dirk Baecker proposes Luhmann's interviews to Merve.

11

DISCO DISPOSITIVE

-2-

der neuen Kybernetik: um den englischen Architekten und Kybernetikphilosophen Ranulph Glanville. Glanville brilliert in Kabinettstückchen erkenntnistheoretischer Reflexionen, kombiniert wie kaum jemand zuvor literarisch einfallsreiches Philosophieren mit ahnungsvollen mathematischen Modellen der Interaktion von Objekten mit Objekten, Subjekten mit Subjekten. Ähnlich wie nach Wittgensteinlektüre ist auch nach einer Glanvillelektüre nichts mehr wie zuvor.

Von Luhmann ebenso wie von Glanville habe ich ein Einverständnis mit diesen Projekten. Sie brauchen also, wenn Sie Interesse haben, nur zuzugreifen.

Über eine positive Antwort würde ich mich freuen und verbleibe einstweilen mit freundlichen Grüßen

It was the *taz* that best captured Jacob Taubes's intellectual persona after his death: 'Talmud in the Paris Bar' was the title of its obituary, written by the Egyptologist and scholar of monotheistic cultures Jan Assmann. Assmann described the philosophical style of a stupendous scholar and reader, but one who did not pursue his passion as a solitary exercise: Taubes was drawn not only to the great texts, but also to the places of elevated society, and was therefore a familiar sight both in the lounge of the Hotel Kempinski and in the Paris Bar in Kantstrasse, which counted him among its regulars as long as he lived. 'It was not professorial virtues such as ambition and determination, asceticism and persistence that defined his temperament. He didn't think much of "scholarship as a way of life".'[1] In the founding phase of the Berlin Institute for Advanced Study, Taubes surprised Senator Glotz with the suggestion of offering fellows not only the villa in Grunewald, but also a more central pied-à-terre at Checkpoint Charlie.[2] The proposal to combat the seclusion of the ivory tower reflects his preference for urban avant-gardes. It did not obtain a majority among the politicians responsible for research and education, however.

Taubes got on better with the restaurateurs. In the summer of 1986, before leaving for Paris, where he would spend a semester as a research fellow at the Maison des Sciences de l'Homme, he gathered his friends and companions at the Paris Bar. 'I have travelled a great deal,' his invitation read,

> but I have always been glad to return to Berlin, and now I would like to say good-bye. On this occasion I invite you 'à table' in the Paris Bar on Saturday, the 5th of July, 1986. The rules of this table are well known: everyone orders what they like. The Paris Bar has permitted me to 'occupy' half the house, from the corner table to the bar. I will be glad if your time allows you to come by the Paris Bar during these hours.

Heidi Paris and Peter Gente were among Taubes's guests. On their invitation, he added in handwriting: 'I'm counting on you.'[3] A friendly pressure, expressing both a long-standing fellowship and a confidence that the publishers didn't need much persuasion to come to a party. It would have been interesting to know who else was invited on that occasion. The guest list would have allowed us to reconstruct an intellectual microcosm which assembled for the last time under Taubes's auspices: in winter of 1986, he learned of his terminal illness; he died the following spring.[4] He would not resume his Talmud studies at his favourite café, whose owner appreciated in turn the patronage of an intellectual. Taubes's last invitation is one of the trophies reproduced in the Paris Bar's jubilee album of 2000.[5]

Diedrich Diederichsen sprinkled in a little theory of night life in *Sexbeat*, his book on the cultural background of the 1980s. He saw the trend towards going out later and later, which became apparent at the beginning of the decade, as the last vestige of leftist faith in a better future: 'We know now that going out is the geometric ray, or vector if you like, the only arrow we have left that points infinitely in one direction.'[6] If that is true, then the pleasure of going out was a compensation for the feeling of having run up against the end of history. It is often said that the ruins of lost beliefs are particularly suited as party venues. In West Berlin, the island of *Posthistoire*, the heyday of nightlife was just getting started.[7]

The Merve publishers were no exception. From 1979 on, they cultivated their contacts in the Paris Bar. 'I tend to go to discos and bars where musicians and painters are, people doing art', Peter Gente later said about his publishing practice.[8] Evenings with Taubes, with Kippenberger and Heiner Müller, gave birth to ideas for books. The dividing line between working and going out was blurred. 'The so-called editors' meetings take place in bars', Heidi Paris explained about the new business methods,[9] and her testimonial to the hospitality industry expresses more than a predilection for late nights: the sleep deprivation training that the Merve publishers underwent in the 1980s is an inseparable part of the theory culture of the time.

Tyrannies of Intimacy

But haven't the creators of intellectual projects always forged their plans in bars and cafés? According to Jürgen Habermas, the Enlightenment had its beginnings in the London coffee-houses. And E. P. Thompson wrote that the revolutionary working class was born in a pub on the banks of the Thames.[10] The theme can be traced throughout the modern era, and usually turns up where political or aesthetic movements take shape. In the Paris of the avant-garde, even the smallest circle had its own café: the Existentialists drank their *petit crème* at the Deux Magots or the Flore; the Situationists boozed around the corner at Chez Moineau. Their leader Guy Debord boasted untiringly of his talent as a drinker. Like Sartre, he lived in a hotel to avoid the abyss of the bourgeois lifestyle.[11]

Berlin had had its artists' bars in the post-war period, such as the jazz cellar Eierschale, where nonconformists danced to Dixieland, and the cabaret Badewanne, the watering hole of a small Surrealist intelligentsia.[12] In 1959, Rolf Eden opened his first Eden Saloon, pursuing a dream of a more sophisticated, American nightlife: 'I had six rooms, each one different. One with jazz, one with a Playboy slide show, one with cushioned bathtub seating.'[13] Merve Lowien tended bar there in the early sixties.

A few years later, that probably would have been unthinkable to her. For a thousand reasons, the Eden clubs were no longer appropriate for young leftists. Over and above their political arguments for or against one place or another, however, the '68 generation developed an ambivalent attitude towards public houses in general. 'Discussions and editorial work take place in homes', Lowien wrote in 1977 about the practice of the leftist publishing collective to which she had belonged for eight years; the prescriptive overtone is unmistakable.[14] Unlike her successor, who would soon plead for going out, the socialist Lowien advocated a philosophy of domesticity. The history of cocooning – if it is ever written – should include a long chapter on the '68 movement. Their utopia of merging the personal into the political expanded the sphere of the political, but by the same token it diminished the relevance of the public sphere. The generation that became politicized in the sixties acted out the avant-gardes' mistrust of the bourgeois burrow in the opposite direction: they were less interested in turning their backs on their interiors than in furnishing them with heightened expectations. The home has rarely been accorded greater importance. It became the laboratory of collectives, communes and flatmates who felt they were the forerunners of the emancipated society. The handbook on the subculture published in 1969 by März Verlag begins, characteristically, with a list of home phone numbers of notable leftists 'who will be happy to help you if you come to Berlin, and perhaps even want to move here'.[15] The list also included the numbers of a few left-wing publishing houses, which probably also operated out of shared flats. That is all: there is no mention of 'in' bars. The trend towards domesticity reached, in an absurd inversion, even into the safe houses of the terrorists. Its echo is still heard in an advertising slogan that the IKEA chain recently publicized throughout Germany: 'Are you still just housed, or have you started living?'[16] 'If people don't go to pubs and cinemas more often, it's because many kitchens are so cosy and warm', the *Kursbuch* explained in one of its ethnographic miniatures of the seventies.[17]

In West Berlin, there was one more reason: the low rents. Hence the scenes that have become emblematic of '68 are set not only in the lecture halls or on the barricades, but also in the faded splendour of coal-heated turn-of-the-century flats: discussions in spacious kitchens; mattresses on parquet floors beneath stuccoed ceilings.[18] The city's tenements offered ample space for the lifestyle experiments of a generation of cultural revolutionaries. The 'tyrannies of intimacy' that Richard Sennett found in the American counter-culture in 1976 flourished not only in Chicago and New York, but also in Charlottenburg.[19] In West Berlin, their theoretical justification was declared in the idiom of neo-Marxism: 'doing commune', we read in *Subkultur Berlin*, is also a legitimate form of production.[20]

In the early sixties, the student movement had attained intellectual stature by distancing themselves from the existentialist harmlessness of their elder siblings. The SDS delegate Elisabeth Lenk's speech to her fellow students, quoted on page 35, is symptomatic: to be revolutionary, it was not enough to sit 'in jazz basements' with haircuts 'à la Enzensberger'.[21] Instead, she demanded 'theory work' – an activity which required the discipline of 8-hour days. Those who still went to the pub afterwards either did so with a guilty conscience or were 'the movement's round-dancers', despised by the political avant-garde.[22] In Germany, too, there were hippies who would not have dreamed of getting high on difficult texts, and hippie entrepreneurs who saw the demand for a new amusements industry. Bernd Cailloux made a bundle with strobe lights and psychedelic light shows, and reinvested it in a lush drug career. But, even as a member of Hamburg's 'underground royalty' who surrounded himself with women and dealers, he was happiest partying within the four walls of his own psychedelically decorated attic flat: 'Electronics, projectors ... not everyone had that kind of home, on the interface of genuine subculture and pop hedonics ... I almost even bought a monkey for my new flat.'[23] Even if it wasn't intended to anticipate the future society, his full refrigerator stood for self-sufficiency. Cailloux continued to be a generous host until his company attracted the attention of the revenue authorities and he had to escape to West Berlin.

The barren spaces of the German cities, dramatized by Alexander Kluge in his 1966 film *Yesterday Girl*, must have harmonized with the domestic tendencies of their hipsters. It is surprising to read, in reminiscences of the sixties, that the New Left was afflicted with a pub deficit. According to the Berlin SDS activist and later Kamper adversary Klaus Laermann, 'in 1968 there was only the now almost legendary "Schotten", where people met after the big demonstrations and teach-ins.'[24] That would probably have been a corner bar, a place for a sausage and a shot-and-a-beer: the Munich equivalent is familiar from Fassbinder's early films. In those days, the *bohémien* Andreas Baader frequented a watering-hole in Charlottenburg called the S-Bahn-Quelle which no doubt looked much the same. 'In the sixties, pubs still had horse collars on the walls and mirror balls on the ceiling,' recalls Bernd Cailloux.[25] The famous 'bar scene', now the pride of every small town, wasn't even born yet. Until '68, the German bar – proverbial exceptions aside – was firmly in the hands of the demimonde and the proletariat.[26]

Pub Blather

A few years later, Klaus Laermann retraced in *Kursbuch* how West Berlin's pub landscape had evolved – one that even 'connoisseurs of the scene' could hardly keep up with. 'None of the big European cities has anything comparable, neither Amsterdam nor Rome nor London, nor any West German university town, Munich, Heidelberg or Düsseldorf.' But, even as bar owners, the '68 generation confirmed once again their weakness for home sweet home: they spread out mattresses on the floors of their discos; their pubs were piled deep with upholstered furniture. 'The ironic quotation of grandma's plush upholstery,' Laermann notes, 'serves to remove the space of the pub from the present, to make it nostalgically immune to what is happening outside.'[27] The sanctum of the living room and the bedroom proved tenacious: long after it seemed to have been overcome in the communes, it surfaced like a repressed truth in the pubs.

Merve Lowien was no friend of the 'Berlin "pub scene"'.[28] Gente had met her rival Heidi Paris in a bar in Schöneberg; when Paris joined the publishing collective, the fate of Lowien's marriage was sealed and the group's dynamic was thrown out of kilter. But Lowien's criticism of nights on the town was not fuelled merely by personal motives. To the heirs of the Frankfurt School, the 'escape from the home to the pub' seemed like selling out the ideas of '68. They watched as the utopia of the Left dissolved in beer fumes. The participant observation that Laermann published in the *Kursbuch* depicts a stifling atmosphere which still survives in a segment of the bar scene today: the furniture from junk shops, the dim lights and the rock music – to which, the ethnographer notes with a shake of his head, one did not dance in bars. The guests of the new 'nonstop party' preferred standing around. The abolition of the saloon bar's seating order, Laermann found, made it easy for them to strike up conversations. 'There is such a high degree of mobility that one gets the feeling the whole interior of the pub is within arm's reach of the bar.'[29] The increase in mobility did not seem to improve the atmosphere, however. 'That was such a depressive scene; they drank, stood around the place,' Peter Gente recalled.[30] The left that sought refuge in the pub, according to Laermann's interpretation, could no longer cope with its theory work. What helped was the bad habit of beer drinking.

But drinking played only a supporting role in this scenario of decline. 'If consuming alcohol had been the pub-goers' primary goal, they could just as well have drunk at home,' Laermann reasoned. The real problem was not the inebriation of disillusioned revolutionaries, but the 'pub blather,' growing louder by the year, that drowned out the intellectual discourse. The doctor of German letters distastefully recorded the language of Spontis at the bar: 'Woman: "Like, it's not my thing, man, I'm just not into it, I'm totally past all that relationship shit.' Man: "Yeah, like, just being together, that'd be cool, without all these silly expectations ..."' Theoretically, the first encounter of Heidi and Peter could have gone something like that too. The dominance of 'disposable language', the disdain for argument, the promiscuity of the moment: in Laermann's view, all of it degraded barroom communication to noncommittal noise. 'Meeting someone during the day whom you spoke to the night before in the bar is usually rather disconcerting. They rarely greet you; more rarely still do they invite you to visit them at home. For the home remains completely insulated from the pub.'[31] And this, in the political topography of the '68 generation, was to the advantage of the home and the detriment of the pub. It is hard to decide what is more unpleasant in Laermann's critique: the apt portrayal of the sociotope, or the condescending posture of the critic.

A good ten years later, Laermann, by this time a professor at Freie Universität, wrote another polemic in *Kursbuch*, which is remembered even today for its title: 'Lacancan und Derridada' poked fun at the fashion of French theory, blaming it for the nonsense in the German social sciences. Laermann's diagnosis of dereliction in a certain style of thinking and writing was a continuation of his criticism of Schöneberg nightlife. There is an argument to be drawn from the monotony of Laermann's allergic reaction, however: the 'ramblings of obscurantism' with which he reproaches his bosom enemy Dietmar Kamper might conceivably be a logical consequence of the 'pub blather' of the seventies ....[32]

Anyone who so vehemently opted for the language of reason must be a Habermasian. And, in fact, Habermas's theory of communicative action, as he first outlined it in 1971 in a debate with Niklas Luhmann, was Laermann's primary theoretical reference. Peter Sloterdijk once jotted down the idea of a 'book of the Eye of the World': 'One and the same state of the world looks completely different depending on whether you're looking upwards at it from chaos or downwards from the ideal. From the first angle, anything approaching order is a miracle; from the second, even the best possible reality looks scandalous.'[33] The red Suhrkamp volume in which Habermas and Luhmann developed their theories is such a book: while Luhmann observed communication from below in order to analyse the mechanisms which – against all probability – make it possible at all,

Habermas set communication in relation to a linguistical utopia.[34] The idea he developed of the ideal speech situation was so apt for comparison with all kinds of real speech situations that it was inevitable that some disciple would turn up – as Klaus Laermann did, in the event – to measure the rituals of the night out against that standard.[35] In a sense, nightlife even furnished a precedent: as the expectations of the '68 generation contracted in the seventies to the experiential space of their evenings, those evenings became a mass communication event.[36] As Bernd Cailloux recounts, many of his cohort experienced the 'most communicative era of their lives' in the pubs.[37] For them, the empowerment to speak – one of the achievements of the student movement – first occurred in the bar.[38] A theory which viewed not labour, but communication, as the constituent matter of society had to take that event seriously.

In Habermas's early work, the coffee-houses of the Glorious Revolution of 1688 are still present as the germinators of bourgeois Enlightenment, serving as the venue of a 'discussion among private people that tended to be ongoing.' But, in spite of that honour, the successors of those coffee-houses are absent from Habermas's later books. To assess the role of the hospitality industry, he limits himself to evaluating 'the literary tradition,' Luhmann notes.[39] Under the conditions of the capitalist logic of exploitation, Habermas mistrusted the emancipatory potential of evening 'leisure behaviour' – in his view, the scenario of decay probably included the substitution of alcohol for 'coffee ... which stimulated sociability.'[40] The small talk in the bars of the 1970s, as the production of a decadent culture, did not bear mentioning. At best, Klaus Laermann conceded, it had the 'minimal brand recognition of a faded utopia.'[41] The examples which Habermas himself used to defend his theory against Luhmann are drawn from the life of a professor: the 'seminar discussion' is followed by the 'informative didactic conversation,' and the day ends with the 'chat over the garden fence.'[42] These scenes are set in bucolic Upper Bavaria: in the year in which he first presented his ideas, Habermas had retreated from the Sponti capital Frankfurt to the shores of Lake Starnberg to serve as Director of the Max Planck Institute for the Study of the Scientific and Technical World. Pub blather played no part in pastoral theory design.

The Art of Having a Beer

In the late seventies, West Berlin's nightlife began to change. 'Then came punk, new painters and all that, and life shifted to the bars,' Diedrich Diederichsen wrote.[43] After the dissolution of the Merve collective, Paris and Gente too made the bars of Schöneberg their publishing office. That was the period when the art of having a beer crossed the threshold to the present. No one remembers any more the plush pubs in which the ideas of '68 decayed into melancholy: the oldest bars still preserved in the collective memory are those founded in the second wave.[44] Among these – if not an early precursor – is the Austrian restaurant Exil, which landed in 1972 like a UFO on the bank of the Landwehrkanal in Kreuzberg. With white tablecloths, fine food and an atmosphere of excessive gaiety, it disrupted the codes of the subculture. To the Kreuzberg left, bourgeois decadence in their hood may have been tantamount to fascism,[45] but to West Berlin's *bohème*, the place became a school of hedonism. Among the guests who were able to appreciate the Viennese veal cutlet and the nocturnal drinking bouts were the Merve publishers and their growing circle of friends – and celebrities such as Max Frisch, Rainer Werner Fassbinder and David Bowie.[46] The Austrian consul went to the Exil too, and drank, with the enemies of his state, the same beer they had just poured over him:[47] the restaurateurs were only in Berlin in the first place because they were wanted by the Austrian police.[48]

It is odd that it took the Vienna Actionists to bring intellectual savoir-vivre to West Berlin. In Austria, they had gained notoriety through the action 'Art and Revolution,' which has also gone down in the annals of '68 under its tabloid designation, the *Uni-Ferkelei*, or 'uni filth.' In Lecture Hall 1 of the University of Vienna, Otto Muehl, Günter Brus, Oswald Wiener and Peter Weibel had spilled their bodily fluids in front of a large audience. The fact that they did so while singing the national anthem, and sullied an Austrian flag in the process, did not help matters. Thus, the Viennese version of the Year of Rebellion culminated in a performance-art scandal. The charges pressed ranged from 'desecration of the Austrian national emblems' to 'blasphemy': reason enough for the accused to scatter in all directions. While Muehl found a new field of activity as the leader of a commune, Günter Brus and Oswald Wiener took refuge beyond the borders, moving their families to West Berlin, where the Wieners opened a restaurant to earn their living. Within the Berlin Wall, that was not difficult: 'No closing time, no business licence, no regulations.'[49]

The blasphemers against the Republic of Austria served Tafelspitz; their Exil's reputation as the locus of a new aesthetic radicalism was assured from the beginning. In the style of the historic avant-gardes, they held readings and Dadaistic lectures. The walls were soon full of works of art because of the artists who made the restaurant their living room. Günter Brus, previously a specialist in self-mutilation, painted a ceiling fresco; Dieter Roth contributed a wallpaper with a beer-glass motif.[50] Pictures turned up everywhere at that time as emblems of the new epoch – both on the walls of the in places and in the pages of the theory journals.

In the 1980s, the Exil's art collection migrated across town to Charlottenburg. By this time, Oswald Wiener had retired as a restaurateur to study computer science at Technische Universität. In 1984, he published an article in *Kursbuch* on his transition 'from dialectical to binary thinking.'[51] His partner Michel Würthle, meanwhile, after a tip-off from the RAF defence lawyer Otto Schily, had taken over a run-down restaurant in Kantstrasse.[52] Within a few years, the Paris Bar became the top address in West Berlin. With its mixture of *bohème*, celebrities and society, it reflected the booming art business which had finally shaken off the asceticism of the avant-garde. 'Ye who enter here, abandon all hope of getting out before the morning comes,' wrote Heiner Müller, himself a regular.[53] Jacob Taubes pursued his studies of the Talmud in the Paris Bar; Nicolaus Sombart wrote in 1982: 'Clearly one can go nowhere else in Berlin.'[54]

In the Jungle

In reality, there were any number of alternatives: the Risiko, originally a lesbian collective, renowned as a marketplace for hard drugs; the SO36, managed by Martin Kippenberger, which housed Berlin's first punk concerts in 1978; the Anderes Ufer (the 'other shore'),

20 In the original Dschungel at Winterfeldplatz, 1976.

Germany's first 'out' gay bar, where the painter Salomé wrapped his nude body in barbed wire the same year; the Café Mitropa, the 'informal management academy for current pop business', in Bernd Cailloux's description, where Thierry Noir and Kiddy Citny hatched a project in the early 1980s to paint the Berlin Wall. But the most important place for hedonists who were no longer interested in talk, only in partying, was Der Dschungel – 'the jungle'. Gente and Paris, nightlife aficionados, went there up to four times a week.[55]

The metamorphosis of the German student pub had begun in 1976. The battered furniture had been tossed on the junk heap, the walls painted salmon pink, the rooms reforested with plastic palm trees with plush tropical animals climbing about in them. Soon, no more soft toys were allowed; the newer style included scrap metal, tiles and neon lights that set off the guests' outfits. The long-haired regulars were joined by punks and streetwalking transsexuals from Nollendorfplatz, a block away. The bartenders played the Sex Pistols, Kraftwerk and David Bowie. The time was not yet foreseeable when a bar would have to employ DJs to cope with the dancing frenzy: this was before the autumn of '78, when the disco wave would roll across the Atlantic. In this transitional phase, the Dschungel was a place between the decades, where the codes of the left subculture got caught in the maelstrom of a cool carnival.

One evening in January of 1978, David Bowie and Michel Foucault bumped into each other here. Foucault was in Berlin as a guest of the Tunix Conference, and Heidi Paris was showing him around the Schöneberg night spots. David Bowie lived around the corner and often went out in the neighbourhood. He had just released *Heroes*, and Suhrkamp had just published the first volume of Foucault's *History of Sexuality*. The German edition of *Playboy* published articles on Bowie and Foucault in the same issue, stylizing them as opposites: the sex symbol contrasted with the 'Paris left-wing philosopher' whose theory about the interaction of power and sex must be classified, according to the magazine, as anti-pleasure. An epic killjoy, he 'threatened to expand his theory of torture into six volumes', to which the *Playboy* editors sighed: 'Bonjour tristesse.' And yet Foucault too was perfectly capable of enjoying himself in Berlin's bar scene. The narrative of biopower could easily have spun off a wicked little theory of the disco. He never wrote such a theory, however – perhaps he was enchanted by the preening peacocks. Perhaps he found the atmosphere so fascinating that his theoretical acumen went soggy, while his first ideas flashed for a philosophy of the *art de vivre* that he would later pursue in the darkrooms of San Francisco. In the last years of his life, Foucault studied the question of how to master one's life by giving it the beautiful forms of a work of art. The question may well date back to the Dionysian Schöneberg of 1978.[56]

Soon afterwards, the Dschungel moved to a new location, where it supplanted a Chinese restaurant. The metamorphosis which had begun two years before was now complete: the caterpillar of the Sponti bar had blossomed into the butterfly of a chic New Wave club. What Foucault had not furnished was supplied by his translator Ulrich Raulff in the pages of *Tumult* – his study on 'Disco' fit the new Dschungel to a T, describing it as a Berlin counterpart to Studio 54: 'A glittering dance floor, surrounded by darkness, lightning, thunder and voices out of the darkness, palm jungles, billowing fog, dramatic staircases, slightly overexcited staff.'[57] Instead of beer, the drinks were cocktails and vintage champagne. Instead of jeans and leather jackets, a motley fancy-dress ball surged through the night. The only thing that had survived the move was the palm trees, in whose neon-lit shade the crowd was cooler than ever. 'Cool meant transfigured, unfriendly, arrogant, tight-lipped, a wee bit adventurous,' recalls one of the regulars from this period.[58] No wonder Baudrillard was the theoretician of the hour. Those who got in to the Dschungel could count themselves among the elite of West Berlin's nightlife. Raulff decrypts the game of 'exclusion and inclusion' as an essential element of the disco dispositive.[59] Friends of the house were given coloured plastic tokens as admission passes, while everyone else simply had to hope, just as in New York, that either their appearance or their acquaintance would get them in.

Paris and Gente were regulars. They went to the Dschungel to digest their *Anti-Oedipus* discussions, just as they went there to show their Parisian authors a good time. But the disco was also relevant to their work as theory publishers. Some of the texts they began bringing out in German in 1977, written by French professors back in the early seventies, unexpectedly found a context in Schöneberg by night. The ragtag public that gathered night after night in the Dschungel: a 'patchwork of minorities.' The carousel of fashion, spinning faster every year: an ironic repetition of the left subculture's splintering, an 'allusion to nothing.'[60] Norbert Bolz, Taubes's assistant, announced the birth of 'pop philosophy' in 1981 – a genre largely unknown in Germany up to then. Although he garnished his essay with quotations from Jimi Hendrix and the Rolling Stones, he was not pleading for the development of a new field of objects for theory: 'It's about style,' Bolz stated. What he meant was 'a thinking in currents, not concerned with meaning,' which he imagined as 'sexual and decisionistic.' Deleuze and Guattari, the precursors of this style of thinking, played with the idea of a pop philosophy themselves in the 1970s: 'RHIZOMATICS = POP ANALYSIS' was one of the equations they had set in all caps in *A Thousand Plateaus*. In his interviews with Claire Parnet, Deleuze explained that he composed his lectures in the same way as Bob Dylan composed his songs: 'A very lengthy preparation, yet no method, nor rules, nor recipes.' Bolz's recommendation to read *Anti-Oedipus* 'as you would go to the cinema or play a record' was thus right in line with the book's authors.[61]

'Did you know', Peter Gente wrote to the East Berlin Romanist Karlheinz Barck in 1988, 'that Roland Barthes was a passionate disco-goer?'[62] As the publishers' hours grew later, such correlations took on increasing importance. After the French in the 1970s, their discovery of the 1980s was pop music. A short time before Barthes's death, they tried to interest him in writing a book about – reggae! They were planning to publish texts by Patti Smith, and 'do something together with Brian Eno', who lived in West Berlin.[63] A book by the pop conceptualist would have fit the publishers' catalogue perfectly, but no Merve book by Eno, nor by Patti Smith, ever appeared. Instead, they published texts by Blixa Bargeld of Die Toten Hosen, *Geniale Dilletanten* by Wolfgang Müller on the punk festival of the same name, and Shuhei Hosokawa's *Walkman Effect*, of Deleuzian inspiration. While Ulrich Raulff felt an apocalyptic anxiety over the total saturation of cities with sound systems, the Japanese musicologist saw the 'boy with roller skates eating McDonald, drinking Coke, and listening to Michael Jackson through walkman' as the prototype of a new culture.[64] Hosokawa asked the publishers to bring his Merve book to the attention of Paul Virilio, Blixa Bargeld and Umberto Eco.[65] At the international semiotics conference in Urbino where Gente and Hosokawa had met in 1981, Eco too had danced to loud disco music.[66]

Klaus Laermann's scepticism notwithstanding, the theory discourse did not come to a halt after hours. In fact, the weariness with too much 'abstract thought' was propitious to certain theories.[67] 'Always on hand', writes Bernd Cailloux, who moved in the same circles as Gente and Paris, was 'a group discussing Hegel or Heidegger in the less plot-driven corners of the disco'.[68] The philosophy of history's 'difficult signs' was still in circulation, but the new culture was playing its part in the dismantling of dialectics.[69] In the age of 'discourse pogo', as the 1980s have been called, apodictic sleight of hand carried the day against airtight deduction, and names triumphed over arguments.[70] To dialectically trained objectors, this style of thinking was synonymous with 'left-wing Decisionism'. Its 'unambiguous simplicity', Wilhelm Gottschalch wrote in Rowohlt's *Literaturmagazin*, denied the 'ambivalence of all social phenomena'.[71] Stark contrasts tended to short-circuit the discussion – indeed, that was part of the attraction of the new style of thinking. The brightness needed was generated by alcohol, the chroniclers of the present agreed. 'Not drinking makes you sad, gluttonous, fat and stupid', Rainald Goetz found in 1984, after five years of continuous drinking. 'Cautious drinking on the other hand makes you the opposite, that is, good and knackered.'[72] Gilles Deleuze, too, mentioned the philosophical significance of alcohol in his interviews with Claire Parnet.[73] Michael Rutschky, reflecting in 1983 on what was necessary in order for people to talk to one another, described the situation as quite un-dialectical: 'The gradual, subliminal, ultimately complete destruction of inhibitions by drinking white wine is the constantly repeated proof that communication with the outside world is *in general* possible.'[74]

Above the Clouds

No such excesses are associated with Niklas Luhmann. 'At 11:00 p.m. I am usually lying in bed reading a few things that I can still digest at that hour', he testified to the daily *Frankfurter Rundschau* in 1985.[75] The importance given to nightlife in his communication theory, presented in 1971 as an alternative to Habermas, is hence all the more surprising. Among the examples Luhmann contrasts with Habermas's idea of the ideal speech situation, we find queues, 'bigger parties' and 'discussions in bars':[76] Luhmann sees these, not as varieties of chatter, but as paradigmatic – and, therefore, instructive – cases of communication. Berlin intellectuals who had learned to decipher the hidden messages of the philosophers in Jacob Taubes's seminars before going out drinking at night cannot have mistaken the arcane meaning of the Habermas–Luhmann controversy: in reality, it was an obfuscated dispute over the status of barroom conversations.[77]

A dive into the basement of Luhmann's footnotes is necessary to pick up the trail of drinking establishments that runs through his work – a trail that leads straight to California. Luhmann is so notorious for his apocryphal references that some readers say he invented the most important ones himself. Among his sources is the dissertation of an Erving Goffman student named Sherri Cavan, which he cites with a persistence that suggests he is indebted to her for fundamental insights.[78] The anthropologist Cavan had toured the bars of San

Francisco in the mid-sixties to observe their guests drinking. The laconism of her ethnographic miniatures, the best of which recall Raymond Carver, must have appealed to the laconic Luhmann.

But the critical point was something else: Luhmann found in Cavan's work a 'case study of situations in which the making and ending of contact is facilitated.'[79] Whoever walks into a bar in San Francisco tacitly accepts the rules of Californian nightlife, under which anyone may speak to anyone.[80] In this society game, the object was not to examine claims of truth, and by no means to arrive at a consensus – after which the conversation probably would have petered out. The object was to be in contact with one another and, in the ideal case, to get into bed with one another. The fact that that usually didn't work out, and that the undaunted guests nevertheless kept on trying – this, to Luhmann, was the 'everyday miracle' of communication.[81] His theory spelled out the realization that communication was unlikely, and that society consisted of the sum of the precautions taken to make it more probable. Bars practically offered laboratory conditions for corroborating observations. Rainald Goetz, who found confirmation of his own experiences in Luhmann, paraphrased Luhmann's theory in 1983, writing 'that communication is impossible, there's no such thing, and therefore it has to be attempted again and again in a highly controlled, highly calculated, highly impassioned way.'[82] He did so, evening after evening, in the bars of Munich.

As a young *Spex* contributor, Goetz gave short shrift to the 'Francosophical mumblings' disseminated by the 'silly Merve Verlag,'[83] and systems theory was certainly worlds apart from the sound that Paris and Gente imported from Paris. In the course of the 1980s, however, the Merve publishers also succumbed to the charms of the new objectivity. Luhmann's delayed reception history merits a study of its own. Luhmann himself was of the opinion that he found his best readers where neo-Marxism had prepared the ground for abstract thinking.[84] But most of those who converted to systems theory had first broken with dialectics. The disputation with Habermas had earned Luhmann the reputation of a challenger of the Frankfurt School – in fact, according to a 1971 review by Bazon Brock in the *Frankfurter Allgemeine Zeitung*, Bielefeld led Frankfurt by 8 to 7.[85] Luhmann's theory would top the league tables only in the climate of the

1980s, however, when theory and engagement diverged, and difficult thinkers took on the habitus of *impassibilité*. A 1984 debate between Luhmann and the peace and ecology researcher Robert Jungk, later published by Merve, reveals by its tone alone the chasms that yawned between the 'jet-set Christian Democrats' of Bielefeld and the new social movements. Jungk: 'The systems you set up, Mr Luhmann, are in reality all systems of fear.' Luhmann: 'I find this view too simplistic.'[86]

Luhmann's coolness was irresistible to intellectuals who cultivated a posthistorical equanimity. After all the theoretical excitement, it offered a possible last kick. Luhmann first published his theory in its totality the year Foucault died. He expressed its aspirations in an image of flying above a dense blanket of clouds, below which lay the 'extinct volcanoes of Marxism.'[87] For many readers, its conception was most comparable with art. A fellow sociologist wrote that it was 'more closely related to Joseph Beuys than to the sober efforts at a mathematizing analysis of social networks.'[88] Luhmann also offered a good example of the aestheticization of truth, which Jacob Taubes had identified as the signature of the age.[89] For all its scholarly acumen, his theory also had a seductive elegance. And it also plugged into the intellectual situation in another respect: with his message that the world's complexity necessitated differentiation, Luhmann took up the legacy of the radical thinkers of the interwar period – and lent it his politically tempered form. The pathos of decision, which the renegades from dialectics had sought and found first in Walter Benjamin, and later in Carl Schmitt, was encountered again in Luhmann – although couched in the austere formulas of a mathematician by the name of George Spencer-Brown.[90]

In the summer of 1987, the Luhmann student Dirk Baecker proposed to Merve a book of Luhmann's collected interviews: 'All of them are rather witty commentaries on current events and impressions, and can also serve as introductions to Luhmann's characteristic theory style.'[91] The publishers liked the idea. However, in order 'not to be the publisher that always makes these little booklets with the big theoreticians' interviews, but one that explores that genre for its possibilities', they asked Baecker to contribute his thoughts on the epistemology of the interviews by way of an introduction.[92] The resulting book, *Archimedes und wir* [Archimedes and us], went to press just in time for Luhmann's sixtieth birthday. The pieces in it add up to an intellectual character sketch. As proponents of direct contact with their authors, Paris and Gente went to Bielefeld in December of 1987 to present their book in person at the buffet of the university's International Centre. The party which followed was worthy of the name – 'surely not by Berlin standards, but for Bielefeld', Dirk Baecker's co-editor Georg Stanitzek wrote to the publishers a week later. In a break from his habit, they had seen Luhmann by night. The guest of honour seemed to be quite pleased: 'In retrospect,' Stanitzek wrote, 'Luhmann too, who ordinarily looks every gift horse in the mouth, expressed his enjoyment – noteworthy to say the least, when you know his customary reserve.'[93]

Epilogue: After Theory?

When the Berlin Wall collapsed less than two years later, it was more or less incidental to the Merve publishers: in their intellectual geography, the German unification had no significance that might have pushed their work in a particular direction. If anything, it threatened their habitat and shook the ground under their business model. The end of 'the Western world's subsidized madhouse', as Thomas Kapielski once called West Berlin, would also mean the loss of a preserve for precarious forms of enterprise.[1] As if they had seen it coming, Gente and Paris brought out the book *Aisthesis: Wahrnehmung heute, oder Perspektiven einer anderen Ästhetik* [Aesthesis: perception today, or prospects for a different aesthetics] with the East German branch of the historic publishing house Reclam just in time for the unification. In fact, the German–German collaboration between Merve and Reclam had been in preparation since 1988. In spite of an editorial afterword asserting that the book presents a new way of thinking, and not a retrospective on a publishing house project, the essays in *Aisthesis* read like a stock-taking at the end of an era.[2] Deleuze, Foucault, Virilio, Baudrillard – the book was practically a Merve's Greatest Hits compiled for East German readers. In the early 1990s, the Merve publishers were following the founding years of Berlin techno in Mitte, previously the westernmost borough of East Berlin. In the medium term, however, they loosened their territorial ties still further. Heidi Paris accepted a visiting professorship in design at the academy of fine arts in Kassel. Peter Gente began developing an interest in Asia. They were able to place their finances on a secure footing by co-opting an Austrian patron. From 1991 on, Merve was able to afford the production of hardcover books, and, at the same time, the theory that Merve had been importing to West Germany since the 1970s began to be received in German universities.[3]

The 1990s were the decade of Cultural Studies and the breakthrough of pop theory.[4] The front lines of theoretical debates now ran right through the middle of the academic world. Faculties in the US were divided by the 'science wars';[5] intradisciplinary battles were fought in the reunified Germany too. When I returned to Berlin from Bologna in 1997, Foucault was still fair subject matter for a Ph.D. thesis at Humboldt-Universität, but a renowned social historian refused to grade a term paper of mine because of its too-conspicuous Foucault references – thus giving me ample material for conversations at parties. Derrida or Habermas? Lyotard or Luhmann? These were decisions of existential moment. But French theory was in the process of storming the last bastions of the social sciences. Just a short time later, it was to be part of academic business-as-usual in Germany too. What it lost in its triumph was its aura of danger.[6] Michael Hardt and Antonio Negri's *Empire* was a last big theory bestseller in 2000. Soon afterwards, however, well-founded case studies became dominant in the universities. The analysts of the present diagnosed a relapse of reality.[7] In 2001, two airliners demolished the World Trade Center. Two years later, Terry Eagleton, who had once paved the way for theory to enter British literary studies, published a book with the title *After Theory*.[8]

Since then, theory has made a comeback. A second disaster in New York, the bankruptcy of Lehman Brothers, helped to bring the interregnum to its end. They have all returned: the French post-structuralists, the Italian post-Operaists, and those who had remained loyal to Marxism all these years.[9] A situation in which both the market and the state have lost a tremendous amount of credibility should be ideal for new, pathbreaking ideas. But it is hard to avoid the impression that the present-day theory discourse is in the as-if mode. Have difficult ideas returned – as a retro fashion? The German cultural pages have been receptive for some years now to the observation that Foucault in the sixties matched his suits to the beige of his Jaguar.[10] The West German theory publishers have turned over their papers to the archives, and their former readers have written their memoirs. The USA, where the French shaped a generation of college students in the 1980s, has blessed us with the genre of the theory novel. After the theorization of narrative, is the new trend now the narration of theory? Could it be that theory is now more interesting as an object of literature than as an instrument for analysing it?[11] A 2009 conference on 'theory theory', held at the venue of legendary theory symposia in Dubrovnik, came to the conclusion that 'both the theory boom and the farewell to theory, as well as theory apathy and even opposition to theory, denote theoretical positions'. That sounds suspiciously like a rearguard action.[12]

In late summer of 2002, Heidi Paris took her life. A difficult personal situation and the 'gloom of the two-thousands' had toppled her fragile psychic equilibrium.[13] There were authors who advised Peter Gente to give up Merve,[14] but he wasn't ready to do that. Not until five years later did he retire to Southeast Asia. I had nearly completed my research for this book when I received the news of his death: he died at the age of 78 in Chiang Mai in northern Thailand. Four weeks later, after his ashes had been brought to Germany, a burial was held in Berlin. It was a cold, sunny day in March 2014. Those who had gathered at the cemetery in Schöneberg were still wearing their scarves and winter coats. They filled every seat in the chapel. Standing at the back, I tried to see who had come: professors, translators, established figures, ageing bohemians ... I had interviewed some of them in the preceding years; others had mistrusted my inquiries. In their ordinary lives, many of these people probably had little to do with one another, but to me, they all belonged together: here were the minds of old West Berlin assembled. There was a reading of Maurice Blanchot's 'The Name Berlin'; loudspeakers played James Tenney's electronic music. The eulogies called to mind a past era. After the burial, the gathering continued in the publishing offices of Merve with beer, talk and tobacco. The spring catalogue was stacked on tables in preparation for the upcoming Leipzig Book Fair. Happily, there are successors who are continuing the business, and there are new Merve books, in timeless modern covers, printed on cheap paper, with titles such as *Kunst an sich* [Art in itself] and *Akzeleration*. The future of Merve seems to be secure for the time being. The future of theory is uncertain.

Appendix: Translations of Illustrations

Figure 5 Louis Althusser, *Für Marx*, Frankfurt: Suhrkamp, 1968

[The definitive resultant will be the resultant of an infinity of resultants, that is, the product of an] infinite proliferation of parallelograms. Once again, either we trust to the infinite (that is, the indeterminate, epistemological void) for the production in the final resultant of *the* resultant we are hoping to *deduce*: the one that will coincide with economic determination in the last instance, etc., that is, *we trust a void to produce a fullness* (for example, within the limits of the purely *formal* model of the composition of forces, it does not escape Engels that the said forces present might cancel one another out, or oppose one another . . . under such conditions, what is there to prove that the global resultant might not be *nothing*, for example, or at any rate, what is there to prove that *it will be what we want, the economic*, and not something else, politics, or religion? At this formal level *there is no assurance of any kind as to the content of the resultant*, of *any* resultant). Or we surreptitiously *substitute the result we expect for the final resultant*, and duly rediscover in it, along with other, microscopic determinations, the macroscopic determinations which were secreted in the conditioning of the individual at the outset; this expected result, these macroscopic determinations will be the economy. I am obliged to repeat what I have just said of what was beneath the immediate level: either we stay within the *problem* Engels poses for his object (individual wills), in which case we fall into the epistemological void of the infinity of parallelograms and their resultants; or else, quite simply, we *accept* the Marxist solution, but then we have found no *basis* for it, and it was not worth the trouble of *looking for it.*

So the problem we face now is this: why is everything so clear and harmonious at the level of *individual wills,* whereas *beneath this level* or *beyond it,* it all becomes either empty or tautological? How is it that this problem, so *well posed,* corresponding so well to *the object* in which it is posed, should become incapable of solution as soon as we move away from its initial object? A question which must remain the riddle of riddles until we realize that it is *this initial object* which commands both *the transparency of the problem and the impossibility of its solution.*

Indeed, Engels's whole proof hangs by that very particular *object, individual wills* interrelated according to the physical model of the parallelogram of forces. *This is his real presupposition, both in method and in theory.* In this respect the model does have meaning: it can be given a *content,* it can be *manipulated.* It 'describes' apparently 'elementary' bilateral human relations of rivalry, competition or co-operation. At this level what was previously the infinite diversity of microscopic causes might seem to be organized in real, and discrete, and visible unities. At this level accident becomes man, what was movement above becomes conscious will. This is where everything really begins, and it is from this point that *deduction* must begin. But unfortunately this so secure basis establishes nothing at all, this so clear principle merely leads to darkness – unless it withdraws into itself, reiterating *its own transparency* as a fixed proof of all that is expected of it. Precisely what is *this transparency*? We must recognize that *this transparency is nothing but the transparency of the presuppositions of classical bourgeois ideology and bourgeois political economy.* What is the starting-point for this classical ideology, whether it is Hobbes on the composition of the conatus, Locke and Rousseau on the generation of the general will, Helvetius and Holbach on the production of the general interest, Smith and Ricardo (the texts abound) on atomistic behaviour, what is the starting-point if not precisely the confrontation of these famous *individual wills* which are by no means the starting-point for reality, but for a *representation* of reality, for a *myth* intended [to provide a *basis* for] *the objectives.*
(Louis Althusser, *For Marx,* trans. Ben Brewster, New York: Vintage, 1970, 123–5.)

Figure 6 Charles Bettelheim, *Über das Fortbestehen von Warenverhältnissen in den 'sozialistischen Ländern'*, Berlin: Merve, 1970

MERVE-VERLAG of Berlin is a socialist collective which publishes the series INTERNATIONAL MARXIST DISCUSSION.

We do our budgeting, accounting, printing, distribution, etc., communally – that is, sharing the work involved in the publication of the texts. Self-agitation and acquiring the foundations of Marxist theory are an integral part of our work as a collective.

We publish work on issues of Marxist theory and non-revisionist practice regularly (15–20 issues per year) in the series INTERNATIONAL MARXIST DISCUSSION. These works are intended to contribute to clarifying the concept of revisionism and thus to promote the development of theory and strategy, which all revolutionary practice requires. Within this scope are works on the theory of imperialism, class, the state and the party. We will address both the methodological problems of such theories and their expression in the strategies of revolutionary groups.

MERVE-VERLAG is not a profit-making enterprise.

Figure 7 Oskar Negt and Alexander Kluge, *Öffentlichkeit und Erfahrung*, Frankfurt: Suhrkamp, 1972

Translation of right-hand page:

[This is the underlying reason for the predominance of technology and of the industrial model itself, which determines television production, in particular the production of series, and which is expressed not only by its ready-made character[22] but also by its apparent] opposite – the exaggerated insistence of well-known directors on special requests and *idées fixes*. A possible response to this situation would be for directors, writers, or editors to organize themselves. Forerunners of such an organization are the German Writers' Union (VS), the Authors' Publishing House, the filmmakers syndicate and association of cinema and television directors, along with the producers' charters of the networks. One would need to develop these rudimentary forms of organization into a substantive, cooperative operation.

However, one should not regard the manufacturing mode of production used by individual television teams as merely backward. The industrial stage of this production will not consist simply of an intensification or rationalization of current procedures in the making of films and television plays. Rather, this presupposes a discipline, cooperation, and productivity in the creative and intellectual process that does not exist today. Nor can such forms of production be developed among the creators themselves; they demand motivation by the more evolved needs of the audience. In the context of the present situation, it is more correct to say that the artisanal production of individual items, which lags behind even the manufactural state, is in a better [position to respond to the consciousness and fantasy of concrete groups of viewers].

[It possesses amazing capacities for innovation that open up the potential for television to develop] forms of aesthetic expression unknown to any other medium. Recently, individual authors (*Autoren*) have begun to use these means (in the show 'Baff' and in individual show episodes, for example, or in the case of Zadek), nonetheless failing to appreciate the full development potential of this technology with their exclusive privileging of formal tricks. The contradiction arises less because of a lack of goodwill or simply because of the organizational separation of the technical and creative hierarchies, but rather, above all, because of the different levels of cooperation and societilization of the outdated creative and the highly advanced technical components of television production. Because of this, there . . .

(Negt and Kluge, *Public Sphere and Experience*, trans. Labanyi, Daniel and Oksiloff, 113–14.)

Figure 8 Jean-François Lyotard, *Das Patchwork der Minderheiten*, Berlin: Merve, 1977

Back cover:

Jean-François Lyotard, born in 1925, was active during the Algerian War in the radical leftist group associated with the journal *Socialisme ou Barbarie*; later Professor of Philosophy at Nanterre, now at the University of Paris VIII (Vincennes). By now, he is something of a barbarian himself in the 'empire' of socialism – and not only there – an outsider perforating the borders of the Empire and shredding the categories of the Centre.

In the texts collected here, he writes about the minorities, about the polymorphous and precarious patchwork they form. He traces their ruses and feints which skew the monotonous, centralized spaces, their movements in the tricky time of desire, and infiltrates with them the economic, political discourses to install paradoxes that burst their order and logic.

These operations are affirmative through and through, and their method is not criticism so much as a sophisticated game of traps, intensities and perspectives.

Figure 9 Pages 6 and 7 of Gilles Deleuze and Félix Guattari, *Anti-Oedipus*, trans. Bernd Schwibs, Winterthur: Suhrbier, 1974

1 Desiring-Production

It is at work everywhere, functioning smoothly at times, at other times in fits and starts. It breathes, it heats, it eats. It shits and fucks. What a mistake to have ever said the id. Everywhere it is machines – real ones, not figurative ones: machines driving other machines, machines being driven by other machines, with all the necessary couplings and connections. An organ-machine is plugged into an energy-source-machine: the one produces a flow that the other interrupts. The breast is a machine that produces milk, and the mouth a machine coupled to it. The mouth of the anorexic wavers between several functions: its possessor is uncertain as to whether it is an eating-machine, an anal machine, a talking-machine, or a breathing machine (asthma attacks). Hence we are all handymen: each with his little machines. For every organ-machine, an energy-machine: all the time, flows and interruptions. Judge Schreber has sunbeams in his ass. A solar anus. And rest assured that it works: Judge Schreber feels something, produces something, and is capable of explaining the process theoretically. Something is produced: the effects of a machine, not mere metaphors.

A schizophrenic out for a walk is a better [Handwritten note in the margin: Which illness is chic?] model than a neurotic lying on the analyst's couch. A breath of fresh air, a relationship with the outside world. Lenz's stroll, for example, as reconstructed by Büchner. This walk outdoors is different from the moments when Lenz finds himself closeted with his pastor, who forces him to situate himself socially, in relationship to the God of established religion, in relationship to his father, to his mother. While taking a stroll outdoors, on the other hand, he is in the mountains, amid falling snowflakes, with other gods or

without any gods at all, without a family, without a father or a mother, with nature. 'What does my father want? Can he offer me more than that? Impossible. Leave me in peace.' Everything is a machine. Celestial machines, the stars or rainbows in the sky, alpine machines – all of them connected to those of his body. The continual whirr of machines. 'He thought that it must be a feeling of endless bliss to ...
(From Deleuze and Guattari, *Anti-Oedipus*, trans. Hurley, Seem and Lane, 8–9.)

Figure 11 Michel Foucault in West Berlin, Güntzelstrasse, Pension Finck, 1978

We have arrived. I'm at Pension Finck (54 Güntzelstrasse). Restaurant next door until 4:30, then TU. I'll try to phone around 6 or 7 o'clock. Michel.

Figure 14 *Traverses: Revue trimestrielle*, 32 (1984)

The Child in the Bubble

The most original form of epidemic today is no longer the primitive form, it is the subsequent, reactive form of its own antidote, of its counterpart, of its dissuasion. It is no longer illness which is proliferating, but rather security. It is no longer bacteria which proliferates, but antibiotics. It is no longer criminal mentality which proliferates, but police mentality and all the forces – of detection, prevention, dissuasion – which extend their repressive network of anticipation towards states and spirits.

If we therefore distance ourselves from the original fatality of sources of death, it is in order to better approach a collective obsession with life, health, diet and therapies, both mental and biological, of a secular and still ritualised purity, of bodies and the environment, which present with exactly the same qualities as the old lethal epidemics. In the rush to eliminate sources of evil, it is the counter contagion, the proliferation of benefits, of fertility, of vitality, of security, of visibility and of transparency, which risk threatening the existence of the species.

■

The great and lethal epidemics have disappeared. They have made way for a single epidemic: the proliferation of humans themselves. Overpopulation constitutes a kind of slow and irresistible epidemic, the opposite of the plague and cholera. We may always hope that it will come to an end by itself, once sated of living things, as once did the plague, once it had had its fill of cadavers. But will this same regulatory reflex play out with regards to this excess of life as it did towards excess deaths? Because excess of life is even more lethal.

■

From the savage child to the bubble child. This child, protected from all contamination by an artificial, immunising space, caressed by his mother through the glass walls with her plastic gloves, and who laughs and grows up in his extra-terrestrial atmosphere under...
(Jean Baudrillard, 'The Child in the Bubble'.)

Figure 15 Architectural Misunderstandings Would Like to Become a Book: Martin Kippenberger Sends Greetings from Tenerife, 1987

D[ear] H. P., d[ear] P. G.,
Architectural sculpture, intentional and anticipated misunderstandings, which only want to be love, are photographed on Mother Earth and would like to become a book!?
Greetings Martin K.

Figure 17 Endpapers of Ernst Jünger, *Auf den Marmorklippen*, Hamburg: Hanseatische Verlagsanstalt, 1939
Inscription:

For Peter
'... We draw nearer to that secret ...'
hparis, September '83

Figure 19 Dirk Baecker proposes Luhmann's interviews to Merve

Dr Dirk Baecker
Schäferstrasse 15
4800 Bielefeld 1
Tel. 0521/870931
5 August 1987

Merve Verlag GmbH
Crelle Str. 22
1000 Berlin 62

Dear publishers,
A few years ago, it must have been in 1981 after my return from a year studying in Paris, I wrote to you how gratifying I find your innovative audacity in the German book market. I was thinking then mainly of the introduction of translations of a few works by Virilio and Baudrillard, whom everyone is talking about now.

Today, I would like to present to you two book projects of my own which would fit well in your tradition of dispensing with tradition in favour of innovation.

The first project concerns a little volume with the collected interviews of Niklas Luhmann. You have no doubt observed, in the *Frankfurter Rundschau* and in the *taz*, for example, that Luhmann has developed a very cool and ironic, occasionally caustic interview style, sometimes reminiscent in its self-reflexive commentary of [Paul Valéry's] 'Monsieur Teste', restoring to the genre a certain literary energy. All of them are rather witty commentaries on current events and impressions, and can also serve as introductions to Luhmann's characteristic theory style. There are some interviews published in Italy (in *Unità*, *Rinascità*) and some here, which together could make a nice little book.

The second project concerns the publishing exploit of the translation and first compilation of articles by one of the cleverest and most playful advocates of the new cybernetics: the English architect and philosopher of cybernetics Ranulph Glanville. Glanville excels in little showpieces of epistemological reflection; combines as hardly anyone before imaginative literary philosophizing with portentous mathematical models of the interaction of objects with objects, subjects with subjects. After reading Glanville, as after a reading of Wittgenstein, nothing is the same.

I have approval for these projects from Luhmann as well as from Glanville. Thus all you need to do, if you are interested, is take them.

I would be very glad of a positive answer and remain with best regards
[signed]

Notes

Introduction: What Was Theory?

1 Andreas Baader to Ello Michel, 21 August 1968, quoted in Klaus Stern and Jörg Herrmann, *Andreas Baader: Das Leben eines Staatsfeindes*, Munich: dtv, 2007, fig. 40; cf. 110–16, 177.

2 On the 'highly theoretical' motivation of the first-generation Red Army Faction, see Karl Heinz Bohrer, 'The Three Cultures', in *Observations on the 'Spiritual Situation of the Age'*, ed. Jürgen Habermas, trans. Andrew Buchwalter, Cambridge, Mass.: MIT Press, 1984, 147.

3 Quoted in 'Marcuse: Hilfe von Arbeitslosen', in *Der Spiegel*, 21:25 (1967), 103.

4 Cf. Nikolaus Wegmann, 'Wie kommt die Theorie zum Leser? Der Suhrkamp-Verlag und der Ruhm der Systemtheorie', in *Soziale Systeme*, 16:2 (2010), 463.

5 Cf. Sabine Vogel, 'Die Kunst des Verschwindens: Es begann im Geist der 68er Bewegung; Jetzt hat der Berliner Buchverleger Peter Gente sein Lebenswerk, den Merve Verlag, weitergegeben', in *Berliner Zeitung*, 2 January 2008.

6 Ulrich Raulff, 'Tod einer Buchmacherin: Der Merve Verlag und seine Leser haben Heidi Paris verloren', in *Süddeutsche Zeitung*, 19 September 2002; cf. Dietmar Dath, 'Schwester Merve: Zum Tod der Verlegerin Heidi Paris', in *Frankfurter Allgemeine Zeitung*, 20 September 2002.

7 After years of archival research, Marchetti published his findings in a scholarly and voluminous work that should have been translated long

ago: Valerio Marchetti, *L'invenzione della bisessualità: Discussioni fra teologi, medici, e giuristi del XVII secolo sull'ambiguità delle corpi e delle anime*, Milan: Mondadori, 2001.

8 I mean the Merve books Michel Foucault, *Mikrophysik der Macht*, trans. Hans-Joachim Metzger, Berlin: Merve, 1976, and Paul Veyne, *Der Eisberg der Geschichte: Foucault revolutioniert die Historie* [The iceberg of history: Foucault revolutionizes history], trans. Karin Tholen-Struthoff, Berlin: Merve, 1981.

9 Quoted in Merve Lowien, *Weibliche Produktivkraft: Gibt es eine andere Ökonomie? Erfahrungen aus einem linken Projekt* [Female productive power: is there a different economics? Experience of a leftist project], Berlin: Merve, 1977, 153. On Gente's circle of acquaintance, see Jürg Altwegg, 'Die Merve-Kulturen: Ein Verlags- und Verlegerporträt', in *Die Zeit*, 22 July 1983; and Heinz Bude, 'Die Suche nach dem Unmöglichen: Paul Arnheim und die Bücher' [The search for the impossible: Paul Arnheim and books], in Bude, *Das Altern einer Generation: Die Jahrgänge 1938 bis 1948*, Frankfurt: Suhrkamp, 1995, 225. The pseudonymous Paul Arnheim of Bude's study is Peter Gente.

10 Email to the author, 9 December 2011.

11 Altwegg, 'Die Merve-Kulturen', mentions that there were Merve books among the effects of the Stammheim prisoners. According to Stern and Herrmann, *Andreas Baader*, 177, many leftist publishers provided their books to the terrorists at no cost.

12 Jacob Taubes, 'Secondary Recommendation on the Working Plan and Application for a Graduate Stipend of Hans-Peter Gente', 15 July 1974: Merve archives, Karlsruhe Centre for Art and Media Technology (ZKM).

13 Henning Ritter, *Notizhefte*, Berlin Verlag, 2010, 24.

14 A more nuanced view is in order here. As Lorenz Jäger has remarked, the cohort born around 1935 produced the best *observers* of the '68 activists – who were a few years younger than themselves. Peter Gente, born in 1936, could be counted among those observers. See Lorenz Jäger, 'Die Jahre, die ihr nicht mehr kennt: Mission Zeitbruch; Fotos von Abisag Tüllmann im Historischen Museum Frankfurt', in *Frankfurter Allgemeine Zeitung*, 26 November 2010.

15 On the problem of gender roles in the Merve collective, see Lowien, *Weibliche Produktivkraft*. See also Wolfert von Rahden and Ulrich Raulff, 'Distanzgesten: Ein Gespräch über das Zeitschriftenmachen', interview

with Moritz Neuffer and Morten Paul, in *Grundlagerforschung für eine linke Praxis in den Geisteswissenschaften*, 1 (2014), 67–9.

16 The video adaptation of Heiner Müller's text 'Bildbeschreibung' was never made, to my knowledge. See the extensive documentation of the project in the Merve Archives.

17 Merve Verlag to Sylvère Lotringer, 25 March 1981: Merve Archives. The outgoing correspondence of the Merve publishers is quoted here and subsequently from archived drafts, some of which were posted in translation.

18 Heidi Paris, *Drei Reden zum Design: Der Spaghettistuhl* [Three talks on design: the spaghetti chair], Berlin: Merve, 2012, 10. On Berlin's traditional self-identification with the zeitgeist, see Patrick Eiden-Offe, 'Hipster-Biedermeier und Vormärz-Eckensteher (und immer wieder Berlin)', in *Merkur*, 786 (2014), 980–8.

19 George Steiner, 'Adorno: Love and Cognition', in *Times Literary Supplement*, 9 March 1973, 255.

20 According to recent research on literary genres, reader expectations play a key part in the emergence of genres. Cf. Wilhelm Vosskamp, 'Gattungen als literarisch-soziale Institutionen', in *Textsortenlehre: Gattungsgeschichte*, ed. Walter Hinck, Heidelberg: Quelle & Meyer, 1977, 27–44. For new thoughts, see Franco Moretti, *Graphs, Maps, Trees: Abstract Models for a Literary History*, London: Verso, 2005.

21 'The texts we devoured in those days stimulated movement. Whether the middle Marcuse, Walter Benjamin, the early Marx or certain chapters of *Capital* – they were interchangeable. What mattered was definitively escaping the stifling air of the 1950s', Helmut Lethen once said about reading theory in the sixties. 'Fantasia contrappuntistica: Vom Ton der Väter zum Sound der Söhne', interview with Helmut Lethen, in Sabine Sanio, *1968 und die Avantgarde: Politisch-ästhetische Wechselwirkungen in der westlichen Welt*, Sinzig: Studio, 2008, 98. Especially noteworthy among more recent memoirs are Helmut Lethen, *Suche nach dem Handorakel: Ein Bericht*, Göttingen: Wallstein, 2012; and Ulrich Raulff, *Wiedersehen mit den Siebzigern: Die wilden Jahre des Lesens*, Stuttgart: Klett-Cotta, 2014. Important remarks on theory are also found in Karl Heinz Bohrer, 'Sechs Szenen Achtundsechzig', in *Merkur*, 708 (2008), 410–24, and Hans Jörg Rheinberger, *Rekurrenzen: Texte zu Althusser* [Recurrences: texts on Althusser], Berlin: Merve, 2014.

For an American perspective that is analogous to that of Merve Verlag in many respects, see Sylvère Lotringer, 'Doing Theory', in *French Theory in America*, ed. Lotringer and Sande Cohen, New York: Routledge, 2001, 125–62.

22 To name just a few examples: Martin Jay, *The Dialectical Imagination: A History of the Frankfurt School and the Institute of Social Research, 1923–1950*, Boston: Little, Brown, 1973; François Dosse, *History of Structuralism*, 2 vols., trans. Deborah Glassman, Minneapolis: University of Minnesota Press, 1997; Vincent Descombes, *Modern French Philosophy*, trans. L. Scott-Fox and J. M. Harding, Cambridge University Press, 1980, 182f.; Ingo Elbe, *Marx im Westen: Die neue Marx-Lektüre in der Bundesrepublik seit 1965*, Berlin: De Gruyter, 2008.

23 On the importance of Althusser's 'theoretical practice' for the history of science, see Hans-Jörg Rheinberger, 'My Road to History of Science', in *Science in Context*, 26:4 (2013), 639–48; Philipp Felsch, 'Homo theoreticus', in *Eine Naturgeschichte für das 21. Jahrhundert: Hommage à, zu Ehren von, in Honor of Hans-Jörg Rheinberger*, ed. Safia Azzouni, Christina Brandt, Bernd Gausemeier, Julia Kursell, Henning Schmidgen and Barbara Wittmann, Berlin: Max-Planck-Institut, 2011, 204–6. Later concepts to which this book is indebted include the 'discursive practices' introduced by Michel Foucault in the *Archaeology of Knowledge* (trans. A. M. Sheridan Smith, London: Tavistock, 1972), and also the stylistics of 'intellectual practices' proposed by Michel de Certeau (*The Practice of Everyday Life*, vol. I, trans. Steven Rendall, Berkeley and Los Angeles: University of California Press, 1984), and Ivan Illich's 'historical ethology of reading' (*In the Vineyard of the Text: A Commentary to Hugh's Didascalicon*, University of Chicago Press, 1993). For a current attempt to bring together the history of philosophy and the history of science, see Darrin McMahon and Samuel Moyn (eds.), *Rethinking Modern European Intellectual History*, Oxford University Press, 2014.

24 For project outlines of such a concept of the history of theory, see Marcel Lepper, '"Ce qui restera […], c'est un style": Eine institutionengeschichtliche Projektskizze (1960–1989)', in *Jenseits des Poststrukturalismus? Eine Sondierung*, ed. Marcel Lepper, Steffen Siegel and Sophie Wennerscheid, Frankfurt: Peter Lang, 2005, 51–76; Warren Breckman, 'Times of Theory: On Writing the History of French Theory', in *Journal of the History of Ideas*, 71:3 (2010), 339–61.

25 Michel Foucault, 'I "reportages" di idee', in *Corriere della sera*, 12 November 1978, 1. Foucault's project largely remained just that. The only 'reportage' of ideas he wrote himself is his controversial series on the Iranian revolution of 1979.

1 Federal Republic of Adorno

1
1. Rififi
2. To Catch a Thief
3. We're No Angels
4. Gigi
5. Lola Montès
6. Paisà
7. Mädchen in Uniform
8. Daddy Long Legs
9. Millionenstadt Neapel
10. The Cure, The Pilgrim
11. La Belle et la bête
12. The Desperate Hours
13. Mutter Krausens Fahrt ins Glück
14. The Man with the Golden Arm
15. Threepenny Opera
16. To the Ends of the Earth
17. Othello
18. The Lower Depths
19. The Red Shoes
20. The Benny Goodman Story
21. Hôtel du Nord
22. Confidential Report
23. Hi-jack Highway
24. The Diary of Major Thompson
25. Shadows of the Past
26. Le ragazze di San Frediano
27. Ich denke oft an Piroschka
28. Les Belles de nuit
29. Invitation to the Dance
30. Die weisse Schlangenfrau
31. Mädchen m. [illegible]

32. Loser Takes All
33. The Unknown Soldier

2 The speech Khrushchev had given four months before at the 20th Congress of the Communist Party of the Soviet Union was broadcast on 21 June 1956. See Wolfgang Leonhard, 'Die bedeutsamste Rede des Kommunismus', in *Aus Politik und Zeitgeschichte*, 17/18 (2006), 3–5.

3 Gente saw himself as a late bloomer: 'Somehow it took me a long time to come to myself, to my own interests,' he told the sociologist Heinz Bude, who interviewed him for his portrait of the '68 generation. Quoted in Bude, 'Die Suche nach dem Unmöglichen,' 228.

4 On the importance of cinema in the cultural and political landscape of East and West Berlin, see Uta Berg-Ganschow and Wolfgang Jacobsen (eds.), *Film, Stadt, Kino, Berlin*, exhibition catalogue, Deutsche Kinemathek, Berlin: Argon, 1987.

5 Quoted in Lowien, *Weibliche Produktivkraft*, 152.

6 Karl Marx, *Critique of Hegel's Philosophy of Right*, trans. Annette Jolin and Joseph O'Malley, Cambridge University Press, 1970, 135.

7 On Khrushchev's speech and the attendant radio propaganda, see the articles in Thomas Grossbölting and Hermann Wentker (eds.), *Kommunismus in der Krise: Die Entstalinisierung 1956 und die Folgen*, Göttingen: Vandenhoeck & Ruprecht, 2008.

8 Maurice Blanchot, 'The Word Berlin,' trans. James Cascaito, in *The German Issue*, ed. Sylvère Lotringer, 2nd edn, Los Angeles: Semiotext(e), 2009, 60–4.

9 Bude, 'Die Suche nach dem Unmöglichen,' 211. On the cultural significance of latent sexuality, see the interview with Friedrich Kittler, 'Wir haben nur uns selber, um daraus zu schöpfen,' in *Die Welt*, 30 January 2011.

10 Susan Sontag, *Reborn: Journals and Notebooks, 1947–1963*, ed. David Rieff, New York: Farrar, Straus and Giroux, 2008.

11 Quoted in Lowien, *Weibliche Produktivkraft*, 152.

12 Author's interview with Peter Gente, 10 May 2012. See also Bude, 'Die Suche nach dem Unmöglichen,' 218.

13 Theodor W. Adorno, *Minima Moralia: Reflections from Damaged Life*, trans. E. F. N. Jephcott, London: Verso, 1978, 192.

14 Helmut Lethen, a few years younger than Gente, had a similar experience a little later with Walter Benjamin, whom he encountered for the first

time on the radio: 'What I heard was addictive. But I can no longer reconstruct what the drug was that made me high' – Lethen, *Suche nach dem Handorakel*, 51.

15 On Adorno's verdict of a 'rigidification of circumstances,' see Theodor Adorno, 'Commitment,' in Adorno, *Notes to Literature*, ed. Rolf Tiedemann, trans. Shierry Weber Nicholsen, rev. edn, New York: Columbia University Press, 2019, 363. On his relationship to Arnold Gehlen, see Wolf Lepenies, *The Seduction of Culture in German History*, Princeton University Press, 2006, 147.

16 Adorno, *Minima Moralia*, 20, 135, 23, 116, 42f., 39, 40, 113.

17 Ibid., 25. See also Theodor W. Adorno and Elisabeth Lenk, *The Challenge of Surrealism: The Correspondence of Theodor W. Adorno and Elisabeth Lenk*, trans. Susan H. Gillespie, Minneapolis: University of Minnesota Press, 2015, 56.

18 Theodor W. Adorno, 'Notes on Kafka,' in Adorno, *Prisms*, trans. Samuel Weber and Shierry Weber, Cambridge, Mass.: MIT Press, 1981, 260. See also Martin Mittelmeier, *Adorno in Neapel: Wie sich eine Sehnsuchtslandschaft in Philosophie verwandelt*, Munich: Siedler, 2013. My portrayal of Adorno is influenced by that book and by conversations with Martin Mittelmeier.

19 Bude, 'Die Suche nach dem Unmöglichen,' 214; the author's conversations with Peter Gente on 26 September 2010 and 10 May 2012, and with Hannes Böhringer on 20 March 2014. One of Peter Gente's last memories of Halberstadt was of the dancing lessons that he attended together with Alexandra Kluge, a doctor's daughter: the younger sister of the filmmaker and Merve author Alexander Kluge was born in Halberstadt a year after Gente.

20 Quoted in Andreas Bernard, 'Fünfzig Jahre *Minima Moralia*,' in *Theodor W. Adorno:* Minima Moralia *neu gelesen*, ed. Andreas Bernard and Ulrich Raulff, Frankfurt: Suhrkamp, 2003, 8.

21 See Michael Rutschky, 'Erinnerungen an die Gesellschaftskritik,' in *Merkur*, 423 (1984), 28.

22 Heidi Paris and Peter Gente, 'Für *Buch-Markt*,' statement for the industry journal *Buch-Markt*, unpublished typescript, Berlin, 1986 (www.heidi-paris.de/verlag/wider-das-kostbare).

23 Quoted in Bude, 'Die Suche nach dem Unmöglichen,' 219.

24 Quoted in Ulrich Raulff, 'Die *Minima Moralia* nach fünfzig Jahren: Ein

philosophisches Volksbuch im Spiegel seiner frühen Kritik', in *Theodor W. Adorno:* Minima Moralia *neu gelesen*, ed. Bernard and Raulff, 128f. On the reception of *Minima Moralia*, see also Alex Demirović, *Der nonkonformistische Intellektuelle: Die Entwicklung der Kritischen Theorie zur Frankfurter Schule*, Frankfurt: Suhrkamp, 1999, 537–55.

25 'Keine Angst vor dem Elfenbeinturm: Gespräch mit dem Frankfurter Sozialphilosophen Professor Theodor W. Adorno', in *Der Spiegel*, 23:19 (1969), 204.

26 Gottfried Benn, 'Probleme der Lyrik', in Benn, *Gesammelte Werke*, vol. IV, Wiesbaden: Limes, 1968, 1092. See also Wolf Lepenies, 'Gottfried Benn: Der Artist im Posthistoire', in *Literarische Profile: Deutsche Dichter von Grimmelshausen bis Brecht*, ed. Walter Hinderer, Königstein: Athenäum, 1982, 326–37. On the triumph of fragmentary thinking, see Karl Heinz Bohrer, 'Welche Macht hat die Philosophie heute noch?' in Bohrer, *Selbstdenker und Systemdenker: Über agonales Denken*, Munich: Hanser, 2011, 69–88.

27 Theodor W. Adorno, 'The Essay as Form', in *Notes to Literature*, 32.

28 Theodor W. Adorno, 'Cultural Criticism and Society', in Adorno, *Prisms*, 34.

29 So Raulff suggests in 'Die *Minima Moralia* nach fünfzig Jahren', 128. See also Raulff, *Kreis ohne Meister: Stefan Georges Nachleben*, Munich: C. H. Beck, 2009, 498f.

30 Michael Rutschky, *Erfahrungshunger: Ein Essay über die siebziger Jahre*, Cologne: Kiepenheuer & Witsch, 1980, 84. See also the analogous observation in Heinz-Klaus Metzger, 'Das Ende der Musikgeschichte', in *Geist gegen den Zeitgeist: Erinnern an Adorno*, ed. Josef Früchtl and Maria Calloni, Frankfurt: Suhrkamp, 1991, 163: 'In those days I still thought the philosophy of music could *transcend* music' (emphasis in the original).

31 Adorno, *Minima Moralia*, 15. See also Michael Rutschky, 'Fassungslose Traurigkeit: Bewusstseinsstoff für soziale Aufsteiger; Vor 50 Jahren erschien Adornos *Minima Moralia*', in *Die Welt*, 17 November 2001.

32 Adorno, *Minima Moralia*, 25f.

33 Rutschky, 'Erinnerungen an die Gesellschaftskritik', 28f.

34 Joachim Kaiser, 'Was blieb von Adornos Glanz?' in *Süddeutsche Zeitung*, 11 September 2003.

35 Witold Gombrowicz, *Diary*, vol. III, trans. Lillian Vallee, New Haven: Yale

University Press, 2012, 108, 112, 122f. On the post-war modernism of West Berlin, see Emily Pugh, *Architecture, Politics, and Identity in Divided Berlin*, University of Pittsburgh Press, 2014, 62–105; Moritz Föllmer, *Individuality and Modernity in Berlin: Self and Society from Weimar to the Wall*, Cambridge University Press, 2013, 240–64.

36 Bude, 'Die Suche nach dem Unmöglichen,' 214.

37 Quoted in Lowien, *Weibliche Produktivkraft*, 152.

38 Theodor W. Adorno to Leo Lowenthal, 3 January 1949, trans. Donald Reneau, in Lowenthal, *Critical Theory and Frankfurt Theorists: Lectures, Correspondence, Conversations*, Abingdon: Routledge, 2017. On the currency of the motif, which was later used by Jacob Taubes – as mentioned in the introduction – see Lepenies, *The Seduction of Culture*, 148–53. On the eve of the student revolts, Jürgen Habermas assessed the willingness of German students to take political action as rather low. Jürgen Habermas, Ludwig von Friedeburg, Christoph Oehler and Friedrich Weltz, *Student und Politik: Eine soziologische Untersuchung zum politischen Bewusstsein Frankfurter Studenten*, Neuwied: Luchterhand, 1961. On the 'sceptical generation,' see Jens Hacke, 'Helmuth Schelskys skeptische Jugend: Die mythische Geburtsstunde einer bundesrepublikanischen Generation,' in *Sonde 1957: Ein Jahr als symbolische Zäsur für Wandlungsprozesse im geteilten Deutschland*, ed. Alexander Gallus and Werner Müller, Berlin: Duncker & Humblot, 2010, 329–42.

39 Adorno, *Minima Moralia*, 130.

40 Theodor W. Adorno, 'Lyric Poetry and Society,' in *Notes to Literature*, 38.

41 On empowerment to cultural criticism by *Minima Moralia*, see Demirović, *Der nonkonformistische Intellektuelle*, 529f. On art criticism as a supplement to art, see also Rutschky, *Erfahrungshunger*, 227. From 1957 until the mid-seventies, the cinephile Gente was a subscriber to the journal *filmkritik*, which was strongly influenced by Adorno, especially in its early years. Author's interview with Peter Gente, 10 May 2012.

42 Jürgen Kaube, 'So gut wie nichts macht alles wieder gut: Theodor W. Adorno zum einhundertsten Geburtstag,' in *Frankfurter Allgemeine Zeitung*, 6 September 2003; Theodor W. Adorno, 'Die Auferstandene Kultur,' in Adorno, *Gesammelte Schriften*, vol. XX/2, 455, 458, quoted in Lepenies, *Kultur und Politik: Deutsche Geschichten*, Munich: Hanser, 2006, 288; Kaiser, 'Was blieb von Adornos Glanz?'; Gombrowicz, *Diary*, vol.

III, 131. On the growth of aesthetic theory since the 1950s, see Anselm Haverkamp, *Latenzzeit: Wissen im Nachkrieg*, Berlin: Kadmos, 2004, 85f.

43 See Helmut Kreutzer, 'Einleitung', in Max Bense, *Ausgewählte Schriften*, vol. III, Stuttgart: Metzler, 1998, xxviff. On Bense's role in post-war West Germany, see Barbara Büscher, Christoph Hoffmann and Hans-Christian von Herrmann (eds.), *Ästhetik als Programm: Max Bense; Daten und Streuungen*, Berlin: Diaphanes, 2004.

44 See Ilonka Czerny, *Die Gruppe Spur (1957–1965): Ein Künstlerphänomen zwischen Münchner Szene und internationalem Anspruch*, Vienna: Lit, 2008, 207–11; Roberto Ohrt, *Phantom Avantgarde: Eine Geschichte der Situationistischen Internationale und der modernen Kunst*, Hamburg: Nautilus, 1997, 198. In the spirit of the SPUR operation, the artist Hans Imhoff produced lecture-hall dada after the sound of Adorno and Habermas in 1968. See Lorenz Jäger, *Adorno: A Political Biography*, New Haven: Yale University Press, 2004, 205–7. Because parody presupposes expectations on the part of the reader or listener, it is an infallible sign that 'theory' was in the process of establishing itself as a genre. See Vosskamp, 'Gattungen als literarisch-soziale Institutionen'.

45 Quoted in Bude, 'Die Suche nach dem Unmöglichen', 218.

46 Theodor W. Adorno, 'Bibliographische Grillen', in *Frankfurter Allgemeine Zeitung*, 16 October 1959.

47 See, for example, Kathrin Passig, 'Das Buch als Geldbäumchen', in Passig, *Standardsituationen der Technologiekritik*, Frankfurt: Suhrkamp, 2013, 41–54.

48 Ernesto Grassi, *Die zweite Aufklärung: Enzyklopädie heute*, Hamburg: Rowohlt, 1958, 12.

49 Hans Magnus Enzensberger, 'Bildung als Konsumgut: Analyse der Taschenbuch-Produktion', in Enzensberger, *Einzelheiten*, Frankfurt: Suhrkamp, 1962, iii. On the paperback as an a priori medium of the student movement, see Ben Mercer, 'The Paperback Revolution: Mass-Circulation Books and the Cultural Origins of 1968 in Western Europe', in *Journal of the History of Ideas*, 72 (2011), 613–36.

50 According to empirical studies, which supplanted speculation in the course of the 1960s, most paperback readers lived in major cities, were under 30, and were enrolled in post-secondary education: Mercer, 'The Paperback Revolution'. For West Germany, see the book market research publications, beginning in 1963.

51 Heinz Gollhardt, 'Das Taschenbuch im Zeitalter der Massenkultur: Vom Bildungskanon zum "locker geordneten Informationschaos"', in *Das Buch zwischen gestern und morgen: Zeichen und Aspekte*, ed. Georg Ramseger and Werner Schoenicke, Stuttgart: Deutscher Bücherbund, 1969, 131.

52 Hans Schmoller, 'The Paperback Revolution', in *Essays in the History of Publishing: In Celebration of the 250th Anniversary of the House of Longman, 1724–1974*, ed. Asa Briggs, London: Longman, 1974, 314.

53 The following section is based on Philipp Felsch and Martin Mittelmeier, '"Ich war ehrlich überrascht und erschrocken, wie umfangreich Sie geantwortet haben": Theodor W. Adorno korrespondiert mit seinen Lesern', in *Kultur und Gespenster*, 13 (2012), 159–99.

54 Klaus Reichert, 'Adorno und das Radio', in *Sinn und Form*, 62:4 (2010), 454. See also Clemens Albrecht, 'Die Massenmedien und die Frankfurter Schule', in Albrecht, Günter C. Behrmann, Michael Bock, Harald Homann and Friedrich H. Tenbruck, *Die intellektuelle Gründung der Bundesrepublik: Eine Wirkungsgeschichte der Frankfurter Schule*, Frankfurt: Campus, 1999, 203–46.

55 Kaiser, 'Was blieb von Adornos Glanz?'

56 Quoted in Henning Ritter, 'Wenn Adorno spricht', in *Frankfurter Allgemeine Zeitung*, 11 October 2008.

57 As Hans-D. Kempf of Brussels, who wrote to Adorno on 8 April 1968, reports: Theodor W. Adorno Archives, Frankfurt.

58 Quoted in Francis Böckelmann and Herbert Nagel (eds.), *Subversive Aktion: Der Sinn der Organisation ist ihr Scheitern*, Frankfurt: Neue Kritik, 1976, 146f. The episode is also recounted in Jäger, *Adorno*, 273.

59 Adorno, *Minima Moralia*, 136.

60 Adorno to P. G., 19 September 1967: Theodor W. Adorno Archive. On the discourse about intellectuals in post-war West Germany, see Birgit Pape, 'Intellektuelle in der Bundesrepublik 1945–1967', in *Intellektuelle im 20. Jahrhundert in Deutschland*, ed. Jutta Schlich, Tübingen: Niemeyer, 2000, 295–324.

61 P. G. to Adorno, 22 July 1967: Theodor W. Adorno Archives.

62 Baroness von Gersdorff to Adorno, 20 April 1956: Theodor W. Adorno Archives.

63 Ely Amstein to Adorno, 18 September 1962: Theodor W. Adorno Archives.

64 H. N. to Adorno, 14 August 1952: Theodor W. Adorno Archives.

65 D. Gabriel to Adorno, 31 May 1959: Theodor W. Adorno Archives.

66 Ella Schwarz to Adorno, 14 September 1961: Theodor W. Adorno Archives. On Ella Schwarz, see Felsch and Mittelmeier, 'Theodor W. Adorno korrespondiert mit seinen Lesern', 163.
67 H. B.-R. to Adorno, 5 November 1965: Theodor W. Adorno Archives.
68 Adorno to Roland Jaeger, 9 September 1963. Theodor W. Adorno Archives.
69 Adorno to the Government of Lower Franconia, 30 January 1968: Theodor W. Adorno Archives.
70 Adorno to J. A., 12 March 1968: Theodor W. Adorno Archives.
71 Quoted in Reichert, 'Adorno und das Radio', 456.
72 Kurt Bauer to Adorno, 25 July 1959; Ernst Bachmann to Adorno, 12 April 1957: Theodor W. Adorno Archives.
73 See Felsch and Mittelmeier, 'Theodor W. Adorno korrespondiert mit seinen Lesern', 196ff.
74 J. A. to Adorno, 9 March 1968: Theodor W. Adorno Archives.
75 Adorno to J. A., 12 March 1968: Theodor W. Adorno Archives.
76 J. A. to Adorno, 15 March 1968: Theodor W. Adorno Archives. On Adorno's attitude towards homosexuality, see Felsch and Mittelmeier, 'Theodor W. Adorno korrespondiert mit seinen Lesern', 190.
77 H. B. to Adorno, 26 June 1966: Theodor W. Adorno Archives.
78 Adorno to H. B., 1 July 1966. Theodor W. Adorno Archives.
79 H. B. to Adorno, 18 December 1966: Theodor W. Adorno Archives.
80 Peter Gente to Adorno, 30 October 1965: Theodor W. Adorno Archives. Another reason for writing to Adorno lay in the fact that Gente had heard him speak a few days before at the Academy of Fine Arts on 'The Problem of Functionalism Today'. See Michael Schwarz, 'Adorno in der Akademie der Künste: Vorträge 1957–1967', in *Zeitschrift für Kritische Theorie*, 36/7 (2013), 213.
81 Adorno to Peter Gente, 2 November 1965: Theodor W. Adorno Archives.
82 See Gunzelin Schmid Noerr, 'Die Stellung der Dialektik der Aufklärung in der Entwicklung der Kritischen Theorie: Bemerkungen zu Autorschaft, Entstehung, einigen theoretischen Implikationen und späterer Einschätzung durch die Autoren', in Max Horkheimer, *Gesammelte Schriften*, vol. V: *'Dialektik der Aufklärung' und Schriften 1940–1950*, Frankfurt: Fischer, 1987, 423–52.
83 Rolf Tiedemann, 'Editorische Nachbemerkung', in Theodor W. Adorno, *Gesammelte Schriften*, vol. XV: *Komposition für den Film: Der getreue*

Korrepetitor [Composing for films: the faithful répétiteur], Frankfurt: Suhrkamp, 1976, 406.

84 Rainald Goetz, *Hirn*, Frankfurt: Suhrkamp, 1986, 102.

85 On Eisler and Adorno, see Günter Mayer, *Weltbild, Notenbild: Zur Dialektik des musikalischen Materials*, Leipzig: Reclam, 1978; Laura Silverberg, 'Between Dissonance and Dissidence: Socialist Modernism in the German Democratic Republic', in *Journal of Musicology*, 26:1 (2009), 44–84.

86 Rudolph Bauer to Adorno, 21 and 24 November 1965: Theodor W. Adorno Archives. The letter referred to Adorno's commentary on Marx in his lecture course on negative dialectics. In the next lecture, Adorno addressed Bauer's question in detail. Theodor W. Adorno, *Lectures on Negative Dialectics: Fragments of a Lecture Course, 1965/1966*, ed. Rolf Tiedemann, trans. Rodney Livingstone, Cambridge: Polity, 2008, 45–54.

2 In the Suhrkamp Culture

1 Adorno, *Lectures on Negative Dialectics*, 57f. On the atmosphere in Adorno's lecture course, see Kurt Flasch, 'Die Trümmerfrau der Kultur', in *Berliner Zeitung*, 18 July 1998.

2 Theodor W. Adorno, *Metaphysics: Concept and Problems*, ed. Rolf Tiedemann, trans. Edmund Jephcott, Palo Alto: Stanford University Press, 2001, 126.

3 Cf. Marcel Lepper, 'Theoriegenerationen 1945–1989', in *Zeitschrift für Germanistik*, 18:2 (2008), 244–9.

4 Tilman Fichter and Siegward Lönnendonker, *Kleine Geschichte des SDS: Der Sozialistische Deutsche Studentenbund von Helmut Schmidt bis Rudi Dutschke*, 4th edn, Essen: Bundeszentrale für politische Bildung, 2008.

5 Elisabeth Lenk, 'Die sozialistische Theorie in der Arbeit des SDS', in Theodor W. Adorno and Elisabeth Lenk, *Briefwechsel 1962–1969*, Munich: Text & Kritik, 2001, 171–81.

6 On the theory overload of post-war Marxism, see the classic diagnosis by Perry Anderson, *Considerations on Western Marxism*, London: Verso, 1979.

7 Hans-Jürgen Krahl, *Konstitution und Klassenkampf: Zur historischen Dialektik von bürgerlicher Emanzipation und proletarischer Revolution* [Constitution and class struggle: on the historical dialectic of bourgeois emancipation and proletarian revolution], Frankfurt: Neue Kritik, 1971, 236.

8 In the words of Peter Rühmkorf, *Die Jahre, die Ihr kennt: Anfälle und Erinnerungen*, Reinbek: Rowohlt, 1972, 141. On the Argument Club

and the atmosphere at Freie Universität in the sixties, see '"Wenn die Dinge wiederkehren, sind sie schlimmer als zuvor": Gespräch mit Margherita von Brentano', in Margherita von Brentano, *Das Politische und das Persönliche*, ed. Iris Nachum and Susan Neiman, Göttingen: Wallstein, 2010, 223–59.

9 Franz Neumann, *Behemoth: The Structure and Practice of National Socialism*, Toronto: Oxford University Press, 1942.

10 See Helmut Lethen, 'Unheimliche Nähe: Carl Schmitt liest Walter Benjamin', in *Frankfurter Allgemeine Zeitung*, 16 September 1999.

11 Merve Verlag to Pierre Klossowski, 28 May 1979: Merve Archives.

12 Carlo Feltrinelli, *Senior Service*, trans. Alastair McEwen, London: Granta, 2001.

13 In the words of Helmut Lethen, in an email to the author, 9 December 2011.

14 Interview with Helmut Lethen, 30 December 2011.

15 At least, that was what Jacob Taubes said, according to Peter Gente; author's interview of 26 September 2010.

16 Henning Ritter, 'Klaus Heinrich: Die lange Lehre zum kurzen Protest', in Ritter, *Verehrte Denker*, Springe: zu Klampen, 2012, 68.

17 Walter Benjamin, 'The Author as Producer', in Benjamin, *Reflections*, trans. Edmund Jephcott, New York and London: Harcourt Brace Jovanovich, 1978, 250 (translation modified).

18 Bohrer, 'The Three Cultures', 137.

19 Lethen, 'Unheimliche Nähe'.

20 The description of Gente's role in the dispute over Benjamin's estate is based on communications from Helmuth Lethen (see emails of 9 December 2011 and 25 September 2014). On the intervention of *Alternative*, see Moritz Neuffer, 'Theorie als Praxis: Die Zeitschrift *Alternative* (1938–1982)', unpublished MA thesis, Berlin, 2012. On the background of the dispute in the humanities, see also Elke Morlok and Frederek Musall, 'Die Geschichte seiner Freundschaft: Gershom Scholem und die Benjamin-Rezeption in der Bonner Republik', in *Gershom Scholem in Deutschland: Zwischen Seelenverwandtschaft und Sprachlosigkeit*, ed. Gerold Necker, Elke Morlok and Matthias Morgenstern, Tübingen: Mohr Siebeck, 2014, 115–43.

21 Peter Gente, 'Über das Vorwort Georg Lukács' zur zweiten Auflage der Theorie des Romans' [On Georg Lukács's preface to the second edition

of the *Theory of the Novel*], unpublished typescript, Berlin, 1965: Merve Archives.

22 Bude, 'Die Suche nach dem Unmöglichen', 231. On Adorno's attitude, see Adorno and Lenk, *The Challenge of Surrealism*, 183: 'I must confess to you that I am as little persuaded of the decline of the arts today as I was during the surrealist heyday.'

23 Hans Magnus Enzensberger, 'Gemeinplätze, die Neueste Literatur betreffend', in *Kursbuch*, 15 (1968), 195f. On the reception of *Kursbuch* 15, see Henning Marmulla, *Enzensbergers Kursbuch: Eine Zeitschrift um 68*, Berlin: Matthes & Seitz, 2011, 176–98.

24 Sylvère Lotringer, 'German Issues', in *The German Issue*, ed. Lotringer, vi.

25 Lowien, *Weibliche Produktivkraft*, 45.

26 Hans-Peter Gente, 'Versuch über Bitterfeld' [Essay on Bitterfeld], in *Alternative*, 38/9 (1964), 126f.

27 Helmut Lethen, email to the author, 9 December 2011.

28 Peter Gente, 'Editorische Notiz' [Editorial note], in Jacob Taubes, *Ad Carl Schmitt: Gegenstrebige Fügung* [To Carl Schmitt: union of opposites], Berlin: Merve, 1987, 79.

29 Cf. Nicolaus Sombart, *Jugend in Berlin, 1933–1943: Ein Bericht*, Frankfurt: Fischer, 1986, 53.

30 Informative in this regard is Jacob Taubes, 'Ästhetisierung der Wahrheit im Posthistoire', in *Streitbare Philosophie: Margherita von Brentano zum 65. Geburtstag*, ed. Gabriele Althaus and Irmingard Staeuble, Berlin: Metropol, 1988, 41.

31 Jan Assmann, 'Talmud in der Paris-Bar: Zum Tod des jüdischen Philosophen Jacob Taubes (1923–1987)', in *die tageszeitung*, 28 March 1987.

32 Adorno and Lenk, *The Challenge of Surrealism*, 147.

33 Henning Ritter, 'Akosmisch: Zum Tod von Jacob Taubes', in *Frankfurter Allgemeine Zeitung*, 24 March 1987. On Ritter himself, see Wolf Lepenies, 'Der wilde Denker: Erinnerungen an Henning Ritter', in *Die Welt*, 29 June 2013. For another description of the Taubes circle, see Rheinberger, *Rekurrenzen*.

34 'Jacob Taubes', interview, in *Denken, das an der Zeit ist*, ed. Florian Rötzer, Frankfurt: Suhrkamp, 1987, 307.

35 Cord Riechelmann, 'Nachwort', in Harald Fricke, *Texte 1990–2007* [Texts 1990–2007], Berlin: Merve, 2010, 151.

36 See Sara Hakemi, *Anschlag und Spektakel: Flugblätter der Kommune I; Erklärungen von Ensslin/Baader und der frühen RAF*, Bochum: Posth, 2008, 59ff.

37 Taubes was fond of recounting the episode. See Taubes, *Ad Carl Schmitt*, 24. For a vivid description of Kojève's snobbish philosophy of history, see Nicolaus Sombart, *Pariser Lehrjahre, 1951–1954: Leçons de sociologie*, Hamburg: Hoffmann & Campe, 1994, 340–7.

38 Armin Mohler, 'Der messianische Irrwisch: Über Jacob Taubes (1923–1987)', in *Criticón*, 103 (1987), 221. On Taubes's Berkeley association, see Martin Treml, 'Paulinische Feindschaft: Korrespondenzen von Jacob Taubes und Carl Schmitt', in *Jacob Taubes – Carl Schmitt: Briefwechsel mit Materialien*, ed. Herbert Kopp-Oberstebrink, Thorsten Palzhoff and Martin Treml, Munich: Fink, 2012.

39 See Roger Thiel, 'Ästhetik der Aufklärung; Aufklärung der Ästhetik: Eine kritische Physiognomie der edition suhrkamp', in *Wolfenbütteler Notizen zur Buchgeschichte*, 15:1 (1990), 3f.

40 'Einführungsprospekt zur "edition suhrkamp"', in *25 Jahre edition suhrkamp 1963–1988*, Frankfurt: Suhrkamp, 1988, 1.

41 Raimund Fellinger and Wolfgang Schopf (eds.), *Kleine Geschichte der edition suhrkamp*, Frankfurt: Suhrkamp, 2003, 26; cf. 37; see also Jürgen Habermas, 'Kultur des Gegenwartssinns', in *Du: Das Kulturmagazin*, 803 (2010), special issue: *Gibt es eine neue Suhrkamp-Kultur?* 38.

42 'Wissbar wohin: Philosophie', in *Der Spiegel*, 20:29 (1966), 76.

43 Günther C. Behrmann, 'Die Theorie, das Institut, die Zeitschrift und das Buch: Zur Publikations- und Wirkungsgeschichte der Kritischen Theorie 1945 bis 1965', in Albrecht et al., *Die intellektuelle Gründung der Bundesrepublik*, 311.

44 Mercer, 'The Paperback Revolution', 621.

45 Karl Markus Michel to Hans Blumenberg, 20 January 1965: Siegfried Unseld Archives in the German Literature Archive, Marbach.

46 On the relation between minimalism and pop, and on the two Beatles covers, see Diedrich Diederichsen, 'Psychedelische Begabungen: Minimalismus und Pop', in Diederichsen, *Kritik des Auges: Texte zur Kunst*, Hamburg: Fundus, 2008, 75–105; and Walter Grasskamp, *Das Cover von Sgt. Pepper: Eine Momentaufnahme der Popkultur*, Berlin: Wagenbach, 2004.

47 See Jan Bürger, 'Die Stunde der Theorie', in *Zeitschrift für Ideengeschichte*, 6:4 (2012), 5–10.

48 Jacob Taubes to Karl Markus Michel, 26 August 1965: Siegfried Unseld Archives.

49 'Jacob Taubes', 305. See also Morten Paul, 'Vor der Theorie: Jacob Taubes als Verlagsberater', in *Zeitschrift für Ideengeschichte*, 6:4 (2012), 29–34.

50 Jacob Taubes to Karl Markus Michel, 30 November 1965: Siegfried Unseld Archives.

51 Jacob Taubes to Karl Markus Michel, 26 August 1965.

52 Dieter Henrich to Siegfried Unseld, 17 June 1964: Siegfried Unseld Archives.

53 Jacob Taubes to Siegfried Unseld, 4 November 1963: Siegfried Unseld Archives. On Taubes's prior activities in publishing, see Behrmann, 'Die Theorie, das Institut, die Zeitschrift und das Buch', 265; Treml, 'Paulinische Feindschaft', 290f.

54 See Karl Markus Michel to Éditions François Maspero, 30 June 1966: Siegfried Unseld Archives.

55 Jacob Taubes to Siegfried Unseld, 5 May 1964: Siegfried Unseld Archives.

56 Adorno, 'The Essay as Form', 9. On the history of the genre in West Germany, see Georg Stanitzek, *Essay: BRD*, Berlin: Vorwerk, 2011, 8. The pop-culture magazine *Spex* later added another item to the negative definitions of theory: *Gegen die Uni studieren* [Studying against the uni] was the theme of its issue 17:5 (1996), 44–55.

57 Karl Markus Michel to Jacob Taubes, 19 August 1965: Siegfried Unseld Archives.

58 On the distinction between 'old' and 'new' culture, which also corresponds to the difference between hardcover books and paperbacks, see Bohrer, 'The Three Cultures'.

59 Jacob Taubes to Siegfried Unseld, 20 April 1965: Siegfried Unseld Archives. 'Suhrkamp is extremely sceptical of academic philosophy (for good reason, in some cases)', Taubes wrote to Blumenberg on 10 August 1964, 'and therefore I can propose only the best – not commodities': Hans Blumenberg and Jacob Taubes, *Briefwechsel 1961–1981 und weitere Materialien*, Frankfurt: Suhrkamp, 2013, 37.

60 Karl Markus Michel, 'Aktennotiz für Siegfried Unseld: Resume der Gespräche mit Jacob Taubes am 30./31. Juli in Berlin': Siegfried Unseld Archives.

61 Karl Markus Michel to Siegfried Unseld, 1 April 1966: Siegfried Unseld Archives.

62 Dieter Henrich to Siegfried Unseld, 17 June 1964: Siegfried Unseld Archives.
63 Karl Markus Michel to Siegfried Unseld, 1 April 1966: Siegfried Unseld Archives.
64 Jacob Taubes to Siegfried Unseld, 6 April 1965: Siegfried Unseld Archives.
65 Was he thinking of the essayist Adorno? On the mutual disregard of Blumenberg and Adorno, see Christian Voller, 'Kommunikation verweigert: Schwierige Beziehungen zwischen Blumenberg und Adorno', in *Zeitschrift für Kulturphilosophie*, 7:2 (2013), 381–405.
66 Hans Blumenberg to Karl Markus Michel, 21 April 1965: Siegfried Unseld Archives. In the end, however, he yielded to Unseld's efforts. Less than a year later, there is a mention of the 12,000 Deutschmarks he received for *The Legitimacy of the Modern Age*. Siegfried Unseld to Hans Blumenberg, 14 February 1966: Siegfried Unseld Archives.
67 Jacob Taubes to Siegfried Unseld, 2 February 1965: Siegfried Unseld archives.
68 Jacob Taubes to Karl Markus Michel, 29 and 30 November 1965: Siegfried Unseld archives.
69 The same can be said of the critical America expert Adorno, who wrote after his return to Germany that his sojourn in the US had given him 'the capacity to see culture from the outside': 'Scientific Experiences of a European Scholar in America', trans. Donald Fleming, in *The Intellectual Migration: Europe and America, 1930–1960*, ed. Donald Fleming and Bernard Bailyn, Cambridge, Mass.: Belknap, 1969, 367.
70 Taubes, *Ad Carl Schmitt*, 49.
71 Jacob Taubes to Siegfried Unseld, 5 May 1964: Siegfried Unseld Archives.
72 Karl Markus Michel to Siegfried Unseld, 1 April 1966: Siegfried Unseld Archives.
73 Jacob Taubes to Karl Markus Michel, 14 June 1966: Siegfried Unseld Archives.
74 Jacob Taubes to Karl Markus Michel, 21 September 1966: Siegfried Unseld Archives.
75 Karl Markus Michel to Siegfried Unseld, 1 April 1966: Siegfried Unseld Archives.
76 Karl Markus Michel to Jacob Taubes, 13 June 1966. Siegfried Unseld Archives.
77 Karl Markus Michel to Karel Kosík, 9 November 1966: Siegfried Unseld Archives.

78 Jacob Taubes to Karl Markus Michel, 20 April and 12 August 1965: Siegfried Unseld Archives.

79 Bude, 'Die Suche nach dem Unmöglichen', 224ff. The 'Battle of Tegeler Weg' is the name given to the bloody confrontation between parts of the Berlin protest movement and the Berlin police on 4 November 1968.

80 J. W. Stalin, *Marxismus und Fragen der Sprachwissenschaft*, Munich: Rogner & Bernhard, 1968. The editor Hans-Peter Gente gave the book a brief introduction.

81 Quoted in Lowien, *Weibliche Produktivkraft*, 146ff.

82 Ibid., 40f.

3 Ill-Made Books

1 Lowien, *Weibliche Produktivkraft*, 35.

2 Wolfgang Büscher, *Drei Stunden Null: Deutsche Abenteuer*, Reinbek: Rowohlt, 2003, 28.

3 Lowien, *Weibliche Produktivkraft*, 38. On the economic conditions of the West Berlin subculture, see Pugh, *Architecture, Politics, and Identity*, 200–40; Wolfgang Müller, *Subkultur Westberlin, 1979–1989*, Hamburg: Fundus, 2013, 44 and passim. On the project economy of the subculture generally, see Hans-Christian Dany, Ulrich Dörrie and Bettina Sefkow (eds.), *dagegen dabei: Texte, Gespräche und Dokumente zu Strategien der Selbstorganisation seit 1969*, Hamburg: Michael Kellner, 1998.

4 Cf. Gerd Koenen, 'Der transzendental Obdachlose: Hans-Jürgen Krahl', in *Zeitschrift für Ideengeschichte*, 2:3 (2008), 5–22.

5 After *Marxism and Problems of Linguistics*, Gente edited another Stalin title: J. W. Stalin, *Zu den Fragen des Leninismus: Eine Auswahl* [On the problems of Leninism: a selection], Frankfurt: Fischer, 1970.

6 Diedrich Diederichsen, *Sexbeat*, 2nd edn, Cologne: Kiepenheuer & Witsch, 2010, 36.

7 On the decay of the student movement, see Gerd Koenen, *Das rote Jahrzehnt: Unsere kleine deutsche Kulturrevolution, 1967–1977*, Cologne: Kiepenheuer & Witsch, 2001, 141ff.

8 Bohrer, 'Sechs Szenen Achtundsechzig', 413f.; Adelheid von Saldern, 'Markt für Marx: Literaturbetrieb und Lesebewegungen in der Bundesrepublik in den Sechziger- und Siebzigerjahren', in *Archiv für Sozialgeschichte*, 44 (2004), 149–80. On the alternative press and its readers, see Sven Reichardt, *Authentizität und Gemeinschaft: Linksalternatives Leben*

in den siebziger und frühen achtziger Jahren, Frankfurt: Suhrkamp, 2014, 223–317.

9 For a chart, see Lowien, *Weibliche Produktivkraft*, 215.

10 On Althusser and his 'theoretical antihumanism', see Robert Pfaller, *Althusser: Das Schweigen im Text; Epistemologie, Psychoanalyse und Nominalismus in Louis Althussers Theorie der Lektüre*, Munich: Fink, 1997.

11 The term 'hyperintellectualism' is Martin Puder's: 'Der böse Blick des Michel Foucault', in *Neue Rundschau*, 83 (1972), 316.

12 Louis Althusser, *Reading Capital*, trans. Ben Brewster, London: New Left Books, 1970, 58.

13 See also Felsch, 'Homo theoreticus'. On the context in which Foucault's *Archaeology of Knowledge* was conceived and Althusser's influence, see also Dosse, *History of Structuralism*, 234f., 239f.

14 Hans-Jörg Rheinberger, 'Die erkenntnistheoretischen Auffassungen Althussers', in *Das Argument*, 17:11/12 (1975), 931.

15 Althusser, *Reading Capital*, 241; cf. Althusser, *Wie sollen wir* Das Kapital *lesen?* Berlin: n.p. [Merve], 1.

16 Tony Judt, 'Elucubrations: The "Marxism" of Louis Althusser', in Judt, *Reappraisals: Reflections on the Forgotten Twentieth Century*, New York: Penguin, 2008, 108.

17 Theodor W. Adorno, 'Marginalia to Theory and Praxis', in Adorno, *Critical Models: Interventions and Catchwords*, trans. Henry W. Pickford, New York: Columbia University Press, 1998, 261 (translation modified).

18 Anderson, *Considerations on Western Marxism*, 73. Cf. Alex Demirović, 'Bodenlose Politik: Dialoge über Theorie und Praxis', in *Frankfurter Schule und Studentenbewegung: Von der Flaschenpost zum Molotowcocktail, 1946–1995*, vol. III, ed. Wolfgang Kraushaar, Hamburg: Rogner & Bernhard, 1998, 71–94. The discussion carried on by the New Left about the relation between theory and practice is reminiscent in many respects of the debates of the young Hegelians in the 1840s. See Wolfgang Essbach, *Die Junghegelianer: Soziologie einer Intellektuellengruppe*, Munich: Fink, 1988, 270–90.

19 Niklas Luhmann, 'Die Praxis der Theorie', in Luhmann, *Soziologische Aufklärung*, vol. I: *Aufsätze zur Theorie sozialer Systeme*, Opladen: Westdeutscher, 1970, 253.

20 Michel Foucault and Gilles Deleuze, 'Intellectuals and Power', in Michel Foucault, *Language, Counter-Memory, Practice: Selected Essays and*

Interviews, trans. Donald F. Bouchard and Sherry Simon, Ithaca, NY: Cornell University Press, 1977, 206f., 208; cf. Deleuze and Foucault, 'Die Intellektuellen und die Macht', in Deleuze and Foucault, *Der Faden ist gerissen* [The thread is broken], trans. Ulrich Raulff and Walter Seitter, Berlin: Merve, 1977, 87, 89. (An earlier German translation of the 1972 discussion had been published in Michel Foucault, *Von der Subversion des Wissens*, Munich: Hanser, 1974, 106–15.)

21 Heidi Paris and Peter Gente, 'Ping-Pong auf der Hochebene von Tibet: Gespräch mit den Betreibern des Merve Verlages' [Ping-pong on the Tibetan plateau: interview with the people who run Merve Verlag], in *dagegen dabei*, ed. Dany et al., 128.

22 Ulrich Müller, 'Althussers strukturalistische Umdeutung des "Kapital"', in *Das Argument*, 17:1/2 (1975), 92. On the difficult reception of Althusser, see Pfaller, *Althusser: Das Schweigen im Text*, 12f.

23 Jacques Rancière, *Althusser's Lesson*, trans. Emiliano Battista, London: Bloomsbury, 2011, 154, 147; cf. Jacques Rancière, *Wider den akademischen Marxismus*, trans. Wolfgang Hagen, Konrad Honsel, Otto Kallscheuer and Gerline Koch, Berlin: Merve, 1975, back cover, 29f., 36. On Maoism in France, see Julian Bourg, 'Principally Contradiction: The Flourishing of French Maoism', in *Mao's Little Red Book: A Global History*, ed. Alexander G. Cook, Cambridge University Press, 2014, 225–44.

24 See Friedrich Balke, 'Das Ende eines Schweigens: Zu Louis Althussers *L'Avenir dure longtemps*', in *Symptome: Zeitschrift für epistemologische Baustellen*, 10 (1992), 60–2; Judt, 'Elucubrations: The "Marxism" of Louis Althusser', 113.

25 See Louis Althusser, *The Future Lasts Forever: A Memoir*, ed. Olivier Corpet and Yann Moulier Boutang, trans. Richard Veasy, New York: New Press, 1993.

26 Heiner Müller, *Rotwelsch* [Cant], Berlin: Merve, 1982, 173.

27 Louis Althusser to Merve Verlag, 10 August 1973: Merve Archives.

28 Merve publishing collective, West Berlin, 'Artikel für Lexikon Feltrinelli/Fischer: Raubdrucke' [Article for Feltrinelli/Fischer encyclopedia: bootleg printing], typescript, Berlin, 1974. The article is not present in the *Enciclopedia Feltrinelli–Fischer*, vol. XXXIV: *Comunicazione di Massa*, ed. Pio Baldelli, Milan, 1974. On the bootleg printing movement, see also Albrecht Götz von Olenhusen, '"Aufklärung durch Aktion": Kollektiv-Verlage und Raubdrucke', in *Buch, Buchhandel und Rundfunk: 1968*

und die Folgen, ed. Monika Estermann and Edgar Lersch, Wiesbaden: Harrassowitz, 2003, 196–212.

29 Quoted in Albrecht Götz von Olenhusen, *'Der Weg vom Manuscript zum gedruckten Text ist länger, als er bisher je gewesen ist': Walter Benjamin im Raubdruck 1969 bis 1996*, Lengwil: Libelle, 1997, 13.

30 On the history of copyright in Germany, see Monika Dommann, *Autoren und Apparate: Die Geschichte des Copyrights im Medienwandel*, Frankfurt: S. Fischer, 2014.

31 See Ina Hitzenauer, *Der oppositionelle Buchmarkt der 1960er und 1970er Jahre in Deutschland*, Munich: Grin, 2005, 3; von Saldern, 'Markt für Marx', 154f.

32 Cf. Olenhusen, *'Der Weg vom Manuskript zum gedruckten Text'*, 3.

33 By the 1980s, if not before, the Merve rhombus achieved a similar degree of recognition among readers of theory to that of Willy Fleckhaus's rainbow-coloured *edition suhrkamp* covers: Jochen Stankowski and Christof Windgätter, 'Der Rauten-Macher: Gespräch über den Merve-Verlag', in Windgätter, *Verpackungen des Wissens: Materialität und Markenbildung in den Wissenschaften*, Vienna: Böhlau, 2012, 57–70.

34 According to Wolfgang Hagen in Guido Graf, '*Schlau sein, dabei sein*: Querbeat mit Merve', radio feature about Merve Verlag, WDR 3, 7 July 2005.

35 Robert Escarpit, *The Book Revolution*, London: Harrap/Unesco, 1966.

36 Quoted in Georg Stanitzek, 'Gebrauchswerte der Ideologiekritik', in *Theorietheorie: Wider die Theoriemüdigkeit in den Geisteswissenschaften*, ed. Mario Grizelj and Oliver Jahraus, Munich: Fink, 2011, 243.

37 Gollhardt, 'Das Taschenbuch im Zeitalter der Massenkultur', 125. 'Any treatment of the book which claims for it a special respect ... comes from another era', Gilles Deleuze would declare some years later in Gilles Deleuze and Claire Parnet, *Dialogues II*, trans. Hugh Tomlinson and Barbara Habberjam, 2nd edn, New York: Columbia University Press, 2007, 3f.

38 Stanitzek, 'Gebrauchswerte der Ideologiekritik'.

39 The distinction between the two types of books is from Escarpit, *The Book Revolution*, 31ff. Jochen Stankowski, the creator of the Merve rhombus, saw no contradiction in creating corporate logos as a leftist designer. In 1971, he also developed the corporate design of the retail chain Rewe: Stankowski and Windgätter, 'Der Rauten-Macher'.

40 Lowien, *Weibliche Produktivkraft*, 79.
41 Heidi Paris and Peter Gente, 'Fuss-Note', in *Geniale Dilletanten* [Footnote, in Brilliant dilletantes], ed. Wolfgang Müller, Berlin: Merve, 1982, 126.
42 Paris and Gente, 'Für *Buch-Markt*'.
43 Merve collective, 'Warum wir Rancière publizieren' [Why we are publishing Rancière], in Rancière, *Wider den akademischen Marxismus*, 91. Cf. Lowien, *Weibliche Produktivkraft*, 34. On the importance of China, see Altwegg, 'Die Merve-Kulturen'.
44 Lowien, *Weibliche Produktivkraft*, 196. After Merve had become established in the market, left-wing bookshops and bookstalls – in mainland West Germany, as well as West Berlin – bought each title as it appeared, by subscription, which ensured a stable revenue base. The print runs varied in the early seventies between 2,000 and 5,000 copies. Ibid., 52.
45 Adorno, *Minima Moralia*, 128.
46 Lowien, *Weibliche Produktivkraft*, 64, 79.
47 Ibid., 62, 83, 102, 76.
48 Herbert Marcuse to Merve Verlag, 9 April 1977: Merve Archives.
49 On the importance of that volume, see Wegmann, 'Wie kommt die Theorie zum Leser?' On the Habermas–Luhmann controversy, see chapter 11 in this book.
50 At least, that is the thrust of Niklas Luhmann, 'Systemtheoretische Argumentationen: Eine Entgegnung auf Jürgen Habermas', in Jürgen Habermas and Luhmann, *Theorie der Gesellschaft oder Sozialtechnologie: Was leistet die Systemforschung?* [Systems-theoretical argumentations: a rebuttal to Jürgen Habermas, in Theory of society or social technology: what does systems theory achieve?] Frankfurt: Suhrkamp, 1971, 316–41.
51 Lowien, *Weibliche Produktivkraft*, 72, 157, 131, 49, 168.
52 Ibid., 183, 85.
53 Compare, on the minute-taking practice of the West Berlin commune Kommune II, Nina Verheyen, *Diskussionslust: Eine Kulturgeschichte des 'besseren Arguments' in Westdeutschland*, Göttingen: Vandenhoeck & Ruprecht, 2010, 246f.
54 Lowien, *Weibliche Produktivkraft*, 187, 183, 85, 157.
55 Merve Verlag to Jürgen Hoch, 17 August 1978: Merve Archives.
56 On the history of discussion in West Germany, see Verheyen, *Diskussionslust*. On the fondness for drinking and on the Germans' aversion to compromise, see Norbert Elias, *Studies on the Germans*, trans.

Eric Dunning and Stephen Mennell, University College Dublin Press, 2013.

57 Cf. Jean-François Lyotard, 'Ein Denkmal des Marxismus', in Lyotard, *Streifzüge*, Vienna: Passagen, 1989, 96.

58 Lowien, *Weibliche Produktivkraft*, 86.

59 Verena Stefan, *Shedding and Literally Dreaming*, New York: Feminist Press, 1978.

60 Alexander Kluge, *Gelegenheitsarbeit einer Sklavin: Zur realistischen Methode* [Part-time work of a domestic slave: on the realistic method], Frankfurt: Suhrkamp, 1975, 7; cf. 235, 240. Cf. Lowien, *Weibliche Produktivkraft*, 87. On the German women's movement in the seventies, see also Rutschky, *Erfahrungshunger*, 60; Wolfgang Kraushaar, 'Thesen zum Verhältnis von Alternativ- und Fluchtbewegung: Am Beispiel der Frankfurter Scene', in *Autonomie oder Ghetto? Kontroversen über die Alternativbewegung*, ed. Wolfgang Kraushaar, Frankfurt: Neue Kritik, 1978, 48–55.

61 Hélène Cixous, *Die unendliche Zirkulation des Begehrens* [The endless circulation of desire], Berlin: Merve, 1977. On the relation between German and French feminism, see Cornelia Möser, *Féminismes en traductions: théories voyageuses et traductions culturelles*, Paris: Éditions des archives contemporaines, 2013.

62 Lowien, *Weibliche Produktivkraft*, 165.

63 Koenen, *Das rote Jahrzehnt*, 142f.

64 See Jäger, *Adorno*, 284. To Adorno, works of art were 'instructions for the praxis they refrain from'. Adorno, 'Commitment', 362f.

65 On the antagonism between these two tribes of the Left, see Matthis Dienstag (pseudonym of Karl Markus Michel), 'Provinz aus dem Kopf: Neue Nachrichten über die Metropolen-Spontis', in *Autonomie oder Ghetto? Kontroversen über die Alternativbewegung*, ed. Kraushaar, 148–86.

66 Quotations from Krahl, *Konstitution und Klassenkampf: Zur historischen Dialektik von bürgerlicher Emanzipation und proletarischer Revolution*, 26f., 279, 281. See also Detlev Glaussen, 'Hans-Jürgen Krahl: ein philosophisch-politisches Profil', in *Frankfurter Schule und Studentenbewegung*, vol. III, 65–70. On Krahl's tragic 'family novel', see Koenen, 'Der transzendental Obdachlose'. On the organization question, see also Gilles Deleuze, 'Nomadic Thought', in Deleuze, *Desert Islands and Other Texts 1953–1974*, ed. David Lapoujade, trans. Michael Taormina, Los Angeles: Semiotext(e),

2004, 260 (cf. Deleuze, *Nietzsche: Ein Lesebuch* [Nietzsche: a reader by Gilles Deleuze], trans. Ronald Voullié, Berlin: Merve, 1979, 121): 'As we know, the revolutionary problem today is to find some unity in our various struggles without falling back on the despotic and bureaucratic organization of the party or State apparatus: we want a war-machine that would not recreate a State apparatus.'

67 Lowien, *Weibliche Produktivkraft*, 159.

68 Ibid., 114.

69 Michel Foucault, 'The Order of Discourse', trans. Ian McLeod, in *Untying the Text: A Post-structuralist Reader*, Boston: Routledge and Kegan Paul, 1981, 67.

70 The term is from Friedrich Kittler, 'Ein Verwaiser', in *Anschlüsse: Versuche nach Michel Foucault*, ed. Gesa Dane, Wolfgang Essbach and Christa Karpenstein-Essbach, Tübingen: Diskord, 1985, 142.

71 Friedrich Kittler, 'Forgetting', trans. Caroline Wellbery and David Wellbery, in *Discourse*, 3 (1981), 103.

72 Lowien, *Weibliche Produktivkraft*, 125.

4 The Wolfsburg Empire

1 Ibid., 7.

2 Altwegg, 'Die Merve-Kulturen'. An informative source on comrades who went underground is Ulrike Edschmid, *Das Verschwinden des Philip S.*, Frankfurt: Suhrkamp, 2013.

3 'Anmerkung des Merve-Kollektivs', in Otto Schily and Christian Ströbele, *Plädoyers einer politischen Verteidigung: Reden und Mitschriften aus dem Mahler-Prozess* [Afterword by the Merve collective, in Pleadings of a political defence: speeches and transcripts from the Mahler trial], Berlin: Merve, 1973, 145. Incidentally, Peter Gente and Heidi Paris attended the funeral of Ulrike Meinhof in 1975. See Paris and Gente, 'Ping-Pong auf der Hochebene von Tibet', 130.

4 *Plädoyers einer politischen Verteidigung*, 138ff.

5 Horst Mahler, 'Rede vor Gericht', in ibid., 130. Ulrike Meinhof and Gerhard Müller were arrested in June 1972 at the home of the teacher Fritz Rodewald (1939–2009) after he tipped off the police, allegedly encouraged by Oskar Negt. Klaus Rainer Röhl, the publisher of *konkret* from 1964 to 1973 and Meinhof's husband from 1961 to 1968, was a 'moderate' on the issue of political violence.

6 Mahler says so in the documentary *Die Anwälte: Eine deutsche Geschichte* [The lawyers: a German story] by Birgit Schulz, Cologne, 2009.

7 'Anmerkung des Merve-Kollektivs', 145f. (The original cites the corresponding passages in the German original of Negt and Kluge, of course.) On the anti-Semitism of the West German terrorists and on the anti-Zionist turn in the German Left after the Six-Day War, see Jens Benicke, *Von Adorno zu Mao: Über die schlechte Aufhebung der antiautoritären Bewegung*, Freiburg: Ça ira, 2010, 73ff.; Wolfgang Kraushaar, *'Wann endlich beginnt bei euch der Kampf gegen die heilige Kuh Israel?' München 1970: Über die antisemitischen Wurzeln des deutschen Terrorismus*, Reinbek: Rowohlt, 2013.

8 For a contemporary attempt at systematization, see Rolf Schwendter, *Theorie der Subkultur*, Cologne: Kiepenheuer & Witsch, 1971. On the 'counter-culture' in West Germany, see also Detlef Siegfried, *Sound der Revolte: Studien zur Kulturrevolution um 1968*, Weinheim: Juventa, 2008, esp. 123–60.

9 Oskar Negt and Alexander Kluge, *Öffentlichkeit und Erfahrung: Zur Organisationsanalyse von bürgerlicher und proletarischer Öffentlichkeit*, Frankfurt: Suhrkamp, 1972, 10.

10 See Jochen Hörisch, *Theorie-Apotheke: Eine Handreichung zu den humanwissenschaftlichen Theorien der letzten fünfzig Jahre, einschliesslich ihrer Risiken und Nebenwirkungen*, Frankfurt: Suhrkamp, 2005.

11 See Walter Benjamin and Asja Lacis, 'Naples', in Walter Benjamin, *Reflections*, trans. Edmund Jephcott, New York and London: Harcourt Brace Jovanovich, 1978, 163–73. On the importance of Naples for the Frankfurt School, see also Mittelmeier, *Adorno in Neapel*.

12 Dieter Kunzelmann, *Leisten Sie keinen Widerstand! Bilder aus meinem Leben*, Berlin: Transit, 1998, 107; cf. 120. See also Aribert Reimann, *Dieter Kunzelmann: Avantgardist, Protestler, Radikaler*, Göttingen: Vandenhoeck & Ruprecht, 2009, 211ff.

13 See Philipp Felsch, 'Beim Paten: Feltrinelli und die Deutschen', in *Ästhetik & Kommunikation*, 129/30 (2005), special issue: *Mythos BRD*, 115–19; Gerd Koenen, *Vesper, Ensslin, Baader: Urszenen des deutschen Terrorismus*, Cologne: Kiepenheuer & Witsch, 2003, 264–7. According to Koenen, Italy was 'the dream country of all the militarizing elements of the movement in Germany' (262). On the travel culture of the Left in the seventies, see Anja Bertsch, 'Alternative (in) Bewegung: Distinktion und transnationale

Vergemeinschaftung im alternativen Tourismus', in *Das Alternative Milieu: Antibürgerlicher Lebensstil und linke Politik in der Bundesrepublik Deutschland und Europa 1968–1983*, ed. Sven Reichardt and Detlef Siegfried, Göttingen: Wallstein, 2010, 115–30.

14 See Oskar Negt and Alexander Kluge, *Public Sphere and Experience: Analysis of the Bourgeois and Proletarian Public Sphere*, trans. Peter Labanyi, Jamie Owen Daniel and Assenka Oksiloff, London: Verso, 2016, 91ff.

15 Müller, *Rotwelsch*, 60. On the strikes in Turin, see Guido Viale, *Die Träume liegen wieder auf der Strasse: Offene Fragen der deutschen und italienischen Linken nach 1968*, Berlin: Wagenbach, 1979. The workers' slogans are quoted in Daniel Cohn-Bendit, *Der grosse Basar: Gespräche mit Michel Lévy, Jean-Marc Salmon, Maren Sell*, Munich: Trikont, 1975, 99.

16 Lowien, *Weibliche Produktivkraft*, 72.

17 See Philipp Felsch, 'Schafft italienische Zustände! Wolfsburg als linke Utopie und wie sie scheiterte', in *Radikal: Anders*, Karlsruhe: Autostadt Wolfsburg GmbH, 2011, n.p. On the situation of the Italian migrant workers in Wolfsburg, see Anne von Oswald, '"Venite a lavorare con la Volkswagen": "Gastarbeiter" in Wolfsburg 1962–1974', in *Aufbau West – Aufbau Ost: Die Planstädte Wolfsburg und Eisenhüttenstadt in der Nachkriegszeit*, ed. Rosmarie Beier, Ostfildern-Ruit: Hatje, 1997, 199–210.

18 Lowien, *Weibliche Produktivkraft*, 72.

19 Ibid., 83f.

20 That position had been advanced by the New Left in Italy since the early sixties. The origins of Operaism can be found in the pages of the journal *Quaderni rossi*, and especially in the writings of Mario Tronti, who, like Toni Negri, was among the earliest Merve authors. Tronti's principal work, however, was published in Germany by Neue Kritik: see Mario Tronti, *Arbeiter und Kapital*, Frankfurt: Neue Kritik, 1974.

21 Eddy Cherki and Michel Wieviorka, 'Autoreduction Movements in Turin', in *Semiotext(e)*, 3:3 (1980), special issue: *Autonomia; Post-Political Politics*, 72–9.

22 On the theory and history of Operaism, see Steve Wright, *Storming Heaven: Class Composition and Struggle in Italian Autonomist Marxism*, 2nd edn, London: Pluto, 2017; and *Semiotext(e)*, 3:3 (1980), special issue: *Autonomia; Post-Political Politics*. A very informative source on the differences between German and Italian militants is Edschmid, *Das Verschwinden des Philip S.*

23 Cohn-Bendit, *Der grosse Basar*, 98, 102f.; Koenen, *Das rote Jahrzehnt*, 317f.

24 As indicated, for example, by a 1972 newsletter of the Ufficio Internazionale of Potere Operaio, sent to the Merve collective by Toni Negri. The document has been preserved in the Merve Archives.

25 Toni Negri to the Merve collective, 7 July 1972.

26 Bude, 'Die Suche nach dem Unmöglichen,' 226.

27 See Giovanni di Lorenzo, 'VorUrteil: Die Geschichte des Toni Negri,' in *Transatlantik*, 5:3 (1984), 34–41.

28 Michael Hardt and Antonio Negri, *Empire*, Cambridge, Mass.: Harvard University Press, 2000, 413.

29 Lowien, *Weibliche Produktivkraft*, 121, 115.

30 Vogel, 'Die Kunst des Verschwindens.'

31 'Frauentausch'; Lowien, *Weibliche Produktivkraft*, 133.

32 Heidi Paris and Peter Gente, 'Kunst des Büchermachens: Gespräch mit Heide Paris und Peter Gente vom Merve-Verlag' [Art of making books: interview with Heide [*sic*] Paris and Peter Gente of Merve Verlag], in *Kunstforum International*, 100 (1989), 377.

33 Interview with Hannes Böhringer, 20 March 2014. See also Frithjof Thaetner, 'Trauerrede für Heidi Paris,' in *Für Heidi Paris* [For Heidi Paris], Berlin: Merve, 2003, 23.

34 So says Hannes Böhringer in Graf, 'Querbeat mit Merve.' The radio feature is highly informative in regard to Heidi Paris. See also Rainald Goetz, *Loslabern: Bericht Herbst 2008*, Frankfurt: Suhrkamp, 2009, 166f. The characterization of Heidi Paris is also based on the author's conversations: with Marianne Karbe on 1 December 2011; with Peter Gente on 21 April 2008; and with Georg Stanitzek on 5 April 2014.

35 For a readable portrait of the generation, see Reinhard Mohr, *Zaungäste: Die Generation, die nach der Revolte kam*, Frankfurt: S. Fischer, 1992.

36 Henning Ritter's tutorial was titled 'Geschichte der Vernunft oder des Wahnsinns: Einführung in Foucaults Theorie der Epochenschwelle des 19. Jahrhunderts' [History of reason or of madness: introduction to Foucault's theory of the epochal threshold of the 19th century]: *Vorlesungsverzeichnis für das Wintersemester 1973/74*, Berlin: Freie Universität, 1973.

37 Diederichsen, *Sexbeat*, 74ff.

38 Merve Verlag to Jean-François Lyotard, 8 October 1976: Merve Archives.

5 (Possible) Reasons for the Happiness of Thought

1 Merve Verlag to Jean-Francois Lyotard, 8 October 1976: Merve Archives.

2 Jean-François Lyotard to Merve Verlag, 7 November 1976: Merve Archives.

3 Cf. Reinhold Urmetzer, 'Müll-Abfuhr: Lyotards politische Annäherung an Duchamp', in *die tageszeitung*, 26 February 1988.

4 Jean-François Lyotard, *Das Patchwork der Minderheiten: Für eine herrenlose Politik*, trans. Clemens-Carl Haerle, Berlin: Merve, 1977, 16, 37; cf. 28. An English translation of the lead essay has been published, at least online: 'A Brief Putting in Perspective of Decadence and of Several Minoritarian Battles to Be Waged', trans. Taylor Adkins, in Vast Abrupt: https://vastabrupt.com/2018/03/12/lyotard-brief-putting-perspective-decadence. On non-voters, see Sylvère Lotringer and Christian Marazzi, 'The Return of Politics', in *Semiotext(e)*, 3:3 (1980), special issue: *Autonomia: Post-Political Politics*, 11.

5 Merve Verlag to Jean-François Lyotard, 1 October 1977: Merve Archives.

6 Rudolf Augstein, 'Frauen fliessen, Männer schiessen', in *Der Spiegel*, 31:52 (1977), 204.

7 Author's interview with Peter Gente, 10 May 2012.

8 Warren Breckman, *Adventures of the Symbolic: Post-Marxism and Radical Democracy*, New York: Columbia University Press, 2013, 4ff.; Thomas Grossbölting, 'Entstalinisierungskrisen im Westen: Die kommunistischen Bewegungen Westeuropas und das Jahr 1956', in *Kommunismus in der Krise*, ed. Grossbölting and Wentker, 233–49.

9 Jean-François Lyotard, 'A Memorial of Marxism', trans. Cecile Lindsay, in Lyotard, *Peregrinations: Law, Form, Event*, New York: Columbia University Press, 1988, 45–76; cf. Stuart Sim, *Post-Marxism: An Intellectual History*, London: Routledge, 2000, ch. 7.

10 Jean-François Lyotard, 'A "Barbarian" Speaks about Socialism', interview with Bernard-Henri Lévy, trans. Roger McKeon, in Lyotard, *Jean-François Lyotard: The Interviews and Debates*, London: Bloomsbury, 2020, 41; cf. Jean-François Lyotard, *Intensitäten*, trans. Lothar Kurzawa and Volker Schaefer, Berlin: Merve, 1978, 7.

11 Karl Marx, *The Eighteenth Brumaire of Louis Bonaparte*, trans. D. D. L., New York and Berlin: Mondial, 2005, 46. On the relation between lumpenproletariat and *bohème*, see Georg Stanitzek, 'Die Bohème als Bildungsmilieu: Zur Struktur eines Soziotops', in *Soziale Systeme*, 16:2 (2010), 404–18.

12 Gilles Deleuze in the discussion on his and Guattari's 'reports', in *Antipsychiatrie und Wunschökonomie: Materialien des Kongresses 'Psychoanalyse und Politik' in Mailand 8.–9. Mai 1973* [Antipsychiatry and the economy of desire: materials from the conference 'Psychoanalysis and Politics', Milan, 8 and 9 May 1973], ed. Armando Verdiglione, Berlin: Merve, 1976, 24. On the social 'sediment' in systems of power as an object of Foucault's analyses, see also Jürgen Habermas, 'The Genealogical Writing of History: On Some Aporias in Foucault's Theory of Power', in *Canadian Journal of Political and Social Theory*, 10:1–2 (1986), 1–9.

13 Benicke, *Von Adorno zu Mao*, 30f., 94f.

14 Cf. William Burroughs, *Naked Lunch: The Restored Text*, London: Harper Collins, 2010, 201.

15 Lyotard, 'A "Barbarian" Speaks about Socialism', 43; cf. Lyotard, *Intensitäten*, 11.

16 Félix Guattari, 'Everybody Wants to Be a Fascist', trans. Suzanne Fletcher and Catherine Benamou, in Guattari, *Chaosophy: Texts and Interviews 1972–1977*, Los Angeles: Semiotext(e), 2009, p. 157; cf. Félix Guattari, *Mikro-Politik des Wunsches* [Micropolitics of desire], trans. Hans-Joachim Metzger, Berlin: Merve, 1977, 11.

17 Jean-François Lyotard, 'Tomb of the Intellectual', trans. Bill Readings and Kevin Paul Geiman, in Lyotard, *Political Writings*, University College London, 1993, 3.

18 Michel de Certeau, 'Pratiques du pouvoir', in Certeau, *Histoire et psychanalyse: entre science et fiction*, Paris: Gallimard, 1987, 149.

19 Niklas Luhmann, *Archimedes und wir: Interviews* [Archimedes and us: interviews], Berlin: Merve, 1987, 29. For a survey of the discourse on the intellectual in West Germany in the 1970s and 1980s, see Roman Luckscheiter, 'Intellektuelle in der Bundesrepublik 1968–1989', in *Intellektuelle im 20. Jahrhundert in Deutschland*, ed. Jutta Schlich, Tübingen: Niemeyer, 2000, 325–41. The publication of Dietz Bering's now classic study *Die Intellektuellen: Geschichte eines Schimpfworts*, Stuttgart: Klett-Cotta, 1978, is symptomatic of the situation in the late seventies.

20 Merve Verlag to Jean-François Lyotard, 1 June 1978: Merve Archives.

21 Cf. Jean-François Lyotard, *Dérive à partir de Marx et Freud* [Adrift from Marx and Freud], Paris: Union générale d'éditions, 1973.

22 Lyotard, 'Notes on the Return and Kapital', trans. Roger McKeon, in *Semiotext(e)*, 3:1 (1978), 47 (cf. Lyotard, *Intensitäten*, 20); Lyotard,

'Energumen Capitalism', trans. R. Mackay, in *#Accelerate: The Accelerationist Reader*, ed. Armen Avanessian and Robin Mackay, Falmouth: Urbanomic/ Merve, 2014, 191ff.; cf. 'Energieteufel Kapitalismus', in Lyotard, *Intensitäten*, 108ff. On capitalism as a de-territorializing principle, see Descombes, *Modern French Philosophy*, 176f., 181f. For a critique of energetic social theories, see Max Weber's still classic essay '"Energetic" Theories of Culture', trans. Jon Mark Mikkelsen and Charles Schwartz, in *Mid-American Review of Sociology*, 9:2 (1984), 35–58. On the history of the term 'intensity' down to Nietzsche, see Erich Kleinschmidt, 'Intensität: Prospekt zu einem kulturpoetischen Modellbegriff', in *Weimarer Beiträge*, 49 (2003), 165–83.

23 Diedrich Diederichsen, *Eigenblutdoping: Selbstverwertung, Künstlerromantik, Partizipation*, Cologne: Kiepenheuer & Witsch, 2008, 151.

24 Lyotard, 'Notes on the Return and Kapital', 52f.; cf. Lyotard, *Intensitäten*, 32. Other participants in the conference included Gilles Deleuze, Jacques Derrida and Pierre Klossowski: Maurice de Gandillac, 'Le colloque de Cerisy-la-Salle', in *Nietzsche-Studien*, 4 (1975), 324–33.

25 Lyotard, 'Notes on the Return and Kapital', 45 (cf. Lyotard, *Intensitäten*, 17: 'Even the cry belongs – as Nietzsche knows – to representation.'). On the relationship between the philosophical discourse of intensity and the 'text of day-to-day life', see Diederichsen, *Eigenblutdoping*, 153. On the speechlessness of the hippies, see Diederichsen, *Sexbeat*, 26ff.

26 Lyotard, 'Notes on the Return and Kapital', 51f.; cf. Lyotard, *Intensitäten*, 27ff., 32. In the 1980s, after Gente and Paris had met John Cage, he became one of their most cherished authors: author's interview with Peter Gente, 26 September 2010. See also Marcus Klug, *Ein Leben wie eine Komposition von John Cage* [A life like a John Cage composition], video interview with Peter Gente, Berlin, 2007 (www.youtube.com/watch?v=82LiWC6EpmY).

27 Lyotard, 'Notes on the Return and Kapital', 45, 52; cf. Lyotard, *Intensitäten*, 17, 32; Lyotard, 'Apathie in der Theorie' [Apathy in theory], trans. Lothar Kurzawa, in Lyotard, *Apathie in der Theorie*, trans. Clemens-Carl Haerle and Lothar Kurzawa, Berlin: Merve, 1979, 92.

28 Karl Heinz Bohrer, 'Intensität ist kein Gefühl: Nietzsche contra Wagner als Lehrbeispiel', in *Merkur*, 424 (1984), 138–44.

29 See Rudolf E. Künzli, 'Nietzsche und die Semiologie: Neue Ansätze in der französischen Nietzsche-Interpretation', in *Nietzsche-Studien*, 5 (1976), 263–88; Gerd Bergfleth, 'Die Verewigung des Lebens: Zu Klossowskis

Nietzsche-Deutung', in Pierre Klossowski, *Nietzsche und der Circulus vitiosus deus*, trans. Ronald Voullié, Munich: Matthes & Seitz, 1986, 431–49.

30 Bohrer, 'Sechs Szenen Achtundsechzig', 416. Cf. Raulff, *Kreis ohne Meister*, 499.

31 Merve Verlag to Gilles Deleuze, 8 May 1979: Merve Archives. The reference is to Deleuze, *Nietzsche: Ein Lesebuch*, 121.

32 Merve Verlag to Pierre Klossowski, 28 May 1979; Merve Verlag to Sylvère Lotringer, 25 March 1981; Paris and Gente, 'Fuss-Note', 126.

33 Lowien, *Weibliche Produktivkraft*, 122, quoting Jacques Derrida, 'From Restricted to General Economy: A Hegelianism without Reserve', in Derrida, *Writing and Difference*, trans. Alan Bass, Chicago University Press, 1978, 256.

34 See chapter 11.

35 Deleuze, *Nietzsche: Ein Lesebuch*, 116; quoted here from the English translation: Deleuze, 'Nomadic Thought', 257. Is that why he pointed out what fun it was to write together with Guattari? 'It was great fun', Deleuze reports, in 'Gilles Deleuze and Félix Guattari on *Anti-Oedipus*' (interview by Catherine Backès-Clément, 1972), in Gilles Deleuze, *Negotiations: 1972–1990*, trans. Martin Joughin, New York: Columbia University Press, 1995, 14; cf. Deleuze and Guattari, *Rhizom*, Berlin: Merve, 1977, 50.

36 Lyotard, 'Energumen Capitalism', 207; Lyotard, 'Apathie in der Theorie', 92ff. The idea of parodying theory goes back to Klossowski: cf. Pierre Klossowski, 'Circulus vitiosus', in Klossowski, *Nietzsche und der Circulus vitiosus deus*, 413ff., 418ff.; Descombes, *Modern French Philosophy*, 182f.

37 Merve Verlag to Roland Barthes, 9 May 1979: Merve Archives.

38 Rudolf Heinz and Georg Tholen (eds.), *Schizo-Schleichwege: Beiträge zum Anti-Ödipus*, Bremen: Impuls, 1981.

39 Peter Bexte, 'Warum haben Sie keinen Schreibtisch, Herr Gente? Der Mitbegründer des Berliner Merve Verlages im Interview' [Why don't you have a desk, Mr Gente? Interview with the co-founder of Merve Verlag, Berlin], in *Frankfurter Allgemeine Magazin*, 2 October 1987, 107.

40 Michael Rutschky, 'Der Lachkrampf', in *Merkur*, 641/2 (2002), special issue: *Lachen* [Laughter], 931–4. 'I'm afraid my giggles lead us straight to the core of ecstatic philosophy', Rutschky wrote (ibid., 934), 'which is about sovereignty through the loss of the self.' Although he was referring to Bataille, it is just a stone's throw from Bataille to Foucault.

41 Michel Foucault, *The Order of Things: Archaeology of the Human Sciences*,

London: Tavistock, 1970, 342f. On Foucault's unsettling laughter, see Puder, 'Der böse Blick des Michel Foucault', 321.

42 Heidi Paris and Peter Gente, 'Ein Star ist gestorben, ein Planet geboren' [A star has died, a planet is born], typescript: Merve Archives.

43 Kittler, 'Ein Verwaiser', 141.

44 Michel de Certeau, 'The Laugh of Michel Foucault', in Certeau, *Heterologies: Discourse on the Other*, trans. Brian Massumi, Minneapolis: University of Minnesota Press, 1986, 193–8.

45 According to Klaus Heinrich's '"Theorie" des Lachens', in *Lachen, Gelächter, Lächeln: Reflexionen in drei Spiegeln*, ed. Dietmar Kamper and Christoph Wulf, Frankfurt: Syndikat, 1986, 17–38.

46 This hypothesis calls for further study. Gert Mattenklott has confirmed it for education and related disciplines in his 'Versuch über Albernheit', in *Lachen, Gelächter, Lächeln*, ed. Kamper and Wulf, 215: 'Especially in the 1970s, interest in humour and wit, laughing and smiling seems to have eclipsed all other topics in childhood research.'

47 Hans Blumenberg, 'Der Sturz des Protophilosophen: Zur Komik der reinen Theorie; anhand einer Rezeptionsgeschichte der Thales-Anekdote', in *Poetik und Hermeneutik*, vol. VII: *Das Komische*, ed. Wolfgang Preisendanz and Rainer Warning, Munich: Fink, 1976, 60. For remarks on the 'late Romanticism of the proletariat', see ibid., 17; and Blumenberg, 'Wer sollte vom Lachen der Magd betroffen sein? Eine Duplik', in *Das Komische*, ed. Preisendanz and Warning, 437f. This theme is not found in Blumenberg, *Das Lachen der Thrakerin: Eine Urgeschichte der Theorie*, Frankfurt: Suhrkamp, 1987.

48 Odo Marquard, 'Exile der Heiterkeit', in *Das Komische*, ed. Preisendanz and Warning, 133, 149f.

49 Dieter Wellershoff, 'Infantilismus als Revolte oder das ausgeschlagene Erbe: Zur Theorie des Blödelns', in *Das Komische*, ed. Preisendanz and Warning, 354, 351, 356.

50 Mattenklott, 'Versuch über Albernheit', 211.

51 Ariane Barth, 'Luftwurzeln und Wildwuchs verlieben sich', in *Der Spiegel*, 34:53 (1980), 99. *Rhizom* by Deleuze and Guattari was also published in 1977, but before the Book Fair, and in the old A5 format. It may be the most classic of all Merve's classic titles. On the peregrinations of the Pink Panther through subcultures of the Left and Right, see Klaus Birnstiel, 'Wer hat an der Theorie gedreht? In den siebziger Jahren war

er eine Galionsfigur linker Theoriebildung; Dann geisterte Paulchen Panther durch das Mordvideo der Zwickauer Neonazis: Ein Blick auf die Bildsprache des Terrors', in *Frankfurter Allgemeine Zeitung*, 23 June 2012.

52 Merve Verlag to Jean-François Lyotard, 1 June 1978: Merve Archives.

53 For an illuminating discussion of the relationship between decolonization and post-structuralism, see Mark Terkessidis, 'Als die Kämpfe kleiner wurden: In 30 Jahren von der "Internationalen Marxistischen Diskussion" zum "Internationalen Merve Diskurs"', in *Jungle World*, 26 January 2000.

54 Merve Verlag to Jean-François Lyotard, n.d.: Merve Archives. Peter Gente asserts in an untitled handwritten note dated 1990 – certainly not without justification – that the early Suhrkamp translations were 'a kind of insider tip' for academics, and 'unread classics' until the mid-1970s: Merve Archives. A detailed reception history has not yet been written.

55 Most prominently in Theodor W. Adorno, *Jargon of Authenticity*, trans. Knut Tarnowski and Frederic Will, London: Routledge, 1973. On the reciprocal animosities, see Ulrich Raulff, 'Akute Zeichen fiebriger Dekonstruktion: Die Frankfurter Schule und ihre Gegenspieler in Paris; Eine Verkennungsgeschichte aus gegebenem Anlass', in *Süddeutsche Zeitung*, 21 September 2001.

56 Jean Améry, 'Leben wir im Kerker-Archipel? Eine Strafpredigt über die Strafe', in *Die Zeit*, 14 January 1977. Cf. Jean Améry, 'Archäologie des Wissens: Michel Foucault und sein Diskurs der Gegenaufklärung', in *Die Zeit*, 31 March 1978. On Manfred Frank's attacks, see Raulff, *Wiedersehen mit den Siebzigern*, 69.

57 Merve Verlag to Daniel Charles, 16 December 1978: Merve Archives.

58 Gilles Deleuze and Félix Guattari, 'Introduction: Rhizome', in Deleuze and Guattari, *A Thousand Plateaus: Capitalism and Schizophrenia*, trans. Brian Massumi, Minneapolis: University of Missouri Press, 1987, 24f.; cf. Deleuze and Guattari, *Rhizom*, 41.

59 That was the judgement of such diverse Merve readers as Diedrich Diederichsen ('Aus dem Zusammenhang reissen / in den Zusammenhang schmeissen: Zur deutschen Veröffentlichung von "Mille Plateaux" von Gilles Deleuze und Félix Guattari', in Diederichsen, *Freiheit macht arm: Das Leben nach Rock'n'Roll 1990–93*, Cologne: Kiepenheuer & Witsch, 1993, 163) and Friedrich Kittler ('Ein Verwaiser', 141). In the early 1980s, the essayist Lothar Baier wrote a critique of 'Frenchmen's theory' *à la*

Merve, which, in his opinion, was characterized – not least because of deficient translation – by a style 'made in Germany': Lothar Baier, 'Franzosentheorie', in Baier, *Französische Zustände: Berichte und Essays*, Frankfurt: Europäische Verlagsanstalt, 1982.

6 The Reader as Partisan

1 Merve Verlag to Jean-François Lyotard, 1 June 1978: Merve Archives.
2 See *Literaturmagazin*, 9 (1978), special issue: *Der neue Irrationalismus*.
3 Merve Verlag to Jürgen Hoch, 17 August 1978, Merve Archives.
4 Roland Barthes, 'The Death of the Author', in Barthes, *The Rustle of Language*, trans. Richard Howard, New York: Farrar, Straus and Giroux, 1986, 55.
5 Michel Foucault, 'What Is an Author?' trans. Josué V. Harari, in Foucault, *Essential Works of Foucault 1954–1984*, vol. II: *Aesthetics, Method, and Epistemology*, ed. James D. Faubion, New York: New Press, 1998.
6 Roland Barthes, 'Writing Reading', in Barthes, *The Rustle of Language*, 29.
7 Michel Foucault, 'Truth and Power', interview with Alessandro Fontana and Pasquale Pasquino, trans. Colin Gordon, in Foucault, *Power/Knowledge: Selected Interviews and Other Writings 1972–1977*, New York: Pantheon, 1980, 127; cf. Foucault, *Dispositive der Macht* [Dispositives of power], trans. Jutta Kranz, Hans-Joachim Metzger, Ulrich Raulff, Walter Seitter and E. Wehr, Berlin: Merve, 1978, 46.
8 Louis Althusser, 'La philosophie comme arme de la révolution: réponse à huit questions', in Althusser, *Positions (1964–1975)*, Paris: Éditions sociales, 1976, 47.
9 Manfred Naumann, Dieter Schlenstedt, Karlheinz Barck, Dieter Kliche and Rosemarie Lenzer, *Gesellschaft, Literatur, Lesen: Literaturrezeption in theoretischer Sicht*, Berlin: Aufbau, 1973.
10 Quoted in Certeau, 'The Laugh of Michel Foucault', 194.
11 Jorge Luis Borges, *Collected Fictions*, trans. Andrew Hurley, London: Penguin, 1999, 3.
12 Kittler, 'Forgetting', 98f., 104f. From Kittler's perspective, at least, older Merve titles turn out to be the antithesis of hermeneutics, since at the second reading most of them start falling apart.
13 Roland Barthes, *The Pleasure of the Text*, trans. Richard Miller, New York: Hill and Wang, 1975, 13.
14 Bexte, 'Warum haben Sie keinen Schreibtisch, Herr Gente?' 107.

15 Henning Ritter, 'Jacob Taubes: Verstehen, was da los ist', in Ritter, *Verehrte Denker*, 41.

16 On Ritter's 'notorious writing inhibitions', see Lepenies, 'Der wilde Denker'.

17 On Heidi Paris as a reader, see Goetz, *Loslabern*, 167.

18 Paris and Gente, 'Editorische Notiz', in Harald Szeemann, *Museum der Obsessionen* [Editorial note, in Museum of obsessions], Berlin: Merve, 1981, 225.

19 Michel Foucault's characterization of the book in his famous foreword to the American edition: Michel Foucault, 'Preface', in Gilles Deleuze and Félix Guattari, *Anti-Oedipus: Capitalism and Schizophrenia*, trans. Robert Hurley, Mark Seem and Helen R. Lane, Minneapolis: University of Minnesota Press, 1983, xiii; cf. Foucault, *Dispositive der Macht*, 228. On Deleuze and Guattari's Nietzschean version of Freudo-Marxism, see Descombes, *Modern French Philosophy*, 173ff.

20 Wolfgang Hagen in Graf, 'Querbeat mit Merve'.

21 Manfred Frank, *What Is Neostructuralism?* trans. Sabine Wilke and Richard Gray, Minneapolis: University of Minnesota Press, 1989, 317.

22 Paris and Gente, 'Ping-Pong auf der Hochebene von Tibet', 130.

23 Bexte, 'Warum haben Sie keinen Schreibtisch, Herr Gente?' 107. Paris and Gente also read each other their translations (interview with the Merve translator Ronald Voullié, 6 December 2011). On the history of reading aloud and silently between the Middle Ages and the early modern period, see Illich, *In the Vineyard of the Text*.

24 The practice of repeated, collective reading aloud is involved in most of the reading experiments of the seventies. An early example is Althusser, who had challenged his contemporaries as early as 1965 to finally read *Capital* 'to the letter' – 'the text itself, complete, all four volumes, line by line; to return ten times to the first chapters': Althusser, *Reading Capital*, 13. See also Harald Weinrich, 'Lesen, schneller lesen, langsamer lesen', in *Neue Rundschau*, 84:3 (1984), 80–99, who interprets such slow reading as a strategy to counter the general trend towards accelerated reading.

25 On Nietzsche's way of reading, see Matthias Bickenbach, *Von den Möglichkeiten einer 'inneren' Geschichte des Lesens*, Tübingen: Niemeyer, 1999, 40–54.

26 Paris and Gente, 'Fuss-Note', 127.

27 Paris and Gente, 'Ping-Pong auf der Hochebene von Tibet', 130.

28 Hans-Thies Lehmann and Helmuth Lethen, 'Das kollektive Lesen', in *Bertolt Brechts 'Hauspostille': Text und kollektives Lesen*, ed. Lehmann and Lethen, Stuttgart: Metzler, 1978, 2f., 8ff. On the feeling of floating, see Lethen, *Suche nach dem Handorakel*, 126f. On the concept of the wish in the background of this reading, see Ulrich Raulf [Raulff], 'Der nicht-ödipale Wunsch: Notizen zu Deleuze/Guattari: "Anti-Ödipus"', in *Über die Wünsche: Ein Versuch zur Archäologie der Subjektivität*, ed. Dietmar Kamper, Munich: Hanser, 1977, 64–81.

29 Lyotard, 'Notes on the Return and Kapital', 45, 52f.; cf. Lyotard, *Intensitäten*, 32. Lyotard's emphasis.

30 Deleuze and Guattari, 'Introduction: Rhizome', 4; cf. Deleuze and Guattari, *Rhizom*, 7. François Dosse likewise considered 'Rhizome' a 'theory of reading': see Dosse, *Gilles Deleuze and Félix Guattari: Intersecting Lives*, trans. Deborah Glassman, New York: Columbia University Press, 2010, 362.

31 Deleuze in the group interview 'In Flux', in Guattari, *Chaosophy: Texts and Interviews 1972–1977*, ed. Sylvère Lotringer, trans. David L. Sweet, Jarred Becker and Taylor Adkins, Los Angeles: Semiotext(e), 2009, 75; cf. Guattari, *Mikro-Politik des Wunsches*, 46. The child as the ideal addressee of theory occurs again later in Lyotard's *The Postmodern Explained to Children: Correspondence, 1982–1985*, trans. Don Barry, Bernadette Maher, Julian Pefanis, Virginia Spate and Morgan Thomas, Sydney: Power, 1992. On the difficulty of *Anti-Oedipus*, see Raulf, 'Der nicht-ödipale Wunsch', 64.

32 Frank, *What Is Neostructuralism?* 329.

33 Félix Guattari et al., 'In Flux', in Guattari, *Chaosophy*, 71 (cf. 75); cf. Guattari, *Mikro-Politik des Wunsches*, 40 (cf. 46). On Bakhtin's Rabelais as a target of projection in the seventies, see Dirk Schümer, 'Lachen mit Bachtin: ein geisteshistorisches Trauerspiel', in *Merkur*, 641/2 (2002), special issue: *Lachen*, 847–54.

34 Deleuze and Guattari, *Rhizom*, 40f. (The paragraph, apparently added by the authors for the Merve edition, is not present in the English translation of 'Introduction: Rhizome' in *A Thousand Plateaus*, nor in the French.)

35 No wonder the Maoist Alain Badiou found Deleuze and Guattari guilty of the 'tyranny of revisionism'. Quoted in Dosse, *Gilles Deleuze and Félix Guattari: Intersecting Lives*, 366. Post-structuralism as a whole was 'good news for all people who like to read', writes Jörg Lau in 'Der Jargon der

Uneigentlichkeit', in *Merkur*, 594/5 (1998), special issue: *Postmoderne: Eine Bilanz*, 945.

36 Bude, 'Die Suche nach dem Unmöglichen', 201.

37 Barthes, *The Pleasure of the Text*, 3.

38 See also Bude, 'Die Suche nach dem Unmöglichen', 236.

39 Merve collective, 'Warum wir Rancière publizieren', 91.

40 See Agnes Heller, 'Paradigm of Production, Paradigm of Work', in *Dialectical Anthropology*, 6 (1981), 71–9.

41 Guattari, 'Everybody Wants to Be a Fascist', 175; cf. Guattari, *Mikro-Politik des Wunsches*, 37. On the production paradigm of *Anti-Oedipus*, see Raulf, 'Der nicht-ödipale Wunsch', 68ff.

42 Certeau, *The Practice of Everyday Life*, xix, xii, xvii.

43 On the book's origins and background, see François Dosse, *Michel de Certeau: le marcheur blessé*, Paris: La Découverte, 2002, 443ff., 489ff.

44 Hans-Ulrich Wehler, 'Geschichte von unten gesehen', in: *Die Zeit*, 3 May 1985.

45 Michel de Certeau to Merve Verlag, 1 July 1985: Merve Archives.

46 Certeau, *The Practice of Everyday Life*, v.

47 Ibid., 173, xxii, 167ff., 169.

48 Enzensberger, 'Bildung als Konsumgut', iii.

49 On the leftist critique of consumption in the seventies, see Alexander Sedlmaier, 'Konsumkritik und politische Gewalt in der linksalternativen Szene der siebziger Jahre', in *Das Alternative Milieu:* ed. Reichardt and Siegfried, 185–205.

50 On the last two concepts, see Stanitzek, 'Gebrauchswerte der Ideologiekritik'.

51 Jean Baudrillard, *The System of Objects*, trans. James Benedict, London: Verso, 1996, 199f. This new perspective – which Baudrillard was not the only one to develop – has given rise to a whole new research literature since the 1980s. Cf. David Graeber, *Fragments of an Anarchist Anthropology*, Chicago: Prickly Paradigm, 2004, esp. 100.

52 They were the troops assigned to dismantle the 'heroic modern age' whose strong subject would attain a last high point in the Western hemisphere in the days of the student uprisings: Lethen, *Suche nach dem Handorakel*, 33f.

53 Michel Foucault, *The Birth of Biopolitics: Lectures at the Collège de France, 1978–1979*, ed. Michel Snellart, trans. Graham Burchell, Basingstoke: Palgrave, 2008, 226.

54 See Robert T. Michael and Gary S. Becker, 'On the New Theory of Consumer Behavior', in *Swedish Journal of Economics*, 75:4 (1973), 381ff.

55 Adorno, *Minima Moralia*, 156f. On the long-term influence of Adorno's verdict, see Thomas Hecken, *Das Versagen der Intellektuellen: Eine Verteidigung des Konsums gegen seine deutschen Verächter*, Bielefeld: Transkript, 2010.

56 Helmut Lethen, *Cool Conduct: The Culture of Distance in Weimar Germany*, trans. Don Reneau, Berkeley: University of California Press, 2002, 187ff.

57 Paris, *Drei Reden zum Design*, 9. On Berlin ready-made design and the conditions under which it arose, see Christian Borngräber (ed.), *Berliner Design-Handbuch* [Berlin design handbook], Berlin: Merve, 1987, and Borngräber (ed.), *Berliner Wege: Prototypen der Designwerkstatt / Prototypes for the Designwerkstatt*, Berlin: Ernst, 1988.

58 Paris and Gente, 'Für *Buch-Markt*'.

59 Hans Magnus Enzensberger, *Mediocrity and Delusion: Collected Diversions*, trans. Martin Chalmers, London: Verso, 1992, 11.

60 Gerhard Schmidtchen, 'Lesekultur in Deutschland: Ergebnisse repräsentativer Buchmarktstudien für den Börsenverein des Deutschen Buchhandels', in *Börsenblatt für den Deutschen Buchhandel*, 24:70 (1968), 1990. Schmidtchen, who became a sociologist of Catholicism after his time at the Allensbach Institute, had certainly read Carl Schmitt, whose *Theory of the Partisan* discusses the pros and cons of a 'tendency to modify or even dissolve the traditional concepts': 'Any loner or non-conformist can now be called a partisan, whether or not he ever even considers taking up arms. It is permissible as a metaphor; I have used it myself in order to characterize historically influential figures and situations': Carl Schmitt, *The Theory of the Partisan*, trans. A. C. Goodson, *New Centennial Review*, 4:3 (2004), 12f.

7 Foucault and the Terrorists

1 On 5 September 1977, while the Red Army Faction founders Andreas Baader and Gudrun Ensslin were serving life sentences in Stammheim Prison near Stuttgart, their comrades at large kidnapped Hanns Martin Schleyer, the president of the German Employers' Association, killing his bodyguards. Lufthansa Flight 181 from Mallorca to Frankfurt was hijacked on 13 October. Both Schleyer's kidnappers and the hijackers demanded the release of the RAF prisoners. The drama came to a threefold climax

on 18 October: German special forces stormed the aircraft in Mogadishu, Somalia, and liberated the hostages; three members of the RAF leadership died in their cells in Stammheim the same night, apparently by coordinated suicide; and Schleyer's murdered body was found in Mulhouse, France, the next day.

2 Reinhard Lettau, 'Las Vegas der Literatur: Flohzirkus, Schwerpunkttitel und abgeräumte Büfetts', in *Die Zeit*, 28 October 1977.

3 Siegfried Unseld, 'Schmidt, Bonn, Suhrkamp: Aus Siegfried Unseld's "Chronik"', in *Zeitschrift für Ideengeschichte*, 4:4 (2010), 99–106; Jan Bürger, 'Herrenrunde mit Panzerwagen: Ein Kommentar', in *Zeitschrift für Ideengeschichte*, 4:4 (2010), 107–10.

4 The preceding and the following quotations are from that unpublished recording: Michel Foucault in conversation with Heidi Paris, Peter Gente, Walter Seitter, Hans-Joachim Metzger and Pasquale Pasquino, Paris, 1977. A digitized version is in the collection of Merve Verlag. Ulrich Raulff mentions the battery of cassette recorders that surrounded Foucault during his lectures at the Collège de France in *Wiedersehen mit den Siebzigern*, 66.

5 Heiner Müller, *Krieg ohne Schlacht: Leben in zwei Diktaturen*, 4th edn, Cologne: Kiepenheuer & Witsch, 1999.

6 Peter Gente in conversation with the author, 10 May 2012.

7 The observation is by Heidi Paris: see her article 'Die Brille von Foucault' [Foucault's glasses], signed with her pseudonym *die piepsmaus* ['squeaking mouse'], in *die tageszeitung*, 22 June 1979: 'All the books end *c.*1830 (where Marx's begin).'

8 Cf. Uta Liebmann Schaub, 'Foucault, Alternative Presses, and Alternative Ideology in West Germany: A Report', in *German Studies Review*, 12:1 (1989), 139–53.

9 See, e. g., Jean Baudrillard, *Kool Killer oder Der Aufstand der Zeichen* ['Kool Killer, or the Insurrection of Signs'], trans. Hans-Joachim Metzger, Berlin: Merve, 1978, 11; Lyotard, *Patchwork der Minderheiten*, 44; cf. Lyotard, 'A Brief Putting in Perspective'. On the significance of the RAF in the intellectual landscape of the seventies, see also Rutschky, *Erfahrungshunger*, 133–93.

10 Peter Gente in conversation with the author, 10 May 2012. See also Ben Kafka and Jamieson Webster, 'No, Oedipus Does Not Exist', in *Cabinet*, 42 (2011), 27–30. On the code names that the RAF borrowed from *Moby Dick* and their implications, see Stefan Aust, *The Baader–Meinhof Complex*,

trans. Anthea Bell, London: The Bodley Head, 1987, 247–9; Geoffrey Winthrop-Young, 'Kittler und seine Terroristen', in: *Tumult*, 40 (2012), 76ff.

11 Foucault, *The Order of Things*, 262. On Foucault and Althusser, see Didier Eribon, *Foucault et ses contemporains*, Paris: Fayard, 1994, ch. 10.

12 Puder, 'Der böse Blick des Michel Foucault'.

13 Peter Gente, untitled, undated manuscript on the Merve group's relations with Foucault: Merve Archives. On Foucault's handwriting, see Raulff, *Wiedersehen mit den Siebzigern*, 79.

14 Günter Maschke wrote this phrase about Carl Schmitt ('Im Irrgarten Carl Schmitts', in *Intellektuelle im Bann des Nationalsozialismus*, ed. Karl Corino, Hamburg: Hoffmann & Campe, 1980, 204), but perhaps it can be applied to Foucault as well. On the significance of medicine for his way of thinking and writing, see Michel Foucault, *Speech Begins after Death: Conversations with Claude Bonnefoy*, ed. Philippe Artières, trans. Robert Bononno, Minneapolis: University of Minnesota Press, 2013.

15 Paris, 'Die Brille von Foucault'.

16 Ulrich Raulff, 'Auf sie mit Gedrill! Martialisch, monumentalisch, mythisch: Michel Foucault erfand die Historie, von der Friedrich Nietzsche träumte', in *Frankfurter Allgemeine Zeitung*, 2 November 1999.

17 Michel Foucault, *Von der Freundschaft als Lebensweise: Michel Foucault im Gespräch* [On friendship as a way of life: Michel Foucault in conversation], trans. Marianne Karbe and Walter Seitter, Berlin: Merve, 1984, 17. On acute perception and the conceptual realism of the 1920s, see Helmut Lethen, *Verhaltenslehren der Kälte: Lebensversuche zwischen den Kriegen*, Frankfurt: Suhrkamp, 1994, 187.

18 As reported by Walter Seitter in *Michel Foucault in/à Berlin*, a documentary by Agnes Handwerk, Hamburg, 1992/3.

19 On the contemporary discussion about the state of emergency in 1977, see Wolfgang Kraushaar, '"Unsere Aufgabe die Herbeiführung des wirklichen Ausnahmezustands": Walter Benjamin, die Studentenbewegung und der grosse Katzenjammer', in *Der Ausnahmezustand als Regel: Eine Bilanz der kritischen Theorie*, ed. Rüdiger Schmidt-Grépály, Jan Urbich and Claudia Wirsing, Weimar: Verlag der Bauhaus-Universität, 2013, 114–34.

20 Anonymous [Klaus Hülbrock], 'Buback: ein Nachruf', in *Göttinger Nachrichten*, 25 April 1977.

21 On the 'Friends of the German Cinemathèque' and the Berlin art houses, see Berg-Ganschow and Jacobsen (eds.), *Film, Stadt, Kino, Berlin*, 55f.

22 Raulff, *Wiedersehen mit den Siebzigern*, 107.
23 Gente in the taped conversation at Foucault's home in October 1977.
24 Rutschky, *Erfahrungshunger*, 197ff.
25 Peter Sloterdijk, *Zeilen und Tage: Notizen 2008–2011*, Berlin: Suhrkamp, 2012, 74.
26 Heidi Paris in the taped conversation at Foucault's home in October 1977. See also the articles in Irene Bandhauer-Schöffmann and Dirk van Laak (eds.), *Der Linksterrorismus der 1970er Jahre und die Ordnung der Geschlechter*, Trier: WVT, 2013.
27 Michel Foucault, 'Wir fühlten uns als schmutzige Spezies' [We felt like vermin], in *Der Spiegel*, 31 (1977), 52, 78.
28 Merve Verlag to Michel Foucault, 12 December 1977: Merve Archives.
29 Merve Verlag to Roland Barthes, 9 May 1979: Merve Archives.
30 See Sebastian Haumann, '"Stadtindianer" and "Indiani Metropolitani": Recontextualizing an Italian Protest Movement in West Germany', in *Between Prague Spring and French May: Opposition and Revolt in Europe, 1960–1980*, ed. Martin Klimke, Jacco Pekelder and Joachim Scharloth, New York: Berghahn, 2011, 141.
31 For a critical contemporary analysis, see Kraushaar, 'Thesen zum Verhältnis von Alternativ- und Fluchtbewegung', 8–67.
32 All quotations from Dieter Hoffman-Axthelm, Otto Kallscheuer, Eberhard Knödler-Bunte and Brigitte Wartmann, *Zwei Kulturen? Tunix, Mescalero und die Folgen*, Berlin: Ä&K, 1979, 93f., 122. See also Mohr, *Zaungäste*, 36f.
33 Diederichsen, *Sexbeat*, 18. Still very instructive is Herbert Röttgen and Florian Rabe, *Vulkantänze: Linke und alternative Ausgänge*, Munich: Trikont, 1978, esp. 132ff.
34 Merve Verlag to Daniel Defert, 10 January 1978: Merve Archives.
35 Merve Verlag to Jean-François Lyotard, 12 January 1978; Jean-François Lyotard to Merve Verlag, 5 January 1978: Merve Archives.
36 Gente, quoted in Klug, *Ein Leben wie eine Komposition von John Cage*.
37 Matthew G. Hannah, 'Foucault's "German Moment": Genealogy of a Disjuncture', in *Foucault Studies*, 13 (2012), 116–37.

8 Critique of Pure Text

1 Merve Verlag to Michel Foucault, 23 March 1978: Merve Archives.
2 Jürgen Habermas, 'Introduction', in *Observations on the 'Spiritual Situation of the Age'*, ed. Habermas, 22.

3 Merve Verlag to Jacques Rancière, 31 May 1978: Merve Archives.
4 Walter Seitter, 'Was ist die "Neue Philosophie", und wo steht sie zwischen Wissenschaft und "Irrationalismus"?', undated typescript: Dietmar Kamper papers, university archives of Freie Universität, Berlin.
5 André Glucksmann, *The Master Thinkers*, trans. Brian Pearce, New York: Harper and Row, 1980, 37. For a contemporary eulogy of the theory from a German perspective, see Kurt Sontheimer, *Das Elend unserer Intellektuellen: Linke Theorie in der Bundesrepublik Deutschland*, Hamburg: Hoffmann & Campe, 1976.
6 Oskar Negt, 'Nicht das Gold, Wotan ist das Problem: Der jüngste Aufstand gegen die dialektische Vernunft; die "Neuen Philosophen" Frankreichs', in *Literaturmagazin*, 9 (1978), special issue: *Der neue Irrationalismus*, 44.
7 Wilfried Gottschalch, 'Foucaults Denken: Eine Politisierung des Urschreis?' in *Literaturmagazin*, 9 (1978), special issue: *Der neue Irrationalismus*, 66–73.
8 Anonymous [Hülbrock], 'Buback: Ein Nachruf'. E.g. Negt, 'Nicht das Gold, Wotan ist das Problem', 45; also – with a great deal more nuance – Kraushaar, 'Thesen zum Verhältnis von Alternativ- und Fluchtbewegung'.
9 Bohrer, 'The Three Cultures', 153.
10 Mohr, *Zaungäste*, 153.
11 Hildegard Brenner, Peter Krumme and Hans Thies Lehmann, 'Der Ort der Theorie', in *Alternative*, 145/6 (1982), 204.
12 Peter Gente considered the alternative movement's 'antitheoretical affect' to be positively dangerous: taped conversation with Foucault, Paris, 1977.
13 Baudrillard, 'Kool Killer, or The Insurrection of Signs', in Baudrillard, *Symbolic Exchange and Death*, trans. Iain Hamilton Grant, London: Sage, 1993, p. 80; cf. Baudrillard, *Kool Killer oder der Aufstand der Zeichen*, 31.
14 Niklas Luhmann, *Kann die moderne Gesellschaft sich auf ökologische Gefährdungen einstellen?* [Can modern society adjust to ecological dangers?], Opladen: Westdeutscher, 1985, 31.
15 'Warum Ökologie? Eine Diskussion zwischen Libération, Brice Lalonde, Dominique Simonnet, Laurent Samuel und Jean Baudrillard', in Baudrillard, *Kool Killer*, 119–27. On Baudrillard's curriculum vitae, see Jürg Altwegg, 'Alles ist nur noch eine einzige Show: Jean Baudrillards "Der symbolische Tausch und der Tod"; Die Herrschaft des Scheins über das Sein', in *Frankfurter Allgemeine Zeitung*, 20 May 1983.
16 Paul Virilio, 'Projekt für eine Katastrophen-Zeitschrift', in *Tumult*, 2 (1979), 128.

17 Gerd Bergfleth, 'Die Fatalität der Moderne', interview with Jean Baudrillard, in Bergfleth, Georges Bataille, Simone Weil et al., *Zur Kritik der palavernden Aufklärung*, Munich: Matthes & Seitz, 1984, 133.

18 Cf. Jean Baudrillard, *Der Tod tanzt aus der Reihe* [Death does its own thing], Berlin: Merve, 1979.

19 Baudrillard, *Symbolic Exchange and Death*, 4, 37.

20 Gerd Bergfleth, 'Nachwort', in Jean Baudrillard, *Der symbolische Tausch und der Tod*, Munich: Matthes & Seitz, 1982, 366.

21 Author's interview with Peter Gente, 10 May 2012.

22 Jean Baudrillard, *Forget Foucault*, trans. Nicole Dufresne, Los Angeles: Semiotext(e), 1987, 36 (published in German as *Oublier Foucault*, 2nd edn, Munich: Raben, 1983).

23 See, e.g., Paolo Virno, *A Grammar of the Multitude: For an Analysis of Contemporary Forms of Life*, trans. Isabella Bertoletti, James Cascaito and Andrea Casson, Los Angeles: Semiotext(e), 2004, 98f.

24 Baudrillard, *Symbolic Exchange and Death*, 5.

25 'Do the Readers Need References that Badly?' Jean Baudrillard to Mark Sedlacek, n.d.: Merve Archives. Cf. Peter Gente, 'Vorwort' [Preface], in *Philosophie und Kunst: Jean Baudrillard; Eine Hommage zu seinem 75. Geburtstag* [Philosophy and art: in homage to Jean Baudrillard on his 75th birthday], ed. Peter Gente, Barbara Könches and Peter Weibel, Berlin: Merve, 2005, 19f.

26 Quoted in Klaus Laermann, 'Das rasende Gefasel der Gegenaufklärung: Dietmar Kamper als Symptom', in *Merkur*, 433 (1985), 215.

27 Baudrillard, *Symbolic Exchange and Death*, 44, n. 3.

28 See Roman Jakobson, 'What Is Poetry?' in Jakobson, *Language in Literature*, Cambridge, Mass.: Harvard University Press, 1987, 376f.

29 Kittler, 'Ein Verwaiser', 142.

30 Jean Baudrillard to Merve, 8 May 1985: Merve Archives.

31 Peter Sloterdijk, *Critique of Cynical Reason*, trans. Michael Eldred, Minneapolis: University of Minnesota Press, 1987, xxxiv.

32 Jean Baudrillard to Merve, 15 October 1978: Merve Archives.

33 See Florian Rötzer, 'Die Rache der Dinge' (afterword), in Jean Baudrillard, *Das System der Dinge: Über unser Verhältnis zu den alltäglichen Gegenständen*, Frankfurt: Campus, 1991, 251.

34 The expectation of ecological catastrophe was compounded in those days by the scenario of nuclear overkill. On the feeling of genuine menace and

the accompanying impression of unreality, see Jörg Schröder and Uwe Nettelbeck, *Cosmic*, Schlectenwegen: März, 1982.

35 Lorenz Lorenz, 'Lasst Euch nicht verführen!' in *Elaste*, 7 (1983), n.p.

36 Thomas Meineke, 'Die göttliche Linke: Jean Baudrillards Simulations-Theorie', in *Die Zeit*, 6 March 1987.

37 Steiner, 'Adorno: Love and Cognition', 255.

38 The quotation, 'Allein die Schrift!' in the German, alluding to Luther's *sola scriptura*, is taken, along with the observations that follow, from Jost Philipp Klenner, 'Suhrkamps Ikonoklasmus', in *Zeitschrift für Ideengeschichte*, 6:4 (2012), 82–91.

39 Raulff, *Wiedersehen mit den Siebzigern*, 110.

40 Merve Verlag to various addressees, 20 January 1977: Estate of Dietmar Kamper.

41 Frank Böckelmann, Dietmar Kamper, Ellen Künzel et al., *Das Schillern der Revolte*, Berlin: Merve, 1978, back cover.

42 Heidi Paris to the editors of *Tumult*, 3 March 1980: Merve Archives. Cf. Anonymous, 'metro', concept paper, undated: Estate of Dietmar Kamper.

43 Dietmar Kamper, presentation on the launch of *Tumult*, in the book shop Autorenbuchhandlung, Carmerstrasse, West Berlin, 23 February 1982: Estate of Dietmar Kamper.

44 'Who can still recognize', Kamper's colleague Klaus Laermann wrote in 1985, 'which of the following titles, following the current fashion, are not my inventions, but have actually been foisted upon us with a straight face? *Das Textbegehren des Phallus* [The phallus's textual desire]; *Das Murmeln des Diskurses* [The murmur of discourse]; *Vom Geheimnis des Referenten* [On the secret of the signifier]; *Der buchstäbliche Körper* [The literal body]; *Der übersinnliche Leib* [The supersensory body]; *Der all-einstehende Penis* [The all-avowing penis]; *Zur Zirkulation des Begehrens* [On the circulation of desire]; *Das Schweigen der Schrift vor dem Buchstaben* [The silence of writing before the letter]': Laermann, 'Das rasende Gefasel der Gegenaufklärung', 219. On the other hand, see Lyotard's idea, mentioned above, of combating the 'theoretical terror' by parodying rather than criticizing theory: Lyotard, 'Apathie in der Theorie', 92ff.

45 Anonymous, 'Myzel', concept paper, undated: Estate of Dietmar Kamper.

46 Laermann, 'Das rasende Gefasel der Gegenaufklärung', 213. See also Eckhard Henscheid, 'Der rasende Fasler', in Henscheid, *Erledigte Fälle: Bilder deutscher Menschen*, Frankfurt: Zweitausendeins, 1986, 110–17.

47 Frank Böckelmann, 'Bericht über Verhandlungen mit Roger & Bernhard', 5 May 1978: Estate of Dietmar Kamper.

48 Walter Seitter, 'Zum Programmtext', concept paper, undated: Estate of Dietmar Kamper.

49 Seitter in the taped conversation at Foucault's home in October 1977.

50 Cf. Ulrich Raulff, 'Foucaults Versuchung', in *Zeitschrift für Ideengeschichte*, 6:4 (2012), 11–17.

51 Cf. Gente, 'Vorwort', 18–22.

52 Anonymous, 'metro', concept paper, undated: Estate of Dietmar Kamper.

53 See Gérard Genette, 'Sketching an Intellectual Itinerary', trans. Joanna Augustyn, in *French Theory in America*, ed. Lotringer and Cohen, 71–86. On the concept of 'paratext', see also Gérard Genette, *Paratexts: Thresholds of Interpretation*, trans. Jane E. Lewin, Cambridge University Press, 1997.

54 'Versuche, per Unfall zu Denken: Gespräch mit Paul Virilio', in *Tumult*, 1 (1979), 86. On Virilio's Catholicism, see Raulff, *Wiedersehen mit den Siebzigern*, 110.

55 Anonymous, 'Text', concept paper, undated: Estate of Dietmar Kamper.

56 Diederichsen, *Sexbeat*, VI.

57 Ulrich Raulff and Marie Luise Syring, 'Sich quer durch die Kultur schlagen: Über die französische Zeitschrift *Traverses*', in *Tumult*, 1 (1979), 105f. At the same time, the New York theory publisher Sylvère Lotringer was pursuing a very similar strategy: 'For me there was a total equivalence between a great piece of theory and a flyer found in the street': Sylvère Lotringer, '*Pataphysics Magazine* Interview', Melbourne, 1990: www.yanniflorence.net/pataphysicsmagazine/lotringer_interview.html; cf. Lotringer, *Foreign Agent: Kunst in den Zeiten der Theorie* [Foreign agent: art in the time of theory], Berlin: Merve, 1991, 12.

58 On the significance of collage for the historical avant-gardes, and on Benjamin, see Peter Bürger, *Theory of the Avant-Garde*, trans. Michael Shaw, Minneapolis: University of Minnesota Press, 1984, 68ff.

59 Ulrich Giersch, 'Zur Produktivkraft taktiler Schnittstellen: Vom Fotokopieren aus gesehen; life is Xerox, you are just a copy', www.gewebewerk.silvia-klara-breitwieser.cultd.de/giersch/index.htm. As early as 1970, in his 'building blocks for a theory of the media', Enzensberger had praised the photocopier as a device which 'potentially made everyone a printer': Hans Magnus Enzensberger, 'Baukasten zu einer Theorie der Medien', in *Kursbuch*, 20 (1970), 162.

60 On the concept of the separation of styles, see Erich Auerbach, *Mimesis: The Representation of Reality in Western Literature*, trans. Willard R. Trask, Princeton University Press, 2013 [1953]. On the publishing house März Verlag, see Jan-Frederik Bändel, Barbara Kalender and Jörg Schröder, *Immer radikal, niemals konsequent: Der März Verlag; erweitertes Verlegertum, postmoderne Literatur und Business Art*, Hamburg: Philo Fine Arts, 2011.

61 Heidi Paris to the editors of *Tumult*, 3 March 1980: Merve Archives – 'The cost of Issue 1, about DM5000, was higher than actually feasible.'

62 Of course, theoreticians had collaborated with curators in the past. François Burkhardt, the director of the Centre de création industrielle, had worked with Ernst Bloch in 1972 on Documenta 5. What was new was that the theoretician's role merged with that of the curator. See Jean-François Lyotard, 'Design jenseits von Ästhetik,' interview with François Burkhardt, in *Immaterialität und Postmoderne* [Design beyond aesthetics, in Immateriality and postmodernism], trans. Marianne Karbe, Berlin: Merve, 1985, 29.

63 Paul Virilio, *Bunker Archaeology*, Paris: Demi-cercle, 1994. A selection of the photographs is also found in Virilio's Merve book: Paul Virilio, *Geschwindigkeit und Politik* [Speed and politics], trans. Ronald Voullié, Berlin: Merve, 1980.

64 Lyotard, 'Philosophie in der Diaspora,' interview with Jacques Derrida, in *Immaterialität und Postmoderne*, 24. See also Antonia Wunderlich, *Der Philosoph im Museum: Die Ausstellung 'Les Immatériaux' von Jean-François Lyotard*, Bielefeld: Transcript, 2008.

65 Bruno Latour and Peter Weibel (eds.), *Iconoclash: Beyond the Image Wars in Science, Religion and Art*, Cambridge, Mass.: MIT Press, 2002 [originally published as Latour, *Iconoclash oder Gibt es eine Welt jenseits des Bilderkrieges?* trans. Gustav Rossler, Berlin: Merve, 2002].

66 In the 1980s, the Romance philologist Hans Ulrich Gumbrecht 'wanted to revisit materialism as the philosophical core of all Marxist theories': Hans Ulrich Gumbrecht, *After 1945: Latency as Origin of the Present*, Palo Alto: Stanford University Press, 2013, 284. The result was an influential anthology edited by Gumbricht and Karl Ludwig Pfeiffer, *Materialities of Communication*, Palo Alto: Stanford University Press, 1994.

67 Raulff and Syring, 'Sich quer durch die Kultur schlagen,' 107.

68 Anonymous, 'Zeit-Zeichen der Macht,' concept paper, undated: Estate of Dietmar Kamper.

69 Lepenies, 'Gottfried Benn: Der Artist im Posthistoire,' 328.
70 Bohrer, 'The Three Cultures,' 153.

9 Into the White Cube

1 '"Theorie muss aus der Kunstecke rauskommen": Interview mit Tom Lamberty,' in *die tageszeitung*, 19 August 2014.
2 Still eye-opening as a critical conception of art institutions is Arthur C. Danto, 'The Artworld,' in *Journal of Philosophy*, 61 (1964), 571–84.
3 One reason was that Peter Gente, before retiring to Thailand, had commissioned the art collector and publisher Harald Falckenberg to manage his interest in Merve. On the exhibition, see Alexander Cammann, 'Lebendig-museal: 40 Jahre Merve Verlag,' in *Die Zeit*, 18 February 2010, who writes: 'Is it still theory, or has it become art? Or is it perhaps both?'
4 Alix Rule and David Levine, 'International Art English: Zur Karriere der Pressemitteilung in der Kunstwelt,' in *Merkur*, 769 (2013), 516–27.
5 This situation was described as early as the mid-1980s by Hannes Böhringer: see his *Begriffsfelder: Von der Philosophie zur Kunst* [Conceptual fields: from philosophy to art], Berlin: Merve, 1985, 125. The phenomenon is different, Böhringer wrote, from modern art's 'dependency on commentary' diagnosed in 1960 by Arnold Gehlen inasmuch as the commentary no longer serves 'to explain something which is incomprehensible at first glance, but inversely to conceptualize and complicate something which is presented to the first glance as easily understandable.' On the American context, see Sylvère Lotringer, 'Third Wave: Art and the Commodification of Theory,' in *Theories of Contemporary Art*, ed. Richard Hertz, 2nd edn, Englewood Cliffs: Prentice Hall, 1993, 101ff.; cf. Lotringer, *Foreign Agent*, 66ff.
6 Cf. Joseph Kosuth, 'Art after Philosophy,' in Kosuth, *Art after Philosophy and After: Collected Writings, 1966–1990*, Cambridge, Mass.: MIT Press, 1991, 13–32. Cf. Böhringer, *Begriffsfelder*, 92. On the relation between art and criticism since Hegel, see Christian Demand, *Die Beschämung der Philister: Wie die Kunst sich der Kritik entledigte*, 2nd edn, Springe: zu Klampen, 2007.
7 For a eulogy of literary art, see Karl Markus Michel, 'Ein Kranz für die Literatur: Fünf Variationen über eine These,' in *Kursbuch*, 15 (1968), 169–86.

8 Arthur C. Danto, 'Approaching the End of Art,' in Danto, *The State of the Art*, New York: Prentice Hall, 1987, 217.

9 Merve Verlag to Michel Foucault, 9 May 1979: Merve Archives.

10 Harald Szeemann, 'Monte Verità: Berg der Wahrheit,' in *Monte Verità: Berg der Wahrheit; Lokale Anthropologie als Beitrag zur Wiederentdeckung einer neuzeitlichen sakralen Topologie*, ed. Szeemann, Milan: Electa, 1980, 6.

11 Heidi Paris and Peter Gente, 'Psychopathen aller Länder, vereinigt Euch!' [Psychopaths of the world, unite!], in *die tageszeitung*, 20 April 1979.

12 Quoted in Hans Joachim Müller, *Harald Szeemann: Ausstellungsmacher*, Berne: Benteli, 2006, 70f.

13 Ibid., 14–33.

14 'To me, institutions are instruments,' Szeemann wrote, 'for changing, or at least relativizing, the users' notions of possession': quoted in ibid., 20.

15 Another contemporary variant was the 'Musée sentimental,' also conceived in 1979, by Daniel Spoerri and Marie-Luise Plessen. Spoerri and Plessen, too, presented utensils as if they were relics. See Anke te Heesen and Susanne Padberg (eds.), *Musée Sentimental 1979: Ein Ausstellungskonzept*, Ostfildern: Hatje Cantz, 2011.

16 On the critique, and utopian visions, of museums, see Anke te Heesen, *Theorien des Museums zur Einführung*, Hamburg: Junius, 2012, chs. 5 and 7.

17 This is most evident in the catalogue of Szeemann's 1975 exhibition *Junggesellenmaschinen*: Hans Ulrich Reck and Harald Szeemann (eds.), *Junggesellenmaschinen*, revised edn, Vienna: Springer, 1999. The catalogue, originally published in 1975, contains texts by Lyotard, Deleuze, Certeau and others.

18 This and all the previous quotations concerning the encounter with Szeemann are from Paris and Gente, 'Editorische Notiz,' 225ff. See also Paris and Gente, 'Wunschmaschinen: Stellungnahme zu der Frage Was hat der Merve Verlag mit Szeemanns Wunschmaschinen zu tun?' [Desire machines: statement on the question 'What does Merve Verlag have to do with Szeemann's desire machines?'], in Reck and Szeemann (eds.), *Junggesellenmaschinen*, 50–3.

19 Merve Verlag to Michel Foucault, 9 May 1979: Merve Archives.

20 Lethen, *Suche nach dem Handorakel*, 91f.

21 Hannes Böhringer, interview with the author, 20 March 2014.

22 On the 'flowering' of art in Düsseldorf, see Harald Szeemann, *Individuelle Mythologien* [Individual mythologies], Berlin: Merve, 1985, 27.

23 Günter Brus, *Das gute alte West-Berlin* [Good old West Berlin], Salzburg: Jung & Jung, 2010, 23; cf. 40. On the lack of a better Berlin society as a potential audience for art, see Gert Mattenklott and Gundel Mattenklott, *Berlin Transit: Eine Stadt als Station*, Reinbek: Rowohlt, 1987, 239ff.

24 The description of the neighbourhood is Martin Kippenberger's, quoted in Stephan Schmidt-Wulffen, 'Alles in allem: Panorama "wilder" Malerei', in *Tiefe Blicke: Kunst der achtziger Jahre aus der Bundesrepublik Deutschland, der DDR, Österreich und der Schweiz*, Cologne: DuMont, 1985, 62. On the history of the West Berlin art scene and the *Neue Wilde*, see also Wolfgang Max Faust and Gerd de Vries, *Hunger nach Bildern: Deutsche Malerei der Gegenwart*, Cologne: DuMont, 1982.

25 Middendorf, quoted in Schmidt-Wulffen, 'Panorama "wilder" Malerei', 37; *Die Zeit* quoted in ibid., 46; cf. 33–51.

26 He employed a professional sign painter instead of painting himself, and announced in a press release that his action 'in the Expressionist city of Berlin' was intended to contribute to 'full employment'. Quoted in Schmidt-Wulffen, 'Panorama "wilder" Malerei', 68. On Kippenberger's West Berlin phase, see ibid., 51–70, and Susanne Kippenberger, *Kippenberger: The Artist and His Families*, trans. Damion Searls, Atlanta: J&L, 2011, 139–214.

27 On 'business art', see Barbara Kalender and Jörg Schröder, 'Der März Verlag: Geschichte und Geschichten', in Bandel, Kalender and Schröder, *Immer radikal, niemals konsequent*, 49ff.

28 Frieder Butzmann, 'Hamburg, Berlin, Musik, Punk, Kunscht, Gudrun, Diederichsen, die Schranknummer usw.', in *dagegen dabei*, ed. Dany et al., 245.

29 'Kunst des Büchermachens', 377–80. See also Bude, 'Die Suche nach dem Unmöglichen', 233.

30 Cf. Paris and Gente, 'Ping-Pong auf der Hochebene von Tibet', 135: 'The movement of the *Neue Wilde* has defined itself to a high degree through picture books.'

31 Thomas Kapielski, 'Baden-Baden: Juni und Juli 1999', in Kapielski, *Sozialmanierismus* [Social mannerism], Berlin: Merve, 2001, 88.

32 Quoted in 'Heidi + Peter', in *For Sale? A Presentation of New Design on the Border*, Vienna: prodomo, 1989, n.p.: www.heidi-paris.de/design/for-sale-1982. Heidi Paris quotes the title of an interview in which Lyotard quoted Adorno. The phrase is quoted here after Adorno, 'Vers une musique

informelle', in Adorno, *Quasi una Fantasia: Essays on Modern Music*, trans. Rodney Livingstone, London: Verso, 1998, 322.

33 Merve Verlag to Sylvère Lotringer, 25 March 1981. On Kippenberger and the feminist bookshops, see Paris and Gente, 'Ping-Pong auf der Hochebene von Tibet', 131.

34 Martin Kippenberger to Merve Verlag, 15 January 1987: Merve Archives.

35 See John Klein, 'The Dispersal of the Modernist Series', in *Oxford Art Journal*, 21 (1998), 121–35.

36 Marianne Karbe and Hannes Böhringer underscored the importance of Fluxus for Heidi Paris in interviews with the author on 1 December 2011 and 20 March 2014. On artists' books and multiples, see Michael Glasmeier, *Die Bücher der Künstler: Publikationen und Editionen seit den sechziger Jahren in Deutschland; Eine Ausstellung in zehn Kapiteln*, exhibition catalogue, Stuttgart: Hansjörg Mayer, 1994. See also Craig Dworkin, 'Textual Prostheses', in *Comparative Literature*, 57:1 (2005), 1–24.

37 Merve Verlag had invented 'events between theoretical literature and avant-garde art', Ulrich Raulff wrote in his obituary, 'Tod einer Buchmacherin'.

38 Paris and Gente, 'Ping-Pong auf der Hochebene von Tibet', 134.

39 The brief review signed L. W. introduces an anonymous interview, 'translated from the French by Peter Gente', excerpted from *Solo*: 'Der maskierte Philosoph' [The masked philosopher], in *die tageszeitung*, 12 June 1981.

40 Lotringer, '*Pataphysics Magazine* Interview'; cf. Lotringer, *Foreign Agent*, 8.

41 Quoted in David Morris, 'This is the End of the Sixties!' in *Cabinet*, 44 (2012), 24f. Cf. Lotringer, 'Doing Theory', 140f.

42 Lotringer, 'Doing Theory', 128. More recently, the influential curator Hans-Ulrich Obrist in particular has adopted the format of the artist interview. See D. T. Max, 'The Art of Conversation: A Star Curator's Migratory Nature', in *The New Yorker*, 8 December 2014, 64–72.

43 Lotringer, 'Doing Theory', esp. 153. On Derrida's literarization of theory, see Arthur C. Danto, 'Philosophy as/and/of Literature', in Danto, *The Philosophical Disenfranchisement of Art*, New York: Columbia University Press, 2005 [1986], 135–62.

44 For a classic that is still worth reading, see Bürger, *Theory of the Avant-Garde*.

45 Danto, 'The End of Art', 111.

46 Joseph Kosuth, 'Art after Philosophy', 18. Danto situated the decisive breakthrough as early as Andy Warhol, whose *Brillo Boxes*, exhibited at

the Stable Gallery in 1964, demonstrated the last possible position of art arriving at a conclusive self-knowledge. From that point on, asking about the nature of art was obsolete in art. All further reflection was in the ambit of philosophy. Ending his own artistic career to pursue thinking was thus a logical choice. See Danto, 'Approaching the End of Art'.

47 Deleuze, Baudrillard, Virilio and even Niklas Luhmann asserted that they were artists rather than theorists. Cf. Henning Schmidgen, 'Begriffszeichnungen: Über die philosophische Konzeptkunst von Gilles Deleuze', in *Deleuze und die Künste* [Deleuze and the arts], ed. Peter Gente and Peter Weibel, Frankfurt: Suhrkamp, 2007, 26–53; Lotringer, 'Doing Theory', 150, 154; Dirk Käsler, 'Soziologie: "Flug über den Wolken: Dirk Käsler über Niklas Luhmanns "Soziale Systeme"', in *Der Spiegel*, 38:50 (1984), 190.

48 Lotringer, 'German Issues', vi.

49 Sylvère Lotringer to Peter Gente, 11 March 1981: Merve Archives.

50 As a Holocaust survivor, Lotringer stood aloof from West Germany: Sylvère Lotringer, '*Pataphysics Magazine* Interview'; cf. Lotringer, *Foreign Agent*, 14f.

51 Merve Verlag to Sylvère Lotringer, 25 March 1981.

52 Lotringer, 'German Issues', vii.

53 Blanchot, 'The Word Berlin', 60–5.

54 Merve Verlag to Sylvère Lotringer, 25 March 1981.

55 Gert Mattenklott confirms that the German reception of the French postmodern theoreticians began in West Berlin: see his '"Komm ins Offene, Freund!" Transit ins wilde Denken', in *Zeitschrift für Ideengeschichte*, 2:4 (2008), 5–10.

56 Jean-François Lyotard to Merve Verlag, 21 January 1983: Merve Archives.

57 Heiner Müller, 'The Walls of History', interview with Sylvère Lotringer, in *The German Issue*, ed. Lotringer, 52.

58 Mike Davis, *City of Quartz: Excavating the Future in Los Angeles*, New York: Verso, 1992, ch. 1.

59 On the concept of the 'post-war', see Haverkamp, *Latenzzeit*, and Gumbrecht, *After 1945*.

60 Gottfried Benn, 'Der Ptolemäer', in Benn, *Gesammelte Werke*, vol. V, Wiesbaden: Limes, 1968, 1384; Gottfried Benn to Friedrich Wilhelm Oelze, 4 November 1946, in Benn, *Briefe an F. W. Oelze, 1932–1945*,

Wiesbaden: Limes 1977, 55. Cf. Helmuth Lethen, 'Gelegentlich auf Wasser sehen: Benns Inseln', in *Zeitschrift für Ideengeschichte*, 2:4 (2008), 45–53.

61 Gombrowicz, *Diary*, 112, 115. Cf. Föllmer, *Individuality and Modernity in Berlin*, 240ff.

62 Wolf Jobst Siedler and Elisabeth Niggemeyer, *Die Gemordete Stadt: Abgesang auf Putte und Strasse, Platz und Baum*, Berlin: Sammlung Siedler, 1993.

63 Mattenklott, *Berlin Transit*, 229.

64 Michael Rutschky, 'Panzerhaut der DDR: Die Ruinierung der Berliner Mauer', in *Ruinen des Denkens: Denken in Ruinen*, ed. Norbert Bolz and Willem van Reijen, Frankfurt: Suhrkamp, 1996, 60.

65 Cf. Belinda Davis, 'The City as Theater of Protest: West Berlin and West Germany, 1962–1983', in *The Spaces of the Modern City: Imaginaries, Politics, and Everyday Life*, ed. Gyan Prakash and Kevin M. Kruse, Princeton University Press, 2008, 247–74.

66 According to Tobias Rüther, *Heroes: David Bowie and Berlin*, trans. Anthony Mathews, London: Reaktion, 2014, 31ff. On the 'broad present' as a characteristic of now, see Hans Ulrich Gumbrecht, *Our Broad Present: Time and Contemporary Culture*, New York: Columbia University Press, 2014.

67 Cf. Mattenklott, *Berlin Transit*, 229.

68 Nicolaus Sombart, *Journal intime 1982/83: Rückkehr nach Berlin*, Berlin: Elfenbein, 2003, 153, 199; cf. 71f., 97.

69 The conference was being held on the occasion of Adorno's eightieth birthday, and was a milestone on his path to canonization. See Ludwig von Friedeburg and Jürgen Habermas (eds.), *Adorno-Konferenz 1983*, Frankfurt: Suhrkamp, 1983.

70 Taubes, 'Ästhetisierung der Wahrheit im Posthistoire', 41. Interest in *Posthistoire* in the 1980s was initially a Berlin phenomenon. See Lutz Niethammer, *Posthistoire: Has History Come to an End?* trans. Patrick Camiller, London: Verso, 1992, 6.

71 See Taubes, 'Ästhetisierung der Wahrheit im Posthistoire', 45, 47. On the exemplary function of aesthetic judgement in the postmodern era, see Hans Ulrich Gumbrecht, who in turn paraphrases Lyotard, in 'Die Prämisse jeglichen Urteilens: Erinnerung an Frank Schirrmacher', in *Frankfurter Allgemeine Zeitung*, 16 June 2014. On the relationship of Kojève's samurai and Jünger's 'anarch', see Niethammer, *Posthistoire*, 68,

who calls Kojève's idea an 'aesthetic simulation of lordship after its historical demise'.

72 See, for example, Kamper's undated, untitled concept paper on the 'wild academy', which we will look at in the next chapter: 'It combines a posthistoric consciousness with wild thinking'. Estate of Dietmar Kamper.

73 For Taubes's appraisal of the fashionable French philosophers, see the interview 'Jacob Taubes', 312f.

74 Marianne Karbe, 'Protokoll vom 8 Januar 82', typescript: Estate of Dietmar Kamper.

75 Dietmar Kamper to Bruno Hoffmann, 22 September 1982: Estate of Dietmar Kamper.

76 Alexander Dill, 'Protokoll der Sitzung vom 15 November 1982', typescript: Estate of Dietmar Kamper.

10 Prussianism and Spontaneism

1 Gente in the taped conversation at Foucault's home in October 1977.

2 Meg Huber, 'Von wo aus schreiben wir?', concept paper, undated: Estate of Dietmar Kamper. Proceeding from the phenomenon of the New Right after the German unification, Diedrich Diederichsen has reconstructed the rightist current in the German reception of the French philosophers, particularly in the circles surrounding the *Tumult* group: see 'Spirituelle Reaktionäre und völkische Vernunftkritiker', in Diederichsen, *Freiheit macht arm*, 117–57.

3 Ernst Jünger, *Der Waldgang*, Stuttgart: Klett-Cotta, 2008, 30.

4 'Versuche, per Unfall zu Denken: Gespräch mit Paul Virilio', 84. Cf. Virilio, 'Der Urfall (Accidens originale)', in *Tumult*, 1 (1979), 77–82.

5 Ernst Jünger, *The Worker: Dominion and Form*, trans. Bogdan Costea and Laurence Paul Hemming, Evanston, Ill.: Northwestern University Press, 2017, 85; cf. 84. On Jünger's disdain for book learning, see also Jünger, *On Pain*, trans. David C. Durst, New York: Telos, 2008, 29. On the significance of Jünger for Virilio's work, see Karl Prümm, 'Gefährliche Augenblicke: Ernst Jünger als Medientheoretiker', in *Ernst Jünger: Politik; Mythos; Kunst*, ed. Lutz Hagestedt, Berlin: De Gruyter, 2004, 349f.

6 Cf. *Tumult*, 4 (1982); 7 (1985); 8 (1986); and the announcements on the back cover of 2 (1979).

7 Seitter, 'Zum Programmtext'. After the German unification, Seitter made the 'correct use of the French' his programme: learn with Foucault to

think about Germany. Cf. Seitter, 'Vom rechten Gebrauch der Franzosen', in *Tumult*, 15 (1991), 5–14.

8 The 'Forests' issue was ultimately cancelled at short notice, according to Wolfert von Rahden in a telephone conversation with the author, 24 September 2014.

9 Lethen and Heinz Dieter Kittsteiner, '"Jetzt zieht Leutnant Jünger seinen Mantel aus": Überlegungen zur "Ästhetik des Schreckens"', in *Berliner Hefte*, 11 (1979), 22. See also Karl Heinz Bohrer, *Die Ästhetik des Schreckens: Die pessimistische Romantik und Ernst Jüngers Frühwerk*, Frankfurt: Hanser, 1978.

10 Joschka Fischer, quoted in Malte Herwig, 'In Papiergewittern', in *Der Spiegel*, 41:40 (2007), 202. On the reception of Jünger in West Germany and its reversal in the 1970s, see Detlev Schöttker, 'Postalische Jagden: Ernst Jüngers Präsenz in der deutschen Literatur und Publizistik nach 1945', in *Ernst Jünger: Arbeiter am Abgrund*, ed. Stephan Schlak, Heike Gfrereis, Detlev Schöttker, et al., Marbach: Deutsche Schillergesellschaft, 2010, 242ff.; Bohrer, 'Karl Heinz Bohrer im Gespräch mit Stephan Schlak', in *Ernst Jünger: Arbeiter am Abgrund*, ed. Schlak et al., 249–78.

11 Norbert Bolz, Jacob Taubes's assistant, saw Jünger's 'walk in the woods' as 'a theoretical prototype of the vanishing line (not line of escape) and nomadic intensity': Norbert Bolz, 'Pop-Philosophie', in *Schizo-Schleichwege*, ed. Heinz and Tholen, 191. On the postmodern reception of Jünger, see Peter Koslowski, *Der Mythos der Moderne: Die dichterische Philosophie Ernst Jüngers*, Munich: Fink, 1991; and Niethammer, *Posthistoire*, 68–90. See also Daniel Morat, *Von der Tat zur Gelassenheit: Konservatives Denken bei Martin Heidegger, Ernst Jünger und Friedrich Georg Jünger*, Göttingen: Wallstein, 2007.

12 Müller, *Krieg ohne Schlacht*, 281f.

13 Ulrich Raulff, 'Schneid', in *Tumult*, 4 (1982), 125, 128. 'We thought in those days the interest in sexuality would soon pass', writes Raulff: *Wiedersehen mit den Siebzigern*, 103.

14 Michel Foucault, lecture of 21 January 1976, in *'Society Must Be Defended': Lectures at the Collège de France, 1975–76*, trans. David Macey, New York: Picador, 2003, 50f; cf. Michel Foucault, *Vom Licht des Krieges zur Geburt der Geschichte* [From the light of war to the birth of history], trans. Walter Seitter, Berlin: Merve, 1986, 12. See also Raulff, 'Auf sie mit Gedrill!'

15 Raulff, 'Schneid', 128. On the relation between Marxism and military

science, see Bernard Semmel (ed.), *Marxism and the Science of War*, Oxford University Press, 1981.

16 On this topic, see the contemporary descriptions by Jean-Luc Pinard-Legry, 'Alexandre Kojève: Zur französischen Hegel-Rezeption', in *Vermittler: Deutsch-französisches Jahrbuch*, vol. I, ed. Jürgen Siess, Frankfurt: Syndikat, 1981, 105–17; Traugott König, 'Die Abenteuer der Dialektik in Frankreich', in: *Fugen: Deutsch-französisches Jahrbuch für Text-Analytik*, Olten and Freiburg im Breisgau: Walter, 1980, 282–9. For a more recent analysis, see Bruce Baugh, *French Hegel: From Surrealism to Postmodernism*, Abingdon and New York: Routledge, 2003.

17 On the relation between Kojève and the Collège de Sociologie, see Stephan Moebius, *Die Zauberlehrlinge: Soziologiegeschichte des Collège de Sociologie (1937–1939)*, Constance: UVK, 2006, 212–22.

18 See Descombes, *Modern French Philosophy*, 14, 23.

19 See Jan Rehmann, *Postmoderner Links-Nietzscheanismus: Deleuze & Foucault; Eine Dekonstruktion*, Hamburg: Argument, 2004, 136–9; Raulff, 'Auf sie mit Gedrill!'.

20 Deleuze, 'Nomadic Thought', 258ff. (cf. Deleuze, *Nietzsche: Ein Lesebuch*, 118ff.); Certeau, *The Practice of Everyday Life*, xvii (cf. Certeau, *Kunst des Handelns* [Art of action], trans. Ronald Voullié, Berlin: Merve, 1988, 20). On Deleuze's 'war-machines', inspired by Nietzsche, see Rehmann, *Postmoderner Links-Nietzscheanismus*, 60–8. Another important text on the opposition of state and war is the contemporary work of political anthropology by Pierre Clastres, *Archaeology of Violence*, Los Angeles: Semiotext(e), 2010.

21 Pinard-Legry, 'Alexandre Kojève', 109.

22 Ulrich Raulff, 'Disco: Studio 54 Revisited', in *Tumult*, 1 (1979), 64.

23 Hannes Böhringer, 'Avantgarde: Geschichten einer Metapher', in *Archiv für Begriffsgeschichte*, 22 (1978), 90–114.

24 The *bon mot* is from Friedrich Kittler, *Gramophone, Film, Typewriter*, trans. Geoffrey Winthrop-Young and Michael Wutz, Palo Alto: Stanford University Press, 1999, 96f. On the importance of war in Kittler's history of media, see Geoffrey Winthrop-Young, 'Drill and Distraction in the Yellow Submarine: On the Dominance of War in Friedrich Kittler's Media Theory', in *Critical Inquiry*, 28:4 (2002), 825–54.

25 Günter Maschke, 'Positionen inmitten des Hasses: Der Staat, der Feind und das Recht; Der umstrittene Denker Carl Schmitt; Zu seinem Tode',

in *Wir selbst*, 2 (1985). On Schmitt's affinity with theory, see Armin Mohler, 'Links-Schmittisten, Rechts-Schmittisten und Establishment-Schmittisten: Über das erste Carl-Schmitt-Symposium', in *Criticón*, 98 (1986), 266; Volker Neumann, 'Die Wirklichkeit im Lichte der Idee', in *Complexio Oppositorum: Über Carl Schmitt*, ed. Helmut Quaritsch, Berlin: Duncker & Humblot, 1988, 557–75.

26 On the Schmitt circles in the early years of West Germany, see Dirk van Laak, *Gespräche in der Sicherheit des Schweigens: Carl Schmitt in der politischen Geistesgeschichte der frühen Bundesrepublik*, Berlin: De Gruyter, 1993.

27 Sombart, *Journal intime*, 16.

28 See Heinz Dieter Kittsteiner, 'Der Begriff des Politischen in der heroischen Moderne: Carl Schmitt, Leo Strauss, Karl Marx', in *Die (k)alte Sachlichkeit: Herkunft und Wirkungen eines Konzepts*, ed. Moritz Bassler and Ewout van der Knaap, Würzburg: Königshausen & Neumann, 2004, esp. 164f.

29 Walter Seitter, 'Strukturalistische Stichpunkte zur Politik' [Structuralist keywords on politics], in Böckelmann et al., *Das Schillern der Revolte*, 87.

30 Raulff, 'Schneid', 124.

31 Peter Gente, untitled manuscript of a lecture on Carl Schmitt, undated: Merve Archives. The first clipping on Carl Schmitt in Gente's newspaper archive is dated 1967.

32 See Henning Ritter, 'Mein Besuch bei Carl Schmitt', in *Frankfurter Allgemeine Zeitung*, 9 December 2006.

33 Schmitt, *The Theory of the Partisan*, 32. The first copies of Mao's Little Red Book to circulate in West Germany may well have been ordered by young Schmitt readers. Cf. Ritter, 'Mein Besuch bei Carl Schmitt'.

34 Joachim Schickel, *Gespräche mit Carl Schmitt* [Conversations with Carl Schmitt], Berlin: Merve, 1993, 21.

35 Joachim Schickel (ed.), *Guerrilleros, Partisanen: Theorie und Praxis*, Munich: Hanser, 1970.

36 Cord Riechelmann in conversation with the author, 2 April 2014.

37 Maschke, 'Positionen inmitten des Hasses'; Lethen, *Suche nach dem Handorakel*, 36. Cf. Heinz Dieter Kittsteiner, 'Erkenne die Lage: Uber den Einbruch des Ernstfalls in das Geschichtsdenken', in *Sprachen der Ironie; Sprachen des Ernstes*, ed. Karl Heinz Bohrer, Frankfurt: Suhrkamp, 2000, 233–52.

38 Thus Peter Sloterdijk's gist in a panel discussion with Beat Wyss in Salon Kufsteiner Strasse, Berlin, 4 October 2013. On the importance of enmity in Schmitt's work, see Carl Schmitt, *The Concept of the Political*, trans. George Schwab, University of Chicago Press, 1996. Cf. Neumann, 'Die Wirklichkeit im Lichte der Idee', 566.
39 Sombart, *Jugend in Berlin*, 258.
40 Armin Mohler, 'Carl Schmitt und die "konservative Revolution"', in *Complexio Oppositorium*, ed. Quaritsch, 142.
41 Maschke, 'Positionen inmitten des Hasses', 33. On Günter Maschke, see Manuel Seitenbecher, *Mahler, Maschke & Co.: Rechtes Denken in der 68er Bewegung?* Paderborn: Ferdinand Schoeningh, 2013, esp. 261–8.
42 Paris and Gente, 'Ping-Pong auf der Hochebene von Tibet', 133.
43 Peter Gente, untitled manuscript of a lecture on Carl Schmitt, undated: Merve Archives.
44 See, e. g., Christian Linder, *Der Bahnhof von Finnentrop: Eine Reise ins Carl-Schmitt-Land*, Berlin: Matthes & Seitz, 2008.
45 'I am sorry that I do not yet know Lacan, which would apparently be necessary – according to your argument – to understand you.' Quoted in Walter Seitter, *Menschenfassungen: Studien zur Erkenntnispolitikwissenschaft*, 2nd edn, Weilerswist: Velbrück, 2012, 9.
46 Sombart, *Jugend in Berlin*, 258; italics in the original.
47 Edith Seifert and Michaela Ott in conversation with the author, 7 March 2014.
48 Diedrich Diederichsen reported the same thing about the founders of *Spex*: '"So obskur, wie es gerade noch ging": Diedrich Diederichsen erzählt von seinen *Spex*-Jahren', in *Jungle World*, 28 February 2013.
49 Anonymous, 'Zeit-Zeichen der Macht', concept paper, undated; Frank Böckelmann to Pasquale Pasquino, 30 October 1978: Estate of Dietmar Kamper.
50 Cf. Raulff, *Wiedersehen mit den Siebzigern*, 104.
51 Cf. Bude, 'Die Suche nach dem Unmöglichen', 233.
52 After sustained investigations, the narrator feels he has 'seen a fragment of the iridescent veil of this world', and compares the experience with a hike in the mountains: 'As we climb, we draw nearer to that secret whose final mysteries are hidden in the dust. So with every upward step the chance pattern of the horizon is lost among the mountains, but when we have climbed sufficiently it encircles us on every hand, whatever our point

of vantage, with the pure ring that unites us to eternity'– Ernst Jünger, *On the Marble Cliffs*, trans. Stuart Hood, New York: New Directions, 1947, 22–4.

53 Dietmar Kamper, untitled concept paper for the *Wilde Akademie*, undated. Estate of Dietmar Kamper.

54 Sombart, *Journal intime*, 160; cf. 65.

55 Laermann, 'Das rasende Gefasel der Gegenaufklärung', 217, 220. The entry of culinary arts in the social science scene was also observed in the 1980s in connection with the Dubrovnik colloquia organized by Hans-Ulrich Gumbrecht: see Rembert Hüser, 'Etiketten aufkleben', in *Das Populäre der Gesellschaft: Systemtheorie und Populärkultur*, ed. Christian Huck and Carsten Zorn, Wiesbaden: VS, 2007, 239–60. See also Mattenklott, 'Komm ins Offene, Freund!'

56 'Elites are those whose sociology no one dares write', Carl Schmitt had remarked in 1953, adding that his definition had the advantage of 'defining sociology at the same time': Carl Schmitt to Armin Mohler, 26 December 1953, in *Carl Schmitt: Briefwechsel mit einem seiner Schüler*, ed. Armin Mohler, Berlin: Akademie, 1995, 147. It would be worthwhile to examine the growth of interest in elites among sociologists and cultural historians in the 1980s. Another model of the intellectual formation of elites in *Tumult* circles was no doubt Pierre Klossowski's idea, articulated in the context of his Nietzsche interpretations, of a 'little, secret community' of conspirators: see Klossowski, 'Circulus vitiosus', 405.

57 'Elite oder Avantgarde? Jacob Taubes im Gespräch mit Wolfert von Rahden und Norbert Kapferer', in *Tumult*, 4 (1982), 64–76. On the personal background of Taubes's political position, see Raulff, *Kreis ohne Meister*, 494f.

58 Treml, 'Paulinische Feindschaft', 275.

59 Ritter, 'Jacob Taubes', 35f.; and Ritter, 'Akosmisch: Zum Tod von Jacob Taubes'.

60 Quoted from Taubes, 'Ästhetisierung der Wahrheit im Posthistoire', 41.

61 These ideas are taken from the author's conversation with Cord Riechelmann, 2 April 2014.

62 Treml, 'Paulinische Feindschaft', 290.

63 Ritter, 'Jacob Taubes', 35. A summary of Strauss's argument was later published by Merve: see Leo Strauss, Alexandre Kojève and Friedrich Kittler, *Kunst des Schreibens* [Art of writing], Berlin: Merve, 2009.

64 Cf. Sombart, *Jugend in Berlin*, 257ff. Sombart considered Schmitt's reading method modern-day gnosis.
65 Taubes, *Ad Carl Schmitt*, 31.
66 Gente, 'Editorische Notiz', 79.
67 Ibid. On Taubes's Benjamin letter and the background of relations between Schmitt and Benjamin, see Taubes, *Ad Carl Schmitt*; Treml, 'Paulinische Feindschaft'; and especially Ritter, 'Jacob Taubes'.
68 Gente, 'Editorische Notiz', 79.
69 Taubes, *Ad Carl Schmitt*, 16, 22f. On the eschatological themes of Taubes's life, see Jacob Taubes, *Der Preis des Messianismus: Briefe von Jacob Taubes an Gershom Scholem und andere Materialien*, ed. Elettra Stimilli, Würzburg: Königshausen & Neumann, 2006.
70 According to Ritter, 'Jacob Taubes', 41.
71 Mohler, 'Der messianische Irrwisch', 221.
72 Taubes, *Ad Carl Schmitt*, 49f.

11 Disco Dispositive

1 Assmann, 'Talmud in der Paris-Bar'.
2 Martin Treml and Herbert Kopp-Oberstebrink, 'Netzwerker, Projektemacher: Die goldenen Jahre der Philosophie an der Freien Universität Berlin; Ein Gespräch über den abwesenden Herrn Taubes', in *Der Freitag*, 13 October 2010.
3 Jacob Taubes to Heidi Paris and Peter Gente, 16 June 1986: Merve Archives.
4 Jacob Taubes to Heidi Paris, 8 December 1986: Merve Archives.
5 Jacob Taubes, 'Ein Brief', in *Paris Bar, Berlin*, ed. Michel Würthle, Berlin: Quadriga, 2000, 19.
6 Diederichsen, *Sexbeat*, 46.
7 Bernd Cailloux, *Gutgeschriebene Verluste*, Frankfurt: Suhrkamp, 2013, 19. Cailloux also refers to 'gastronomic dance theatre' (ibid., 45). On the connection between disenchantment with theory and nightlife in West Berlin in the early 1980s, see also Thomas E. Schmidt, 'Als ich mal dazugehörte: Szenenbildung Anfang der Achtziger', in *Merkur*, 773/4 (2013), 957–66.
8 Bude, 'Die Suche nach dem Unmöglichen', 241.
9 Paris and Gente, 'Ping-Pong auf der Hochebene von Tibet', 132. Diedrich Diederichsen referred to the mixture of work and social life which began

in the 1980s as the 'Nietzsche economy': 'People of Intensity, People of Power: The Nietzsche-Economy', in *e-flux journal*, 19 (2010), 8–29.

10 Jürgen Habermas, *The Structural Transformation of the Public Sphere*, trans. Thomas Burger, Cambridge, Mass.: MIT Press, 1989, 32f.; E. P. Thompson, *The Making of the English Working Class*, New York: Pantheon, 1964, 17ff.

11 Simon Ford, *The Situationist International: A User's Guide*, London: Black Dog, 2004, 21, 27.

12 Elisabeth Lenk (ed.), *Die Badewanne: Ein Künstlerkabarett der frühen Nachkriegszeit*, Berlin: Hentrich, 1991.

13 '30.000 Euro Unterhalt im Monat', interview with Rolf Eden, in *Süddeutsche Zeitung*, 17 May 2010.

14 Lowien, *Weibliche Produktivkraft*, 38.

15 Hartmut Sander and Ulrich Christians (eds.), *Subkultur Berlin: Selbstdarstellung Text-, Ton-Bilddokumente Esoterik der Kommunen Rocker subversiven Gruppen*, Darmstadt: März, 1969, 2.

16 In German: 'Wohnst du noch, oder lebst du schon?'

17 Norbert Klugmann, 'Selten allein: Szenen einer WG', in *Kursbuch*, 54 (1978), 166.

18 See, e.g., Büscher, *Drei Stunden Null*, 34ff.

19 Richard Sennett, *The Fall of Public Man*, New York: Knopf, 1976, 337.

20 Sander and Christians, *Subkultur Berlin*, 5.

21 Lenk, 'Die sozialistische Theorie in der Arbeit des SDS', 174.

22 Marie-Luise Scherer, 'Der RAF-Anwalt Otto Schily', in Scherer, *Ungeheurer Alltag: Geschichten und Reportagen*, Reinbek: Rowohlt, 1988, 137. On the avoidance of theory work and guilty consciences, see Klaus Laermann, 'Kneipengerede: Zu einigen Verkehrsformen der Berliner "linken" Subkultur', in *Kursbuch*, 37 (1974), 173.

23 Cailloux, *Gutgeschriebene Verluste*, 77ff.

24 Laermann, 'Kneipengerede', 168.

25 Bernd Cailloux, 'Spielzeit 77/78: Die weisse Phase', in *Nachtleben Berlin: 1974 bis heute*, ed. Wolfgang Farkas, Berlin: Metrolit, 2013, 35. On Baader's local bar, see Stern and Herrmann, *Andreas Baader*, 75.

26 Lethen, *Suche nach dem Handorakel*, 29. Also corroborated in the main by Hubert Fichte, *Die Palette*, Reinbek: Rowohlt, 1968.

27 Laermann, 'Kneipengerede', 168, 171. On the alternative pub scene, see Reichardt, *Authentizität und Gemeinschaft*, 572–83. On the discos of the late sixties, see Lorenz Jäger, 'Doch wo sind die Brandstifter geblieben?'

in *Frankfurter Allgemeine Zeitung*, 22 February 2013; Bernd Cailloux, *Das Geschäftsjahr 1968/69*, Frankfurt: Suhrkamp, 2005.

28 Lowien, *Weibliche Produktivkraft*, 121.

29 Laermann, 'Kneipengerede', 173, 169.

30 Quoted in Graf, 'Querbeat mit Merve'.

31 Laermann, 'Kneipengerede', 178.

32 Laermann, 'Das rasende Gefasel der Gegenaufklärung'. Cf. Laermann, 'Lacancan und Derridada: Über die Frankolatrie in den Kulturwissenschaften', in: *Kursbuch*, 84 (1986), 34–43.

33 Sloterdijk, *Zeilen und Tage*, 134.

34 Habermas and Luhmann, *Theorie der Gesellschaft oder Sozialtechnologie*, 1971.

35 On the immediately obvious character of Habermas's theory and its inevitable trivialization, see Verheyen, *Diskussionslust*, 302f.

36 On the disappearance of future and past in nightlife, see Niklas Luhmann, 'Zeit und Handlung: eine vergessene Theorie', in Luhmann, *Soziologische Aufklärung*, vol. III: *Soziales System, Gesellschaft, Organisation*, Opladen: Westdeutscher, 1981, 122.

37 Cailloux, *Gutgeschriebene Verluste*, 34.

38 See Michel de Certeau, 'May 1968', in Certeau, *The Capture of Speech and Other Political Writings*, trans. Tom Conley, Minneapolis: University of Minnesota Press, 1997, 3–76.

39 Niklas Luhmann, 'Öffentliche Meinung', in Luhmann, *Politische Planung: Aufsätze zur Soziologie von Politik und Verwaltung* [Public opinion, in: Political planning: essays on the sociology of politics and administration], Opladen: Westdeutscher, 1971, 30.

40 Habermas, *Structural Transformation of the Public Sphere*, 36, 159f, 163.

41 Laermann, 'Kneipengerede', 180.

42 Jürgen Habermas, 'Vorbereitende Bemerkungen zu einer Theorie der kommunikativen Kompetenz', in Habermas and Luhmann, *Theorie der Gesellschaft oder Sozialtechnologie*, 115, 121.

43 Diederichsen, *Sexbeat*, 46.

44 Hence Wolfgang Farkas, for one, begins his compendium of Berlin nightlife with the year 1974.

45 Müller, *Subkultur Westberlin*, 64.

46 Cf. Max Frisch, *From the Berlin Journal*, ed. Thomas Strässle and Margit Unser, trans. Wieland Hoban, London: Seagull, 2017, 151.

47 Brus, *Das gute alte West-Berlin*, 20.

48 On the Exil, see Oswald Wiener, 'Austria Go Home!,' interview with Friedrich Geyrhofer, trans. Christian-Albrecht Gollub, in *The German Issue*, ed. Lotringer, 222–32; Susanne Kippenberger, 'Wie Ingrid und Oswald Wiener keine Ahnung von der Gastronomie hatten, aber alles richtig machten,' in Kippenberger, *Am Tisch: Die kulinarische Boheme oder Die Entdeckung der Lebenslust*, Berlin-Verlag, 2012, 122–31; Stephan Landwehr, 'Das Schlupfloch der Bohème,' in *Nachtleben Berlin*, ed. Farkas, 76f. On the Austrian restaurants and bars in West Berlin as a school of gastronomy, see Jürgen Kaube, 'Aufklärung ohne Rettungsversprechen: Die Denkfigur, die einem ein Licht aufsteckt; Zum Tod unseres Kollegen Henning Ritter,' in *Frankfurter Allgemeine Zeitung*, 25 June 2013.

49 Brus, *Das gute alte West-Berlin*, 67. On Viennese Actionism, see Eva Badura-Triska and Hubert Klocker (eds.), *Vienna Actionism: Art and Upheaval in 1960s Vienna*, Cologne: Walter König, 2011.

50 Brus, *Das gute alte West-Berlin*, 25.

51 Oswald Wiener, 'Turings Test: Vom dialektischen zum binären Denken,' in *Kursbuch*, 75 (1984), 12–37.

52 On Schily, who took a sabbatical in the Berlin bar scene after the death of his clients in Stammheim Prison, see Sherer, 'Der RAF-Anwalt Otto Schily'; Michael Althen, 'Der Sieg der neuen Mitte: Aus für die "Paris-Bar",' in: *Frankfurter Allgemeine Zeitung*, 25 November 2005.

53 Heiner Müller, 'Traumhölle in Berlin Paris Bar: Eine Ortsbeschreibung,' in *Paris Bar, Berlin*, ed. Würthle, 10. The book extensively documents the history of the Paris Bar. See also Michel Würthle, 'Die Verführung der Kunst,' in *Nachtleben Berlin*, ed. Farkas, 78–85.

54 Sombart, *Journal intime*, 33.

55 Cailloux, *Gutgeschriebene Verluste*, 41f. On all the bars and clubs named here, see Müller, *Subkultur Westberlin*. On the drug scene in West Berlin, see Klaus Weinhauer, 'Heroinszenen in der Bundesrepublik Deutschland und in Grossbritannien der siebziger Jahre: Konsumpraktiken zwischen staatlichen, medialen und zivilgesellschaftlichen Einflüssen,' in *Das Alternative Milieu*, ed. Reichardt and Siegfried, 244–63. From 1979 at the latest, when Christiane F. became famous, West Berlin was reputed to be the 'heroin capital of the world,' in the words of Iggy Pop, who had come to Berlin in 1976 to kick his cocaine addiction: quoted in Rüther, *Heroes*, 116.

56 Cf. Rüther, *Heroes*, 95–6. *Playboy* quoted in Rüther.
57 Raulff, 'Disco: Studio 54 Revisited,' 596.
58 Adriano Sack et al., 'Dschungel: Yes, We Could,' in *Liebling*, 11/12 (2008).
59 Raulff, 'Disco: Studio 54 Revisited,' 60.
60 Diedrich Diederichsen, 'Die Auflösung der Welt: Vom Ende und Anfang,' in Diederichsen et al., *Schocker: Stile und Moden der Subkultur*, Reinbek: Rowohlt, 1980, 178; cf. 166.
61 Norbert Bolz, 'Pop-Philosophie,' in *Schizo-Schleichwege*, ed. Heinz and Tholen, 192; Deleuze and Guattari, 'Introduction: Rhizome,' 24; cf. Deleuze and Guattari, *Rhizom*, 38; Gilles Deleuze and Claire Parnet, *Dialogues*, London: Athlone, 1987, 8. On Deleuze and Guattari's 'pop analysis,' see Diederichsen, 'Aus dem Zusammenhang reissen,' 163, 182; Tom Holert, '"Dispell Them": Anti-Pop und Pop-Philosophie; Ist eine andere Politik des Populären möglich?,' in *Deleuze und die Künste*, ed. Peter Gente and Peter Weibel, Frankfurt: Suhrkamp, 2007, 168–89.
62 Peter Gente to Karlheinz Barck, 6 November 1988, quoted in Karlheinz Barck, Peter Gente, Heidi Paris and Stefan Richter, 'Statt eines Nachwortes,' in *Aisthesis: Wahrnehmung heute oder Perspektiven einer anderen Ästhetik* [In lieu of an afterword, in: Aisthesis: perception today, or prospects for a different aesthetics], ed. Barck et al., Leipzig: Reclam, 1990, 447.
63 Merve Verlag to Gilles Deleuze, 8 May 1979; Merve Verlag to Roland Barthes, 9 May 1979: Merve Archives.
64 Shuhei Hosokawa, 'The Walkman Effect,' in *Popular Music* 4 (1984), 176; cf. Hosokawa, *Der Walkman-Effekt*, trans. Birger Ollrogge, Berlin: Merve, 1987.
65 Shuhei Hosokawa to Merve Verlag, 15 September 1987: Merve Archives.
66 Peter Gente to Karlheinz Barck, 6 November 1988, quoted in Barck et al., 'Statt eines Nachwortes,' 447.
67 Bohrer, 'The Three Cultures,' 149.
68 Cailloux, *Gutgeschriebene Verluste*, 31.
69 Diederichsen, 'Die Auflösung der Welt,' 166.
70 See Enno Stahl, 'Bolz, Hörisch, Kittler und Winkels tanzen im Ratinger Hof; Was körperlich-sportiv begann, setzt sich auf anderer Ebene fort: Diskurs-Pogo,' in *Kultur & Gespenster*, 6 (2008), 108–17. 'Intensity has to do with proper names,' Deleuze had written in his Nietzsche reader (*Nietzsche: Ein Lesebuch*, 115). Cf. Peter Gente's self-assessment ('Ping Pong auf der Hochebene von Tibet,' 131): 'It didn't turn out how we

imagined it, and perhaps it couldn't have done. Furthermore, the further we went in the art field, the more we were concerned with the individual authors. Just following Deleuze, Cage or even Foucault was enough for us to go on with. As we did so, our militancy fell by the wayside in favour of an epicureanism.' For a characterization of the intellectual situation, see Diedrich Diederichsen, 'Virtueller Maosismus: Das Wissen von 1984', in Diederichsen, *Freiheit macht arm*, 227–45.

71 Gottschalch, 'Foucaults Denken', 72. See also Negt, 'Nicht das Gold, Wotan ist das Problem', 44f.

72 Goetz, *Hirn*, 89.

73 Gilles Deleuze and Claire Parnet, 'Boisson', in Deleuze and Parnet, *Gilles Deleuze from A to Z*, dir. Pierre-André Boutang, trans. Charles J. Stivale, DVD video, 2011: Semiotext(e).

74 Michael Rutschky, *Wartezeit: Ein Sittenbild*, Cologne: Kiepenheuer & Witsch, 1983, 177. Emphasis in the original.

75 Niklas Luhmann, 'Biographie, Attitüden, Zettelkasten' [Biography, attitudes, card file], in Luhmann, *Archimedes und wir*, 145. Luhmann moved awkwardly in society. See, e.g., Andrea Frank, 'Weder Naserümpfen noch Augenaufschlag', in *Gibt es eigentlich den Berliner Zoo noch? Erinnerungen an Niklas Luhmann*, ed. Theodor M. Bardmann and Dirk Baecker, Constance: UVK, 1999, 70.

76 Luhmann, 'Systemtheoretische Argumentationen', 329, 331.

77 For a contemporary Berliner's view of the Habermas–Luhmann debate, see Norbert Bolz, 'Niklas Luhmann und Jürgen Habermas: Eine Phantomdebatte', in *Luhmann Lektüren*, ed. Wolfram Burckhardt, Berlin: Kadmos, 2010, 34–52.

78 Luhmann cites Cavan in the following works: 'Systemtheoretische Argumentationen', 331; 'Öffentliche Meinung', 30; 'Einfache Sozialsysteme', in Luhmann, *Soziologische Aufklärung*, vol. II: *Aufsätze zur Theorie sozialer Systeme*, Opladen: Westdeutscher, 1975, 37; 'Zeit und Handlung: eine vergessene Theorie', 122; *Love as Passion*, trans. Jeremy Gaines and Doris L. Jones, Cambridge, Mass.: Harvard University Press, 1986, 237; *Social Systems*, trans. John Bednarz, Jr, and Dirk Baecker, Palo Alto: Stanford University Press, 1995, 602; *A Sociological Theory of Law*, trans. Elizabeth King-Utz and Martin Albrow, Abingdon: Routledge, 2013, 35; 'Die Form "Person"', in Luhmann, *Soziologische Auklärung*, vol. VI: *Die Soziologie und der Mensch*, Opladen: Westdeutscher, 1995, 147; *Theory of Society*, trans.

Rhodes Barrett, vol. II, Palo Alto: Stanford University Press, 2013, 390. On Luhmann's apocryphal references, see Hans Ulrich Gumbrecht, '"Old Europe" and "The Sociologist": How Does Niklas Luhmann's Theory Relate to Philosophical Tradition?' in *e-compós*, 15:3 (2012), 1–14, www.e-compos.org.br/e-compos/article/download/866/628/0.

79 Luhmann, *Social Systems*, 602.

80 Sherri Cavan, *Liquor License: An Ethnography of Bar Behavior*, Chicago: Aldine, 1966, 49; cf. 30.

81 Among many other possible citations for this point, see Niklas Luhmann, 'The Improbability of Communication', in *International Social Science Journal*, 33:1 (1981), 122–32.

82 Goetz, *Hirn*, 66. In a later book, Goetz called this the 'theory of blabbing away', which is directly opposed to the theory of chatter: Goetz, *Loslabern*, 17.

83 Goetz, *Hirn*, 47, 79.

84 Luhmann, *Archimedes und wir*, 115.

85 Bazon Brock, 'Gegen das Chaos der Möglichkeiten: Zur Debatte zwischen Habermas und Luhmann', in *Frankfurter Allgemeine Zeitung*, 12 October 1971. On the significance of that debate for intellectual politics, see Wegmann, 'Wie kommt die Theorie zum Leser?'

86 Luhmann, *Archimedes und wir*, 102, 104. The characterization of systems theorists as 'jet-set Christian Democrats': ibid., 58.

87 Luhmann, *Social Systems*, l (lower-case Roman numeral L).

88 Käsler, 'Soziologie: Flug über den Wolken', 190.

89 According to Jürgen Kaube, it is difficult to place Luhmann's ideas in a historical context since he was responding primarily to intra-academic stimuli: Jürgen Kaube, 'Theorieproduktion ohne Technologiedefizit: Niklas Luhmann, sein Zettelkasten und die Ideengeschichte der Bundesrepublik', in *Was war Bielefeld? Eine ideengeschichtliche Nachfrage*, ed. Sonja Asal and Stephan Schlak, Göttingen: Wallstein, 2009, 161–70.

90 Dietrich Schwanitz, 'Der Zauberer hext sich selber weg: Operation Systemtheorie abgeschlossen; Niklas Luhmann macht die unsichtbare Gesellschaft sichtbar', in *Frankfurter Allgemeine Zeitung*, 14 October 1997.

91 Dirk Baecker to Merve Verlag, 3 August 1987: Merve Archives.

92 Peter Gente to Dirk Baecker, 2 September 1987: Merve Archives.

93 Georg Stanitzek to Merve Verlag, 15 December 1987: Merve Archives.

Epilogue: After Theory?

1 Kapielski, 'Baden-Baden', 89.

2 Karlheinz Barck et al., 'Statt eines Nachwortes', 445, 456.

3 Michel Serres, *Hermes I: Kommunikation* [Hermes I: communication], trans. Michael Bischoff, Berlin: Merve, 1991. Bude mentions the new investor in 'Die Suche nach dem Unmöglichen', 192.

4 Rolf Lindner, *Die Stunde der Cultural Studies*, Vienna: Universitätsverlag, 2000, 9ff.

5 The American physicist Alan Sokal submitted a paper to the literary journal *Social Text* in 1996, in which he claimed to deconstruct quantum theory. After the article was published, he publicized his hoax, sparking a highly polemical discussion. See Keith Parsons (ed.), *The Science Wars: Debating Scientific Knowledge and Technology*, Amherst: Prometheus, 2003. For an earlier example of US hostility to theory, see Walter Benn Michaels and Steven Knapp, 'Against Theory', in *Critical Inquiry*, 8:4 (1982), 723–42.

6 For a critical summary, see, e.g., *Merkur*, 594/5 (1998), special issue: *Postmoderne: Eine Bilanz*.

7 See, e.g., *Merkur*, 677/8 (2005), special issue: *Wirklichkeit! Wege in die Realität*.

8 Terry Eagleton, *After Theory*, New York: Basic, 2003.

9 See Benjamin Kunkel, 'How Much Is Too Much?' in *London Review of Books*, 33:3 (2011), 9–14.

10 Andreas Rosenfelder, 'Der hedonistische Mönch: Was hätte er zur Verstaatlichung des Finanzwesens gesagt? Was zur Lage in Iran? 25 Jahre nach seinem Tod fehlt uns Foucault mehr denn je', in *Frankfurter Allgemeine Sonntagszeitung*, 21 June 2009.

11 Nicholas Dames suspects so in 'The Theory Generation', in *n+1*, 14 (2012).

12 Mario Grizelj and Oliver Jahraus, 'Einleitung: Theorietheorie; Geisteswissenschaft als Ort avancierter Theoriebildung; Theorie als Ort avancierter Geisteswissenschaft', in *Theorietheorie: Wider die Theoriemüdigkeit in den Geisteswissenschaften*, ed. Grizelj and Jahraus, Munich: Fink, 2011, 9.

13 Goetz, *Loslabern*, 166. Cf. the eulogies in *Für Heidi Paris*.

14 Author's conversation with Marianne Karbe, 1 December 2011.

Bibliography

Archives

Theodor W. Adorno Archives: Institute for Social Research, Senckenberganlage 26, 60325 Frankfurt am Main, Germany.

Dietmar Kamper Estate: University Archives, Freie Universität, Malteserstrasse 74–100, 12249 Berlin, Germany.

Merve Archives: Centre for Art and Media Technology (ZKM), Lorenzstrasse 19, 76135 Karlsruhe, Germany.

Siegfried Unseld Archives: *Theorie* series, German Literature Archives (DLA), Schillerhöhe 8–10, 71672 Marbach am Neckar, Germany.

Author's Interviews and Conversations

Hannes Böhringer, 20 March 2014.

Peter Gente, 21 April 2008, 26 September 2010 and 10 May 2012.

Wolfgang Hagen, 5 March 2008.

Marianne Karbe, 1 December 2011.

Helmut Lethen, 30 December 2011.

Michaela Ott and Edith Seifert, 7 March 2014.

Wolfert von Rahden, 24 September 2014.

Ulrich Raulff, 12 July 2012.

Hans-Jörg Rheinberger, 4 November 2013.

Cord Riechelmann, 2 April 2014.

Henning Schmidgen, 15 March 2008.

Walter Seitter, 25 October 2013.

Georg Stanitzek, 5 April 2014.
Jochen Stankowski, 11 March 2008.
Ronald Voullié, 6 December 2011.

Audio and Video Recordings

Die Anwälte: Eine deutsche Geschichte, film documentary, dir. Birgit Schulz, Cologne, 2009.

Michel Foucault in conversation with Heidi Paris, Peter Gente, Walter Seitter, Hans-Joachim Metzger and Pasquale Pasquino, unpublished tape recording, Paris, 1977. Collection of Merve Verlag.

Foucault in/à Berlin, film documentary, dir. Agnes Handwerk, Hamburg, 1992/3.

Gilles Deleuze from A to Z, Gilles Deleuze in conversation with Claire Parnet, dir. Pierre-André Boutang, trans. Charles J. Stivale, DVD video, Semiotext(e), 2011.

Ein Leben wie eine Komposition von John Cage, Peter Gente interviewed by Marcus Klug, Berlin, 2007: www.youtube.com/watch?v=82LiWC6EpmY.

'*Schlau sein, dabei sein*: Querbeat mit Merve', radio feature by Guido Graf about Merve Verlag, WDR 3, Cologne, 7 July 2005.

Literature

Theodor W. Adorno, 'Bibliographische Grillen', in *Frankfurter Allgemeine Zeitung*, 16 October 1959.

——, 'Commitment', in Adorno, *Notes to Literature*, 348–63.

——, 'Cultural Criticism and Society', in *Prisms*, trans. Samuel Weber and Shierry Weber, Cambridge, Mass.: MIT Press, 1981

——, 'The Essay as Form', in Adorno, *Notes to Literature*, 3–23.

——, *Jargon of Authenticity*, trans. Knut Tarnowski and Frederic Will, London: Routledge, 1973.

——, *Lectures on Negative Dialectics: Fragments of a Lecture Course, 1965/1966*, ed. Rolf Tiedemann, trans. Rodney Livingstone, Cambridge: Polity, 2008.

——, 'Lyric Poetry and Society', in Adorno, *Notes to Literature*, 37–54.

——, 'Marginalia to Theory and Praxis', in Adorno, *Critical Models: Interventions and Catchwords*, trans. Henry W. Pickford, New York: Columbia University Press, 1998.

——, *Metaphysics: Concept and Problems*, ed. Rolf Tiedemann, trans. Edmund Jephcott, Palo Alto: Stanford University Press, 2001.

——, *Minima Moralia: Reflections from Damaged Life*, trans. E. F. N. Jephcott, London: Verso, 1978.

——, 'Notes on Kafka,' in Adorno, *Prisms*, trans. Samuel Weber and Shierry Weber, Cambridge, Mass.: MIT Press, 1981, 243–70.

——, *Notes to Literature*, ed. Rolf Tiedemann, trans. Shierry Weber Nicholsen, rev. edn [in one volume], New York: Columbia University Press, 2019.

——, 'Scientific Experiences of a European Scholar in America,' trans. Donald Fleming, in *The Intellectual Migration: Europe and America, 1930–1960*, ed. Donald Fleming and Bernard Bailyn, Cambridge, Mass.: Belknap, 1969, 367.

——, 'Vers une musique informelle,' in Adorno, *Quasi una Fantasia: Essays on Modern Music*, trans. Rodney Livingstone, London: Verso, 1998, 269–322.

—— and Elisabeth Lenk, *Briefwechsel 1962–1969*, Munich: Text & Kritik, 2001.

—— ——, *The Challenge of Surrealism: The Correspondence of Theodor W. Adorno and Elisabeth Lenk*, trans. Susan H. Gillespie, Minneapolis: University of Minnesota Press, 2015.

Clemens Albrecht, 'Die Massenmedien und die Frankfurter Schule,' in Albrecht, Günter C. Behrmann, Michael Bock, Harald Homann and Friedrich H. Tenbruck, *Die intellektuelle Gründung der Bundesrepublik: Eine Wirkungsgeschichte der Frankfurter Schule*, Frankfurt: Campus, 1999, 203–46.

Michael Althen, 'Der Sieg der neuen Mitte: Aus für die "Paris-Bar",' in *Frankfurter Allgemeine Zeitung*, 25 November 2005.

Louis Althusser, *For Marx*, trans. Ben Brewster, New York: Vintage, 1970.

——, *The Future Lasts Forever: A Memoir*, ed. Olivier Corpet and Yann Moulier Boutang, trans. Richard Veasy, New York: New Press, 1993.

——, 'La Philosophie comme arme de la révolution,' in Althusser, *Positions (1964–1975)*, Paris: Éditions sociales, 1976, 35–48.

——, *Reading Capital*, trans. Ben Brewster, London: New Left Books, 1970.

——, *Wie sollen wir* Das Kapital *lesen?* Berlin: n.p. [Merve], 1970.

Jürg Altwegg, 'Alles ist nur noch eine einzige Show: Jean Baudrillards "Der symbolische Tausch und der Tod"; Die Herrschaft des Scheins über das Sein,' in *Frankfurter Allgemeine Zeitung*, 20 May 1983.

——, 'Die Merve-Kulturen: Ein Verlags- und Verlegerporträt,' in *Die Zeit*, 22 July 1983.

Jean Améry, 'Archäologie des Wissens: Michel Foucault und sein Diskurs der Gegenaufklärung,' in *Die Zeit*, 31 March 1978.

——, 'Leben wir im Kerker-Archipel? Eine Strafpredigt über die Strafe', in *Die Zeit*, 14 January 1977.

Perry Anderson, *Considerations on Western Marxism*, London: Verso, 1979.

Anonymous [Klaus Hülbrock], 'Buback: Ein Nachruf', in *Göttinger Nachrichten*, 25 April 1977.

Jan Assmann, 'Talmud in der Paris-Bar: Zum Tod des jüdischen Philosophen Jacob Taubes (1923–1987)', in *die tageszeitung*, 28 March 1987.

Erich Auerbach, *Mimesis: The Representation of Reality in Western Literature*, trans. Willard R. Trask, Princeton University Press, 2013 [1953].

Rudolf Augstein, 'Frauen fliessen, Männer schiessen', in *Der Spiegel*, 31:52 (1977), 204.

Stefan Aust, *The Baader–Meinhof Complex*, trans. Anthea Bell, London: The Bodley Head, 1987.

Eva Badura-Triska and Hubert Klocker (eds.), *Vienna Actionism: Art and Upheaval in 1960s Vienna*, Cologne: Walter König, 2012.

Lothar Baier, 'Franzosentheorie', in Baier, *Französische Zustande: Berichte und Essays*, Frankfurt: Europäische Verlagsanstalt, 1982, 21–6.

Friedrich Balke, 'Das Ende eines Schweigens: Zu Louis Althussers *L'Avenir dure longtemps*', in *Symptome: Zeitschrift für epistemologische Baustellen*, 10 (1992), 60–2.

Jan-Frederik Bändel, Barbara Kalender and Jörg Schröder, *Immer radikal, niemals konsequent: Der März Verlag; erweitertes Verlegertum, postmoderne Literatur und Business Art*, Hamburg: Philo Fine Arts, 2011.

Irene Bandhauer-Schöffmann and Dirk van Laak (eds.), *Der Linksterrorismus der 1970er Jahre und die Ordnung der Geschlechter*, Trier: WVT, 2013.

Karlheinz Barck, Peter Gente, Heidi Paris and Stefan Richter, 'Statt eines Nachwortes', in *Aisthesis: Wahrnehmung heute oder Perspektiven einer anderen Ästhetik*, ed. Barck, Gente, Paris and Richter, Leipzig: Reclam, 1990, 445–68.

Ariane Barth, 'Luftwurzeln und Wildwuchs verlieben sich', in *Der Spiegel*, 34:53 (1980), 98–102.

Roland Barthes, 'The Death of the Author', in Barthes, *The Rustle of Language*, trans. Richard Howard, New York: Farrar, Straus and Giroux, 1986, 49–55.

——, *The Pleasure of the Text*, trans. Richard Miller, New York: Hill and Wang, 1975.

——, 'Writing Reading', in Barthes, *The Rustle of Language*, trans. Richard Howard, New York: Farrar, Straus and Giroux, 1986, 29–32.

Jean Baudrillard, *Forget Foucault*, trans. Nicole Dufresne, Los Angeles: Semiotext(e), 1987.

——, 'Kool Killer, or The Insurrection of Signs', in Baudrillard, *Symbolic Exchange and Death*, 76–84.

——, *Kool Killer oder Der Aufstand der Zeichen*, trans. Hans-Joachim Metzger, Berlin: Merve, 1978.

——, *Symbolic Exchange and Death*, trans. Iain Hamilton Grant: London: Sage, 1993.

——, *Der symbolische Tausch und der Tod*, trans. Gerd Bergfleth, Gabriele Ricke and Ronald Voullié, Munich: Matthes & Seitz, 1982.

——, *Das System der Dinge: Über unser Verhältnis zu den alltäglichen Gegenständen*, Frankfurt: Campus, 1991.

——, *The System of Objects*, trans. James Benedict, London: Verso, 1996.

——, *Der Tod tanzt aus der Reihe*, Berlin: Merve, 1979.

Bruce Baugh, *French Hegel: From Surrealism to Postmodernism*, Abingdon and New York: Routledge, 2003.

Günther G. Behrmann, 'Die Theorie, das Institut, die Zeitschrift und das Buch: Zur Publikations- und Wirkungsgeschichte der Kritischen Theorie 1945 bis 1965', in Clemens Albrecht, Günter C. Behrmann, Michael Bock, Harald Homann and Friedrich H. Tenbruck, *Die intellektuelle Gründung der Bundesrepublik: Eine Wirkungsgeschichte der Frankfurter Schule*, Frankfurt: Campus, 1999, 247–311.

Jens Benicke, *Von Adorno zu Mao: Über die schlechte Aufhebung der antiautoritären Bewegung*, Freiburg: Ça ira, 2010.

Walter Benjamin, 'The Author as Producer', in Benjamin, *Reflections*, trans. Edmund Jephcott, New York and London: Harcourt Brace Jovanovich, 1978, 232–51.

Walter Benjamin and Asja Lacis, 'Naples', in Benjamin, *Reflections*, trans. Edmund Jephcott, New York and London: Harcourt Brace Jovanovich, 1978, 173–86.

Gottfried Benn, *Briefe an F. W. Oelze, 1932–1945*, Wiesbaden: Limes, 1977.

——, 'Probleme der Lyrik', in Benn, *Gesammelte Werke*, vol. IV, Wiesbaden: Limes, 1968, 1058–96.

——, 'Der Ptolemäer', in Benn, *Gesammelte Werke*, vol. V, Wiesbaden: Limes, 1968.

Gerd Bergfleth, 'Die Fatalität der Moderne', interview with Jean Baudrillard, in Bergfleth et al., *Zur Kritik der palavernden Aufklärung*, Munich: Matthes & Seitz, 1984, 133–44.

——, 'Nachwort', in Jean Baudrillard, *Der symbolische Tausch und der Tod*, Munich: Matthes & Seitz, 1982, 363–430.

——, 'Die Verewigung des Lebens: Zu Klossowskis Nietzsche-Deutung', in Pierre Klossowski, *Nietzsche und der Circulus vitiosus deus*, Munich: Matthes & Seitz, 1986, 431–49.

Uta Berg-Ganschow and Wolfgang Jacobsen (eds.), *Film, Stadt, Kino, Berlin*, exhibition catalogue, Berlin: Argon, 1987.

Dietz Bering, *Die Intellektuellen: Geschichte eines Schimpfworts*, Stuttgart: Klett-Cotta, 1978.

Andreas Bernard, 'Fünfzig Jahre *Minima Moralia*', in *Theodor W. Adorno:* Minima Moralia *neu gelesen*, ed. Andreas Bernard and Ulrich Raulff, Frankfurt: Suhrkamp, 2003, 7–10.

Anja Bertsch, 'Alternative (in) Bewegung: Distinktion und transnationale Vergemeinschaftung im alternativen Tourismus', in *Das Alternative Milieu*, ed. Reichardt and Siegfried, 115–30.

Charles Bettelheim, *Über das Fortbestehen von Warenverhältnissen in den 'sozialistischen Ländern'* [On the persistence of commodity relations in the 'socialist countries'], Berlin: Merve, 1970

Peter Bexte, 'Warum haben Sie keinen Schreibtisch, Herr Gente? Der Mitbegründer des Berliner Merve Verlages im Interview', in *Frankfurter Allgemeine Magazin*, 2 October 1987, 106f.

Matthias Bickenbach, *Von den Möglichkeiten einer 'inneren' Geschichte des Lesens*, Tübingen: Niemeyer, 1999.

Klaus Birnstiel, 'Wer hat an der Theorie gedreht? In den siebziger Jahren war er eine Galionsfigur linker Theoriebildung; Dann geisterte Paulchen Panther durch das Mordvideo der Zwickauer Neonazis: Ein Blick auf die Bildsprache des Terrors', in *Frankfurter Allgemeine Zeitung*, 23 June 2012.

Maurice Blanchot, 'The Word Berlin', trans. James Cascaito, in *The German Issue*, ed. Sylvère Lotringer, 2nd edn, Los Angeles: Semiotext(e), 2009, 60–4.

Hans Blumenberg, *Das Lachen der Thrakerin: Eine Urgeschichte der Theorie*, Frankfurt: Suhrkamp, 1987.

——, 'Der Sturz des Protophilosophen: Zur Komik der reinen Theorie; anhand einer Rezeptionsgeschichte der Thales-Anekdote', in *Poetik und Hermeneutik*, vol. VII: *Das Komische*, ed. Wolfgang Preisendanz and Rainer Warning, Munich: Fink, 1976, 11–64.

——, 'Wer sollte vom Lachen der Magd betroffen sein? Eine Duplik', in

Poetik und Hermeneutik, vol. VII: *Das Komische*, ed. Wolfgang Preisendanz and Rainer Warning, Munich: Fink, 1976, 437–41.

—— and Jacob Taubes, *Briefwechsel 1961–1981 und weitere Materialien*, Frankfurt: Suhrkamp, 2013.

Frank Böckelmann et al., *Das Schillern der Revolte*, Berlin: Merve, 1978.

Frank Böckelmann and Herbert Nagel (eds.), *Subversive Aktion: Der Sinn der Organisation ist ihr Scheitern*, Frankfurt: Neue Kritik, 1976.

Karl Heinz Bohrer, *Die Ästhetik des Schreckens: Die pessimistische Romantik und Ernst Jüngers Frühwerk*, Frankfurt: Hanser, 1978.

——, 'Intensität ist kein Gefühl: Nietzsche contra Wagner als Lehrbeispiel', in *Merkur*, 424 (1984), 138–44.

——, 'Karl Heinz Bohrer im Gespräch mit Stephan Schlak', in *Ernst Jünger: Arbeiter am Abgrund* (Marbacher Kataloge 64), ed. Stephan Schlak, Heike Gfrereis, Detlev Schöttker, et al., Marbach: Deutsche Schillergesellschaft, 2010, 249–78.

——, 'Sechs Szenen Achtundsechzig', in *Merkur*, 708 (2008), 410–24.

——, 'The Three Cultures', in *Observations on the 'Spiritual Situation of the Age'*, ed. Jürgen Habermas, trans. Andrew Buchwalter, Cambridge, Mass.: MIT Press, 1984, 125–56.

——, 'Welche Macht hat die Philosophie heute noch?', in Bohrer, *Selbstdenker und Systemdenker: Über agonales Denken*, Munich: Hanser, 2011, 69–88.

Hannes Böhringer, 'Avantgarde: Geschichten einer Metapher', in *Archiv für Begriffsgeschichte*, 22 (1978), 90–114.

——, *Begriffsfelder: Von der Philosophie zur Kunst*, Berlin: Merve, 1985.

Norbert Bolz, 'Niklas Luhmann und Jürgen Habermas: Eine Phantomdebatte', in *Luhmann Lektüren*, ed. Wolfram Burckhardt, Berlin: Kadmos, 2010, 34–52.

——, 'Pop-Philosophie', in *Schizo-Schleichwege: Beiträge zum Anti-Ödipus*, ed. Rudolf Heinz and Georg Tholen, Bremen: Impuls, 1981, 183–93.

Jorge Luis Borges, *Collected Fictions*, trans. Andrew Hurley, London: Penguin, 1999.

Christian Borngräber (ed.), *Berliner Design-Handbuch*, Berlin: Merve, 1987.

—— (ed.), *Berliner Wege: Prototypen der Designwerkstatt/Prototypes for the Designwerkstatt*, Berlin: Ernst, 1988.

Julian Bourg, 'Principally Contradiction: The Flourishing of French Maoism', in *Mao's Little Red Book: A Global History*, ed. Alexander G. Cook, Cambridge University Press, 2014, 225–44.

Warren Breckman, *Adventures of the Symbolic: Post-Marxism and Radical Democracy*, New York: Columbia University Press, 2013.

——, 'Times of Theory: On Writing the History of French Theory', in *Journal of the History of Ideas*, 71:3 (2010), 339–61.

Hildegard Brenner, Peter Krumme and Hans Thies Lehmann, 'Der Ort der Theorie', in *Alternative*, 145/6 (1982), 202–12.

Margherita von Brentano, *Das Politische und das Persönliche*, ed. Iris Nachum and Susan Neiman, Göttingen: Wallstein, 2010.

Bazon Brock, 'Gegen das Chaos der Möglichkeiten: zur Debatte zwischen Habermas und Luhmann', in *Frankfurter Allgemeine Zeitung*, 12 October 1971.

Günter Brus, *Das gute alte West-Berlin*, Salzburg: Jung & Jung, 2010.

Heinz Bude, 'Die Suche nach dem Unmöglichen: Paul Arnheim und die Bücher' in Bude, *Das Altern einer Generation: Die Jahrgänge 1938 bis 1948*, Frankfurt: Suhrkamp, 1995, 191–241.

Jan Bürger, 'Herrenrunde mit Panzerwagen: Ein Kommentar', in *Zeitschrift für Ideengeschichte*, 4:4 (2010), 107–10.

——, 'Die Stunde der Theorie', in *Zeitschrift für Ideengeschichte*, 6:4 (2012), 5–10.

Peter Bürger, *Theory of the Avant-Garde*, trans. Michael Shaw, Minneapolis: University of Minnesota Press, 1984.

William Burroughs, *Naked Lunch: The Restored Text*, London: HarperCollins, 2010.

Barbara Büscher, Christoph Hoffmann and Hans-Christian von Herrmann (eds.), *Ästhetik als Programm: Max Bense; Daten und Streuungen*, Berlin: Diaphanes, 2004.

Wolfgang Büscher, *Drei Stunden Null: Deutsche Abenteuer*, Reinbek: Rowohlt, 2003.

Frieder Butzmann, 'Hamburg, Berlin, Musik, Punk, Kunscht, Gudrun, Diederichsen, die Schranknummer usw', in *dagegen dabei*, ed. Dany et al., 242–6.

Bernd Cailloux, *Das Geschäftsjahr 1968/69*, Frankfurt: Suhrkamp, 2005.

——, *Gutgeschriebene Verluste*, Frankfurt: Suhrkamp, 2013.

——, 'Spielzeit 77/78: Die weisse Phase', in *Nachtleben Berlin*, ed. Farkas, 34–9.

Alexander Cammann, 'Lebendig-museal: 40 Jahre Merve Verlag', in *Die Zeit*, 18 February 2010.

Sherri Cavan, *Liquor License: An Ethnography of Bar Behavior*, Chicago: Aldine, 1966.

Michel de Certeau, *Kunst des Handelns*, trans. Ronald Voullié, Berlin: Merve, 1988.

——, 'The Laugh of Michel Foucault', in Certeau, *Heterologies: Discourse on the Other*, trans. Brian Massumi, Minneapolis: University of Minnesota Press, 1986, 193–8.

——, 'May 1968', in Certeau, *The Capture of Speech and Other Political Writings*, trans. Tom Conley, Minneapolis: University of Minnesota Press, 1997, 3–76.

——, *The Practice of Everyday Life*, trans. Steven Rendall, Berkeley and Los Angeles: University of California Press, 1984.

——, 'Pratiques du pouvoir', in *Histoire et psychanalyse: entre science et fiction*, Paris: Gallimard, 1987, 144–52.

Eddy Cherki and Michel Wieviorka, 'Autoreduction Movements in Turin', in *Semiotext(e)* 3:3 (1980), special issue: *Autonomia: Post-Political Politics*, 72–9.

Hélène Cixous, *Die unendliche Zirkulation des Begehrens*, Berlin: Merve, 1977.

Pierre Clastres, *Archaeology of Violence*, Los Angeles: Semiotext(e), 2010.

Daniel Cohn-Bendit, *Der grosse Basar: Gespräche mit Michel Lévy, Jean-Marc Salmon, Maren Sell*, Munich: Trikont, 1975.

Ilonka Czerny, *Die Gruppe Spur (1957–1965): Ein Künstlerphänomen zwischen Münchner Szene und internationalem Anspruch*, Vienna: Lit, 2008.

Nicholas Dames, 'The Theory Generation', in *n+1*, 14 (2012).

Arthur C. Danto, 'Approaching the End of Art', in Danto, *The State of the Art*, New York: Prentice Hall, 1987, 202–18.

——, 'The Artworld', in *Journal of Philosophy*, 61 (1964), 571–84.

——, 'The End of Art', in Danto, *The Philosophical Disenfranchisement of Art*, New York: Columbia University Press, 2005 [1986], 81–116.

——, 'Philosophy as/and/of Literature', in Danto, *The Philosophical Disenfranchisement of Art*, New York: Columbia University Press, 2005 [1986], 135–62.

Hans-Christian Dany, Ulrich Dörrie and Bettina Sefkow (eds.), *dagegen dabei: Texte, Gespräche und Dokumente zu Strategien der Selbstorganisation seit 1969*, Hamburg: Michael Kellner, 1998.

Dietmar Dath, 'Schwester Merve: Zum Tod der Verlegerin Heidi Paris', in *Frankfurter Allgemeine Zeitung*, 20 September 2002.

Belinda Davis, 'The City as Theater of Protest: West Berlin and West Germany, 1962–1983', in *The Spaces of the Modern City: Imaginaries, Politics, and Everyday Life*, ed. Gyan Prakash and Kevin M. Kruse, Princeton University Press, 2008, 247–74.

Mike Davis, *City of Quartz: Excavating the Future in Los Angeles*, New York: Verso, 1992, 15–97.

Gilles Deleuze, *Nietzsche: Ein Lesebuch*, trans. Ronald Voullié, Berlin: Merve, 1979.

——, 'Nomadic Thought', in Deleuze, *Desert Islands and Other Texts 1953–1974*, ed. David Lapoujade, trans. Michael Taormina, Los Angeles: Semiotext(e), 2004, 252–61.

——, 'Referat', in *Antipsychiatrie und Wunschökonomie: Materialien des Kongresses 'Psychoanalyse und Politik' in Mailand, 8.–9. Mai 1973*, ed. Armando Verdiglione, Berlin: Merve, 1976, 1–30.

—— and Michel Foucault, *Der Faden ist gerissen*, trans. Ulrich Raulff and Walter Seitter, Berlin: Merve, 1977.

—— ——, 'Intellectuals and Power', in Foucault, *Language, Counter-Memory, Practice: Selected Essays and Interviews*, trans. Donald F. Bouchard and Sherry Simon, Ithaca, NY: Cornell University Press, 1977, 205–17.

—— and Félix Guattari, *Anti-Oedipus: Capitalism and Schizophrenia*, trans. Robert Hurley, Mark Seem and Helen R. Lane, Minneapolis: University of Minnesota Press, 1983.

—— ——, 'Gilles Deleuze and Félix Guattari on *Anti-Oedipus*', interview by Catherine Backès-Clément, 1972, in Deleuze, *Negotiations: 1972–1990*, trans. Martin Joughin, New York: Columbia University Press, 1995, 13–24.

—— ——, 'Introduction: Rhizome', in *A Thousand Plateaus: Capitalism and Schizophrenia*, trans. Brian Massumi, Minneapolis: University of Minnesota Press, 1987, 3–25.

—— ——, *Rhizom*, Berlin: Merve, 1977.

—— and Claire Parnet, *Dialogues*, London: Athlone, 1987.

—— ——, *Dialogues II*, trans. Hugh Tomlinson and Barbara Habberjam, 2nd edn, New York: Columbia University Press, 2007.

Christian Demand, *Die Beschämung der Philister: Wie die Kunst sich der Kritik entledigte*, 2nd edn, Springe: zu Klampen, 2007.

Alex Demirović, 'Bodenlose Politik: Dialoge über Theorie und Praxis', in *Frankfurter Schule und Studentenbewegung: Von der Flaschenpost zum*

Molotowcocktail, 1946–1995, vol. III, ed. Wolfgang Kraushaar, Hamburg: Rogner & Bernhard, 1998, 71–94.

——, *Der nonkonformistische Intellektuelle: Die Entwicklung der Kritischen Theorie zur Frankfurter Schule*, Frankfurt: Suhrkamp, 1999.

Jacques Derrida, 'From Restricted to General Economy: A Hegelianism without Reserve', in Derrida, *Writing and Difference*, trans. Alan Bass, University of Chicago Press, 1978, 251–77.

Vincent Descombes, *Modern French Philosophy*, trans. L. Scott-Fox and J. M. Harding, Cambridge University Press, 1980.

Diedrich Diederichsen, 'Die Auflösung der Welt: Vom Ende und Anfang', in Diederichsen et al., *Schocker: Stile und Moden der Subkultur*, Reinbek: Rowohlt, 1980, 165–88.

——, 'Aus dem Zusammenhang reissen / in den Zusammenhang schmeissen: Zur deutschen Veröffentlichung von "Mille Plateaux" von Gilles Deleuze und Félix Guattari', in Diederichsen, *Freiheit macht arm*, 159–82.

——, *Eigenblutdoping: Selbstverwertung, Künstlerromantik, Partizipation*, Cologne: Kiepenheuer & Witsch, 2008.

——, *Freiheit macht arm: Das Leben nach Rock'n'Roll 1990–93*, Cologne: Kiepenheuer & Witsch, 1993.

——, 'People of Intensity, People of Power: The Nietzsche-Economy', in *e-flux journal*, 19 (2010), 8–29.

——, 'Psychedelische Begabungen: Minimalismus und Pop', in Diederichsen, *Kritik des Auges: Texte zur Kunst*, Hamburg: Fundus, 2008, 75–105.

——, *Sexbeat*, 2nd edn, Cologne: Kiepenheuer & Witsch, 2010.

——, '"So obskur, wie es gerade noch ging": Diedrich Diederichsen erzählt von seinen *Spex*-Jahren', in *Jungle World*, 28 February 2013.

——, 'Spirituelle Reaktionäre und völkische Vernunftkritiker', in Diederichsen, *Freiheit macht arm*, 117–57.

——, 'Virtueller Maosismus: Das Wissen von 1984', in Diederichsen, *Freiheit macht arm*, 227–45.

Matthis Dienstag [Karl Markus Michel], 'Provinz aus dem Kopf: Neue Nachrichten über die Metropolen-Spontis', in *Autonomie oder Ghetto? Kontroversen über die Alternativbewegung*, ed. Wolfgang Kraushaar, Frankfurt: Neue Kritik, 1978, 148–86.

Monika Dommann, *Autoren und Apparate: Die Geschichte des Copyrights im Medienwandel*, Frankfurt: S. Fischer, 2014.

François Dosse, *Gilles Deleuze and Félix Guattari: Intersecting Lives*, trans. Deborah Glassman, New York: Columbia University Press, 2010.

——, *History of Structuralism*, trans. Deborah Glassman, vol. II: *The Sign Sets, 1967–Present*, Minneapolis: University of Minnesota Press, 1997.

——, *Michel de Certeau: Le marcheur blessé*, Paris: La Découverte, 2002.

Craig Dworkin, 'Textual Prostheses', in *Comparative Literature*, 57:1 (2005), 1–24.

Terry Eagleton, *After Theory*, New York: Basic, 2003.

Rolf Eden, '30.000 Euro Unterhalt im Monat', interview, in *Süddeutsche Zeitung*, 17 May 2010.

Ulrike Edschmid, *Das Verschwinden des Philip S.*, Frankfurt: Suhrkamp, 2013.

Patrick Eiden-Offe, 'Hipster-Biedermeier und Vormärz-Eckensteher (und immer wieder Berlin)', in *Merkur*, 786 (2014), 980–8.

'Einführungsprospekt zur "edition suhrkamp"', in *25 Jahre edition suhrkamp 1963–1988*, Frankfurt, 1988, 1.

Ingo Elbe, *Marx im Westen: Die neue Marx-Lektüre in der Bundesrepublik seit 1965*, Berlin: De Gruyter, 2008.

Norbert Elias, *Studies on the Germans*, trans. Eric Dunning and Stephen Mennell, University College Dublin Press, 2013.

Hans Magnus Enzensberger, 'Baukasten zu einer Theorie der Medien', in *Kursbuch*, 20 (1970), 159–86.

——, 'Bildung als Konsumgut: Analyse der Taschenbuch-Produktion', in Enzensberger, *Einzelheiten*, Frankfurt: Suhrkamp, 1962, 110–36.

——, 'Gemeinplätze, die Neueste Literatur betreffend', in *Kursbuch*, 15 (1968), 187–97.

——, *Mediocrity and Delusion: Collected Diversions*, trans. Martin Chalmers, London: Verso, 1992.

Didier Eribon, *Foucault et ses contemporains*, Paris: Fayard, 1994.

Robert Escarpit, *The Book Revolution*, London: Harrap/Unesco, 1966.

Wolfgang Essbach, *Die Junghegelianer: Soziologie einer Intellektuellengruppe*, Munich: Fink, 1988.

Wolfgang Farkas (ed.), *Nachtleben Berlin: 1974 bis heute*, Berlin: Metrolit, 2013.

Wolfgang Max Faust and Gerd de Vries, *Hunger nach Bildern: Deutsche Malerei der Gegenwart*, Cologne: DuMont, 1982.

Raimund Fellinger and Wolfgang Schopf (eds.), *Kleine Geschichte der edition suhrkamp*, Frankfurt: Suhrkamp, 2003.

Philipp Felsch, 'Beim Paten: Feltrinelli und die Deutschen', in *Ästhetik & Kommunikation*, 129/30 (2005), special issue: *Mythos BRD*, 115–19.

——, 'Homo theoreticus', in *Eine Naturgeschichte für das 21. Jahrhundert: Hommage à, zu Ehren von, in Honor of Hans-Jörg Rheinberger*, ed. Safia Azzouni, Christina Brandt, Bernd Gausemeier, Julia Kursell, Henning Schmidgen and Barbara Wittmann, Berlin: Max-Planck-Institut, 2011, 204–6.

——, 'Schafft italienische Zustände! Wolfsburg als linke Utopie und wie sie scheiterte', in *Radikal: Anders*, Karlsruhe: Autostadt Wolfsburg GmbH, 2011, n.p.

—— and Martin Mittelmeier, '"Ich war ehrlich überrascht und erschrocken, wie umfangreich Sie geantwortet haben": Theodor W. Adorno korrespondiert mit seinen Lesern', in *Kultur und Gespenster*, 13 (2012), 159–99.

Carlo Feltrinelli, *Senior Service*, trans. Alastair McEwen, London: Granta, 2001.

Hubert Fichte, *Die Palette*, Reinbek: Rowohlt, 1968.

Tilman Fichter and Siegward Lönnendonker, *Kleine Geschichte des SDS: Der Sozialistische Deutsche Studentenbund von Helmut Schmidt bis Rudi Dutschke*, 4th edn, Essen: Bundeszentrale für politische Bildung, 2008.

Kurt Flasch, 'Die Trümmerfrau der Kultur', in *Berliner Zeitung*, 18 July 1998.

Moritz Föllmer, *Individuality and Modernity in Berlin: Self and Society from Weimar to the Wall*, Cambridge University Press, 2013.

Simon Ford, *The Situationist International: A User's Guide*, London: Black Dog, 2004.

Michel Foucault, *Archaeology of Knowledge*, trans. A. M. Sheridan Smith, London: Tavistock, 1972.

——, *The Birth of Biopolitics: Lectures at the Collège de France, 1978–1979*, ed. Michel Snellart, trans. Graham Burchell, Basingstoke: Palgrave, 2008.

——, *Dispositive der Macht*, trans. Jutta Kranz, Hans-Joachim Metzger, Ulrich Raulff, Walter Seitter and E. Wehr, Berlin: Merve, 1978.

——, *Mikrophysik der Macht: Über Strafjustiz, Psychiatrie und Medizin*, trans. Hans-Joachim Metzger, Berlin: Merve, 1976.

——, 'The Order of Discourse', trans. Ian McLeod, in *Untying the Text: A Post-structuralist Reader*, Boston: Routledge and Kegan Paul, 1981, 47–78.

——, *The Order of Things: Archaeology of the Human Sciences*, London: Tavistock, 1970.

——, 'Preface', in Gilles Deleuze and Félix Guattari, *Anti-Oedipus: Capitalism and Schizophrenia*, trans. Robert Hurley, Mark Seem and Helen R. Lane, Minneapolis: University of Minnesota Press, 1983, xi–xiv.

——, 'I "reportages" di idee', *Corriere della sera*, 12 November 1978, 1.

——, *'Society Must Be Defended': Lectures at the Collège de France, 1975–76*, trans. David Macey, New York: Picador, 2003.

——, *Speech Begins after Death: Conversations with Claude Bonnefoy*, ed. Philippe Artières, trans. Robert Bononno, Minneapolis: University of Minnesota Press, 2013.

——, 'Truth and Power', interview with Alessandro Fontana and Pasquale Pasquino, trans. Colin Gordon, in Foucault, *Power/Knowledge: Selected Interviews and Other Writings 1972–1977*, New York: Pantheon, 1980, 109–33.

——, *Vom Licht des Krieges zur Geburt der Geschichte*, trans. Walter Seitter, Berlin: Merve, 1986.

——, *Von der Freundschaft als Lebensweise: Michel Foucault im Gespräch*, trans. Marianne Karbe and Walter Seitter, Berlin: Merve, 1984.

——, *Von der Subversion des Wissens*, ed. Walter Seitter, Munich: Hanser, 1974, 106–15.

——, 'What Is an Author?' trans. Josué V. Harari, in Foucault, *Essential Works of Foucault 1954–1984*, vol. II: *Aesthetics, Method, and Epistemology*, ed. James D. Faubion, New York: New Press, 1998, 205–22.

——, 'Wir fühlten uns als schmutzige Spezies', in *Der Spiegel*, 31 (1977), 52, 77f.

—— and Gilles Deleuze, 'Intellectuals and Power', in Foucault, *Language, Counter-Memory, Practice: Selected Essays and Interviews*, trans. Donald F. Bouchard and Sherry Simon, Ithaca, NY: Cornell University Press, 1977, 205–17.

Andrea Frank, 'Weder Naserümpfen noch Augenaufschlag', in *Gibt es eigentlich den Berliner Zoo noch? Erinnerungen an Niklas Luhmann*, ed. Theodor M. Bardmann and Dirk Baecker, Constance: UVK, 1999, 67–71.

Manfred Frank, *What Is Neostructuralism?* trans. Sabine Wilke and Richard Gray, Minneapolis: University of Minnesota Press, 1989.

Ludwig von Friedeburg and Jürgen Habermas (eds.), *Adorno-Konferenz 1983*, Frankfurt: Suhrkamp, 1983.

Max Frisch, *From the Berlin Journal*, ed. Thomas Strässle and Margit Unser, trans. Wieland Hoban, London: Seagull, 2017.

Maurice de Gandillac, 'Le colloque de Cerisy-la-Salle', in *Nietzsche-Studien*, 4 (1975), 324–33.

Gérard Genette, '*Paratexts: Thresholds of Interpretation*, trans. Jane E. Lewin, Cambridge University Press, 1997.

——, 'Sketching an Intellectual Itinerary', trans. Joanna Augustyn, in *French Theory in America*, ed. Sylvère Lotringer and Sande Cohen, New York: Routledge, 2001, 71–86.

Hans-Peter Gente, 'Versuch über Bitterfeld', in *Alternative*, 38/9 (1964), 126f.

Peter Gente, 'Editorische Notiz', in Jacob Taubes, *Ad Carl Schmitt: Gegenstrebige Fügung*, Berlin: Merve, 1987, 79f.

——, 'Vorwort', in *Philosophie und Kunst: Jean Baudrillard; Eine Hommage zu seinem 73. Geburtstag*, ed. Gente, Barbara Könches and Peter Weibel, Berlin: Merve, 2005, 18–23.

Ulrich Giersch, 'Zur Produktivkraft taktiler Schnittstellen: Vom Fotokopieren aus gesehen; Life Is Xerox, You Are Just a Copy': www.gewebewerk.silvia-klara-breitwieser.cultd.de/giersch/index.htm.

Michael Glasmeier, *Die Bücher der Künstler: Publikationen und Editionen seit den sechziger Jahren in Deutschland; Eine Ausstellung in zehn Kapiteln*, exhibition catalogue, Stuttgart: Hansjörg Mayer, 1994.

Detlev Glaussen, 'Hans-Jürgen Krahl: ein philosophisch-politisches Profil', in *Frankfurter Schule und Studentenbewegung*, vol. III, 65–70.

André Glucksmann, *The Master Thinkers*, trans. Brian Pearce, New York: Harper and Row, 1980.

Rainald Goetz, *Hirn*, Frankfurt: Suhrkamp, 1986.

——, *Loslabern: Bericht Herbst 2008*, Frankfurt: Suhrkamp, 2009.

Heinz Gollhardt, 'Das Taschenbuch im Zeitalter der Massenkultur: Vom Bildungskanon zum "locker geordneten Informationschaos"', in *Das Buch zwischen gestern und morgen: Zeichen und Aspekte*, ed. Georg Ramseger and Werner Schoenicke, Stuttgart: Deutscher Bücherbund, 1969, 122–32.

Witold Gombrowicz, *Diary*, vol. III, trans. Lillian Vallee, New Haven: Yale University Press, 2012.

Wilfried Gottschalch, 'Foucaults Denken – eine Politisierung des Urschreis?', in *Literaturmagazin*, 9 (1978), special issue: *Der neue Irrationalismus*, 66–73.

David Graeber, *Fragments of an Anarchist Anthropology*, Chicago: Prickly Paradigm, 2004.

Ernesto Grassi, *Die zweite Aufklärung: Enzyklopädie heute*, Hamburg: Rowohlt, 1958.

Walter Grasskamp, *Das Cover von Sgt. Pepper: Eine Momentaufnahme der Popkultur*, Berlin: Wagenbach, 2004.

Mario Grizelj and Oliver Jahraus, 'Einleitung: Theorietheorie; Geisteswissenschaft als Ort avancierter Theoriebildung; Theorie als Ort avancierter Geisteswissenschaft', in *Theorietheorie: Wider die Theoriemüdigkeit in den Geisteswissenschaften*, ed. Grizelj and Jahraus, Munich: Fink, 2011, 9–14.

Thomas Grossbölting, 'Entstalinisierungskrisen im Westen: Die kommunistischen Bewegungen Westeuropas und das Jahr 1956', in *Kommunismus in der Krise*, ed. Grossbölting and Wentker, 233–49.

—— and Hermann Wentker (eds.), *Kommunismus in der Krise: Die Entstalinisierung 1956 und die Folgen*, Göttingen: Vandenhoeck & Ruprecht, 2008.

Félix Guattari, *Chaososophy: Texts and Interviews 1972–1977*, ed. Sylvère Lotringer, trans. David L. Sweet, Jarred Becker and Taylor Adkins, Los Angeles: Semiotext(e), 2009.

——, 'Everybody Wants to Be a Fascist', trans. Suzanne Fletcher and Catherine Benamou, in Guattari, *Chaosophy: Texts and Interviews 1972–1977*, 154–75.

——, *Mikro-Politik des Wunsches*, trans. Hans-Joachim Metzger, Berlin: Merve, 1977.

Hans Ulrich Gumbrecht, *After 1945: Latency as Origin of the Present*, Palo Alto: Stanford University Press, 2013.

——, '"Old Europe" and "The Sociologist": How Does Niklas Luhmann's Theory Relate to Philosophical Tradition?' in *e-compós*, 15:3 (2012), 1–14: www.e-compos.org.br/e-compos/article/download/866/628/0.

——, *Our Broad Present: Time and Contemporary Culture*, New York: Columbia University Press, 2014.

——, 'Die Prämisse jeglichen Urteilens: Erinnerung an Frank Schirrmacher', in *Frankfurter Allgemeine Zeitung*, 16 June 2014.

Jürgen Habermas, 'The Genealogical Writing of History: On Some Aporias in Foucault's Theory of Power', in *Canadian Journal of Political and Social Theory*, 10:1–2 (1986), 1–9.

——, 'Introduction', in *Observations on the 'Spiritual Situation of the Age'*, ed. Habermas, trans. Andrew Buchwalter, Cambridge, Mass.: MIT Press, 1984, 1–28.

——, 'Kultur des Gegenwartssinns', in *Du: Das Kulturmagazin*, 803 (2010), special issue: *Gibt es eine neue Suhrkamp-Kultur?* 36–9.

——, *The Structural Transformation of the Public Sphere*, trans. Thomas Burger, Cambridge, Mass.: MIT Press, 1989.

——, 'Vorbereitende Bemerkungen zu einer Theorie der kommunikativen Kompetenz,' in Habermas and Luhmann, *Theorie der Gesellschaft oder Sozialtechnologie*, 101–41.

—— and Niklas Luhmann, *Theorie der Gesellschaft oder Sozialtechnologie: Was leistet die Systemforschung?* Frankfurt: Suhrkamp, 1971.

—— and Karl Ludwig Pfeiffer (eds.), *Materialities of Communication*, Palo Alto: Stanford University Press, 1994.

—— Ludwig von Friedeburg, Christoph Oehler and Friedrich Weltz, *Student und Politik: Eine soziologische Untersuchung zum politischen Bewusstsein Frankfurter Studenten*, Neuwied: Luchterhand, 1961.

Jens Hacke, 'Helmuth Schelskys skeptische Jugend: Die mythische Geburtsstunde einer bundesrepublikanischen Generation,' in *Sonde 1957: Ein Jahr als symbolische Zäsur für Wandlungsprozesse im geteilten Deutschland*, ed. Alexander Gallus and Werner Müller, Berlin: Duncker & Humblot, 2010, 329–42.

Sara Hakemi, *Anschlag und Spektakel: Flugblätter der Kommune I; Erklärungen von Ensslin/Baader und der frühen RAF*, Bochum: Posth, 2008.

Matthew G. Hannah, 'Foucault's "German Moment": Genealogy of a Disjuncture,' in *Foucault Studies*, 13 (2012), 116–37.

Michael Hardt and Antonio Negri, *Empire*, Cambridge, Mass.: Harvard University Press, 2000.

Sebastian Haumann, '"Stadtindianer" and "Indiani Metropolitani": Recontextualizing an Italian Protest Movement in West Germany,' in *Between Prague Spring and French May: Opposition and Revolt in Europe, 1960–1980*, ed. Martin Klimke, Jacco Pekelder and Joachim Scharloth, New York: Berghahn, 2011, 141–53.

Anselm Haverkamp, *Latenzzeit: Wissen im Nachkrieg*, Berlin: Kadmos, 2004.

Thomas Hecken, *Das Versagen der Intellektuellen: Eine Verteidigung des Konsums gegen seine deutschen Verächter*, Bielefeld: Transkript, 2010.

Anke te Heesen, *Theorien des Museums zur Einführung*, Hamburg: Junius, 2012.

—— and Susanne Padberg (eds.), *Musée sentimental 1979: Ein Ausstellungskonzept*, Ostfildern: Hatje Cantz, 2011.

Klaus Heinrich, '"Theorie" des Lachens,' in *Lachen, Gelächter, Lächeln: Reflexionen in drei Spiegeln*, ed. Dietmar Kamper and Christoph Wulf, Frankfurt: Syndikat, 1986, 17–38.

Rudolf Heinz and Georg Tholen (eds.), *Schizo-Schleichwege: Beiträge zum Anti-Ödipus*, Bremen: Impuls, 1981.

Agnes Heller, 'Paradigm of Production, Paradigm of Work', in *Dialectical Anthropology*, 6 (1981), 71–9.

Eckhard Henscheid, 'Der rasende Fasler', in Henscheid, *Erledigte Fälle: Bilder deutscher Menschen*, Frankfurt: Zweitausendeins, 1986, 110–17.

Malte Herwig, 'In Papiergewittern', in *Der Spiegel*, 41:40 (2007), 200–2.

Ina Hitzenauer, *Der oppositionelle Buchmarkt der 1960er und 1970er Jahre in Deutschland*, Munich: Grin, 2005.

Dieter Hoffmann-Axthelm, Otto Kallscheuer, Eberhard Knödler-Bunte and Brigitte Wartmann, *Zwei Kulturen? Tunix, Mescalero und die Folgen*, Berlin: Ä&K, 1979.

Tom Holert, '"Dispell Them": Anti-Pop und Pop-Philosophie; Ist eine andere Politik des Populären möglich?' in *Deleuze und die Künste*, ed. Peter Gente and Peter Weibel, Frankfurt: Suhrkamp, 2007, 168–89.

Jochen Hörisch, *Theorie-Apotheke: Eine Handreichung zu den humanwissenschaftlichen Theorien der letzten fünfzig Jahre, einschliesslich ihrer Risiken und Nebenwirkungen*, Frankfurt: Suhrkamp, 2005.

Shuhei Hosokawa, 'The Walkman Effect', in *Popular Music*, 4 (1984), 165–80.

——, *Der Walkman-Effekt*, trans. Birger Ollrogge, Berlin: Merve, 1987.

Rembert Hüser, 'Etiketten aufkleben', in *Das Populäre der Gesellschaft: Systemtheorie und Populärkultur*, ed. Christian Huck and Carsten Zorn, Wiesbaden: VS, 2007, 239–60.

Ivan Illich, *In the Vineyard of the Text: A Commentary to Hugh's Didascalicon*, University of Chicago Press, 1993.

Lorenz Jäger, *Adorno: A Political Biography*, New Haven: Yale University Press, 2004.

——, 'Doch wo sind die Brandstifter geblieben?', in *Frankfurter Allgemeine Zeitung*, 22 February 2013.

——, 'Die Jahre, die ihr nicht mehr kennt: Mission Zeitbruch; Fotos von Abisag Tüllmann im Historischen Museum Frankfurt', in *Frankfurter Allgemeine Zeitung*, 26 November 2010.

Roman Jakobson, 'What Is Poetry?' in Jakobson, *Language in Literature*, Cambridge, Mass.: Harvard University Press, 1987, 368–78.

Martin Jay, *The Dialectical Imagination: A History of the Frankfurt School and the Institute of Social Research, 1923–1950*, Boston: Little, Brown, 1973.

Tony Judt, 'Elucubrations: The "Marxism" of Louis Althusser', in Judt,

Reappraisals: Reflections on the Forgotten Twentieth Century, New York: Penguin, 2008, 106–15.

Ernst Jünger, *On the Marble Cliffs*, trans. Stuart Hood, New York: New Directions, 1947.

——, *On Pain*, trans. David C. Durst, New York: Telos, 2008.

——, *Der Waldgang*, Stuttgart: Klett-Cotta, 2008.

——, *The Worker: Dominion and Form*, trans. Bogdan Costea and Laurence Paul Hemming, Northwestern University Press, 2017.

Ben Kafka and Jamieson Webster, 'No, Oedipus Does Not Exist', in *Cabinet*, 42 (2011), 27–30.

Joachim Kaiser, 'Was blieb von Adornos Glanz?' in *Süddeutsche Zeitung*, 11 September 2003.

Barbara Kalender and Jörg Schröder, 'Der März Verlag: Geschichte und Geschichten', in Jan-Frederik Bändel, Barbara Kalender and Jörg Schröder, *Immer radikal, niemals konsequent: Der März Verlag; erweitertes Verlegertum, postmoderne Literatur und Business Art*, Hamburg: Philo Fine Arts, 2011, 7–163.

Thomas Kapielski, 'Baden-Baden: Juni und Juli 1999', in Kapielski, *Sozialmanierismus*, Berlin: Merve, 2001, 83–139.

Dirk Käsler, 'Soziologie: "Flug über den Wolken"; Dirk Käsler über Niklas Luhmanns "Soziale Systeme"', in *Der Spiegel*, 38:50 (1984), 184–90.

Jürgen Kaube, 'Aufklärung ohne Rettungsversprechen: Die Denkfigur, die einem ein Licht aufsteckt; Zum Tod unseres Kollegen Henning Ritter', in *Frankfurter Allgemeine Zeitung*, 25 June 2013.

——, 'So gut wie nichts macht alles wieder gut: Theodor W. Adorno zum einhundertsten Geburtstag', in *Frankfurter Allgemeine Zeitung*, 6 September 2003.

——, 'Theorieproduktion ohne Technologiedefizit: Niklas Luhmann, sein Zettelkasten und die Ideengeschichte der Bundesrepublik', in *Was war Bielefeld? Eine ideengeschichtliche Nachfrage*, ed. Sonja Asal and Stephan Schlak, Göttingen: Wallstein, 2009, 161–70.

'Keine Angst vor dem Elfenbeinturm: Gespräch mit dem Frankfurter Sozialphilosophen Professor Theodor W. Adorno', in *Der Spiegel*, 23:19 (1969), 204

Susanne Kippenberger, *Kippenberger: The Artist and His Families*, trans. Damion Searls, Atlanta: J&L, 2011.

——, 'Wie Ingrid und Oswald Wiener keine Ahnung von der Gastronomie hatten, aber alles richtig machten', in Kippenberger, *Am Tisch: Die kulinarische Boheme oder Die Entdeckung der Lebenslust*, Berlin-Verlag, 2012, 122–31.

Friedrich Kittler, 'Forgetting', trans. Caroline Wellbery and David Wellbery, in *Discourse* 3 (1981), 88–121.

———, *Gramophone, Film, Typewriter*, trans. Geoffrey Winthrop-Young and Michael Wutz, Palo Alto: Stanford University Press, 1999.

———, 'Ein Verwaiser', in *Anschlüsse: Versuche nach Michel Foucault*, ed. Gesa Dane, Wolfgang Essbach and Christa Karpenstein-Essbach, Tübingen: Diskord, 1985, 141–6.

———, 'Wir haben nur uns selber, um daraus zu schöpfen', interview, in *Die Welt*, 30 January 2011.

Heinz Dieter Kittsteiner, 'Der Begriff des Politischen in der heroischen Moderne: Carl Schmitt, Leo Strauss, Karl Marx', in *Die (k)alte Sachlichkeit: Herkunft und Wirkungen eines Konzepts*, ed. Moritz Bassler and Ewout van der Knaap, Würzburg: Königshausen & Neumann, 2004, 161–87.

———, 'Erkenne die Lage: Über den Einbruch des Ernstfalls in das Geschichtsdenken', in *Sprachen der Ironie; Sprachen des Ernstes*, ed. Karl Heinz Bohrer, Frankfurt 2000, 233–52.

John Klein, 'The Dispersal of the Modernist Series', in *Oxford Art Journal*, 21 (1998), 121–35.

Erich Kleinschmidt, 'Intensität: Prospekt zu einem kulturpoetischen Modellbegriff', in *Weimarer Beiträge*, 49 (2003), 165–83.

Jost Philipp Klenner, 'Suhrkamps Ikonoklasmus', in *Zeitschrift für Ideengeschichte*, 6:4 (2012), 82–91.

Pierre Klossowski, 'Circulus vitiosus', in Klossowski, *Nietzsche und der Circulus vitiosus deus*, trans. Ronald Voullié, Munich: Matthes & Seitz, 1986, 403–29.

Alexander Kluge, *Gelegenheitsarbeit einer Sklavin: Zur realistischen Methode*, Frankfurt: Suhrkamp, 1975.

Norbert Klugmann, 'Selten allein: Szenen einer WG', in *Kursbuch*, 54 (1978), 163–73.

Gerd Koenen, *Das rote Jahrzehnt: Unsere kleine deutsche Kulturrevolution, 1967–1977*, Cologne: Kiepenheuer & Witsch, 2001.

———, 'Der transzendental Obdachlose: Hans-Jürgen Krahl', in *Zeitschrift für Ideengeschichte*, 2:3 (2008), 5–22.

———, *Vesper, Ensslin, Baader: Urszenen des deutschen Terrorismus*, Cologne: Kiepenheuer & Witsch, 2003.

Traugott König, 'Die Abenteuer der Dialektik in Frankreich', in *Fugen:*

Deutsch-französisches Jahrbuch für Text-Analytik, Olten and Freiburg im Breisgau: Walter, 1980, 282–9.

Peter Koslowski, *Der Mythos der Moderne: Die dichterische Philosophie Ernst Jüngers*, Munich: Fink, 1991.

Joseph Kosuth, 'Art after Philosophy', in Kosuth, *Art after Philosophy and After: Collected Writings, 1966–1990*, Cambridge, Mass.: MIT Press, 1991.

Hans-Jürgen Krahl, *Konstitution und Klassenkampf: Zur historischen Dialektik von bürgerlicher Emanzipation und proletarischer Revolution*, Frankfurt: Neue Kritik, 1971.

Wolfgang Kraushaar, 'Thesen zum Verhältnis von Alternativ- und Fluchtbewegung: Am Beispiel der Frankfurter Scene', in *Autonomie oder Ghetto? Kontroversen über die Alternativbewegung*, ed. Kraushaar, Frankfurt: Neue Kritik, 1978, 8–67.

——, '"Unsere Aufgabe die Herbeiführung des wirklichen Ausnahmezustands": Walter Benjamin, die Studentenbewegung und der grosse Katzenjammer', in *Der Ausnahmezustand als Regel: Eine Bilanz der kritischen Theorie*, ed. Rüdiger Schmidt-Grépály, Jan Urbich and Claudia Wirsing, Weimar: Verlag der Bauhaus-Universität, 2013, 114–34.

——, *'Wann endlich beginnt bei euch der Kampf gegen die heilige Kuh Israel?' München 1970: Über die antisemitischen Wurzeln des deutschen Terrorismus*, Reinbek: Rowohlt, 2013.

Helmut Kreutzer, 'Einleitung', in Max Bense, *Ausgewählte Schriften*, vol. III, Stuttgart: Metzler, 1998, VII–XXX.

Benjamin Kunkel, 'How Much Is Too Much?' in *London Review of Books*, 33:3 (2011), 9–14.

Dieter Kunzelmann, *Leisten Sie keinen Widerstand! Bilder aus meinem Leben*, Berlin: Transit, 1998.

Rudolf E. Künzli, 'Nietzsche und die Semiologie: Neue Ansätze in der französischen Nietzsche-Interpretation', in *Nietzsche-Studien*, 5 (1976), 263–88.

Dirk van Laak, *Gespräche in der Sicherheit des Schweigens: Carl Schmitt in der politischen Geistesgeschichte der frühen Bundesrepublik*, Berlin: De Gruyter, 1993.

Klaus Laermann, 'Kneipengerede: Zu einigen Verkehrsformen der Berliner "linken" Subkultur', in *Kursbuch*, 37 (1974), 168–80.

——, 'Lacancan und Derridada: Über die Frankolatrie in den Kulturwissenschaften', in *Kursbuch*, 84 (1986), 34–43.

——, 'Das rasende Gefasel der Gegenaufklärung: Dietmar Kamper als Symptom', in *Merkur*, 433 (1985), 211–20.

Tom Lamberty, 'Theorie muss aus der Kunstecke rauskommen', interview, in *die tageszeitung*, 19 August 2014.

Stephan Landwehr, 'Das Schlupfloch der Boheme', in *Nachtleben Berlin*, ed. Farkas, 76f.

Bruno Latour, *Iconoclash oder Gibt es eine Welt jenseits des Bilderkrieges?* trans. Gustav Rossler, Berlin: Merve, 2002.

—— and Peter Weibel (eds.), *Iconoclash: Beyond the Image Wars in Science, Religion and Art*, Cambridge, Mass.: MIT Press, 2002.

Jörg Lau, 'Der Jargon der Uneigentlichkeit', in *Merkur*, 594/5 (1998), special issue: *Postmoderne: Eine Bilanz*, 944–55.

Hans-Thies Lehmann and Helmuth Lethen, 'Das kollektive Lesen', in *Bertolt Brechts 'Hauspostille': Text und kollektives Lesen*, ed. Lehmann and Lethen, Stuttgart: Metzler, 1978, 1–20.

Elisabeth Lenk, 'Die sozialistische Theorie in der Arbeit des SDS', in Adorno and Lenk, *Briefwechsel*, 171–81.

—— (ed.), *Die Badewanne: Ein Künstlerkabarett der frühen Nachkriegszeit*, Berlin: Hentrich, 1991.

Wolfgang Leonhard, 'Die bedeutsamste Rede des Kommunismus', in *Aus Politik und Zeitgeschichte*, 17/18 (2006), 3–5.

Wolf Lepenies, 'Gottfried Benn: Der Artist im Posthistoire', in *Literarische Profile: Deutsche Dichter von Grimmelshausen bis Brecht*, ed. Walter Hinderer, Königstein: Athenäum, 1982, 326–37.

——, *Kultur und Politik: Deutsche Geschichten*, Munich: Hanser, 2006.

——, *The Seduction of Culture in German History*, Princeton University Press, 2006.

——, 'Der wilde Denker: Erinnerungen an Henning Ritter', in *Die Welt*, 29 June 2013.

Marcel Lepper, '"Ce qui restera [...], c'est un style": Eine institutionengeschichtliche Projektskizze (1960–1989)', in *Jenseits des Poststrukturalismus? Eine Sondierung*, ed. Marcel Lepper et al., Frankfurt: Peter Lang, 2005, 51–76.

——, 'Theoriegenerationen 1945–1989', in *Zeitschrift für Germanistik*, 18:2 (2008), 244–9.

Helmut Lethen, *Cool Conduct: The Culture of Distance in Weimar Germany*, trans. Don Reneau, Berkeley: University of California Press, 2002.

——, 'Fantasia contrappuntistica: Vom Ton der Väter zum Sound der Söhne', interview, in Sabine Sanio, *1968 und die Avantgarde: Politisch-ästhetische Wechselwirkungen in der westlichen Welt*, Sinzig: Studio, 2008, 97–107.

——, 'Gelegentlich auf Wasser sehen: Benns Inseln', in *Zeitschrift für Ideengeschichte*, 2:4 (2008), 45–53.

——, *Suche nach dem Handorakel: Ein Bericht*, Göttingen: Wallstein, 2012.

——, 'Unheimliche Nähe: Carl Schmitt liest Walter Benjamin', in *Frankfurter Allgemeine Zeitung*, 16 September 1999.

——, *Verhaltenslehren der Kälte: Lebensversuche zwischen den Kriegen*, Frankfurt: Suhrkamp, 1994.

—— and Heinz Dieter Kittsteiner, '"Jetzt zieht Leutnant Jünger seinen Mantel aus": Überlegungen zur "Ästhetik des Schreckens"', in *Berliner Hefte*, 11 (1979), 20–50.

Reinhard Lettau, 'Las Vegas der Literatur: Flohzirkus, Schwerpunkttitel und abgeräumte Büfetts', in *Die Zeit*, 28 October 1977.

Christian Linder, *Der Bahnhof von Finnentrop: Eine Reise ins Carl-Schmitt-Land*, Berlin: Matthes & Seitz, 2008.

Rolf Lindner, *Die Stunde der Cultural Studies*, Vienna: Universitätsverlag, 2000.

Literaturmagazin, 9 (1978), special issue: *Der neue Irrationalismus*.

Lorenz Lorenz, 'Lasst Euch nicht verführen!' in *Elaste*, 7 (1983), n.p.

Giovanni di Lorenzo, 'VorUrteil: Die Geschichte des Toni Negri', in *Transatlantik*, 5:3 (1984), 34–41.

Sylvère Lotringer, 'Doing Theory', in *French Theory in America*, ed. Lotringer and Sande Cohen, New York: Routledge, 2001, 125–62.

——, *Foreign Agent: Kunst in den Zeiten der Theorie*, Berlin: Merve, 1991.

——, 'German Issues', in *The German Issue*, ed. Lotringer, 2nd edn, Los Angeles: Semiotext(e), 2009, v–viii.

——, '*Pataphysics Magazine* Interview', Melbourne, 1990, hwww.yanniflorence.net/pataphysicsmagazine/lotringer_interview.html.

——, 'Third Wave: Art and the Commodification of Theory', in *Theories of Contemporary Art*, ed. Richard Hertz, 2nd edn, Englewood Cliffs: Prentice Hall, 1993, 93–103.

—— and Christian Marazzi, 'The Return of Politics', in *Semiotext(e)* 3:3 (1980), special issue: *Autonomia: Post-Political Politics*, 8–21.

Leo Lowenthal, *Critical Theory and Frankfurt Theorists: Lectures, Correspondence, Conversations*, Abingdon: Routledge, 2017.

Merve Lowien, *Weibliche Produktivkraft: Gibt es eine andere Ökonomie? Efahrungen aus einem linken Projekt*, Berlin: Merve, 1977.

Roman Luckscheiter, 'Intellektuelle in der Bundesrepublik 1968–1989', in *Intellektuelle im 20. Jahrhundert in Deutschland*, ed. Jutta Schlich, Tübingen: Niemeyer, 2000, 325–41.

Niklas Luhmann, *Archimedes und wir: Interviews*, Berlin: Merve, 1987.

———, 'Einfache Sozialsysteme', in Luhmann, *Soziologische Aufklärung*, vol. II: *Aufsätze zur Theorie sozialer Systeme*, Opladen: Westdeutscher, 1975, 25–47.

———, 'Die Form "Person"', in Luhmann, *Soziologische Auklärung*, vol. VI: *Die Soziologie und der Mensch*, Opladen: Westdeutscher, 1995, 137–48.

———, 'The Improbability of Communication', in *International Social Science Journal*, 33:1 (1981), 122–32.

———, *Kann die moderne Gesellschaft sich auf ökologische Gefährdungen einstellen?* (Rheinisch-Westfälische Akademie der Wissenschaften Vorträge G278), Opladen: Westdeutscher, 1985.

———, *Love as Passion*, trans. Jeremy Gaines and Doris L. Jones, Cambridge, Mass.: Harvard University Press, 1986.

———, 'Öffentliche Meinung', in Luhmann, *Politische Planung: Aufsätze zur Soziologie von Politik und Verwaltung*, Opladen: Westdeutscher, 1971, 9–34.

———, 'Die Praxis der Theorie', in: Luhmann, *Soziologische Aufklärung*, vol. I: *Aufsätze zur Theorie sozialer Systeme*, Opladen: Westdeutscher, 1970, 253–67.

———, *Social Systems*, trans. John Bednarz, Jr, and Dirk Baecker, Palo Alto: Stanford University Press, 1995.

———, *A Sociological Theory of Law*, trans. Elizabeth King-Utz and Martin Albrow, Abingdon: Routledge, 2013.

———, 'Systemtheoretische Argumentationen: Eine Entgegnung auf Jürgen Habermas', in Habermas and Luhmann, *Theorie der Gesellschaft oder Sozialtechnologie*, 291–405.

———, *Theory of Society*, 2 vols., trans. Rhodes Barrett, Palo Alto: Stanford University Press, 2012–13.

———, 'Zeit und Handlung: eine vergessene Theorie', in Luhmann, *Soziologische Aufklärung*, vol. III: *Soziales System, Gesellschaft, Organisation*, Opladen: Westdeutscher, 1981, 115–42.

Jean-François Lyotard, 'Apathie in der Theorie', trans. Lothar Kurzawa, in Lyotard, *Apathie in der Theorie*, trans. Clemens-Carl Haerle and Lothar Kurzawa, Berlin: Merve, 1979, 73–96.

———, 'A "Barbarian" Speaks about Socialism', interview with Bernard-Henri

Lévy, trans. Roger McKeon, in Lyotard, *Jean-François Lyotard: The Interviews and Debates*, London: Bloomsbury, 2020, 41–3.

——, 'A Brief Putting in Perspective of Decadence and of Several Minoritarian Battles to be Waged,' trans. Taylor Adkins, in *Vast Abrupt*, https://vastabrupt.com/2018/03/12/lyotard-brief-putting-perspective-decadence.

——, 'Ein Denkmal des Marxismus,' in Lyotard, *Streifzüge*, Vienna: Passagen, 1989.

——, *Dérive à partir de Marx et Freud*, Paris: Union générale d'éditions, 1973.

——, 'Design jenseits von Ästhetik,' interview with François Burkhardt, in Lyotard, *Immaterialität und Postmoderne*, 27–34.

——, 'Energumen Capitalism,' trans. R. Mackay, in *#Accelerate: The Accelerationist Reader*, ed. Armen Avanessian and Robin Mackay, Falmouth: Urbanomic/Merve, 2014, 163–208.

——, *Immaterialität und Postmoderne*, trans. Marianne Karbe, Berlin: Merve, 1985.

——, *Intensitäten*, trans. Lothar Kurzawa and Volker Schaefer, Berlin: Merve, 1978.

——, 'A Memorial of Marxism,' trans. Cecile Lindsay, in Lyotard, *Peregrinations: Law, Form, Event*, New York: Columbia University Press, 1988, 45–76.

——, 'Notes on the Return and Kapital,' trans. Roger McKeon, in *Semiotext(e)*, 3:1 (1978).

——, *Das Patchwork der Minderheiten: Für eine herrenlose Politik*, trans. Clemens-Carl Haerle, Berlin: Merve, 1977.

——, 'Philosophie in der Diaspora,' interview with Jacques Derrida, in Lyotard, *Immaterialität und Postmoderne*, 19–26.

——, *The Postmodern Explained to Children: Correspondence, 1982–1985*, trans. Don Barry, Bernadette Maher, Julian Pefanis, Virginia Spate and Morgan Thomas, Sydney: Power, 1992.

——, 'Tomb of the Intellectual,' trans. Bill Readings and Kevin Paul Geiman, in Lyotard, *Political Writings*, University College London 1993.

Valerio Marchetti, *L'invenzione della bisessualità: Discussioni fra teologi, medici, e giuristi del XVII secolo sull'ambiguità delle corpi e delle anime*, Milan: Mondadori, 2001.

'Marcuse: Hilfe von Arbeitslosen,' in *Der Spiegel*, 21:25 (1967), 103f.

Henning Marmulla, *Enzensbergers Kursbuch: Eine Zeitschrift um 68*, Berlin: Matthes & Seitz, 2011.

Odo Marquard, 'Exile der Heiterkeit', in *Poetik und Hermeneutik*, vol. VII: *Das Komische*, ed. Wolfgang Preisendanz and Rainer Warning, Munich: Fink, 1976.

Karl Marx, *Critique of Hegel's Philosophy of Right*, trans. Annette Jolin and Joseph O'Malley, Cambridge University Press, 1970.

——, *The Eighteenth Brumaire of Louis Bonaparte*, trans. D. D. L., New York and Berlin: Mondial, 2005.

Günther Maschke, 'Im Irrgarten Carl Schmitts', in *Intellektuelle im Bann des Nationalsozialismus*, ed. Karl Corino, Hamburg: Hoffmann & Campe, 1980, 204–41.

——, 'Positionen inmitten des Hasses: Der Staat, der Feind und das Recht; Der umstrittene Denker Carl Schmitt; Zu seinem Tode', in *Wir selbst*, 2 (1985).

'Der maskierte Philosoph', anonymous interview, trans. Peter Gente, in *die tageszeitung*, 12 June 1981.

Gert Mattenklott, '"Komm ins Offene, Freund!" Transit ins wilde Denken', in *Zeitschrift für Ideengeschichte*, 2:4 (2008), 5–10.

——, 'Versuch über Albernheit', in *Lachen, Gelächter, Lächeln: Reflexionen in drei Spiegeln*, ed. Dietmar Kamper and Christoph Wulf, Frankfurt: Syndikat, 1986, 210–23.

—— and Gundel Mattenklott, *Berlin Transit: Eine Stadt als Station* [Berlin transit: a city as station], Reinbek: Rowohlt, 1987.

D. T. Max, 'The Art of Conversation. A Star Curator's Migratory Nature', in *The New Yorker*, 8 December 2014, 64–72.

Günther Mayer, *Weltbild, Notenbild: Zur Dialektik des musikalischen Materials*, Leipzig: Reclam, 1978.

Darrin McMahon and Samuel Moyn (eds.), *Rethinking Modern European Intellectual History*, Oxford University Press, 2014.

Thomas Meineke, 'Die göttliche Linke: Jean Baudrillards Simulations-Theorie', in *Die Zeit*, 6 March 1987.

Ben Mercer, 'The Paperback Revolution: Mass-Circulation Books and the Cultural Origins of 1968 in Western Europe', in *Journal of the History of Ideas*, 72 (2011), 613–36.

Merkur, special issue: *Postmoderne: Eine Bilanz*, 594/5 (1998).

Merkur, special issue: *Wirklichkeit! Wege in die Realität*, 677/8 (2005).

Merve collective, 'Warum wir Rancière publizieren', in Rancière, *Wider den akademischen Marxismus*, 91–2.

Heinz-Klaus Metzger, 'Das Ende der Musikgeschichte', in *Geist gegen den Zeitgeist: Erinnern an Adorno*, ed. Josef Früchtl and Maria Calloni, Frankfurt: Suhrkamp, 1991, 163–78.

Robert T. Michael and Gary S. Becker, 'On the New Theory of Consumer Behavior', in *Swedish Journal of Economics*, 75:4 (1973), 378–96.

Walter Benn Michaels and Steven Knapp, 'Against Theory', in *Critical Inquiry*, 8:4 (1982), 723–42.

Karl Markus Michel, 'Ein Kranz für die Literatur: Fünf Variationen über eine These', in *Kursbuch*, 15 (1968), 169–86.

Martin Mittelmeier, *Adorno in Neapel: Wie sich eine Sehnsuchtslandschaft in Philosophie verwandelt*, Munich: Siedler, 2013.

Stephan Moebius, *Die Zauberlehrlinge: Soziologiegeschichte des Collège de Sociologie (1937–1939)*, Constance: UVK, 2006.

Armin Mohler, 'Carl Schmitt und die "Konservative Revolution"', in *Complexio Oppositorium: Über Carl Schmitt*, ed. Helmut Quaritsch, Berlin: Duncker & Humblot, 1988, 129–51.

——, 'Links-Schmittisten, Rechts-Schmittisten und Establishment-Schmittisten: Über das erste Carl-Schmitt-Symposium', in *Criticón*, 98 (1986), 265–7.

——, 'Der messianische Irrwisch: Über Jacob Taubes (1923–1987)', in *Criticón*, 103 (1987), 219–21.

Reinhard Mohr, *Zaungäste: Die Generation, die nach der Revolte kam*, Frankfurt: S. Fischer, 1992.

Daniel Morat, *Von der Tat zur Gelassenheit: Konservatives Denken bei Martin Heidegger, Ernst Jünger und Friedrich Georg Jünger 1920–1960*, Göttingen: Wallstein, 2007.

Franco Moretti, *Graphs, Maps, Trees: Abstract Models for a Literary History*, London: Verso, 2005.

Elke Morlok and Frederek Musall, 'Die Geschichte seiner Freundschaft: Gershom Scholem und die Benjamin-Rezeption in der Bonner Republik', in *Gershom Scholem in Deutschland: Zwischen Seelenverwandtschaft und Sprachlosigkeit*, ed. Gerold Necker, Matthias Morgenstern and Elke Morlok, Tübingen: Mohr Siebeck, 2014, 115–43.

David Morris, 'This is the End of the Sixties!' in *Cabinet*, 44 (2012), 21–6.

Cornelia Möser, *Féminismes en traductions: Théories voyageuses et traductions culturelles*, Paris: Éditions des archives contemporaines, 2013.

Hans-Joachim Müller, *Harald Szeemann: Ausstellunsgmacher*, Berne: Benteli, 2006.

Heiner Müller, *Krieg ohne Schlacht: Leben in zwei Diktaturen*, 4th edn, Cologne: Kiepenheuer & Witsch, 1999.

——, *Rotwelsch*, Berlin: Merve, 1982.

——, 'Traumhölle in Berlin Paris Bar: Eine Ortsbeschreibung', in *Paris Bar, Berlin*, ed. Würthle, 2000.

——, 'The Walls of History', interview with Sylvère Lotringer, *The German Issue*, ed. Lotringer, 2nd edn, Los Angeles: Semiotext(e), 2009, 36–76.

Ulrich Müller, 'Althussers strukturalistische Umdeutung des "Kapital"', in *Das Argument*, 17:1/2 (1975), 85–92.

Wolfgang Müller, *Subkultur Westberlin, 1979–1989*, Hamburg: Fundus, 2013.

—— (ed.), *Geniale Dilletanten*, Berlin: Merve, 1982.

Manfred Naumann, Dieter Schlenstedt, Karlheinz Barck, Dieter Kliche and Rosemarie Lenzer, *Gesellschaft, Literatur, Lesen: Literaturrezeption in theoretischer Sicht*, Berlin: Aufbau, 1973.

Oskar Negt, 'Nicht das Gold, Wotan ist das Problem: Der jüngste Aufstand gegen die dialektische Vernunft; die "Neuen Philosophen" Frankreichs', in *Literaturmagazin*, 9 (1978), special issue: *Der neue Irrationalismus*, 37–51.

—— and Alexander Kluge, *Öffentlichkeit* und Erfahrung: Zur Organisationsanalyse von bürgerlicher und proletarischer Öffentlichkeit, Frankfurt: Suhrkamp, 1972.

—— and Alexander Kluge, *Public Sphere and Experience: Analysis of the Bourgeois and Proletarian Public Sphere*, trans. Peter Labanyi, Jamie Owen Daniel and Assenka Oksiloff, London: Verso, 2016.

Uwe Nettelbeck and Jörg Schröder, *Cosmic*, Schlechtenwegen: März, 1982.

Moritz Neuffer, 'Theorie als Praxis: Die Zeitschrift *Alternative* (1938–1982)', unpublished MA thesis, Berlin, 2012.

Franz Neumann, *Behemoth: The Structure and Practice of National Socialism*, Toronto: Oxford University Press, 1942.

Volker Neumann, 'Die Wirklichkeit im Lichte der Idee', in *Complexio Oppositorum: Über Carl Schmitt*, ed. Helmut Quaritsch, Berlin: Duncker & Humblot, 1988, 557–75.

Lutz Niethammer, *Posthistoire: Has History Come to an End?* trans. Patrick Camiller, London: Verso, 1992.

Roberto Ohrt, *Phantom Avantgarde: Eine Geschichte der Situationistischen Internationale und der modernen Kunst*, Hamburg: Nautilus, 1997.

Albrecht Götz von Olenhusen, '"Aufklärung durch Aktion": Kollektiv-Verlage und Raubdrucke', in *Buch, Buchhandel und Rundfunk: 1968 und die Folgen*, ed. Monika Estermann and Edgar Lersch, Wiesbaden: Harrassowitz, 2003.

——, *'Der Weg vom Manuscript zum gedruckten Text ist länger, als er bisher je gewesen ist': Walter Benjamin im Raubdruck 1969 bis 1996*, Lengwil: Libelle, 1997.

Anne von Oswald, '"Venite a lavorare con la Volkswagen": "Gastarbeiter" in Wolfsburg 1962–1974', in *Aufbau West – Aufbau Ost: Die Planstädte Wolfsburg und Eisenhüttenstadt in der Nachkriegszeit*, ed. Rosmarie Beier, Ostfildern-Ruit: Hatje, 1997, 199–210.

Birgit Pape, 'Intellektuelle in der Bundesrepublik 1945–1967', in *Intellektuelle im 20. Jahrhundert in Deutschland*, ed. Jutta Schlich, Tübingen: Niemeyer, 2000, 295–324

Heidi Paris, 'Die Brille von Foucault', in *die tageszeitung*, 22 June 1979.

——, *Drei Reden zum Design: Der Spaghettistuhl*, Berlin: Merve, 2012.

Heidi Paris and Peter Gente, 'Editorische Notiz', in Szeemann, *Museum der Obsessionen*, 225–30.

——, 'Für *Buch-Markt*', unpublished typescript, Berlin, 1986, www.heidi-paris.de/verlag/wider-das-kostbare.

——, 'Fuss-Note', in *Geniale Dilletanten*, ed. Wolfgang Müller, Berlin: Merve, 1981, 126f.

——, 'Heidi + Peter' in *For Sale? A Presentation of New Design on the Border*, Vienna: prodomo, 1989, n.p.: www.heidi-paris.de/design/for-sale-1982.

——, 'Kunst des Büchermachens: Gespräch mit Heide Paris und Peter Gente vom Merve-Verlag', interview, in *Kunstforum International*, 100 (1989), 377–80.

——, 'Ping-Pong auf der Hochebene von Tibet: Gespräch mit den Betreibern des Merve Verlages', interview, in *dagegen dabei: Texte, Gespräche und Dokumente zu Strategien der Selbstorganisation seit 1969*, ed. Dany et al., 127–36.

——, 'Psychopathen aller Länder, vereinigt Euch!' in *die tageszeitung*, 20 April 1979.

——, 'Wunschmaschinen; Stellungnahme zu der Frage: Was hat der Merve Verlag mit Szeemanns Wunschmaschinen zu tun?' in *Junggesellenmaschinen*, ed. Reck and Szeemann, 50–3.

Keith Parsons (ed.), *The Science Wars: Debating Scientific Knowledge and Technology*, Amherst: Prometheus, 2003.

Kathrin Passig, 'Das Buch als Geldbäumchen', in Passig, *Standardsituationen der Technologiekritik*, Frankfurt: Suhrkamp, 2013, 41–54.

Morten Paul, 'Vor der Theorie: Jacob Taubes als Verlagsberater', in *Zeitschrift für Ideengeschichte*, 6:4 (2012), 29–34.

Robert Pfaller, *Althusser: Das Schweigen im Text; Epistemologie, Psychoanalyse und Nominalismus in Louis Althussers Theorie der Lektüre*, Munich: Fink, 1997.

Jean-Luc Pinard-Legry, 'Alexandre Kojève: Zur französischen Hegel-Rezeption', in *Vermittler: Deutsch-französisches Jahrbuch*, vol. I, ed. Jürgen Siess, Frankfurt: Syndikat, 1981, 105–17.

Karl Prümm, 'Gefährliche Augenblicke: Ernst Jünger als Medientheoretiker', in *Ernst Jünger: Politik; Mythos; Kunst*, ed. Lutz Hagestedt, Berlin: De Gruyter, 2004, 349–70.

Martin Puder, 'Der böse Blick des Michel Foucault', in *Neue Rundschau*, 83 (1972), 315–24.

Emily Pugh, *Architecture, Politics, and Identity in Divided Berlin*, University of Pittsburgh Press, 2014.

Wolfert von Rahden and Ulrich Raulff, 'Distanzgesten: Ein Gespräch über das Zeitschriftenmachen', interview with Moritz Neuffer and Morten Paul, in *Grundlagerforschung für eine linke Praxis in den Geisteswissenschaften*, 1 (2014), 65–87.

Jacques Rancière, *Althusser's Lesson*, trans. Emiliano Battista, London: Bloomsbury, 2011.

———, *Wider den akademischen Marxismus*, trans. Wolfgang Hagen, Konrad Honsel, Otto Kallscheuer and Gerline Koch, Berlin: Merve, 1975.

Ulrich Raulf [Raulff], 'Der nicht-ödipale Wunsch: Notizen zu Deleuze/Guattari: "Anti-Ödipus"', in *Über die Wünsche: Ein Versuch zur Archäologie der Subjektivität*, ed. Dietmar Kamper, Munich: Hanser, 1977, 64–81.

Ulrich Raulff, 'Akute Zeichen fiebriger Dekonstruktion: Die Frankfurter Schule und ihre Gegenspieler in Paris; Eine Verkennungsgeschichte aus gegebenem Anlass', in *Süddeutsche Zeitung*, 21 September 2001.

———, 'Auf sie mit Gedrill! Martialisch, monumentalisch, mythisch: Michel Foucault erfand die Historie, von der Friedrich Nietzsche träumte', in *Frankfurter Allgemeine Zeitung*, 2 November 1999.

———, 'Disco: Studio 54 Revisited', in *Tumult*, 1 (1979), 55–65.

———, 'Foucaults Versuchung', in *Zeitschrift für Ideengeschichte*, 6:4 (2012), 11–17.

———, *Kreis ohne Meister: Stefan Georges Nachleben*, Munich: C. H. Beck, 2009.

——, 'Die *Minima Moralia* nach fünfzig Jahren: Ein philosophisches Volksbuch im Spiegel seiner frühen Kritik', in *Theodor W. Adorno:* Minima Moralia *neu gelesen*, ed. Andreas Bernard and Raulff, Frankfurt: Suhrkamp, 2003, 123–31.

——, 'Schneid', in *Tumult*, 4 (1982), 122–9.

——, 'Tod einer Buchmacherin: Der Merve Verlag und seine Leser haben Heidi Paris verloren', in *Süddeutsche Zeitung*, 19 September 2002.

——, *Wiedersehen mit den Siebzigern: Die wilden Jahre des Lesens*, Stuttgart: Klett-Cotta, 2014.

—— and Marie Luise Syring, 'Sich quer durch die Kultur schlagen: Über die französische Zeitschrift *Traverses*', in *Tumult*, 1 (1979), 103–7.

Hans Ulrich Reck and Harald Szeemann (eds.), *Junggesellenmaschinen*, rev. edn, Vienna: Springer, 1999.

Jan Rehmann, *Postmoderner Links-Nietzscheanismus: Deleuze & Foucault; Eine Dekonstruktion*, Hamburg: Argument, 2004.

Sven Reichardt, *Authentizität und Gemeinschaft: Linksalternatives Leben in den siebziger und frühen achtziger Jahren*, Frankfurt: Suhrkamp, 2014.

—— and Detlef Siegfried (eds.), *Das Alternative Milieu: Antibürgerlicher Lebensstil und linke Politik in der Bundesrepublik Deutschland und Europa 1968–1983*, Göttingen: Wallstein, 2010.

Klaus Reichert, 'Adorno und das Radio', in *Sinn und Form*, 62:4 (2010), 454–65.

Aribert Reimann, *Dieter Kunzelmann: Avantgardist, Protestler, Radikaler*, Göttingen: Vandenhoeck & Ruprecht, 2009.

Hans-Jörg Rheinberger, 'Die erkenntnistheoretischen Auffassungen Althussers', in *Das Argument* 17:11/12 (1975), 922–51.

——, 'My Road to History of Science', in *Science in Context*, 26:4 (2013), 639–48.

——, *Rekurrenzen: Texte zu Althusser*, Berlin: Merve, 2014.

Cord Riechelmann, 'Nachwort', in Harald Fricke, *Texte 1990–2007*, Berlin: Merve, 2010, 149–54.

Henning Ritter, 'Akosmisch: Zum Tod von Jacob Taubes', in *Frankfurter Allgemeine Zeitung*, 24 March 1987.

——, 'Jacob Taubes: Verstehen, was da los ist', in Ritter, *Verehrte Denker*, Springe: zu Klampen, 2012, 27–66.

——, 'Klaus Heinrich: Die lange Lehre zum kurzen Protest', in Ritter, *Verehrte Denker*, Springe: zu Klampen, 2012, 67–78.

——, 'Mein Besuch bei Carl Schmitt', in *Frankfurter Allgemeine Zeitung*, 9 December 2006.

——, *Notizhefte*, Berlin Verlag, 2010.

——, 'Wenn Adorno spricht', in *Frankfurter Allgemeine Zeitung*, 11 October 2008.

Andreas Rosenfelder, 'Der hedonistische Mönch: Was hätte er zur Verstaatlichung des Finanzwesens gesagt? Was zur Lage in Iran? 25 Jahre nach seinem Tod fehlt uns Foucault mehr denn je', in *Frankfurter Allgemeine Zeitung*, 21 June 2009.

Herbert Röttgen and Florian Rabe, *Vulkantänze: Linke und alternative Ausgänge*, Munich: Trikont, 1978.

Florian Rötzer, 'Die Rache der Dinge' (afterword), in Baudrillard, *Das System der Dinge*, 250–61.

—— (ed.), *Denken, das an der Zeit ist*, Frankfurt: Suhrkamp, 1987.

Peter Rühmkorf, *Die Jahre, die Ihr kennt: Anfälle und Erinnerungen*, Reinbek: Rowohlt, 1972.

Alix Rule and David Levine, 'International Art English: Zur Karriere der Pressemitteilung in der Kunstwelt', in *Merkur*, 769 (2013), 516–27.

Tobias Rüther, *Heroes: David Bowie and Berlin*, trans. Anthony Mathews, London: Reaktion, 2014.

Michael Rutschky, *Erfahrungshunger: Ein Essay über die siebziger Jahre*, Cologne: Kiepenheuer & Witsch, 1980.

——, 'Erinnerungen an die Gesellschaftskritik', in *Merkur*, 423 (1984), 28–38.

——, 'Fassungslose Traurigkeit: Bewusstseinsstoff für soziale Aufsteiger; Vor 50 Jahren erschien Adornos *Minima Moralia*', in *Die Welt*, 17 November 2001.

——, 'Der Lachkrampf', in *Merkur*, 641/2 (2002), special issue: *Lachen*, 931–4.

——, 'Panzerhaut der DDR: Die Ruinierung der Berliner Mauer', in *Ruinen des Denkens: Denken in Ruinen*, ed. Norbert Bolz and Willem van Reijen, Frankfurt: Suhrkamp, 1996, 59–90.

——, *Wartezeit: Ein Sittenbild*, Cologne: Kiepenheuer & Witsch, 1983.

Adriano Sack et al., 'Dschungel: Yes, We Could', in *Liebling*, 11/12 (2008).

Adelheid von Saldern, 'Markt für Marx: Literaturbetrieb und Lesebewegungen in der Bundesrepublik in den Sechziger- und Siebzigerjahren', in *Archiv für Sozialgeschichte*, 44 (2004), 149–80.

Hartmut Sander and Ulrich Christians (eds.), *Subkultur Berlin: Selbstdarstellung*

Text-, Ton-Bilddokumente Esoterik der Kommunen Rocker subversiven Gruppen, Darmstadt: März, 1969.

Uta Liebmann Schaub, 'Foucault, Alternative Presses, and Alternative Ideology in West Germany: A Report', in *German Studies Review*, 12:1 (1989), 139–53.

Marie-Luise Scherer, 'Der RAF-Anwalt Otto Schily', in Scherer, *Ungeheurer Alltag: Geschichten und Reportagen*, Reinbek: Rowohlt, 1988, 132–43.

Joachim Schickel (ed.), *Gespräche mit Carl Schmitt*, Berlin: Merve, 1993.

—— (ed.), *Guerilleros, Partisanen: Theorie und Praxis*, Munich: Hanser, 1970.

Otto Schily and Christian Ströbele, *Plädoyers einer politischen Verteidigung: Reden und Mitschriften aus dem Mahler-Prozess*, Berlin: Merve, 1973.

Gunzelin Schmid Noerr, 'Die Stellung der "Dialektik der Aufklärung" in der Entwicklung der Kritischen Theorie: Bemerkungen zu Autorschaft, Entstehung, einigen theoretischen Implikationen und späterer Einschätzung durch die Autoren', in Max Horkheimer, *Gesammelte Schriften*, vol. V: *'Dialektik der Aufklärung' und Schriften 1940–1950*, Frankfurt: Fischer, 1987, 423–52.

Henning Schmidgen, 'Begriffszeichnungen: Über die philosophische Konzeptkunst von Gilles Deleuze', in *Deleuze und die Künste*, ed. Peter Gente and Peter Weibel, Frankfurt: Suhrkamp, 2007, 26–53.

Thomas E. Schmidt, 'Als ich mal dazugehörte: Szenenbildung Anfang der Achtziger', in *Merkur*, 773/4 (2013), 957–66.

Gerhard Schmidtchen, 'Lesekultur in Deutschland: Ergebnisse repräsentativer Buchmarktstudien für den Börsenverein des Deutschen Buchhandels', in *Börsenblatt für den Deutschen Buchhandel*, 24:70 (1968), 1977–2152.

Stephan Schmidt-Wulffen, 'Alles in allem: Panorama "wilder" Malerei', in *Tiefe Blicke: Kunst der achtziger Jahre aus der Bundesrepublik Deutschland, der DDR, Österreich und der Schweiz*, Cologne: DuMont, 1985, 17–95.

Carl Schmitt, *Carl Schmitt: Briefwechsel mit einem seiner Schüler*, ed. Armin Mohler, Berlin: Akademie, 1995.

——, *The Concept of the Political*, trans. George Schwab, Chicago, 1996.

——, *The Theory of the Partisan*, trans. A. C. Goodson, *New Centennial Review*, 4:3 (2004), 1–78.

Hans Schmoller, 'The Paperback Revolution', in *Essays in the History of Publishing: In Celebration of the 250th Anniversary of the House of Longman, 1724–1974*, ed. Asa Briggs, London: Longman, 1974, 283–319.

Detlev Schöttker, 'Postalische Jagden: Ernst Jüngers Präsenz in der deutschen Literatur und Publizistik nach 1945', in *Ernst Jünger: Arbeiter am Abgrund*

(Marbacher Kataloge 64), ed. Stephan Schlak, Heike Gfrereis, Detlev Schöttker, et al., Marbach: Deutsche Schillergesellschaft, 2010, 221–45.

Dirk Schümer, 'Lachen mit Bachtin: ein geisteshistorisches Trauerspiel', in *Merkur*, 641/2 (2002), special issue: *Lachen*, 847–54.

Dietrich Schwanitz, 'Der Zauberer hext sich selber weg: Operation Systemtheorie abgeschlossen; Niklas Luhmann macht die unsichtbare Gesellschaft sichtbar', in *Frankfurter Allgemeine Zeitung*, 14 October 1997.

Michael Schwarz, 'Adorno in der Akademie der Künste: Vorträge 1957–1967', in *Zeitschrift für Kritische Theorie*, 36/7 (2013), 207–16.

Rolf Schwendter, *Theorie der Subkultur*, Cologne: Kiepenheuer & Witsch, 1971.

Alexander Sedlmaier, 'Alexander Sedlmaier, 'Konsumkritik und politische Gewalt in der linksalternativen Szene der siebziger Jahre', in *Das Alternative Milieu*, ed. Reichardt and Siegfried, 185–205.

Manuel Seitenbecher, *Mahler, Maschke & Co.: Rechtes Denken in der 68er Bewegung?* Paderborn: Ferdinand Schoeningh, 2013.

Walter Seitter, *Menschenfassungen: Studien zur Erkenntnispolitikwissenschaft*, 2nd edn, Weilerswist: Velbrück, 2012.

——, 'Strukturalistische Stichpunkte zur Politik', in Frank Böckelmann et al., *Das Schillern der Revolte*, Berlin: Merve, 1978, 83–91.

——, 'Vom rechten Gebrauch der Franzosen', in *Tumult*, 15 (1991), 5–14.

Bernard Semmel (ed.), *Marxism and the Science of War*, Oxford University Press, 1981.

Richard Sennett, *The Fall of Public Man*, New York: Knopf, 1976.

Michel Serres, *Hermes I: Kommunikation*, trans. Michael Bischoff, Berlin: Merve, 1991.

Wolf Jobst Siedler and Elisabeth Niggemeyer, *Die Gemordete Stadt: Abgesang auf Putte und Strasse, Platz und Baum*, Berlin: Sammlung Siedler, 1993.

Detlef Siegfried, *Sound der Revolte: Studien zur Kulturrevolution um 1968*, Weinheim: Juventa, 2008.

Laura Silverberg, 'Between Dissonance and Dissidence: Socialist Modernism in the German Democratic Republic', in *Journal of Musicology*, 26:1 (2009), 44–84: https://doi.org/10.1525/jm.2009.26.1.44.

Stuart Sim, *Post-Marxism: An Intellectual History*, London: Routledge, 2000.

Peter Sloterdijk, *Critique of Cynical Reason*, trans. Michael Eldred, Minneapolis: University of Minnesota Press, 1987.

——, *Zeilen und Tage: Notizen 2008–2011*, Berlin: Suhrkamp, 2012.

Nicolaus Sombart, *Journal intime 1982/83: Rückkehr nach Berlin*, Berlin: Elfenbein, 2003.

——, *Jugend in Berlin, 1933–1943: Ein Bericht*, Frankfurt: Fischer, 1986.

——, *Pariser Lehrjahre, 1951–1954: Leçons de sociologie*, Hamburg: Hoffmann & Campe, 1994.

Susan Sontag, *Reborn: Journals and Notebooks, 1947–1963*, ed. David Rieff, New York: Farrar, Straus and Giroux, 2008.

Kurt Sontheimer, *Das Elend unserer Intellektuellen: Linke Theorie in der Bundesrepublik Deutschland*, Hamburg: Hoffmann & Campe, 1976.

Spex, special issue: *Gegen die Uni studieren*, 17:5 (1996), 44–55.

Enno Stahl, 'Bolz, Hörisch, Kittler und Winkels tanzen im Ratinger Hof; Was körperlich-sportiv begann, setzt sich auf anderer Ebene fort: Diskurs-Pogo', in *Kultur & Gespenster*, 6 (2008), 108–17.

J. W. Stalin, *Marxismus und Fragen der Sprachwissenschaft*, Munich: Rogner & Bernhard, 1968.

——, *Zu den Fragen des Leninismus: Eine Auswahl*, ed. Hans-Peter Gente, Frankfurt: Fischer, 1970.

Georg Stanitzek, 'Die Boheme als Bildungsmilieu: Zur Struktur eines Soziotops', in *Soziale Systeme*, 16:2 (2010), 404–18.

——, *Essay: BRD*, Berlin: Vorwerk, 2011.

——, 'Gebrauchswerte der Ideologiekritik', in *Theorietheorie: Wider die Theoriemüdigkeit in den Geisteswissenschaften*, ed. Mario Grizelj and Oliver Jahraus, Munich: Fink, 2011, 231–59.

Jochen Stankowski and Christof Windgätter, 'Der Rauten-Macher: Gespräch über den Merve-Verlag', in Christof Windgätter, *Verpackungen des Wissens: Materialität und Markenbildung in den Wissenschaften*, Vienna: Böhlau, 2012, 57–70.

Verena Stefan, *Shedding and Literally Dreaming*, New York: Feminist Press, 1978.

George Steiner, 'Adorno: Love and Cognition', in *Times Literary Supplement*, 9 March 1973, 253–5.

Klaus Stern and Jörg Herrmann, *Andreas Baader: Das Leben eines Staatsfeindes*, Munich: dtv, 2007.

Leo Strauss, Alexandre Kojève and Friedrich Kittler, *Kunst des Schreibens*, Berlin: Merve, 2009.

Harald Szeemann, *Individuelle Mythologien*, Berlin: Merve, 1985.

——, 'Monte Verità: Berg der Wahrheit', in *Monte Verità: Berg der Wahrheit;*

Lokale Anthropologie als Beitrag zur Wiederentdeckung einer neuzeitlichen sakralen Topologie, ed. Szeemann, Milan: Electa, 1980, 5–9.

——, *Museum der Obsessionen*, Berlin: Merve, 1981.

Jacob Taubes, *Ad Carl Schmitt: Gegenstrebige Fügung*, Berlin: Merve, 1987.

——, 'Ästhetisierung der Wahrheit im Posthistoire', in *Streitbare Philosophie: Margherita von Brentano zum 65. Geburtstag*, ed. Gabriele Althaus and Irmingard Staeuble, Berlin: Metropol, 1988, 41–51.

——, 'Ein Brief', in *Paris Bar, Berlin*, ed. Würthle, 19.

——, 'Elite oder Avantgarde?' interview with Wolfert von Rahden and Norbert Kapferer, in *Tumult*, 4 (1982), 64–76.

——, 'Jacob Taubes', interview, in *Denken, das an der Zeit ist*, ed. Florian Rötzer, Frankfurt: Suhrkamp, 1987.

——, *Der Preis des Messianismus: Briefe von Jacob Taubes an Gershom Scholem und andere Materialien*, ed. Elettra Stimilli, Würzburg: Königshausen & Neumann, 2006.

Mark Terkessidis, 'Als die Kämpfe kleiner wurden: In 30 Jahren von der "Internationalen Marxistischen Diskussion" zum "Internationalen Merve Diskurs"', in *Jungle World*, 26 January 2000.

Frithjof Thaetner, 'Trauerrede für Heidi Paris', in *Für Heidi Paris*, Berlin: Merve, 2003, 21–4.

Roger Thiel, 'Ästhetik der Aufklärung; Aufklärung der Ästhetik: Eine kritische Physiognomie der *edition suhrkamp*', in *Wolfenbütteler Notizen zur Buchgeschichte*, 15:1 (1990), 1–47.

Edward P. Thompson, *The Making of the English Working Class*, New York: Pantheon, 1964.

Rolf Tiedemann, 'Editorische Nachbemerkung', in Theodor W. Adorno, *Gesammelte Schriften*, vol. XV: *Komposition für den Film: Der getreue Korrepetitor*, Frankfurt: Suhrkamp, 1976, 405f.

Martin Treml, 'Paulinische Feindschaft: Korrespondenzen von Jacob Taubes und Carl Schmitt', in *Jacob Taubes – Carl Schmitt: Briefwechsel mit Materialien*, ed. Herbert Kopp-Oberstebrink, Thorsten Palzhoff and Martin Treml, Munich: Fink, 2012, 273–99.

—— and Herbert Kopp-Oberstebrink, 'Netzwerker, Projektemacher: Die goldenen Jahre der Philosophie an der Freien Universität Berlin; Ein Gespräch über den abwesenden Herrn Taubes', in *Der Freitag*, 13 October 2010.

Mario Tronti, *Arbeiter und Kapital*, Frankfurt: Neue Kritik, 1974.

Siegfried Unseld, 'Schmidt, Bonn, Suhrkamp: Aus Siegfried Unselds "Chronik"', in *Zeitschrift fur Ideengeschichte*, 4:4 (2010), 99–106.

Reinhold Urmetzer, 'Müll-Abfuhr: Lyotards politische Annäherung an Duchamp', in *die tageszeitung*, 26 February 1988.

Armando Verdiglione (ed.), *Antipsychiatrie und Wunschökonomie: Materialien des Kongresses 'Psychoanalyse und Politik' in Mailand 8.–9. Mai 1973*, Berlin: Merve, 1976.

Nina Verheyen, *Diskussionslust: Eine Kulturgeschichte des 'besseren Arguments' in Westdeutschland*, Göttingen: Vandenhoeck & Ruprecht, 2010.

Paul Veyne, *Der Eisberg der Geschichte: Foucault revolutioniert die Historie*, trans. Karin Tholen-Struthoff, Berlin: Merve, 1981.

Guido Viale, *Die Träume liegen wieder auf der Strasse: Offene Fragen der deutschen und italienischen Linken nach 1968*, Berlin: Wagenbach, 1979.

Paul Virilio, *Bunker Archaeology*, Paris: Demi-cercle, 1994.

——, *Geschwindigkeit und Politik*, trans. Ronald Voullié, Berlin: Merve, 1980.

——, 'Projekt für eine Katastrophen-Zeitschrift', in *Tumult*, 2 (1979), 128.

——, 'Der Urfall (Accidens originale)', in *Tumult*, 1 (1979), 77–82.

——, 'Versuche, per Unfall zu Denken: Gespräch mit Paul Virilio', interview, in *Tumult*, 1 (1979), 83–7.

Paolo Virno, *A Grammar of the Multitude: For an Analysis of Contemporary Forms of Life*, trans. Isabella Bertoletti, James Cascaito and Andrea Casson, Los Angeles: Semiotext(e), 2004, 98f.

Sabine Vogel, 'Die Kunst des Verschwindens: Es begann im Geist der 68er Bewegung; Jetzt hat der Berliner Buchverleger Peter Gente sein Lebenswerk, den Merve Verlag, weitergegeben', in *Berliner Zeitung*, 2 January 2008.

Christian Voller, 'Kommunikation verweigert: Schwierige Beziehungen zwischen Blumenberg und Adorno', in *Zeitschrift für Kulturphilosophie*, 7:2 (2013), 381–405.

Vorlesungsverzeichnis für das Wintersemester 1973/74, Berlin: Freie Universität, 1973.

Wilhelm Vosskamp, 'Gattungen als literarisch-soziale Institutionen', in *Textsortenlehre: Gattungsgeschichte*, ed. Walter Hinck, Heidelberg: Quelle & Meyer, 1977, 27–44.

Max Weber, '"Energetic" Theories of Culture', trans. Jon Mark Mikkelsen and Charles Schwartz, in *Mid-American Review of Sociology*, 9:2 (1984), 35–58.

Nikolaus Wegmann, 'Wie kommt die Theorie zum Leser? Der Suhrkamp-Verlag und der Ruhm der Systemtheorie', in *Soziale Systeme*, 16:2 (2010), 463–70.

Hans-Ulrich Wehler, 'Geschichte von unten gesehen', in *Die Zeit*, 3 May 1985.

Klaus Weinhauer, 'Heroinszenen in der Bundesrepublik Deutschland und in Grossbritannien der siebziger Jahre: Konsumpraktiken zwischen staatlichen, medialen und zivilgesellschaftlichen Einflüssen', in *Das Alternative Milieu*, ed. Reichardt and Siegfried, 244–63.

Harald Weinrich, 'Lesen, schneller lesen, langsamer lesen', in *Neue Rundschau*, 84:3 (1984), 80–99.

Dieter Wellershoff, 'Infantilismus als Revolte oder das ausgeschlagene Erbe: Zur Theorie des Blödelns', in *Poetik und Hermeneutik*, vol. VII: *Das Komische*, ed. Wolfgang Preisendanz and Rainer Warning, Munich: Fink, 1976, 335–57.

Oswald Wiener, 'Austria Go Home!', interview with Friedrich Geyrhofer, trans. Christian-Albrecht Gollub, in *The German Issue*, ed. Lotringer, 2nd edn, Los Angeles: Semiotext(e), 2009, 222–32.

———, 'Turings Test: Vom dialektischen zum binären Denken', in *Kursbuch*, 75 (1984), 12–37.

Geoffrey Winthrop-Young, 'Drill and Distraction in the Yellow Submarine: On the Dominance of War in Friedrich Kittler's Media Theory', in *Critical Inquiry*, 28:4 (2002), 825–54.

———, 'Kittler und seine Terroristen', in *Tumult*, 40 (2012), 70–8.

'Wissbar wohin: Philosophie', in *Der Spiegel*, 20:29 (1966), 76.

Steve Wright, *Storming Heaven: Class Composition and Struggle in Italian Autonomist Marxism*, 2nd edn, London: Pluto, 2017.

Antonia Wunderlich, *Der Philosoph im Museum: Die Ausstellung 'Les Immatériaux' von Jean-François Lyotard*, Bielefeld: Transcript, 2008.

Michel Würthle, 'Die Verführung der Kunst', in *Nachtleben Berlin*, ed. Farkas, 78–85.

——— (ed.), *Paris Bar, Berlin*, Berlin: Quadriga, 2000.

Index